The AMERICAN HERITAGE®
New History of

The Civil War

ibooks

The AMERICAN HERITAGE®
New History of
The Civil War

Narrative by
BRUCE CATTON

Edited and with an introduction by
JAMES M. McPHERSON

Contributing Editor, Noah Andre Trudeau

ibooks

Published by ibooks, inc.
24 West 25th Street
New York NY 10010
Distributed by Simon & Schuster, Inc.
1230 Avenue of the Americas
New York, NY 10020

The ibooks World Wide Web Site Address is:
http://www.ibooksinc.com

ISBN 0-7434-3480-3
First ibooks printing November 2001
10 9 8 7 6 5 4 3 2 1

A Byron Preiss Book
Editor: Laura Krakowec Schoeffel
Design: Laura Hammond Hough
Editoral Assistant: Katherine Miller
Picture Reasearch: Sarah Johnson
Executive Editor: Michael Sagalyn
3-D Computer Maps: Paul J. Pugliese
Historical Consultant: Ted Alexander

This work was published in an earlier edition as *The American Heritage Picture History of the Civil War.*

LIBRARY OF CONGRESS CATALOGING IN PUBLICATION DATA
AVAILABLE UPON REQUEST.

This book is printed on acid-free paper.
Printed in China
Set in Bembo

Contents

Introduction

The first edition of *The American Heritage Picture History of the Civil War* was published in 1960 on the eve of the centennial commemoration of the war. The superb text by Bruce Catton and the hundreds of illustrations, ranging from vintage photographs, drawings, and paintings to haunting modern photographs of long-ago battlefields, made this work an instant classic. It helped awaken the interest of millions of Americans in that bloody conflict of 1861–1865, which so shaped this nation.

One-third of a century after the centennial, interest in the Civil War is greater than ever. Some two hundred and fifty Civil War Round Tables meet monthly in all parts of the country to discuss "the War." Millions of tourists visit Civil War battlefields every year. An estimated forty thousand re-enactors don their replica wool uniforms, pick up their replica Springfield rifled muskets, and travel long distances for re-enactments of Civil War battles. Civil War books outsell those on any other aspect of American history, by a large margin. An estimated forty million Americans watched the eleven hours of Ken Burns' television series on the Civil War. Millions of those viewers have also watched the numerous movies, television miniseries, and Civil War documentaries that have appeared on both large and small screens in the 1990's.

What explains this extraordinary interest in a war that has been over for more than 130 years? Part of the answer lies in the scope of a conflict fought on a continental scale—*this* continent, not some foreign land—on battlefields from Pennsylvania to New Mexico and from Florida to Kansas, battlefields that Americans can walk today to understand what happened there more than a century ago. Another part of the answer lies in the near-mythical figures who have come to represent the war. Deified or demonized, they seem to dwarf the ordinary mortals of our own time: Abraham Lincoln and Robert E. Lee, Ulysses S. Grant and Thomas J. "Stonewall" Jackson, William T. Sherman and Nathan Bedford Forrest, Clara Barton and Belle Boyd.

Above all other reasons for our fascination with the Civil War, however, are the sheer drama of the story, the momentous issues at stake, and the tragic, awe-inspiring human cost of the conflict. More than 620,000 Union and Confederate soldiers gave their last full measure of devotion in the war, nearly as many as the number of American soldiers killed in all the other wars this country has fought—*combined*. On one day, September 17, 1862, more American soldiers were killed and mortally wounded in the Battle of Antietam than in all the other wars fought by the United States in the nineteenth century put together: the War of 1812, the Mexican-American War, the Spanish-American War, and the Indian wars. If the same percentage of the American population lost their lives in a war fought at the end of the twentieth century as in that war of 1861–1865, the number of American war dead would total more than five million.

Americans in both North and South were willing to fight on despite such casualties, because they considered the very survival of their respective nations and societies to be at stake. The war began because a compromise did not exist that could solve the differences between the free and slave states regarding the power of the national government to prohibit slavery in territories that had not yet become states. But this issue was merely the surface manifestation of a fundamental conflict over the future direction of national development. Would America move toward a free-labor capitalist economy and a democratic polity in all regions, or would a slave-labor plantation economy and a hierarchical society persist in half of the country? Abraham Lincoln won the Presidency in 1860 on a platform pledged to keep slavery out of the territories; a first step, Lincoln had said in his "House Divided" speech two years earlier, toward the "ultimate extinction" of slavery everywhere in the United States. Southern leaders saw Lincoln's election as the handwriting on the wall, foretelling the ultimate extinction of their way of life, if they remained in the Union. So, the seven deep South states seceded and formed a new nation, which they named the Confederate States of America.

The Lincoln administration and most of the Northern people refused to recognize the legitimacy of secession. They feared that it would discredit the idea of majority-rule democracy and create a fatal precedent for breaking up the dis-United States into several small, squabbling nations. Tensions escalated, until they exploded into war at Fort Sumter in Charleston Bay on April 12, 1861. Claiming this United States fort as their own, the Confederate army that day opened fire on the federal garrison and forced it to lower the American flag in surrender. Lincoln called out the militia to suppress this "insurrection." Four more slave states seceded and joined the Confederacy.

By the end of 1861 nearly a million armed men faced each other along a line stretching twelve hundred miles from Virginia to Missouri. Small battles had already taken place on both ends of that line and in the mountains of what became West Virginia after Union victories there. But the real fighting began in 1862. Huge battles, like Shiloh and Stones River in Tennessee; the Seven Days' Battles, Second Manassas, and Fredricksburg in Virginia, and Antietam in Maryland, foreshadowed even bigger campaigns and battles in subsequent years, from Gettysburg in Pennsylvania and the Wilderness, Spotsylvania, Cold Harbor, Petersburg, Cedar Creek, and a host of others in Virginia to Vicksburg in Mississippi and Chickamauga and Atlanta in Georgia.

By 1864 the original Northern goal of waging a limited war to restore the Union had evolved into a "total war" to destroy the Old South and its basic institution of slavery. Such a victory would give the Union a "new birth of freedom," as Lincoln put it in his address at Gettysburg, in dedication of a cemetery for Union soldiers killed in the battle there. While Grant and Lee remained locked in a deadly embrace at Petersburg, Sherman led his army deep into the Confederate heartland of Georgia and South Carolina, destroying their economic infrastructures. Philip Sheridan's Union forces carried out a similar scorched-earth policy in the Shenandoah Valley of Virginia and George Thomas' bluecoats virtually destroyed John Bell Hood's Confederate Army of Tennessee at the Battle of Nashville. On April 9, 1865, Grant brought Lee to bay at Appomattox. The surrender of other Confederate armies soon followed. The long and painful process of binding up the nation's wounds began.

What was accomplished by all this death and destruction? The war of 1861–1865 resolved two festering questions that the Revolution of 1776 and the Constitution of 1789 had left unresolved: whether this fragile republican experiment called the *United* States would survive as one nation, indivisible; and whether this nation born of a declaration that all men are created with an equal right to liberty would persist as the largest slave-holding country in the world. Both of these questions had remained unanswered before 1865. Many Americans, painfully aware of the unhappy fate of most republics through history, worried whether theirs would also be swept into the dustbin of history. European conservatives gleefully predicted such a fate. Before the Civil War, some Americans had advocated the right of secession and periodically threatened to invoke it; eleven states did invoke it in 1860–61. But since 1865 no state or responsible political leader has seriously threatened secession, not even during the "massive resistance" to desegregation from 1954 to 1964, years of tension that overlapped and in some ways overshadowed the Civil War centennial.

In 1854 Abraham Lincoln said that the "monstrous injustice of slavery . . . deprives our republican example of its just influence in the world—enables the enemies of free institutions, with plausibility, to taunt us as hypocrites." Since 1865 that particular "monstrous injustice" has existed no more.

If the Civil War is of continuing interest to us today, one can readily imagine the all-consuming nature of the experience for those who lived through it. "The excitement of the war, & interest in its incidents, have absorbed everything else," wrote Virginia's zealous secessionist Edmund Ruffin as early as August, 1861. "We think and talk of nothing else." At about the same time, the Yankee sage Ralph Waldo Emerson declared that "the war . . . has assumed such huge proportions that it threatens to engulf us all—no preoccupation can exclude it, & no hermitage hide us." In faraway London, where young Henry Adams served his father as a private secretary at the American legation, he wondered "whether any of us will ever be able to live contented in times of peace and laziness. Our generation has been stirred up from its lower layers and there is that in its history which will stamp every member of it until we are all in our graves. We cannot be commonplace. . . . One does every day and without a second thought, what at another time would be the event of a year, perhaps of a life."

Large crowds gathered around newspaper and telegraph offices during military campaigns, waiting for news from the front. Their mood was one "of painful suspense that unfits the mind for mental activity." These were "fearfully critical, anxious days," wrote a New York diarist in 1864, "in which the destiny of the continent for centuries will be decided." Newspaper circulation doubled, trebled, quadrupled. The Civil War was one of the best-reported wars in history, as scores of reporters traveled with the armies and many soldiers themselves wrote weekly letters for their home-town newspapers.

But words alone did not satisfy the hunger for news. People wanted to *visualize* what it was like at the front. For such images, they turned to the popular illustrated weeklies, to *Harper's* and *Leslie's* and other magazines, which sent skilled artists to report the war in pictures: Winslow Homer, Edwin Forbes, Alfred and William Waud, and many others. They drew soldiers in camp and battle, navies at anchor and in action, nurses and surgeons on the battlefield or in the hospital, and then they rushed their drawings to New York or other cities to be engraved on woodblocks for print-ing in the next issue. Winslow Homer painted his first pictures of Civil War scenes. Other talented artists painted the war on canvas, at the time and later. From these drawings and paintings, some in rich color, we have an unprecedented portrait of men and women at war. Hundreds of these illustrations are reproduced in this book.

The Civil War broke out at the dawn of field photography. The images of death on the battlefield, of suffering, endurance, perseverance, and triumph that leap out from the remarkable wet-plate photographs of that era are literally worth a thousand words. The technology did not yet exist to take action photographs or to print photographs in newspapers or magazines. But the still pictures of officers and enlisted men, of guns and ships, and above all of soldiers killed in battle could be carried in a purse or framed for exhibit. Two days after Antietam, Alexander Gardner and James Gibson, who then worked for Mathew Brady, took a series of grimly eloquent photographs of slain soldiers lying unburied on the battlefield. A month later these pictures went on exhibit in New York City, where thousands of people could, for the first time, vicariously witness such a harvest of death. "Mr. Brady has done something to bring home to us the terrible reality and earnestness of war," wrote a reviewer of the exhibit in *The New York Times*. "If he has not brought bodies and laid them in our door-yards and along streets, he has done something very like it. . . . [But] there is one side of the picture that the sun did not catch, one phase that has escaped photographic skill. It is the background of widows and orphans. . . . Homes have been made desolate, and the light of life in thousands of hearts has been quenched forever. All of this desolation imagination must paint—broken hearts cannot be photographed."

Hundreds of Civil War photographs are reproduced in the pages that follow. The text and captions will help readers imagine those broken hearts. The narration by that master narrator, the late Bruce Catton, remains unchanged from the 1960 edition. But most of the illustrations, some never before published, and all of the captions and sidebars are wholly new to this edition. Stephen W. Sears and Noah Andre Trudeau have scoured archives and collections for new material and have updated the interpretations of those illustrations to bring the insights of the last thir-ty-five years of Civil War scholarship to readers of this new edition. Those "fearfully critical, anxious days in which the destinies of the continent for centuries" were decided come alive again in these pages.

James M. McPherson
May, 1996

CHAPTER 1

A House Divided

The American people in 1860 believed that they were the happiest and luckiest people in all the world, and in a way they were right. Most of them lived on farms or in very small towns, they lived better than their fathers had lived, and they knew that their children would do still better. The landscape was predominantly rural, with unending sandy roads winding leisurely across a country which was both drowsy with enjoyment of the present and vibrant with eagerness to get into the future. The average American then was in fact what he has been since only in legend, an independent small farmer, and in 1860—for the last time in American history—the products of the nation's farms were worth more than the output of its factories.

This may or may not have been the end of America's golden age, but it was at least the final, haunted moment of its age of innocence. Most Americans then, difficult as the future might appear, supposed that this or something like it would go on and on, perhaps forever. Yet infinite change was beginning, and problems left unsolved too long would presently make the change explosive, so that the old landscape would be blown to bits forever, with a bewildered people left to salvage what they could. Six hundred and twenty thousand young Americans, alive when 1860 ended, would die of this explosion in the next four years.

At bottom the coming change simply meant that the infinite ferment of the industrial revolution was about to work its way with a tremendously energetic and restless people who had a virgin continent to exploit. One difficulty was that two very different societies had developed in America, one in the North and the other in the South, which would adjust themselves to the industrial age in very different ways. Another difficulty was that the differences between these two societies were most infernally complicated by the existence in the South of the institution of chattel slavery. Without slavery, the problems between the sections could probably have been worked out by the ordinary give-and-take of politics; with slavery, they became insoluble. So in 1861 the North and the South went to war, destroying one America and beginning the building of another which is not even yet complete.

Abraham Lincoln was inaugurated as the sixteenth U.S. President on March 4, 1861, against the backdrop of the half-completed Capitol dome (opposite). He entered the office beneath the banner of the Republican Party, the platform of which promised a coast-to-coast railroad and a homestead law to encourage western settlement. It also declared that the "normal condition of all the territory of the United States is that of freedom." This antislavery plank, heralded in the Republican Party campaign coins (above), had not only distinguished Lincoln from the other candidates in the election, but had also served to deepen the rift between North and South. In taking the oath of office, Lincoln swore to "preserve, protect, and defend" a nation that was, for the first time in its brief history, in imminent danger of coming apart. Already, seven slave states had declared their independence and seven more were poised to depart the Union. Amid the patriotic drumrolls and ominous tread of marching militia, few were disposed to listen when the lanky new President proclaimed, "We are not enemies, but friends." The United States had reached a terrible point of no return on its course toward civil war.

Even after several wars of national expansion, Americans still thought of themselves in bucolic terms. Eastman Johnson's 1860 painting (right) of cornhusking on the farm touched a common aspiration for the simple life. In reality, however, life in mid-century America was anything but simple. At the time Lincoln took office, 75 per cent of the American people lived in the countryside. Most occupied small or medium-sized farms, often many miles from anything large enough to be called a town, and these towns were loosely linked by unpaved roads. Technology had improved the quality of life for America's rural population, though; mechanical harvesters (patented in 1834) and steel plows (introduced around 1837) more than doubled the nation's production of wheat between 1830 and 1860. If not farmers, young people aspired to become tanners, shoemakers, blacksmiths, carpenters, masons, tailors, dressmakers, or millers. Largely excluded from such opportunities were 4.5 million black Americans, 4 million of whom were slaves. Their participation in the U.S. experience was limited to the background, a position of docile subservience characterized in George Bingham's drawing, *Negro Boy* (below).

In the beginning slavery was no great problem. It had existed all across colonial America, it died out in the North simply because it did not pay, and at the turn of the century most Americans, North and South alike, considered that eventually it would go out of existence everywhere. But in 1793 Yankee Eli Whitney had invented the cotton gin—a simple device which made it possible for textile mills to use the short-staple cotton which the Southern states could grow so abundantly—and in a very short time the whole picture changed. The world just then was developing an almost limitless appetite for cotton, and in the deep South enormous quantities of cotton could be raised cheaply with slave labor. Export figures show what happened. In 1800 the United States had exported $5,000,000 worth of cotton—7 per cent of the nation's total exports. By 1810 this figure had tripled, by 1840 it had risen to $63,000,000, and by 1860 cotton exports were worth $191,000,000—57 per cent of the value of all American exports. The South had become a cotton empire, nearly four million slaves were employed, and slavery looked like an absolutely essential element in Southern prosperity.

But if slavery paid, it left men with uneasy consciences. This unease became most obvious in the North, where a man who demanded the abolition of slavery could comfort himself with the reflection that the financial loss which abolition would entail would, after all, be borne by somebody else—his neighbor to the south. In New England the fanatic William Lloyd Garrison opened a crusade, denouncing slavery as a sin and slaveowners as sinners. More effective work to organize antislavery sentiment was probably done by such Westerners as James G. Birney and Theodore Weld, but Garrison made the most noise—and, making it, helped to arouse most intense resentment in the South. Southerners liked being called sinners no better than anyone else. Also, they undeniably had a bear by the tail. By 1860 slave property was worth at least two billion dollars, and the abolitionists who insisted that this property be outlawed were not especially helpful in showing how this could be done without collapsing the whole Southern economy. In a natural reaction to all of this, Southerners closed ranks. It became first unhealthy and then impossible for anyone in the South to argue for the end of slavery; instead, the institution was increasingly justified as a positive good. Partly from economic pressure and partly in response to the shrill outcries of men like Garrison, the South bound itself emotionally to the institution of slavery.

Yet slavery (to repeat) was not the only source of discord. The two sections were very different, and they wanted different things from their national government.

The population of America's countryside had quadrupled in the first sixty years of the nineteenth century, and the rural impulse was still strong in 1860. Even stronger, however, was the growth of the urban population: in that same sixty-year period in America, the number of city dwellers grew at a rate that was six times that found in the countryside. The coming forces of change were touchingly portrayed by the American painter George Inness in his work *The Lackawanna Valley* (below). The land along the simple sweep of the railroad track has been cleared, presaging future growth, even as the pastoral view of the distant mountains is already obscured by industrial smoke.

Images of productive, happy farmers were popular in American art. At about the same time that painter William Sydney Mount produced his *Dance of the Haymakers*, composer George F. Root wrote a grand cantata on the subject, in which one chorus proclaimed, " 'Tis a bright summer morn and our harvest day/Every creature around us seems to say, 'Good morning!' "

4

In the North, society was passing more rapidly than most people realized to an industrial base. Immigrants were arriving by the tens of thousands, there were vast areas in the West to be opened, men who were developing new industries demanded protection from cheap European imports, systems of transportation and finance were mushrooming in a fantastic manner—and, in short, this dynamic society was beginning to clamor for all sorts of aid and protection from the Federal government at Washington.

In the South, by contrast, society was much more static. There was little immigration, there were not many cities, the factory system showed few signs of growth, and this cotton empire which sold in the world market wanted as many cheap European imports as it could get. To please the South, the national government must keep its hands off as many things as possible; for many years Southerners

A French economist who visited the expanding United States observed that the railroad links between towns effectively reduced "the distance not only between different places, but between different classes." It also created a dynamic population movement. New states in the West were settled largely by people from the East and South, attracted by promises such as those made by the Lakeshore Railroad (right). Newcomers to the frontier identified themselves with the economies and the interests of their new regions, and their elected officials became strident spokesmen for a growing sectionalism. George Bingham's sketch *Stump Speaker* (above) gently satirizes a political aspirant's personal appeal for support.

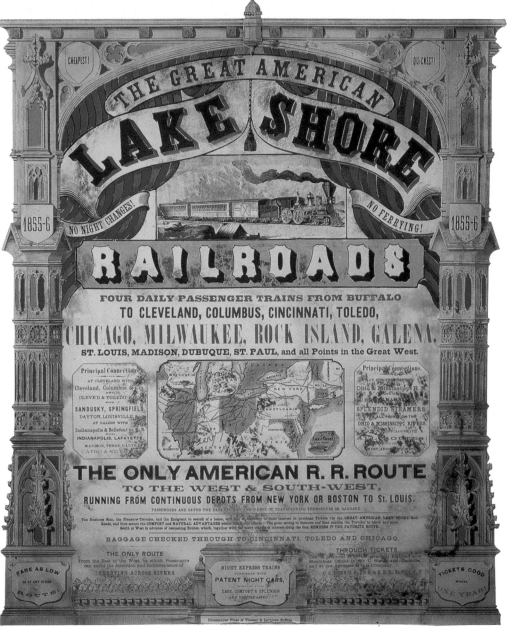

had feared that if the North ever won control in Washington it would pass legislation ruinous to Southern interests.

John C. Calhoun of South Carolina had seen this first and most clearly. Opposing secession, he argued that any state could protect its interests by nullifying, within its own borders, any act by the Federal government which it considered unconstitutional and oppressive. Always aware that the North was the faster-growing section, the South foresaw the day when the North would control the government. Then, Southerners believed, there would be legislation—a stiff high-tariff law, for instance—that would ruin the South. More and more, they developed the theory of states' rights as a matter of self-protection.

ALTHOUGH THERE WERE serious differences between the sections, all of them except slavery could have been settled through the democratic process. Slavery poisoned the whole situation. It was the issue that could not be compromised, the issue that made men so angry they did not want to compromise. It put a cutting edge on all arguments. It was not the only cause of the Civil War, but it was unquestionably the one cause without which the war would not have taken place. The antagonism between the sections came finally, and tragically, to express itself through the slavery issue.

Many attempts to compromise this issue had been made. All of them

Thomas Burnham's painting of Detroit's first election (above) evokes something of the roughneck spectacle of democracy-in-action on America's early frontier. "An American cannot converse," wrote a foreign visitor, "but he can discuss. . . . He speaks to you as if he were addressing a society." The power of oratory was highly regarded in nineteenth-century American society. People from all walks of life would travel many miles to hear a politician speak on a particular issue or a minister preach a sermon. Famous speeches of the time were published and widely distributed; their catch phrases helped crystallize complex issues for the American electorate. During the 1830 Senate debate over public land policy, for example, when Southern sectionalist Robert Hayne of South Carolina proclaimed that states possessed ultimate sovereignty over the national government, he was answered by Massachusetts' Daniel Webster, who cried, "Liberty and Union, now and forever, one and inseparable!" Lines were being drawn.

Francis Grund, an Austrian observer who came to the United States in 1826, believed that the American character was composed of a strong personal drive for material security, a deep-seated religious sentiment, and an almost mystical sense of mission. This satirical mid-century drawing (artist unknown) lampooned the follies of the age, including free love, Jenny Lind's celebrated U.S. singing tour, abolitionists helping slaves escape, railroad safety, medical quackery, and sea bathing. The bedraggled militia company in the center underscored the growing militarism entering the American debate.

For nineteenth-century Americans, technology represented not only material prosperity, but also triumphant proof of the vitality of republican virtues. The proud advertisement produced by the Lawrence Machine Shop (right) speaks of the company's confidence in the future destiny of the country. This utopianism extended into the very design of U.S. factory towns, such as the one in Lowell, Massachusetts (below), which was created to serve as a model in an enlightened republican society. These early, planned communities, boasted one New England businessman, "rendered our manufacturing population the wonder of the world."

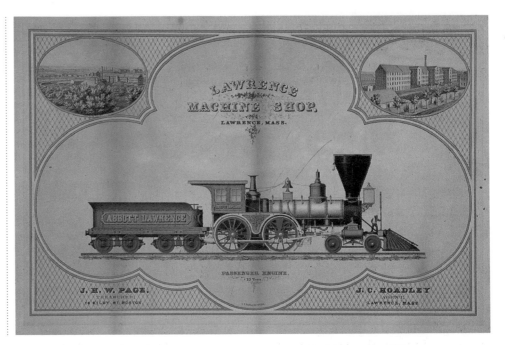

worked for a while; none of them lasted. Perhaps the most that can be said is that they postponed the conflict until the nation was strong enough—just barely so—to survive the shock of civil war.

There had been the Missouri Compromise, in 1820, when North and South argued whether slavery should be permitted in the land acquired by the Louisiana Purchase. Missouri was admitted as a slave state, but it was decreed that thereafter there should be no new slave states north of the parallel that marked Missouri's southern boundary. Men hoped that this would end the whole argument, although dour John Quincy Adams wrote that he considered the debate over the compromise nothing less than "a title-page to a great, tragic volume."

Then there was the Compromise of 1850, which followed the war with Mexico. Immense new territory had been acquired, and Congressman David Wilmot of Pennsylvania introduced legislation stipulating that slavery would never be permitted in any of these lands. The Wilmot Proviso failed to pass, but it was argued furiously, in Congress and out of it, for years, and immense heat was generated. In the end the aging Henry Clay engineered a new compromise. California was to be admitted as a free state, the territories of New Mexico and Utah were created without reference to the Wilmot Proviso, the slave trade in the District of Columbia was abolished, and a much stiffer act to govern the return of

This pastoral view of Samuel Colt's firearms factory (below) belies the profound impact that its products had on American society. The Colt revolver became the ultimate recourse to maintain order. "The six-shooter," declared the fictional hero of an 1852 adventure novel, "is my license, certificate, and deed." Colt was only sixteen when he designed the multishot pistol, using a rotating cylinder, that was so quickly enshrined in popular lore. His manufacturing process was based on the European production method of interchangeable parts. In Europe, however, the various parts were handmade to be fitted together; Colt and others, using what the British called "the American system of manufactures," created parts on machines that were capable of producing great quantities with exacting tolerances. Efficient manufacturers such as Colt could thus provide weapons at low cost, allowing countless local militia companies to drill with the real thing on their shoulders.

Cities in the North had shaped social values and customs from the very first settlements. In the West, cities were injected into empty places by the railroads and they quickly rose to wield influence. In the South, however, the rural culture of the countryside, firmly established well before any larger settlements had reached maturity, was powerfully imprinted upon the character and virtues of its cities. The insular world and self-reliant outlook nurtured on plantations (as idealized in C. Giroux's painting, right) became the determining force of the region.

Industrialization, while not unknown in the South, paled there in comparison with that in the North. Richmond's Tredegar Iron Works (shown in an 1857 engraving, left) was one of about 21,000 factories below the Mason-Dixon Line; at the same time, the total north of that boundary was more than 110,000. Some Southern cities even passed ordinances against new inventions such as steam engines: complained one frustrated businessman in Charleston (the waterfront of which is seen above left as it appeared in 1831), "This power is withheld lest the smoke of an engine should disturb the delicate nerves of an agriculturist . . . while he is indulging in fanciful dreams."

OVERLEAF: James Cameron's 1858 portrait *Colonel and Mrs. James A. Whiteside, Their Son Charles, and Servants* is set on the family terrace overlooking the Chattanooga Valley, Tennessee. Behind Colonel Whiteside (one of the city's leading businessmen), the neatly ordered city of Chattanooga is barely marked by industrial intrusion.

Slavery enveloped white, red, and black people in Colonial American society. It had all but disappeared in the North by the early 1800's, but conditions in the South resulted in its becoming deeply intertwined with the laws, culture, and philosophy of that region. Slavery soon became known as the South's "peculiar institution." The photograph at right, taken in 1862, shows black Americans who had been held in a state of bondage only a short time before the picture was taken. Although the importation of slaves from overseas was legally banned in 1808, the slave trade remained legal within sections of the United States through 1865. Posters announcing slave auctions (like the one above) belied the profound anxiety felt by the victims: "We have a dread constantly on our minds," said a Virginia slave interviewed in 1841, "for we don't know how long master may keep us, nor into whose hands we may fall."

fugitive slaves was adopted. Neither North nor South was entirely happy with this program, but both sections accepted it in the hope that the slavery issue was now settled for good.

This hope promptly exploded. Probably nothing did more to create anti-Southern, antislavery sentiment in the North than the Fugitive Slave Act. It had an effect precisely opposite to the intent of its backers: it aroused Northern sentiment in favor of the runaway slave, and probably caused a vast expansion in the activities of the Underground Railroad, the informal and all but unorganized system whereby Northern citizens helped black fugitives escape across the Canadian border. With this excitement at a high pitch, Harriet Beecher Stowe in 1852 brought out her novel *Uncle Tom's Cabin*, which sold three hundred thousand copies in its first year, won many converts to the antislavery position in the North, and, by contrast, aroused intense new resentment in the South.

On the heels of all of this, in 1854 Senator Stephen A. Douglas of Illinois introduced the fateful Kansas-Nebraska Act, which helped to put the whole controversy beyond hope of settlement.

Douglas was a Democrat, friendly to the South and well liked there. He cared little about slavery, one way or the other; what he wanted was to see the long argument settled so that the country could go about its business, which, as he saw it, included the development of the new Western country between the Missouri River and California. Specifically, Douglas wanted a transcontinental railroad, and he wanted its eastern terminus to be Chicago. Out of this desire came the Kansas-Nebraska Act.

Building the road would involve grants of public land. If the northerly

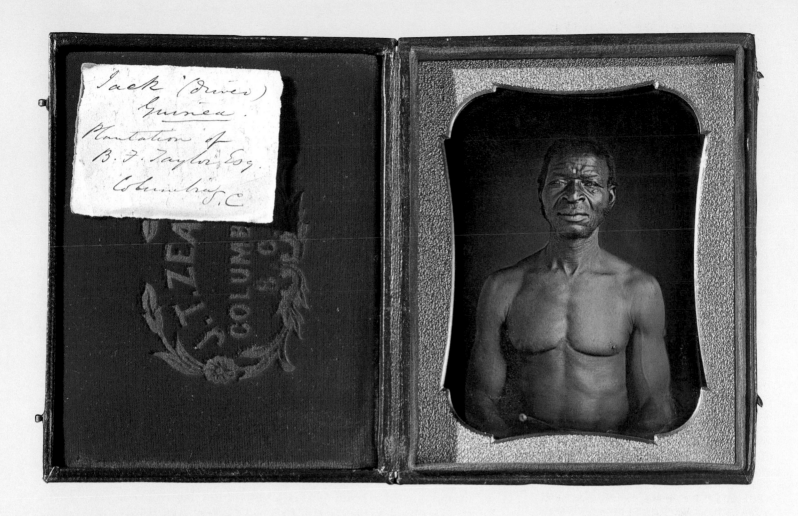

A Slave Narrative

Images of slaves are rare, as is their direct testimony. The daguerreotype above was made in 1850 at the behest of the celebrated Swiss-born natural scientist, Louis Agassiz; it shows a Guinean slave (who was known as "Jack") of B. F. Taylor. Among the records stored in the National Archives is a collection of slave interviews conducted by representatives of the American Freedmen's Inquiry Commission. Solomon Bradley was 27 when he made this statement in South Carolina in 1863: . . . *the most shocking thing that I have seen was on the plantation of Mr. Farrarby, on the line of the railroad. I went up to his house one morning from* *my work for drinking water, and heard a woman screaming awfully in the dooryard. On going up to the fence and looking over I saw a woman stretched out, face downwards, on the ground her hands and feet being fastened to stakes. Mr. Farrarby was standing over and striking her with a leather trace belonging to his carriage-harness. . . . Sometimes when the poor thing cried too loud from the pain Farrarby would kick her in the mouth. After he had exhausted himself whipping her, he sent to his house for sealing wax and a lighted candle and, melting the wax, dropped it upon the woman's lacerated back. He then got a riding whip and, standing over the woman, picked off the hardened wax by switching at it. Mr. Farrarby's grown* *daughters were looking at all this from a window of the house through the blinds. This punishment was so terrible that I was induced to ask what offence the woman had committed and was told by her fellow servants that her only crime was in burning the edges of the waffles that she had cooked for breakfast. The sight of this thing made me wild almost that day. . . . I felt I could not stand it much longer.*

Slave revolts ran nearly the full course of antebellum U.S. history. One of the first was in New York in 1712 when several Africans plotted to burn the city. In 1800, a slave named Gabriel sparked a short-lived killing frenzy in Virginia's Henrico County. A larger uprising took place in Louisiana in 1811, led by a freed black, Charles Deslondes. Charleston was nearly the site of another revolt when, in 1822, a freed black named Denmark Vesey was arrested just before he set an elaborate plot into action. Perhaps the most notorious slave revolt took place in 1831, when Nat Turner—by all accounts a well-treated, docile slave—came to believe that he had been chosen by God to lead his people out of bondage. Turner and his followers (numbering seventy at the most) marched through the countryside of Southampton, Virginia, killing some fifty-five whites. The insurrection, like those before it, was met with overwhelming force. The movement defeated, the other plotters dispersed or captured, Turner himself was apprehended on October 30 by a poor farmer named Benjamin Phipps, in an incident depicted above. A white lawyer, Thomas R. Gray, recorded Turner's confession as he awaited his execution, including the slave's chilling account of a vision in which he had seen "white spirits and black spirits engaged in battle, and the sun was darkened—the thunder rolled in the Heavens, and blood flowed in streams. . . ."

route were adopted the country west of Iowa and Missouri must be surveyed and platted, and for this a proper territorial organization of the area was needed. But the South wanted the road to go to the Pacific coast by way of Texas and New Mexico. To get Southern support for his plan, the Illinois Senator had to find powerful bait.

He found it. When he brought in a bill to create the territories of Kansas and Nebraska he put in two special provisions. One embodied the idea of "popular sovereignty"—the concept that the people of each territory would decide for themselves, when time for statehood came, whether to permit or exclude slavery—and the other specifically repealed the Missouri Compromise. The South took the bait, the bill was passed—and the country moved a long stride nearer to war.

For the Kansas-Nebraska Act raised the argument over slavery to a desperate new intensity. The moderates could no longer be heard; the stage was set for the extremists, the fire-eaters, the men who invited violence with violent words. Many Northerners, previously friendly to the South, now came to feel that the "slave power" was dangerously aggressive, trying not merely to defend slavery where it already existed but to extend it all across the national domain. Worse yet, Kansas was thrown open for settlement under conditions which practically guaranteed bloodshed.

Settlers from the North were grimly determined to make Kansas free soil; Southern settlers were equally determined to win Kansas for slavery. Missouri sent over its Border Ruffians—hardfisted drifters who crossed the line to cast illegal votes, to intimidate free-soil settlers, now and then to raid an abolitionist town. New England shipped in boxes of rifles, known as Beecher's Bibles in derisive reference to the Reverend Henry Ward Beecher, the Brooklyn clergyman whose

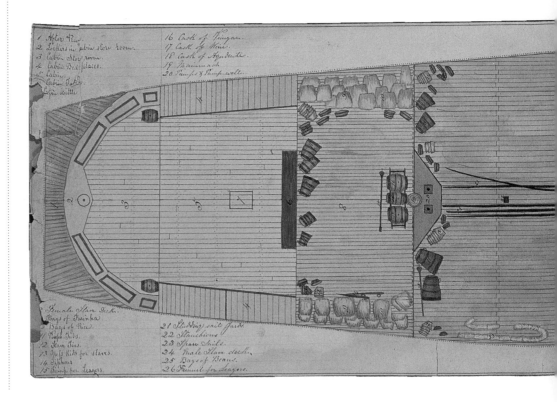

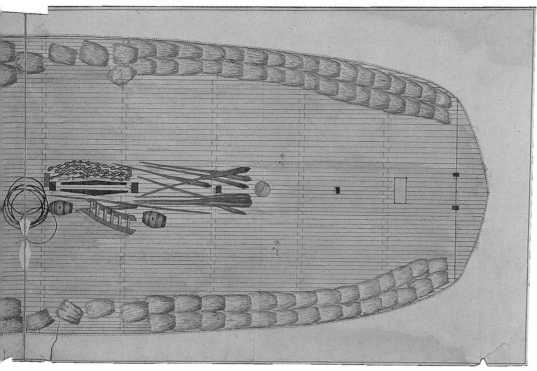

It is estimated that about ten million African slaves were brought to the New World between the sixteenth and the mid-nineteenth century. The precise rendering of the slave deck of the ship *Sapphira* (left) utterly fails to suggest the horrors of a typical crossing. Stacked aboard these vessels like so much cordwood, as many as 16 per cent of the Africans transported failed to survive the dreaded "Middle Passage," which could last from three weeks to three months. Disease took many, but others chose suicide over enslavement. Once in America, slaves were sold on consignment at public auctions or in private deals between owners. There followed another dreaded passage as the slaves (depicted above in Englishman Eyre Crowe's 1853 painting *After the Sale: Slaves Going South*) were hauled off to an uncertain fate. Once the bartered slaves crossed state lines they were subject to Federal controls regulating interstate commerce.

Although painter John Antrobus' *A Plantation Burial* (1860) has no specific story behind it, the recollections of slave Sella Martin provide some context. "My mother died in 1852," he wrote. "She was buried in unconsecrated ground, outside the graveyard for the whites, and her grave was walked over every day of the week by the beasts of the field. After my mother was buried I went to that part of the country, and got a man, at considerable expense, to point out the place where she was sleeping. I put a board at the head of it, and measured its distance from a tree, so that I might know it again."

antislavery fervor had led him to say that there might be spots where a gun was more useful than a Bible. The North also sent down certain free-lance fanatics, among them a lantern-jawed character named John Brown.

By 1855 all of this was causing a great deal of trouble. Proslavery patrols clashed with antislavery patrols, and there were barn-burnings, horse-stealings, and sporadic shootings. The free-soil settlement of Lawrence was sacked by a proslavery mob; in retaliation, John Brown and his followers murdered five Southern settlers near Pottawatomie Creek. When elections were held, one side or the other would complain that the polls were unfairly rigged, would put on a boycott, and then would hold an election of its own; presently there were two territorial legislatures, of clouded legality, and when the question of a constitution arose there were more boycotts, so that no one was quite sure what the voters had done.

. . .

As the nineteenth century moved toward its midpoint, Southern leaders became increasingly aggressive, protecting slavery on every legal front. State after state acted to strip away the complexities surrounding slave law, until its victims were nothing more than rightless chattel. On the national level, Southerners in the House of Representatives succeeded briefly in imposing a gag rule over Congressional debate on the issue in 1836. Efforts to rescind this censorship, such as the 1841 debate depicted at left, finally prevailed in December, 1844. Prominent in the national dialogue was South Carolina Senator John C. Calhoun, who believed that the line between the races was so strong that it was "impossible for them to exist together in the community," without the network of slave laws. Calhoun is depicted below in an 1848 cartoon, futilely attempting to stop antislavery publications, as a modern Joshua trying to halt the sun. At left, below, are pictures of other men who joined with Calhoun: William L. Yancey of Alabama ("all directness, all earnestness . . . unsparing logic"), and Robert Barnwell Rhett, influential editor of the Charleston *Mercury*.

FAR FROM KANSAS, extremists on both sides whipped up fresh tensions. Senator Charles Sumner, the humorless, self-righteous abolitionist from Massachusetts, addressed the Senate on "the crime against Kansas," loosing such unmeasured invective on the head of Senator Andrew Butler of South Carolina that Congressman Preston Brooks, also of South Carolina, a relative of Senator Butler, caned him into insensibility on the Senate floor a few days afterward. Senator William H. Seward of New York spoke vaguely but ominously of an "irrepressible conflict"

William L. Yancey

Robert Barnwell Rhett

"I profoundly loved Henry Clay," wrote crusading newspaperman Horace Greeley. "He was more fitted to win and enjoy popularity than any other American who ever lived." Clay, born in Virginia in 1777, moved to Kentucky as a young man, and became a national figure as a U.S. Congressman, Senator, and three-time candidate for President. Renowned for his diplomatic skills and as the promoter of an "American System," based on tariff protection and governmental infrastructure support, Clay's last years were spent in a desperate effort to stave off the breaking up of the Union. He effected a series of legislative compromises that attempted to mediate a middle course between slave and non-slave interests. In one of his finest speeches, depicted above, as he addressed the Senate on behalf of the Compromise of 1850.

Henry Clay

Daniel Webster

Southerners zealously watched for any sign that the precarious equilibrium they enjoyed with Northern states in the U.S. Senate might be upset. To that end, disaster seemed imminent when California petitioned to join the Union as a free state. Seizing the moment to enact a broad spectrum of laws designed to defuse the incendiary situation once and for all, Henry Clay, with fellow senators Daniel Webster and Thomas Hart Benton, engineered the Compromise of 1850. Southerners accepted the end of slave trafficking in the District of Columbia, in return for the assurance that in the future, states carved out of the Western territories would be allowed to select their own status as "slave" or "free." For their part, Northerners got California into the Union as a free state, but were saddled with national enforcement of the "peculiar institution" through the Fugitive Slave Act.

Thomas Hart Benton

John C. Calhoun

that was germinating. Senator Robert Toombs of Georgia predicted a vast extension of slavery and said that he would one day auction slaves on Boston Common itself. In Alabama the eloquent William Lowndes Yancey argued hotly that the South would never find happiness except by leaving the Union and setting up an independent nation.

Now the Supreme Court added its bit. It had before it the case of Dred Scott, a Negro slave whose master, an army surgeon, had kept him for some years in Illinois and Wisconsin, where there was no slavery. Scott sued for his freedom,

William Lloyd Garrison: Uncompromise in an Age of Compromise

With the ringing editorial declaration, "I am in earnest—and I will not equivocate—I will not excuse—I will not retreat a single inch—and I will be heard," William Lloyd Garrison (left) launched his abolitionist journal, *The Liberator*, in Boston on January 1, 1831. The Massachusetts newspaperman was then twenty-five years old. His calls for immediate emancipation for slaves and civil rights for free blacks aroused antagonism North and South. In 1835, a mob of white Boston laborers who feared competition for jobs with blacks forced Garrison to take refuge in a nearby prison. Despite his belief that slaves "more than any people on the face of the earth" were justified in using violence to break their chains, Garrison was a pacifist who refused to endorse any appeal for direct action. His name became anathema throughout the white South, though ironically, in his fervent hatred of slavery, Garrison believed it was better for Southern states to secede. For years the masthead of *The Liberator* carried the slogan: "No union with slave-holders!"

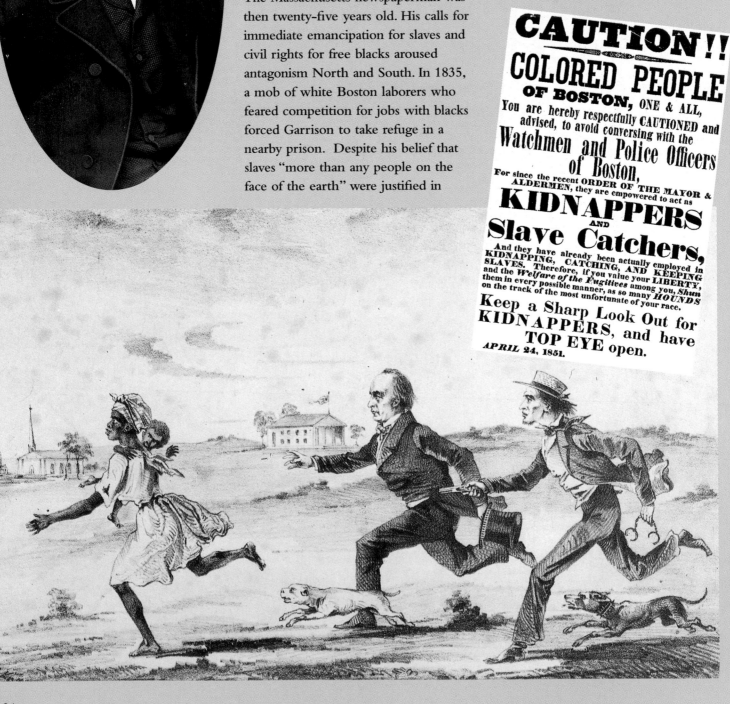

135,000 SETS, 270,000 VOLUMES SOLD.

UNCLE TOM'S CABIN

FOR SALE HERE.

AN EDITION FOR THE MILLION, COMPLETE IN 1 Vol., PRICE 37 1-2 CENTS.

" " IN GERMAN, IN 1 Vol., PRICE 50 CENTS.

" " IN 2 Vols,. CLOTH, 6 PLATES, PRICE $1.50.

SUPERB ILLUSTRATED EDITION, IN 1 Vol., WITH 153 ENGRAVINGS,

PRICES FROM $2.50 TO $5.00.

The Greatest Book of the Age.

Mrs. Harriet Beecher Stowe had been writing with modest success for eighteen years when her concern over slavery led her to write a book to show "the best side of the thing" and "something faintly approaching the worst." She came to her moral position naturally, as one of the daughters of the leading Congregational minister of the age, Lyman Beecher (shown above, flanked by his daughters and some of his sons: Harriet is sitting on the extreme right). The book she wrote, *Uncle Tom's Cabin*, was a phenomenal success, selling out its first print run of 5,000 copies in just forty-eight hours. Stage versions launched a year after the book appeared were even more successful in spreading its message. Offered as "moral, religious, and instructive," the productions (from which Stowe received no royalties) appealed to respectable people, even those who normally avoided the theater.

OPPOSITE: Daniel Webster's support of the Compromise of 1850 cost him dearly, especially because of the Fugitive Slave Act that was part of it. Federal law could reach across the Mason-Dixon Line to capture and return escaped slaves to their masters in the South, a prospect that inspired warning posters in abolitionist strongholds such as Boston (middle). In the same backlash, Daniel Webster was pilloried in the national press and the subject of cutting cartoons, showing him in league with the slave catchers (bottom).

and in 1857 Chief Justice Roger Taney delivered the Court's opinion. That Scott's plea for freedom was denied was no particular surprise, but the grounds on which the denial was based stirred the North afresh. A Negro of slave descent, said Taney, was an inferior sort of person who could not be a citizen of any state and hence could not sue anyone; furthermore, the act by which Congress had forbidden slavery in the Northern territories was invalid because the Constitution gave slavery ironclad protection. There was no legal way in which slavery could be excluded from any territory.

An intense political ferment was working. The old Whig Party had collapsed utterly, and the Democratic Party was showing signs of breaking into sectional wings. In the North there had risen the new Republican Party, an amalgamation of former Whigs, freesoilers, business leaders who wanted a central government that would protect industry, and ordinary folk who wanted a homestead act that would provide free farms in the West. The party had already polled an impressive number of votes in the Presidential campaign of 1856, and it was likely to do better in 1860. Seward of New York hoped to be its next Presidential nominee; so did Salmon P. Chase, prominent antislavery leader from Ohio; and so, also, did a lawyer and former congressman who was not nearly so well known as these two, Abraham Lincoln of Illinois.

In 1858 Lincoln ran for the Senate against Douglas. In a series of famous debates which drew national attention, the two argued the Kansas-Nebraska Act and the slavery issue up and down the state of Illinois. In the end Douglas

OPPOSITE: There was no greater voice than Frederick Douglass' to speak for the millions of slaves who could not themselves be heard. A runaway slave, Douglass worked with the Massachusetts Anti-Slavery Society in the early 1840's, speaking frequently in the Northern states. Through his public pronouncements and writings, Douglass sought to educate Americans about the evils of slavery and to urge them to action. Asked to speak at a Fourth of July celebration, he demurred, saying that the holiday held no real meaning for black Americans. On another occasion, he told his white audience that the continued existence of slavery "brands your republicanism as a sham, your humanity as a base pretense, your Christianity as a lie."

While most drawings of slaves before and during the Civil War tended to follow racial stereotypes by depicting them as simple and content with their meager lives, Eastman Johnson's painting *A Ride for Liberty—the Fugitive Slaves* (below) reflects instead traits of resolution, determination, and courage.

Slaves who attempted to run away faced almost insurmountable obstacles. Escape often meant leaving behind families and loved ones, to take a chance on freedom that few actually attained. For those caught, the punishment could be extreme. "I was making a leap in the dark," Frederick Douglass said of his decision to run. "I was like one going to war without weapons—ten chances of defeat to one of victory." A few years after Douglass successfully slipped out of bondage and became a national spokesman, his prominence would inspire all manner of tributes, including the dedication of *The Fugitive's Song* (opposite page). The numbers who managed to escape north were relatively small in relation to the total slave population, but their very existence vexed slaveholders, one of whom avowed he would "rather a negro would do anything Else than runaway." Some escaped slaves themselves helped others to follow the trail of friendly houses known collectively as the "Underground Railroad." One of its most famous "conductors" was Harriet Tubman, shown here (sitting right) with a few of the former slaves she led to freedom. Another was an ex-slave from Kentucky named Richard Daly, who would guide the fugitives across the Ohio River in his boat. "I would fire my revolver when I was crossing the Ohio River, and my white friend, who was an agent of the Underground Railroad, would fire his revolver to say he was ready. Then I would land the fugitives, and he would . . . pass them along the road to Canada."

won re-election, but he won on terms that may have cost him the Presidency two years later. Lincoln had pinned him down: Was there any lawful way in which the people of a territory could exclude slavery? (In other words, could Douglas' "popular sovereignty" be made to jibe with the Supreme Court's finding in the Dred Scott case?) Douglas replied that the thing was easy. Slavery could not live a day unless it were supported by protective local legislation. In fact, if a territorial legislature simply refused to enact such legislation, slavery would not exist regardless of what the Supreme Court had said. The answer helped Douglas win re-election, but it mortally offended the South. The threatened split in the Democratic Party came measurably nearer, and such a split could mean nothing except victory for the Republicans.

The 1850's were the tormented decade in American history. Always the tension mounted, and no one seemed able to provide an easement. The Panic of 1857 left a severe business depression, and Northern pressure for higher tariff rates and a homestead act became stronger than ever. The depression had hardly touched the South, since world demand for cotton was unabated, and Southern leaders became more than ever convinced that their society and their economy were

sounder and stronger than anything the North could show. There would be no tariff revision, and although Congress did pass a homestead act President James Buchanan, a Pennsylvanian but a strong friend of the South, promptly vetoed it. The administration, indeed, seemed unable to do anything. It could not even make a state out of Kansas, in which territory it was clear, by now, that a strong majority opposed slavery. The rising antagonism between the sections had almost brought paralysis to the Federal government.

And then old John Brown came out of the shadows to add the final touch.

With a mere handful of followers, Brown undertook, on the night of October 16, 1859, to seize the Federal arsenal at Harpers Ferry and with the weapons thus obtained to start a slave insurrection in the South. He managed to get possession of an enginehouse, which he held until the morning of the eighteenth; then a detachment of U.S. marines—temporarily led by Colonel Robert E. Lee of the U.S. Army—overpowered him and snuffed out his crackbrained conspiracy with bayonets and clubbed muskets. Brown was quickly tried, was convicted of treason, and early in December he was hanged. But what he had done had a most disastrous effect on men's minds. To people in the South, it seemed that Brown

With the Kansas-Nebraska Act of 1854, Congress set the stage for an agonizing period of Kansas history. By opting to let settlers there decide by ballot whether the new state would be slave or free, the door was thrown open to partisans on both sides to rush supporters into the territory. The rhetoric quickly escalated to violence, followed by the formation of armed bands (like the Free Staters, also called Free Soilers, photographed alongside their cannon, above right). Before the votes were finally counted, more than 200 settlers had been killed. Some fell in semi-organized brawls (like the one at Hickory Point, below), while others were hunted down and murdered in their sleep. Among those who came to national attention during the struggle was an intimidating ramrod of vengeance with a grim face like a "carnivorous bird." His name was John Brown. He and his followers spread a gospel of violence across bloody Kansas, but presented it as noble abolitionism. According to Frederick Douglass, "His . . . will impressed all."

OPPOSITE: John Brown of Kansas.

confirmed their worst fears: this was what the Yankee abolitionists really wanted—a servile insurrection, with unlimited bloodshed and pillage, from one end of the South to the other! The fact that some vocal persons in the North persisted in regarding Brown as a martyr simply made matters worse. After the John Brown raid the chance that the bitter sectional argument could be harmonized faded close to the vanishing point.

IT WAS IN THIS ATMOSPHERE that the 1860 election was held. The Republicans nominated Lincoln, partly because he was considered less of an extremist than either Seward or Chase; he was moderate on the slavery question, and agreed that the Federal government lacked power to interfere with the peculiar institution in the states. The Republican platform, however, did represent a threat to Southern interests. It embodied the political and economic program of the North—upward revision of the tariff, free farms in the West, railroad subsidies, and all the rest.

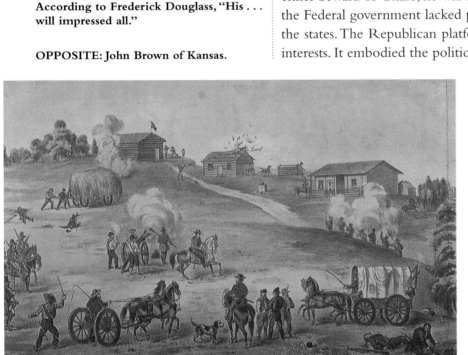

But by now a singular fatalism gripped the nation. The campaign could not be fought on the basis of these issues; men could talk only about slavery, and on that subject they could neither talk nor, for the most part, even think, with moderation. Although it faced a purely sectional opposition, the Democratic Party promptly split into halves. The Northern wing nominated Douglas, but the Southern wing flatly refused to accept the man because of his heresy in regard to slavery in the territories; it named John C. Breckinridge of Kentucky, while a fourth party, hoping desperately for compromise and conciliation, put forward John Bell of Tennessee.

Charles Sumner

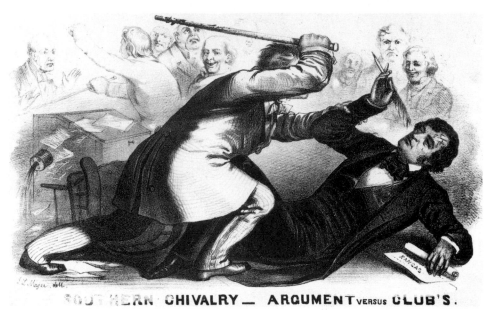

SOUTHERN CHIVALRY — ARGUMENT versus CLUB'S.

LIBERTY, THE FAIR MAID OF KANSAS—IN THE HANDS OF THE "BORDER RUFFIANS".

No longer was the spirit of compromise alive in the land. In the Senate extremists on both sides dominated arguments over the great issues of the day. Prominent for the Northern cause was Charles Sumner of Massachusetts (top left). An astute performer, Sumner used his hands, the poet Henry Wadsworth Longfellow said, "like a cannoneer ramming down cartridges." On May 22, 1856, following a patented Sumner speech in which he cruelly ridiculed his South Carolina colleague, Andrew Butler, he was brutally caned on the Senate floor by Butler's nephew, Preston Brooks (top right). Sumner never fully recovered, while Brooks returned home to a hero's welcome and gifts of additional canes. The excesses of "Bloody Kansas" were the backdrop to an 1856 cartoon (above) attacking the bankrupt policies of Democratic leaders James Buchanan, Franklin Pierce, Lewis Cass, and Stephen Douglas.

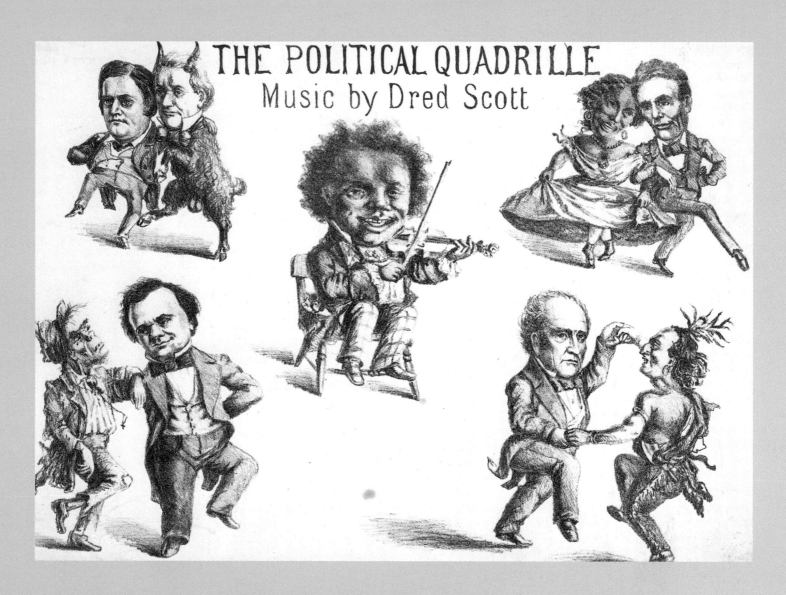

THE POLITICAL QUADRILLE
Music by Dred Scott

A Supreme Court Decision Splits the Nation

Dred Scott was an illiterate Missouri slave who sued to the Supreme Court for his freedom, arguing that as a one-time resident of Wisconsin Territory, where slavery had been prohibited by the Missouri Compromise (1820), he had been legally emancipated. Scott's case came before the Court at a time when there was great political pressure from President James Buchanan for the Court to clarify the issue of "popular sovereignty" and whether or not Congress could impose slave or free status on territories before they became states. The panel of nine justices included seven Democrats, five of them Southern, who ruled in 1857 that the Missouri Compromise was itself unconstitutional and that Congress could not interfere by designating certain territories as "free." The Court also decreed that since Dred Scott was a slave he did not possess the right to sue in a Federal court. The political ramifications of the Dred Scott decision were felt by the four major candidates in the 1860 Presidential election. The cartoon pairs each as a dancing partner with a constituent (clockwise from upper left): John C. Breckinridge with James Buchanan, Abraham Lincoln with a black woman, John Bell with a Native American, and Stephen A. Douglas with a territorial settler. The Dred Scott decision made a perilous situation even worse for black people, and contributed to increased militancy in free black communities. This activism, in turn, led the abolitionist John Brown to believe that a great slave rebellion was ready to explode, needing only the right spark to set it off.

The 1858 Senatorial race in Illinois pitted the nationally known incumbent, Stephen A. Douglas (right), against the relatively unknown Abraham Lincoln (opposite page). At first, the two stumped across the state, separately raising and answering charges, with Lincoln usually appearing in an area after Douglas had spoken. It was then proposed that the two appear together to debate the issues relating to the election. After some bargaining, the two agreed to share the same platform in seven Illinois districts—Ottawa, Freeport, Jonesboro, Charleston, Galesburg, Quincy, and Alton.

Not surprisingly, the Democratic newspapers praised every point made by Douglas, while the Republican organs touted their man, Lincoln. After the Ottawa debate, the pro-Douglas Chicago *Times* reported: "Lincoln . . . stood upon the

POLITICAL DEBATES

BETWEEN

HON. ABRAHAM LINCOLN

AND

HON. STEPHEN A. DOUGLAS,

In the Celebrated Campaign of 1858, in Illinois;

INCLUDING THE PRECEDING SPEECHES OF EACH, AT CHI-
CAGO, SPRINGFIELD, ETC.; ALSO, THE TWO GREAT
SPEECHES OF MR. LINCOLN IN OHIO, IN 1859,

AS

CAREFULLY PREPARED BY THE REPORTERS OF EACH PARTY, AND PUBLISHED
AT THE TIMES OF THEIR DELIVERY.

COLUMBUS:
FOLLETT, FOSTER AND COMPANY.
1860.

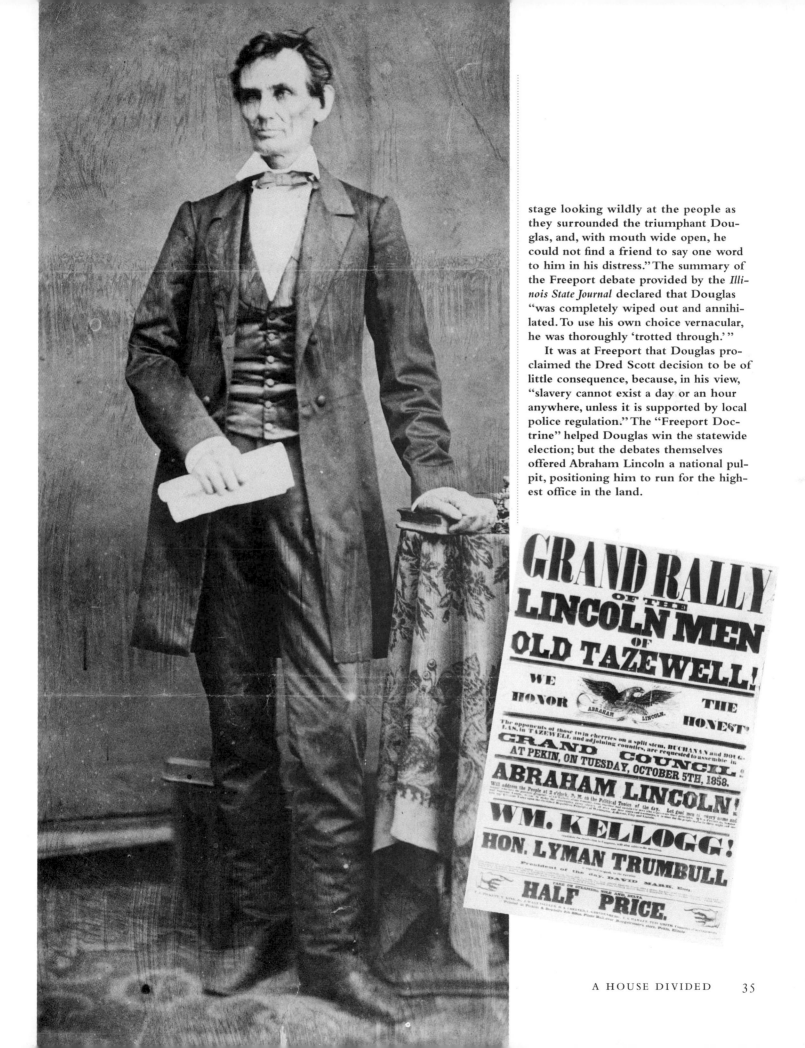

stage looking wildly at the people as they surrounded the triumphant Douglas, and, with mouth wide open, he could not find a friend to say one word to him in his distress." The summary of the Freeport debate provided by the *Illinois State Journal* declared that Douglas "was completely wiped out and annihilated. To use his own choice vernacular, he was thoroughly 'trotted through.'"

It was at Freeport that Douglas proclaimed the Dred Scott decision to be of little consequence, because, in his view, "slavery cannot exist a day or an hour anywhere, unless it is supported by local police regulation." The "Freeport Doctrine" helped Douglas win the statewide election; but the debates themselves offered Abraham Lincoln a national pulpit, positioning him to run for the highest office in the land.

ABOVE: Harpers Ferry, showing the engine house (left foreground) where Brown and his group made their stand.

RIGHT: A sketch by James E. Taylor based on testimony from the hostages taken by Brown, showing one of them arguing with the raid's leader.

OPPOSITE: In death John Brown received admiration and adulation that eluded him in life. When the French writer Victor Hugo learned of Brown's act he was so moved by the story that he drew this bitter sketch.

Victor Hugo 1860

John Brown's Hanging

By 1859, John Brown had taken his blood-soaked crusade against slavery to a new level. Bitterly inspired by the guerrilla wars of Kansas, he now nurtured plans for nothing less than a total slave revolt. In search of funds to achieve his goals, Brown successfully cultivated the abolitionists of New England. The monies raised were enough to equip a small force which Brown planned to use in a strike at the U.S. arsenal in Harpers Ferry, Virginia.

Late on October 16, 1859, Brown led his tiny army—16 whites, 4 free blacks, 1 runaway slave—into Harpers Ferry, where they took over the arsenal with almost no opposition. Hostages were taken and a proclamation was issued, inviting Virginia's slaves to flock to Brown for their salvation. At this crucial moment, though, the slaves held back. Meanwhile, U.S. troops under Colonel Robert E. Lee surrounded the raiders and, after a day of bloody standoff, stormed the building, capturing Brown and four survivors in his band.

A trial swiftly followed, the verdict of treason a foregone conclusion. On December 2, 1859, John Brown was executed by hanging before a guard force numbering 1,500. Extremists either hailed him as a martyr or denounced him as a traitor. The Reverend Henry Ward Beecher saw in Brown's death a condemnation of the North's failure to act decisively on the slavery issue. "What is average citizenship when a lunatic is a hero?" he asked.

In a great example of political prescience, Jeriah Bonham, of the Illinois *Gazette,* headlined his editorial for November 4, 1858: ABRAHAM LINCOLN FOR PRESIDENT IN 1860. Making canny use of the momentum provided by the debates with Douglas, Lincoln drove an impressive bandwagon of support to the Republican nominating convention in Chicago. In its February 16 issue, the Chicago *Tribune* provided four reasons to vote for him: "1st. A gentleman of unimpeachable purity of public life. . . . 2d. A man of, at once, great breadth and great acuteness of intellect. . . . 3d. Right on the record. . . . 4th. A man of executive capacity."

The building specially constructed for the Chicago convention became known as the "Wigwam" (above right). There the Lincoln bandwagon could not be stopped and he came away at the head of the ticket, with Maine's Hannibal Hamlin as his running mate (their campaign poster is shown below right). The Presidential contest was on, but at least in the eyes of the cartoonist responsible for "A Political Race" (below), Lincoln was outdistancing the pack.

THE REPUBLICAN WIGWAM AT CHICAGO, ILLINOIS, IN WHICH THE REPUBLICAN CONVENTION WILL BE HELD, MAY 16, 1860.

The road led steadily downhill after this. The Republicans won the election, as they were bound to do under the circumstances. Lincoln got less than a majority of the popular votes, but a solid majority in the electoral college, and on March 4, 1861, he would become President of the United States . . . but not, it quickly developed, of all of the states. Fearing the worst, the legislature of South Carolina had remained in session until after the election had been held. Once it saw the returns it summoned a state convention, and this convention, in Charleston on December 20, voted unanimously that South Carolina should secede from the Union.

This was the final catalytic agent. It was obvious that one small state could not maintain its independence; equally obvious that if South Carolina should now

"SEE THEM IN THEIR WINDING WAY"

MOHAWK WIDE AWAKES AND BAND
Parade, in honor of the Republican Victories, November, 1860.

Photograph by Stanton.

Lincoln, as was typical in the era, maintained a low profile during the campaign (he can be seen standing to the right of the doorway of his Springfield home in the above photograph taken in August, 1860), while his supporters demonstrated in massed rallies, such as the "Wide Awakes" shown left. Helped by a split within the Democratic Party that resulted in disaffected Southerners nominating John C. Breckinridge on a states' rights platform, while the regulars put forward Stephen A. Douglas, Lincoln took the largest number of popular votes (though he failed to obtain an absolute majority). Lincoln's victory was more lopsided in the electoral college, where he won with 180 votes, while his closest competitor, Breckinridge, racked up 72.

Even before voters went to the polls for the Presidential election of 1860, Southern governors, prompted by South Carolina's W. H. Gist, were conferring among themselves regarding secession. Although Governor Gist preferred not to make the first move, he quickly learned that the cotton states were badly split on the issue, with only three—Mississippi, Alabama, and Florida—ready to follow if some other state pulled out of the Union first. Driven by the firebrand spirit of young Congressmen like Lawrence Keitt ("If we submit [to the Lincoln government]," he wrote, "the South is done"), an elected convention of delegates gathered in Charleston in what would be called Secession Hall (seen at right in an 1861 image). In two intense days (December 19 and 20, 1860), these men shaped a new nation that they hoped would re-establish once and for all the social and philosophical basis of the South. "We, the people of the State of Carolina, in Convention assembled, do declare and ordain . . . that the union now subsisting between South Carolina and other States under the name of 'The United States of America' is hereby dissolved."

be forced back into the Union no one in the South ever need talk again about secession. The cotton states, accordingly, followed suit. By February, South Carolina had been joined by Mississippi, Alabama, Georgia, Florida, Louisiana, and Texas, and on February 8 delegates from the seceding states met at Montgomery, Alabama, and set up a new nation, the Confederate States of America. A provisional constitution was adopted (to be replaced in due time by a permanent document, very much like the Constitution of the United States), and Jefferson Davis of Mississippi was elected President, with Alexander Stephens of Georgia as Vice-President.

Perhaps it still was not too late for an adjustment. A new nation had come into being, but its creation might simply be a means of forcing concessions from the Northern majority; no blood had been shed, and states which voluntarily left the old Union might voluntarily return if their terms were met. Leaders in Congress worked hard, that winter of 1861, to perfect a last-minute compromise, and a committee led by Senator John J. Crittenden of Kentucky worked one out. In effect, it would re-establish the old line of the Missouri Compromise, banning slavery in territories north of the line and protecting it south; it would let future states enter the Union on a popular sovereignty basis; it called for enforcement of the fugitive slave law, with Federal funds to compensate slaveowners whose slaves

Respectfully dedicated to the MINUTE MEN of GEORGIA

Secession Quick Step

The SOUTH, The WHOLE South, and NOTHING but the SOUTH. NOLI ME TANGERE!!

by Herman L. Schreiner of MACON, Georgia,

also by the same Author:

"Cotton Planters CONVENTION Schottish." "JULIA Schottish."

&c. ~ &c.

MACON, GA.
Published by John C. Schreiner & Sons.

W.D. ZOGBAUM & CO. SAVANNAH, GA.

South Carolina's secession, as announced in broadsides such as the one below, set off an inexorable train of events. The years of divergent destinies, radically polarized social agendas, and sectional separation had settled on this time and this place to pass beyond the boundaries of reasoned discourse. When word of this dramatic action spread to other deep South states, six more ended their equivocation. Mississippi followed suit on January 9, Florida on January 10, Alabama on January 11, Georgia on January 19, Louisiana on January 26, and Texas on February 1. These actions were quickly celebrated in verse and song (left). When word reached Frederick Douglass he was elated. "Happily for the cause of human freedom, and for the final unity of the American nation," he wrote afterward, "the South was mad, and would listen to no concessions."

CHARLESTON
MERCURY
EXTRA:

Passed unanimously at 1.15 o'clock, P. M., December 20th, 1860.

AN ORDINANCE

To dissolve the Union between the State of South Carolina and other States united with her under the compact entitled " The Constitution of the United States of America."

We, the People of the State of South Carolina, in Convention assembled, do declare and ordain, and it is hereby declared and ordained,

That the Ordinance adopted by us in Convention, on the twenty-third day of May, in the year of our Lord one thousand seven hundred and eighty-eight, whereby the Constitution of the United States of America was ratified, and also, all Acts and parts of Acts of the General Assembly of this State, ratifying amendments of the said Constitution, are hereby repealed; and that the union now subsisting between South Carolina and other States, under the name of "The United States of America," is hereby dissolved.

THE
UNION
IS
DISSOLVED!

got away; and it provided that the Constitution could never be amended in such a way as to give Congress power over slavery in any of the states.

The Crittenden Compromise hung in the balance, and then collapsed when Lincoln refused to accept it. The sticking point with him was the inclusion of slavery in the territories; the rest of the program he could accept, but he wrote to a Republican associate to "entertain no proposition for a compromise in regard to the extension of slavery."

So the last chance to settle the business had gone, except for the things that might happen in the minds of two men—Abraham Lincoln and Jefferson Davis. They were strangers, very unlike each other, and yet there was an odd linkage. They were born not far apart in time or space; both came from Kentucky, near the Ohio River, and one man went south to become spokesman for the planter aristocracy, while the other went north to become representative of the best the frontier Northwest could produce. In the haunted decade that had just ended, neither man had been known as a radical. Abolitionists considered Lincoln too conservative, and Southern fire-eaters like South Carolina's Robert B. Rhett felt that Davis had been cold and unenthusiastic in regard to secession.

Now these two men faced one another, figuratively, across an ever-widening gulf, and between them they would say whether a nation already divided by mutual misunderstanding would be torn apart physically by war.

On February 4, 1861, little more than a week after the Louisiana legislature adopted an ordinance of secession, delegates from the six states already committed met in convention at Montgomery (the town is depicted in Theodore Davis' drawing below), to form a Southern republic. Within a week, they had hammered out a national constitution (heavily based on that of the United States but clarifying certain of its ambiguities along Southern lines), created a flag (the "Stars and Bars"), and selected their leadership team. As President, the delegates chose a Mississippean who had served the old United States as a military officer, Congressman, Senator, and Secretary of War—Jefferson Davis (opposite). Alexander H. Stephens of Georgia was named Vice-President. In his inaugural speech, Davis said: "If we may not hope to avoid war, we may at least expect that posterity will acquit us of having needlessly engaged in it."

On February 11, 1861, a day before his fifty-second birthday, Abraham Lincoln left his home in Springfield for the journey to the national capital. He parted, he told his supporters, "to assume a task more difficult than that which devolved upon General Washington." His route took him to Indianapolis, Columbus, and Pittsburgh, then along the Lake Erie shore into Buffalo, New York, across the state to Albany, down the Hudson to New York, through New Jersey into Pennsylvania (stopping in Philadelphia where, as shown in Thomas Nast's drawing at right, he was warmly welcomed), and finally to Baltimore for a change of cars to Washington. Convinced by his bodyguard that an ambush was planned in Baltimore, Lincoln allowed himself to be spirited through the city after dark, an action that left him open to unfriendly caricature, as in Adalbert John Volck's cartoon (below right).

OPPOSITE: Shortly before his inauguration, Lincoln agreed to sit for Washington's premiere photographer, Mathew Brady. The New York *Tribune*'s Horace Greeley found Lincoln's determination to preserve the Union "unequivocal, unhesitating, firm, and earnest."

CHAPTER 2

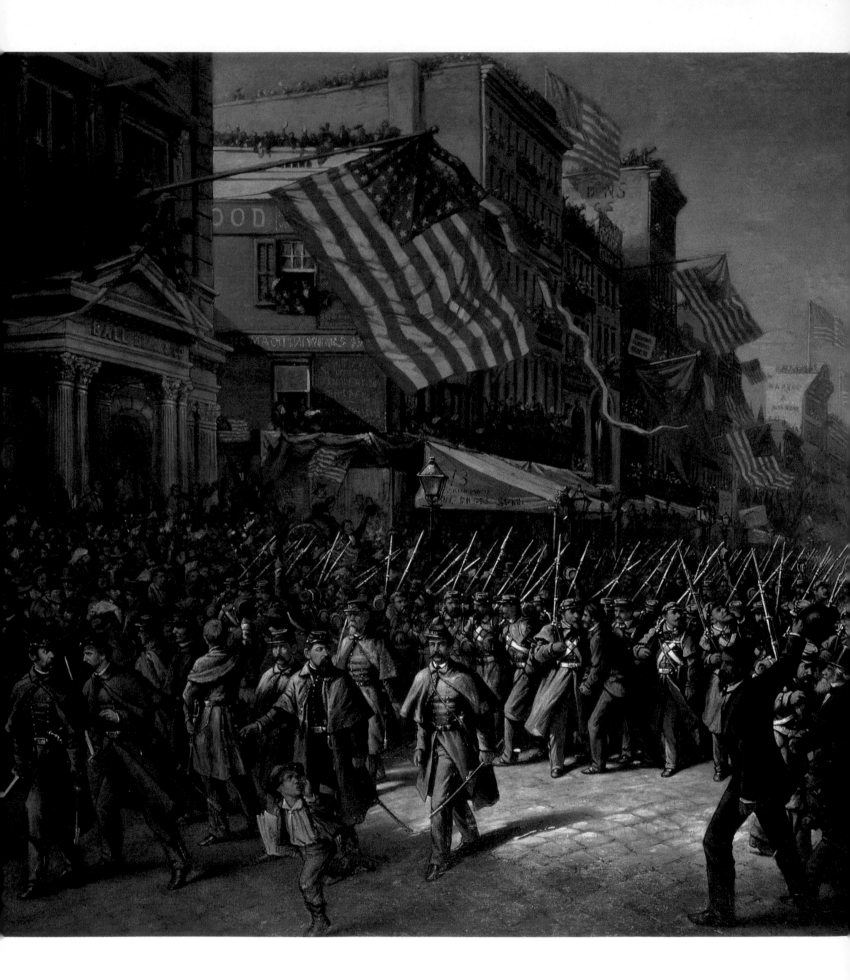

The Opening Guns

There had been many woeful misunderstandings between North and South in the years that led up to the Civil War, but the most tragic misunderstanding of all was that neither side realized, until it was too late, that the other side was desperately in earnest. Not until the war had actually begun would men see that their rivals really meant to fight. By that time it was too late to do anything but go on fighting.

Southerners had been talking secession for many years, and most people in the North had come to look on such talk as a counter in the game of politics. You wanted something, and you threatened that dire things would happen if you did not get what you wanted; but you didn't necessarily mean to do what you were threatening to do, and there was no sense in taking brash words at their face value. America as a nation of poker players understood all about the business of calling bluffs. Not until the guns began to go off would the North realize that when men like Jefferson Davis talked about seceding from the Union they meant every word of it.

The same was true, in reverse, in the South. It seemed incomprehensible there that the Federal Union meant so much in the North that millions of people would be ready to make war to preserve it. The North seemed to dislike both slavery and slaveowners; to the average Southerner, it stood to reason that the

In the words of the poet Walt Whitman, 1861 was an "Arm'd year—year of the struggle." The unleashing of national power and emotion is vividly captured in Thomas Nast's epic canvas (left) showing New York's crack 7th Regiment marching to war on April 19, 1861. To counter the "Stars and Stripes," Southerners had their own "Stars and Bars" standard (above).

Theodore R. Davis was a top Civil War combat artist for *Harper's Weekly*. In the 1880's, he completed a series of drawings for *Century Magazine* showing historical highlights of the conflict, many based on sketches he made at the time. This one (above) depicts the U.S. Army garrison in Charleston Harbor secretly abandoning Fort Moultrie on December 26, 1860, for the more easily defended Fort Sumter. Major Robert Anderson's men spiked the guns they left behind at Moultrie and, in a final symbolic act, cut down the flagstaff to forestall having a secessionist flag raised over the United States property.

North would be happy to get rid of both. Furthermore, it was not supposed that the North could fight even if it wanted to do so. It was a nation of mudsills and undigested immigrants, ruled by money-mad Yankees, and any army it raised would dissolve like the morning mists once it ran into real soldiers. The Southern orator who promised to wipe up, with his handkerchief, all of the blood that would be spilled because of secession was expressing a very common viewpoint.

For a while it looked as if the doubters on both sides might be right. Lincoln was inaugurated in Washington, and in his inaugural address he gave plain warning that he would do all in his power to "hold, occupy and possess" the property and places belonging to the Federal government which lay in Confederate territory. But after this speech was made nothing much seemed to happen, and the new Lincoln administration began to look strangely like that of the departed Buchanan.

When Lincoln said that he would hold all Federal property he referred chiefly to Fort Sumter, a pentagonal brick stronghold on an island near the mouth of Charleston Harbor. The commanding officer there was Major Robert Anderson, a regular army officer from Kentucky, and Anderson had sixty-eight soldiers, enough food to last a few more weeks, and a United States flag which he was determined to keep flying until he was compelled to haul it down. The sight of that flag was an offense to South Carolinians, and through them to the entire Confederacy. An independent nation could not countenance the existence of a foreign fort in the middle of one of its most important harbors, and the Confederate authorities tried hard but unsuccessfully to induce Washington to evacuate the place. They also put some thousands of Southern troops in gun pits and encampments all around the harbor, planting batteries where they would do the most good. In the end, negotiations having failed, and Lincoln having sent word that he was going to run supplies into the beleaguered fort, a clear indication that he proposed to hold it indefinitely, Jefferson Davis gave the word to open fire and bombard the place into submission. The Confederate commander at Charleston was

The Balance Sheet as War Began

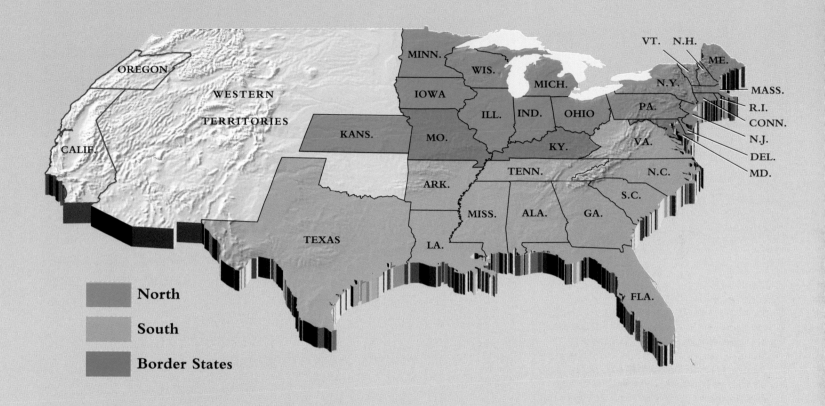

North

South

Border States

"Dependent upon Europe and the North for almost every yard of cloth, and every coat and boot and hat that we wear, for our axes, scythes, tubs, and buckets, in short, for everything except our bread and meat, it must occur to the South that if our relations with the North are ever severed . . . we should . . . be reduced to a state more abject than we are willing to look at even prospectively." Had Southern leaders paused to consider this warning from the editor of the Lynchburg *Virginian*, they would have seen how outnumbered they were in virtually every measurable category. The Union had more than twice the Confederacy's population, and 40 per cent of the latter was in slavery. In edible crops common to both sides, farmers in the North produced much more corn, wheat, and oats. Rebel munitions and foodstuffs would have to move on about a third of the total railroad mileage available to Northern merchants, and Southern commercial shipping was virtually nonexistent. The North's economic advantages extended to personal property (three dollars of value to every Southern one), bank capital (four to one), and the worth of manufactured products (ten to one). Concluded the Lynchburg *Virginian*'s Cassandra-like editor: "And yet, all of these things staring us in the face, we shut our eyes and go in blindfold."

Major Robert Anderson was an unlikely candidate to become a Northern hero. A loyal Kentuckian with a Georgian wife, he was a former slaveowner whose sympathies tended toward the South. He was also a career officer in the U.S. Army with an overriding sense of duty. These dual allegiances placed the dedicated soldier in a difficult position. How large his subsequent actions loomed in the popular mind can be gauged from Alban Jasper Conant's postwar portrait (right), heroic in every aspect. The simmering situation that confronted Anderson is expressed in William Waud's wash drawing (below), showing South Carolinians boldly placing cannon at a strategic point to target Fort Sumter.

the flamboyant General P. G. T. Beauregard, and he obeyed orders promptly. Sumter was ringed with fire, and after a thirty-four-hour bombardment Anderson hauled down his flag, turned the fort over to the Confederacy, and embarked his men on a steamer for New York. And the war was on.

The bombardment of Fort Sumter was spectacular, momentous—and, somehow, anticlimactic. It was the visible symbol that the war had begun—the thunderous announcement, to America and to all nations, that the New World's experiment in democracy had taken a strange new turn—yet when the guns were fired they merely ratified decisions which Lincoln and Davis had already made. Both men had made up their minds to fight rather than to yield, and each man had come to see Fort Sumter as the place for the showdown. (Oddly enough, the long bombardment killed no one on either side, and the war which was to be so costly began with a bloodless battle. The only lives lost at Sumter were lost after the

When Robert Anderson taught at West Point in the mid-1830's, one of his favorite pupils was a dashing dynamo from Louisiana named Pierre Gustave Toutant Beauregard (left). On March 3, 1861, Beauregard, now a brigadier general serving the Confederate States of America, took command of all secessionist forces in Charleston. Upon learning of this, Major Anderson warned Washington that Beauregard's presence "insures . . . the exercise of skill and sound judgment in all operations of the South Carolinians." Included among Beauregard's military assets was Castle Pinckney (below), an island fortification near Charleston over which a Palmetto State flag had been raised on December 27, 1860, in what some consider to be the first overt action of the Civil War.

surrender, when Major Anderson was firing a last salute to his flag; spare ammunition exploded and killed one gunner and mortally wounded another.)

A hysterical wave of emotion swept across the country when the news of Fort Sumter came out. War actually seemed to be welcomed, as if a tension which had grown completely unendurable had at last been broken. Whatever might happen next, at least the years of drift and indecision were over. Grim knowledge of the reality of war would come quickly enough, but right at first an unsophisticated people surged out under waving flags with glad cries and with laughter, as if the thing that had happened called for rejoicing.

The first move was up to Lincoln, and he made it without delay. He announced to the nation that "combinations too

A Fierce Defender of the South

If the entire course of Southern thought and action leading to civil war could be represented in a single individual, then Edmund Ruffin would be the most likely candidate. Born in the earliest days of the American republic, Ruffin was a Virginia farmer whose experiments in soil chemistry markedly improved the productivity of Southern agriculture. He became widely known for his writings on farm subjects, then he used this pulpit to preach the doctrines of slavery, states' rights, and secession. By 1861, Ruffin had come to hate the North with every ounce of his sixty-seven-year-old body. He admitted to having prayed on his knees that Lincoln might be elected (though he had voted for Breckinridge), certain that it would bring on a war for Southern independence. Ruffin was accorded a seat of honor at the South Carolina Secession Convention in Charleston and afterwards was gratified to see his picture sold all over town as the wave of Rebel patriotism began to swell toward its violent climax. When the moment of decision arrived, Ruffin was made a temporary gun captain, allowing him to fire one of the first cannon to open on Sumter. Six days later, uniformed as an honorary member of the Palmetto Guard, he sat for a victory portrait (left) that symbolizes Southern defiance.

powerful to be suppressed" by the ordinary machinery of peacetime government had assumed control of various Southern states; to restore order and suppress these combinations he called on the states to place 75,000 militia at the service of the Federal government. This call to arms brought a rush of enthusiastic recruiting all across the North, but at the same time it immediately put four more states into the Southern Confederacy. Virginia, North Carolina, Tennessee, and Arkansas had not yet left the Union; their sympathies were with the states which had seceded, but they had been clinging to the hope that the schism might yet be healed without bloodshed. Now they had to choose, and they chose promptly: all four left the Union and entered the Confederacy, and the Davis administration began to make arrangements to transfer the Confederate capital from Alabama to Richmond.

NEITHER NORTH NOR SOUTH was in the least ready for a war, and very few people in either section had any conception of the immense demands which the war was going to make. When the conflict began, the country's regular army consisted of no more than 16,000 men—barely enough to police the Indian country and the frontier and to man the coastal fortifications on a skeletonized basis. For whatever it might be worth, the army was at the disposal of the Federal government. It was obvious, however, that even if all of it could be massed in one spot (which was out of the question), it would not be nearly large enough for the job

For an age that accepted violence as the ultimate recourse in any dispute, the end of the Fort Sumter drama was as predictable as it was terrible. When talks for a peaceful evacuation of the post reached an impasse at 3:20 A.M., April 12, Southern negotiators delivered an ultimatum stating that their guns would open fire at the end of one hour. At the appointed time, a visiting V.I.P., former Virginia Congressman Roger Pryor, was offered the honor of starting things, but demurred. "I could not fire the first gun of the war," he said. Theodore R. Davis' watercolor (above) depicts the very instant that a Rebel signal shell exploded directly over Sumter, commencing a general bombardment. The time was 4:30 on the morning of April 12.

at hand. The load would have to be carried mainly by volunteers—which, at the beginning, meant state militia—and neither the weapons which the volunteers would use nor the uniforms they would wear, to say nothing of the officers who would lead them, as yet existed. Both sides were going to have to improvise.

The states did have their militia regiments, and these went to the colors at once. They were of uneven quality; none of them had ever had anything resembling combat training, and the best of them were drilled almost solely for parade-ground maneuvers. Even for parade, most units were poorly prepared. The average militia regiment was composed of one company from this town, another from that town, and so on, the ten companies scattered all across the state, and in many cases the individual companies had never been brought together to maneuver as a regiment. This was a serious handicap. By the military tactics of the 1860's, the ability of troops to maneuver as regiments or brigades was extremely important. To get from column into line—that is, from the formation in which they could march into the formation in which they could fight—called for a variety of highly intricate movements, for which incessant drill was required. A first-rate militia company which had never worked as part of a larger unit would be of little use on the battlefield until it had put in many hours of regimental and brigade drill.

Still, both sides were equally unready, and in both sections the work of preparation went on with excited haste if not with complete efficiency. All of these assorted military outfits went in for gaudy and impractical uniforms; most of them adopted flamboyant names, not realizing that the separate companies would quickly lose their identities as cogs in a larger machine. There were Frontier Guards, Rough-and-Ready Grays, Susquehanna Blues, and the like, and there were Game Cocks, Tigers, Invincibles, Fencibles, and Rangers beyond computation. (Some of the Blues, at this stage, were Southern, and some of the Grays were Northern; the adoption of recognizable national uniforms would come later, after a certain amount of battlefield confusion.) These separate companies were led by officers elected by the rank and file, which was also the case with most of the regiments. In most cases the officers owed their election to their talents as vote-getters, or simply to the fact that they were "leading citizens." Very few were chosen because they had any especial qualifications for military command. In time, field experience would weed out most of the misfits, but in the beginning the rival armies would consist of amateurs led by amateurs.

There were regular officers on hand, to be sure, but in the North the government did not quite know what to do with them. Lieutenant General Winfield Scott was general in chief; a fine soldier and an able strategist once, but very old now, physically all but helpless, perhaps touched with senility. He hoped to keep the regular army more or less intact, as the hard core around which the army of militiamen and volunteers would be built, and he did not want to see regular officers resign to take commissions with the amateurs. From the regulars, to be sure, would come the general officers—but not all of the general officers, at that,

Fort Sumter is shown here under fire, April 12, 1861. Wrote a correspondent for the Charleston *Mercury*: "Shell followed shell in quick succession; the harbor seemed to be surrounded with miniature volcanos belching forth fire and smoke."

Major Anderson was not the only Fort Sumter soldier hailed as a hero in the North. Early in the afternoon, Sergeant John Carmody, disobeying Anderson's orders, went out alone to the exposed barbette tier to fire its powerful guns (which were already loaded) at the enemy. Theodore R. Davis' drawing (right) presents "the war of Carmody against the Confederate States," as another Sumter man described it. Isolated heroism could not save the garrison, though, and after resisting until 1:30 P.M., April 13, Major Anderson hauled down his flag. Fort Sumter was formally occupied the next day, when jubilant Southerners raised their colors over the conquered outpost (opposite page).

for the administration was going to make generals out of a certain number of political leaders, and some of these would be given very important commands. The army immediately in front of Washington, which would be known as the Army of the Potomac, was given to Brigadier General Irvin McDowell, a regular. An army which was being raised in Ohio, which presently would invade western Virginia, was led by Major General George B. McClellan, a brilliant young West Pointer who had served in the Mexican War and then had left the army to become a railroad president. In St. Louis command was held by another regular, Brigadier General William A. Harney; he would be replaced before long by Major General John Charles Frémont, who had served in the regular army and had won fame as "The Pathfinder" of Far Western exploration. He was no West Pointer, and his service had been with the topographical engineers rather than with the line. Many new brigadiers would be named, some of them West Pointers, others not. For some time to come the administration would feel its way toward its new command setup, with no fixed program.

The Confederacy was a little more systematic. Jefferson Davis was a West Pointer himself, with a good deal of field experience, and he had served as Secretary of War. He had a good understanding of the military arts, although he apparently believed that his talents in this field were a bit more extensive than was actually the case, and as far as possible he intended to use trained soldiers for his general officers. About a third of the West Pointers in the regular army had resigned to serve with the South; one of the Confederacy's assets lay in the fact that these included some of the most capable men on the army roster. There was Robert E. Lee, for instance, to whom at the outbreak of the war command of the Federals' principal field army had been offered. Lee had rejected the offer and had gone with his state, Virginia, and Davis would make him a full general. The Beauregard who had taken Fort Sumter, and who now commanded the chief Confederate army in Virginia, was a professional soldier, highly regarded. From the West was coming another West Pointer of substantial reputation, General

"The assault upon Fort Sumter started us all to our feet, as one man," wrote a Philadelphia lawyer named Horace Binney. "There is among us but one thought, one object, one end, one symbol—the Stars and Stripes." On April 15, President Lincoln called for 75,000 volunteers, an appeal spread across the country through newspapers such as the New York *Herald* (above). A patriotic image of the time shows a determined Union eagle rooting the Rebel varmints out of its nest (right).

Albert Sidney Johnston. Still another former regular who would play a prominent part was General Joseph E. Johnston, who had many talents, but who would prove utterly unable to get along with President Davis.

One oddity about the whole situation was the fact that the regular army before the war had been very small, with an officer corps whose members knew one another quite intimately. A Civil War general, as a result, was quite likely to be very well acquainted with the man who was commanding troops against him, knowing his strengths and his weaknesses. There would be times when this mutual knowledge would have a marked effect on strategic and tactical decisions.

THE WAR AIMS OF the two sides were very simple. The Confederacy would fight for independence, the North for re-establishment of the Union. So far, slavery itself was definitely not an issue. The North was far from unity on this point; it was vitally important for Lincoln to keep the support of Northern Democrats, most of whom had little or no objection to the continued existence of slavery in the South; and both he and the Congress itself were explicit in asserting that they wanted to restore the Union without interfering with the domestic institutions of any of the states. In addition, there were the border states, Maryland and Kentucky and Missouri, slave states where sentiment apparently was pro-Union by a rather narrow margin, but where most people had no use at all for abolitionists or the abolitionist cause. If these states should join the Confederacy, the Union cause was as good as lost; probably the most momentous single item on Lincoln's program was the determination to hold these states in the Union. If he could help it, Lincoln was not going to fight a straight Republican war.

War aims would govern war strategy. The Confederacy was a going concern:

THE EAGLE'S NEST.

it had built a government, it was building an army, it considered itself an independent nation and it was functioning as such, and as far as Davis was concerned there would be no war at all unless the Lincoln administration forced one. The Confederacy, then, would act strictly on the defensive, and the opposite side of this coin was the fact that it was up to the North to be aggressive. Unless he could successfully take the offensive and keep at it until all of the "combinations too powerful to be suppressed" had been overthrown, Lincoln would have lost the war. In plain English, Northern armies had to invade the South and destroy the opposing government. This fact would go far to counterbalance the enormous advantages which the Federal government possessed in respect to manpower, riches, and the commercial and industrial strength that supports armies.

These advantages were impressive—so much so that Northern officers like

OUR COUNTRY'S FLAG HAS BEEN INSULTED !
REBELLION HAS BEEN INAUGURATED!
INVASION OF THE CAPITAL IS THREATENED !

FREEMEN, RALLY

PATRIOTS OF MARSHALL COUNTY, are called to meet at Lacon, on Saturday the 20th inst., at 1 o'clock P. M., to organize a Volunteer Company, to be tendered to the Government to support the *Constitution* and the *Laws*, in answer to the President's call.

"To Arms, to Arms ye Braves—
Our God and our Country."

Lacon, April 18th, A. D. 1861.

"Beat! beat! drums—blow! bugles, blow!" Walt Whitman's words recall something of the hot winds of patriotism that swept across the country "like a ruthless force." Spurred by a blizzard of recruiting posters, such as the one at left, young men rushed to join. An underage Indiana farm boy enviously watched his older friends sign up. "I know the Hale boys would fight with their fists . . . ," he wrote, "and I believe they would fight with guns too if needs be." Every image in the patriotic arsenal was brought to the fore, including a stalwart liberty maiden (above) dubbed "The Spirit of '61."

Border State Citizens Confront Bay State Soldiers

Unfortunately, Northern troops intended for the defense of Washington had to be shuttled or marched though the city of Baltimore since there was no through railroad service to the Capital. Baltimore's residents, wrote one observer, "loved the old flag; but they loved their brethren of the South, also."

Near midday on April 19, 1861, rumors spread that a large contingent of Federal soldiers was moving via the horse-drawn railroad track from President Street station along Pratt Street to the Camden Street depot. "The news . . . spread like wildfire," recalled a civilian, "and in a comparatively short time an immense crowd gathered . . . with the intention of preventing the passage of the troops."

These soldiers were all Massachusetts boys, members of that state's 6th Regiment under Colonel Edward F. Jones. Upon reaching the town, Colonel Jones made the ill-advised decision to shuttle his 800-man unit one company at a time instead of marching it in a large, compact body. Seven cars successfully ran the gauntlet; the eighth car either broke down or was stopped, forcing the soldiers to step out and confront a mob that was soon pelting them with stones. A shot rang out, a soldier in the front rank fell dead, and the officer in command ordered his men to return fire. The battered company eventually reached the Camden Street station, where the regiment continued on its way, leaving four of its number dead, along with twelve civilians killed. The bloody confrontation instantly became subject matter for popular lithography (above).

William T. Sherman and James B. McPherson warned Southern friends at the outbreak of the war that the Confederacy was bound to fail. In the North there were over eighteen million people; the South had hardly more than nine million, of whom more than a third were Negro slaves. Nine-tenths of the country's manufacturing capacity was situated in the North, which also had two-thirds of the railway mileage, to say nothing of nearly all of the facilities for building rails, locomotives, and cars. The North contained most of the country's deposits of iron, coal, copper, and precious metals. It controlled the seas and had access to all of the factories of Europe; it was also producing a huge surplus of foodstuffs which Europe greatly needed, and these would pay for enormous quantities of munitions. Taken altogether, its latent advantages were simply overpowering.

They did not, however, mean that Northern victory would be automatic. For the North had to do the invading, and in any war the invader must have a substantial advantage in numbers. The Confederacy occupied an immense territory, and the supply lines of the invader would be long, immobilizing many troops for their protection. Although the North controlled the seas, the Confederacy's coast line was almost endless; to seal the Southland off from the outside world would require a navy far larger than anything the United States previously had dreamed of possessing. Finally, the terms on which the war would be

At first Lincoln was willing to leave Baltimore's prickly residents alone. "Keep your rowdies in Baltimore and there will be no bloodshed," he told the city's mayor. But in May, with the Capital secured, Baltimore was pacified by force. Union troops entered the city on May 12 (as sketched by Frank H. Schell, below), while checkpoints were set up at strategic locations around the city (above).

"I don't believe there is any North!" a frustrated Abraham Lincoln declared in Washington as he anxiously awaited the arrival of the 7th New York and militia units from Rhode Island. The 7th was coming. Following a grand send-off parade in New York (above), the troops boarded ships that landed them at Annapolis (right), from which they marched into Washington to a delirious welcome.

fought meant that the average Southerner would always have a clearer, more emotionally stimulating picture of what he was fighting for than the average Northerner could hope to have. For the Southerner would see himself as fighting to protect the home place from the invader; the Northerner, on the other hand, was fighting for an abstraction, and the sacred cause of "the Union" might look very drab once real war weariness developed. To put it in its simplest terms, the North could lose the war if its people lost the desire to go on with the offensive; it could win only if it could destroy the Confederate people's *ability* to fight. In the end it would need every ounce of advantage it could get.

OLD WINFIELD SCOTT had sketched in a plan. It would take time to raise, equip, and train armies big enough to beat the South; start, therefore, by blockading the seacoast, seal off the inland borders as well, then drive down the Mississippi, constricting the vitality out of the Confederacy—and, at last, send in armies of invasion to break the Southern nation into bits. As things worked out, this was not unlike the plan that was actually followed, but when it was first proposed— news of it leaked out immediately, Washington's ability to keep things secret being very limited—the newspapers derided it, calling it the "Anaconda Plan" and intimating that it was far too slow for any use. Very few men, either in the North or in the South, were ready to admit that the war would be a long one. The militia had been called into Federal service for just ninety days, the limit

The 7th New York was a showcase regiment, accustomed to strutting along in carefully tailored gray uniforms. Some of the unit's tidy élan can be discerned in this camp photo of several of its members. "We are here," wrote an Irish private soon after the 7th reached Washington, ". . . we all feel somewhat as Mr. Caesar Augustus must have felt when he had crossed the Rubicon."

By mid-May, Northern troops were pouring into Washington and their encampments spread across the city. The artist-correspondent Arthur Lumley sketched some of those troops—as he titled the drawing—*Awaiting the Enemy* (right). It was a time of military pageantry, including formal reviews by the President (below) along with all sorts of drills and demonstrations. "There seemed to be one continual drumbeat," wrote a visitor to the city. "People were awakened by the reveille, walked with measured tread during the day, and were lulled by the tattoo at night."

under existing law; it seemed reasonable to many people to suppose that before their term of service expired they ought to win the war.

Before the war could be won, however, the border states had to be secured, and to secure them the Lincoln administration used a strange combination of tactful delicacy and hardfisted ruthlessness.

Kentucky got the delicate handling. This state had a secessionist governor and a Unionist legislature, and in sheer desperation it was trying to sit the war out, having proclaimed its neutrality. For the time being both Lincoln and Davis were willing to respect this neutrality. They knew that it could not last, but the side that infringed it was apt to be the loser thereby, and until the situation elsewhere began to jell, both leaders were willing to leave Kentucky alone. (Both sides unofficially raised troops there, and there was a home guard organization which might turn out to be either Unionist or Confederate.)

If Kentucky got delicate handling, what Maryland and Missouri got was the back of the Federal government's hand.

The death of the dashing New York colonel, Elmer Ellsworth, killed during the Union occupation of Alexandria after he had removed a Confederate flag from a hotel roof (Alonzo Chappel painting, left), deeply affected Abraham Lincoln. The twenty-four-year-old Ellsworth had been one of the four members of the military escort accompanying the President-elect from Springfield to Washington. His boyish enthusiasm, utter confidence, and unwavering determination drew him close to Lincoln, who called him "the greatest little man I ever met." John Hay and John G. Nicolay, then White House secretaries, remembered of Ellsworth that "the echoes of his cheery and manly voice seemed yet to linger in the corridors and rooms of the Executive Mansion."

Not long after Fort Sumter, the 6th Massachusetts Regiment was marching through Baltimore en route to Washington. There were many ardent Southerners in Baltimore, and these surrounded the marching column, jeering and catcalling. Inevitably, people began to shove and throw things, and finally the troops opened fire and there was a bloody fight in the streets. Soldiers and civilians were killed—more civilians than soldiers, as it happened—and although the 6th Regiment finally got to Washington, railroad connection via Baltimore was temporarily broken, and Lincoln took speedy action. Federal troops occupied Baltimore. Secessionist members of the legislature were thrown in jail, as were various city officials of Baltimore, and they were kept there until the Unionists got things firmly in hand. All of this, of course, was plainly illegal, but the Federal government was not going to let the secessionists cut Washington off from the rest of the North, no matter what it had to do to prevent it; with dissident legislators in jail, the Unionist governor of Maryland had little trouble holding the state in the Union.

What happened in Missouri was somewhat similar. The state had refused to secede, sentiment apparently being almost evenly divided, but like Kentucky it had a pro-Southern governor, and he maintained a camp of state troops on the edge of St. Louis. The presence of these troops worried the Federal commander, General Harney, not at all, but it worried other Unionists a great deal, the fear being that the state troops would seize the government arsenal in St. Louis. With the weapons taken there the governor could arm enough secessionist Missourians to take the state out of the Union. So Washington temporarily replaced General Harney with a fiery young regular, Captain Nathaniel S. Lyon—putting a captain in a brigadier's job was stretching things a bit, but not all of the old rules would be valid in this war—and Lyon took his soldiers out, arrested the state troops, disarmed them, and broke up their camp. As he marched his men back to barracks a street crowd collected; as in Baltimore there was jostling, shoving, name-calling, and a display of weapons; and at last the troops opened fire, killing more than a score of civilians. It may be instructive to note that the first fighting in the Civil War, after Fort Sumter, involved men in uniform shooting at men who were not in uniform—the classic pattern of a civil war.

Lyon was all flame and devotion, too impetuous by half. In an effort to keep some sort of peace in Missouri, Harney had worked out an informal truce with the governor of the state, the essence of it being that nobody would make any hostile moves until the situation had taken more definite shape. Lyon swiftly disavowed this truce, drove the governor away from the machinery of government, and marched his little army clear down into southwest Missouri in an effort to rid the state of all armed Confederates. He got into a sharp fight at Wilson's Creek and lost his life. His army had to retreat, and the Confederates continued to hold

Lincoln's first call for 75,000 volunteers was followed in May by his executive decree adding 42,000 places to the volunteer list and expanding the regular army by 23,000. On July 22, Congress weighed in by passing legislation for 500,000 more. Leaving states from Maine to Kansas, volunteers came and by July, more than 180,000 had been enrolled in the Northern ranks. This photo shows the 1st Michigan receiving its regimental colors in Detroit on May 1, 1861. One of the earliest Western regiments to reach Washington, the 1st Michigan fought at the First Battle of Bull Run.

The prospect of war awakened in many Northern women a fierce sense of national loyalty. "It seems as if we never were alive till now," said one, "never had a country till now." In this picture a group of Philadelphia ladies are sewing a regimental battle flag. "Republicanism will wash," a New England woman assured one of her friends in May, "*is* washed already in the water and the fire of this fresh baptism, 'clothed in white samite, mystic, wonderful,' and has a new name, which is *Patriotism*."

southwestern Missouri; and partly because of the bitterness growing out of Lyon's high-handed actions the unhappy state was plagued for the rest of the war by the most virulent sort of partisan warfare. But Missouri did not leave the Union, which was all that Washington cared about at the moment. Legally or otherwise, the Federal government was making the border secure.

Western Virginia also had to be dealt with, but that was easier.

The western counties of Virginia had long been antipathetic to the tidewater people, and when Virginia left the Union, the westerners began to talk about seceding from Virginia. Young General McClellan got an army over into the mountain country and without too great difficulty defeated a small Confederate force which he found there. With victorious Federal troops in their midst, the western Virginia Unionists perked up; in due course they would organize their own state of West Virginia, which the Federal government would hasten to admit to the Union; and although there might be a good deal to be said about the legal ins and outs of the business, the government had at least made certain that the Ohio River was not going to be the northern border of the Confederacy.

But if the border states had been held, the gain was negative. The South seemed unworried, and it was visibly building up its strength. Richmond now was the capital, new troops were pouring in for its defense, and cadets from the Virginia Military Institute were putting in busy days acting as drillmasters. (They had been led to Richmond by a blue-eyed, ungainly professor, a West Pointer who would soon be a Confederate general of renown, Thomas J. Jackson.) The North was never going to win the war by thwarting secessionist designs in Missouri and Maryland. It could win it only by moving south and giving battle; and as the summer of 1861 came on the time for such a move was at hand.

THE WAY GENERAL SCOTT had planned it, the first year of the war would be spent, mostly, in getting ready. The old general had a poor opinion of volunteer troops—like most West Pointers, he felt that they had behaved badly in the Mexican War—and he believed that it would take a long time to prepare them for field service. It would also take a long time to get the supply service organized, so that boots and pants and coats and tents and muskets and all of the other things the new armies would need could be produced in adequate quantities. It would be absurd to start offensive operations until properly trained armies, fully supplied and equipped, were ready to move.

In all of this General Scott was quite correct, by the standards of military logic. Unfortunately, however, military logic was not going to be controlling in this war. What was going on between North and South was a violent extension of a political contest, and the rules and axioms of formalized warfare were not going to mean much.

By those rules and axioms, for instance, Mr. Davis' Confederacy was in hopeless shape. Some of the best manpower any soldier ever saw was flocking to the colors—lean, sinewy men used to handling weapons and to outdoor life, men who could get along very well on poor rations and skimpy equipment, violent men who had a positive taste for fighting—but much of this manpower could not be used because there were no arms. At the beginning of the war the U.S. government arsenals held more than 500,000 small arms, and 135,000 of these were in the South. These, of course, the Confederacy had promptly seized, but it needed a great many more, and anyway only 10,000 of the confiscated guns were modern rifles. The rest were old-fashioned smoothbores, many of them flintlocks little different from the Brown Bess of Revolutionary War days. Frantic state governors had tried to collect weapons from their backwoods owners—shotguns, country rifles, and whatnot—but very little could be done with these; their use would complicate the ammunition supply pattern beyond solution.

To make things worse, the Confederate government had made a miscalculation in respect to cotton which would have a permanently crippling effect.

The Northern blockade was not yet effective, and it would be many months before it would be. The markets of Europe were open, and all of the munitions which the South so desperately needed were for sale in them. Furthermore, they could very easily be paid for with cotton, of which the South had millions of

Off to War: The North

Samuel Cormany (above), who was to become a Union cavalry officer, wrote this entry in his diary the day he signed up: *The air is full of calls for men who are patriotic to enlist—I really inwardly feel that I want to go and do my part—as a man . . . and Darling is likeminded. . . . She calmly consents— That if I desire to go and make the sacrifice for our Country—our Homes, our firesides, she calmly says, though hard to say it—"Yes I am willing." "There will be a way" and thus we wrestled with the problem. Spending a great deal of time on our knees, before our God—and agreed that as a loyal, patriotic Man I should Enlist.*

The clarion call to arms was heard in the South as well as the North. Throughout Virginia's lower Shenandoah Valley, militia units formed in small villages and marched to larger towns such as Martinsburg, where they came together to form regiments, as depicted in Alfred Wordsworth Thompson's sketch (opposite page). "Spurs jingled, sabres rattled, horses neighed, and the voices of officers were heard in every direction marshaling their troops," remembered an observer. Many of these young warriors entered the ranks after having been lovingly outfitted by proud family and friends, as shown in W. L. Sheppard's painting, *Equipment '61* (above). According to one Tennessee Rebel, "Every person, almost, was eager for the war, and we were all afraid it would be over and we not be in the fight."

bales. Energetic action in the first few months of the war could have solved all of the Confederacy's problems of equipment.

But the Southern leaders had chanted "Cotton is King" so long that they had come to believe it. If England and France, and most particularly England, could not get the cotton which their mills needed, it was believed, they would presently intervene in this war, break the Union blockade (which did not yet really exist), and underwrite the Confederacy's independence in order to insure their own supply of cotton. Consequently, the Confederate government in its wisdom refused to export cotton, in order to make certain that England and France would feel the pressure. In effect, it made the Federal blockade effective until such time as the Federal navy could handle the job unaided; and what it had failed to figure on was that because there had been heavy cotton crops during the years just before the war began, there was a substantial carry-over on the world market in 1861. England and France could get along nicely for months to come; so nicely that even in 1862 England was actually shipping some of its cotton back to New England.

Because of all this the Confederacy was not getting the weapons it wanted at the time when it needed them most, and when it could unquestionably have got them without the slightest difficulty. So it could not arm all of the men who were clamoring to get into the army, and the ones who were armed were armed most imperfectly. In time, this problem of weapons would be adjusted. Meager as its industrial facilities were, the South would do wonders with what was available and would produce artillery, small arms, powder, and bullets; it would eventually import European goods in spite of the tightening blockade; and from first to last

"South Carolina troops pass every day," wrote a proud Palmetto State diarist on a visit to Richmond in July, 1861. "They go by with a gay step." The companies that made up the regiments came from throughout the state. Some sported colorful names like the Enoree Mosquitoes, the Carolina Bees, or the Horry Rebels. Pictured above are the Charleston Zouave Cadets, present in full armament, uniform, and accompanied (at left) by two carefully outfitted black orderlies. Also answering their new country's appeal were Georgians of the Sumter Light Guards (right), neatly formed under the Stars and Bars.

The solemn faces of Virginia privates Charles A. Pace (far left) and John Werth (near left) mask the anxiety faced by all soldiers confronting combat for the first time. Another Virginia soldier, Carlton McCarthy, put the thoughts of those young men into words: "In a thousand ways he is tried . . . every quality is put to the test. If he shows the least cowardice he is undone. His courage must never fail."

it would capture a great deal of war material from the Yankees. But in 1861 it was in dire straits, with untrained armies, inadequate in size and very poorly outfitted. By military logic it was little better than helpless.

But the North was not a great deal better off. To be sure, it had more weapons than the South had, and its means of adding to its supply were much broader. Washington by now was ringed with camps, very martial-looking, with some of the new three-year volunteer regiments mingling with the ninety-day militia units, and to Northern editors and politicians it seemed that it was high time for a little action. That the generals who would control these formless levies had never handled large bodies of troops before, that the soldiers themselves were mere civilians in arms with very little discipline and no understanding of the need for any, that what was believed to be an army was simply a collection of independent companies and regiments hopelessly unready to maneuver or fight as a coherent mass—of all of these things few people had any comprehension. The pressure for an immediate advance on the new Confederate capital at Richmond became stronger. Horace Greeley, the forceful but eccentric editor of the powerful New York *Tribune*, was sounding off with his "Forward to Richmond!" war-cry; and although General McDowell, commander of the troops around Washington, knew perfectly well that it would be a long time before his men were ready for a battle, there was nothing he could do about it. Ready or not, he was going to have to move.

EVENTS IN WESTERN VIRGINIA in June and early July seemed to show that the time for a big offensive campaign was at hand.

General McClellan had taken some 20,000 men across the Ohio River and was moving east from Parkersburg along the line of the Baltimore and Ohio Railroad. With a portion of his army he surprised and routed a small contingent of Confederates at the town of Philippi, winning a very small victory which a jubilant press enlarged into a major achievement. With other troops he made an

Whatever their visions of glory, the young men who marched off to war first had to part from loved ones at home. The unsigned illustration *Off to the Front* (right) is filled with the awkward poignancy of the moment, while in George Cochran Lambdin's painting *The Consecration, 1861* (opposite page) the mood is one of reverent benediction. Behind it all was an innocence that would not long survive; as a Georgia woman put it: "We had an idea that when our soldiers got upon the ground and showed . . . they were really . . . willing to fight . . . the whole trouble would be declared at an end."

advance to Beverly, on the turnpike that led via Staunton to the upper end of the Shenandoah Valley, and at Rich Mountain, near Beverly, he routed a Confederate army of 4,500 men. Western Virginia apparently was safe for the Union now, and McClellan's dispatches spoke enthusiastically of the way his men had "annihilated two armies . . . intrenched in mountain fastnesses fortified at their leisure." To a country hungry for good news this was most welcome. Furthermore, McClellan's troops were no better trained than McDowell's. If they could campaign in rough mountain country, annihilating their foes and storming lofty passes, it seemed reasonable to suppose that McDowell's men could do as well in the more open country between Washington and Richmond. Early in July, McDowell was directed to organize and launch a thrust at the principal Confederate army, which lay at and around Manassas Junction, some twenty-five miles from Washington, behind a meandering little river known as Bull Run.

The military situation in Virginia was slightly complicated.

Federal troops under one of the newly created political generals, Ben Butler of Massachusetts, occupied Fort Monroe, at the tip of the Virginia Peninsula. Butler had essayed a mild advance up the Peninsula but had given it up when his advance guard lost a sharp little skirmish at a place known as Big Bethel. He would be inactive, his force not large enough to require more than a small Confederate contingent to watch it.

Up the Potomac River, in the vicinity of Harpers Ferry, there were 16,000 Federal troops commanded by an aged regular, Major General Robert Patterson.

The arrival of the Original Contraband
At Fortress Monroe—

PREVIOUS SPREAD: When America turned to civil war in 1861 no one in authority wanted the nation's blacks involved. "The existing war has no direct relation to slavery," declared one influential newspaper. When a few slaves actually fled to Union strongholds at the Confederate perimeter they were returned to their masters by Federal officers who felt obligated to enforce the Fugitive Slave Act. All this changed in late May, 1861, when, as depicted here in Theodore R. Davis' painting, several slaves escaped to Fortress Monroe on the tip of the Virginia Peninsula and said that their master had used them to dig a Confederate battery position. The U.S. officer commanding there, a shrewd Massachusetts lawyer and politician named Benjamin F. Butler, reasoned that since the owner's property—in this case human property—had been used against the Union, those same slaves could be seized as legitimate contraband-of-war. Federal soldiers thereby had a legal means to offer sanctuary to escaped slaves.

The need to choose sides caused deep divisions within families, communities, and states. In Missouri, the outbreak of the Civil War merely added a national dimension to bitter fighting that had been taking place for years between pro-Union "jayhawkers" and pro-Southern "border ruffians." Though guerrilla warfare would continue unabated, both sides raised formally organized units such as the 9th Missouri (below), which entered Federal service. Eventually 109,000 Missourians wore blue, while 40,000 donned gray.

Patterson meant well, but he was far past his prime and would very shortly demonstrate that he was much too infirm for field command. Facing him were perhaps 9,000 Confederates under the canny Joe Johnston.

Behind Bull Run there were approximately 20,000 Confederates under Beauregard. Johnston outranked Beauregard, but while Johnston remained in the Shenandoah Valley, Beauregard was virtually independent. Since Beauregard had the biggest force, and since he lay squarely across the line of the Orange and Alexandria Railroad, which looked like the best way for a Federal army to approach Richmond, Beauregard's army was the chosen target.

McDowell, therefore, would march down overland to make his attack. He noted that a railway line ran from Manassas Junction to the Shenandoah Valley, within convenient range of Johnston's men; if Johnston could give Patterson the slip he could quite easily move his troops down to the Bull Run area and reinforce Beauregard. Patterson, accordingly, was instructed to keep pressure on Johnston so that he could not detach any troops. McDowell, whose army would total about 35,000 men, thus would have what ought to be a decisive numerical advantage when he made his fight. On the afternoon of July 16 his troops started out.

There is nothing in American military history quite like the story of Bull Run. It was the momentous fight of the amateurs, the battle where everything went wrong, the great day of awakening for the whole nation, North and South together. It marked the end of the ninety-day militia, and it also ended the rosy time in which men could dream that the war would be short, glorious, and bloodless. After Bull Run the nation got down to business.

WHEN IT SET OUT from Washington, McDowell's army was at least brilliant to look at. The militia regiments wore a variety of uniforms. Many of the contingents were dressed in gray. Others wore gaudy clothing patterned after the French Zouaves—baggy red breeches, short blue coats, yellow or scarlet sashes about the

Camp Las Moras' C.S.A. near Fort Clark, Texas, March 1861. This was the first war sketch rec'd by Harpers. Following the surrender of Gen'l Twiggs

Another state split by conflicting allegiances was Tennessee, where, as the 1861 drawing below shows, rival Union and Confederate meetings in Knoxville drew equal crowds. The issue was much less in doubt in Texas, where the pro-Southern U.S. Army commander obligingly surrendered his men and munitions to Texas authorities on February 18. These weapons helped arm newly raised Rebel units such as the one shown in the sketch (left) at Camp Las Moras, Texas, in March. The U.S. capitulation in Texas briefly detained an army officer in transit from his frontier post to Washington for reassignment. The officer was a Virginian; as his state had not yet decided its course, so his own course remained uncertain. His name was Robert E. Lee.

Missouri's entry into the Confederacy seemed inevitable when its secessionist governor, Claiborne Jackson, called out the state militia to resist Lincoln's call for troops. Jackson was opposed by Congressman Frank Blair who found a ready ally in a wiry U.S. Army officer named Nathaniel Lyon, whom one friendly observer found consumed with an "anger that was almost insane." Acting quickly, Lyon protected the U.S. arsenal in St. Louis and disarmed the pro-Jackson militia. The pro-Confederate forces were not suppressed without bloodshed however. When a volunteer company of loyal German-Americans was attacked by a secessionist crowd in the center of the city, the inexperienced troops opened fire (above).

waist, turbans or fezzes for the head. There was a New York regiment which called itself the Highlanders, and it had kilts for dress parade, although on this campaign the men seem to have worn ordinary pants. Regimental flags were of varicolored silk, all new and unstained. Baggage trains, which were somewhat tardy, were immense. A regiment at that time had as many wagons as a brigade would have a little later. From McDowell on down no one knew anything about the mechanics of handling a large army on the march, and logistics were badly fouled up. The fact that most of the soldiers would break ranks as the mood took them—to wander into a field to pick blackberries, to visit a well for drinking water, or simply to take a breather in the shade—did not help matters much. No more informal, individualistic collection of men in uniform ever tried to make a cross-country march. The weather was hot, and great clouds of dust settled over the fancy uniforms.

Beauregard, at Manassas Junction, knew that the Yankees were coming. He had a good intelligence service, with spies in Washington who kept him posted, and in any case there was nothing secret about this move; half of the country knew about it, and Beauregard had ample time to make preparations. He was an able soldier, this Beauregard, but rather on the flashy side, given to the construction of elaborate plans, and he considered that he would smite this invading host by a clever flank attack without waiting for it to assault him. His troops were in line along eight miles of Bull Run, covering the bridges and the fords, and Beauregard planned to swing his right over the stream and strike the Union left before McDowell was ready. Oddly enough, McDowell was planning a somewhat similar move himself—to demonstrate before the Confederate center, cross the bulk of his troops a few miles upstream, and come down hard on the Confederate left.

McDowell's army moved very slowly—which, considering everything, is hardly surprising—and contact with the Confederates was not made until July 18. On this day a Union division prowled forward to Blackburn's Ford, near the center of the line, to make a demonstration; it prowled too far, and was driven back with losses, and the Confederates were mightily encouraged.

Meanwhile, in the Shenandoah Valley, Joe Johnston had given Patterson the slip. He had moved forward and had made menacing gestures, which led Patterson to believe that he was about to be attacked; then, while the old Federal took thought for his defenses, Johnston got most of his men away and took the cars for Manassas. His men would arrive at Bull Run just in time. Johnston himself, ranking Beauregard, would be in command of the united armies, although this was a point that Beauregard never quite seemed to understand.

In any case, the great battle finally took place on July 21, 1861. This was the day on which Beauregard was to make his flank attack, modeled, he proudly remarked, on Napoleon's battle plan at Austerlitz. (Most professional soldiers then had the Napoleon complex, and of all armies that of the French was the most respected.) Beauregard's move, however, was a complete fiasco. Like McDowell, he had no staff worthy of the name, and routine staff work in

The firm actions taken by Nathaniel Lyon (above) may have forestalled, but they did not halt, the Confederacy's efforts to claim Missouri. With a pro-Union state convention in the statehouse acting as if it were the duly elected legislature, Governor Jackson convened the secessionist members of the legislature to proclaim the state's independence, backed by an 11,000-man army under Sterling Price gathered at Wilson's Creek. Though leading a smaller force, Lyon impetuously attacked Price, only to be soundly defeated. The Union officer fell while trying to rally his troops, a dramatic moment depicted in Henri Lovie's battlefield sketch (left).

A Confederate

"There is now 75 thousand men in front of—& in the City of Washington—& one universal grumble at Genl Scotts do nothing policy with such immense means." Elizabeth Blair Lee was a well-bred forty-three-year old Washingtonian writing in June, 1861. The object of her impatience was General Winfield Scott, then commanding the Union armies. A certified hero in the War of 1812, and an architect of the U.S. victory in the Mexican War, Scott (with his staff, right) was seventy-five years old in 1861, proud and irascible.

Battery previous to the Battle of Bulls-Run

Physically unable to take to the field and distrusting the hordes of volunteer soldiers camped around Washington, Scott hoped for time to properly train his rabble and their officers. Brigadier General Irvin McDowell (with his staff, left) was selected for the active command, even though he had never directed any significant body of troops. Under increasing public pressure, he agreed to strike at the Confederate troops gathered some twenty-five miles southwest of the Capital. What those Rebels lacked in resources was made up in ingenuity, such as the battery pictured above which found a way to do without horses. It took the name "bull," but oxen proved more manageable in the yolk.

Beginning in May and continuing through June into July, Confederates assembled most of their army near the strategically important town of Manassas Junction. Marveled one Rebel soldier, "It is the place for meeting people, not unlike New York City." Local residents tried to lead a normal life, including attending regular services at Sudley Church in a quiet stand of trees on a hill (right). Meanwhile, young men from North Carolina, Louisiana, South Carolina, Mississippi, Alabama, Virginia, Tennessee, Georgia, and Maryland drilled in nearby fields as they prepared to meet the enemy.

consequence never got done. Orders went astray, those that did reach their destination were not understood or followed, and the advance of the Confederate right amounted to nothing more than a series of convulsive twitches by a few brigades.

All in all, this was a lucky break for the Confederates. The Rebel army at Bull Run was in no better shape than the Federal army, but when the showdown came it was able to fight on the defensive—which, as numerous battles in this war would show, was infinitely easier for untrained troops. For McDowell's flank move was actually made, and although it was inordinately slow and confused, it did at last put a solid segment of the Union army across Bull Run at a place called Sudley Church, in position to march down and hit the Confederates' left flank. A doughty Confederate brigadier commanding troops at the Stone Bridge, where the main road to Washington crossed Bull Run, saw the Yankees coming and fought a stout delaying action which held them off until Johnston and Beauregard could form a new line, on the wooded plateau near the Henry House, to receive the attack. McDowell sent forward two excellent regular army batteries, and the battle was on.

For men who had never fought before, and who had been given no training of any real consequence, the Northerners and Southerners who collided here did a great deal better than anyone had a right to expect. A good many men ran away, to be sure, but most of them stayed and fought, and the struggle was a hot one. For a time it seemed that the Confederate line would be broken and that the "Forward to Richmond" motif would come to a triumphant crescendo. The two regular batteries that had been doing such good work were advanced to the crest

One of the more prosperous residents of the Manassas Junction area was Wilmer McLean, whose 1,400-acre plantation spread along both sides of a large, meandering creek known as Bull Run. McLean's substantial home (left) would be used as a headquarters by Confederate officers and was precariously close to the bloody fighting of the upcoming battle. It would all prove too much for McLean, who afterwards moved his family to Appomattox Court House, Virginia, where, he assured everyone, "the sound of battle would never reach them."

of Henry House Hill, infantry came surging along with them, and a number of the Confederate units weakened and began to drift to the rear.

THEN CAME ONE of those moments of dramatic inspiration that men remember. Brigadier General Barnard Bee sought to rally some of the wavering Confederate regiments. Not far away he saw a Virginia brigade of Johnston's troops, standing fast and delivering a sharp fire: a brigade led by that former Virginia Military Institute professor, Brigadier General T. J. Jackson.

"There is Jackson standing like a stone wall!" cried Bee, gesturing with his sword. "Rally behind the Virginians!"

So a great name was born. From that moment on the man would be Stonewall Jackson.

Bee's troops rallied. Fresh Confederate troops, just off the train from the Valley, kept coming in on their flank. The two pestiferous Union batteries, placed too far forward to get proper support from their own infantry, were taken by a sudden Confederate counterattack—the Rebels here wore blue uniforms, and the gunners held their fire until too late, supposing the attacking wave to be Unionists coming up to help—and suddenly the Union offensive, which had come so near to success, collapsed, all the heart gone out of it, and the soldiers who had been involved in it turned and headed for the rear.

There was no rout here. The Union attack had failed and the men were withdrawing, but there was no panic. One trouble apparently lay in the fact that the tactical maneuver by which troops fighting in line would form column and go to the rear was very complicated, and most of these green Union troops did not have it down pat; a withdrawal under fire was bound to become disordered

This painting (right) by Union battle participant James Hope shows one of the dramatic last actions in the fighting at Bull Run, around Henry Hill. In a final effort to wrest the hill away from Confederate troops, Colonel Oliver O. Howard's brigade, made up of regiments from New England, formed an assault on Chinn Ridge just south of that point. The attack failed, killing 50 of the Yankees and wounding 116. Howard watched his men move up into the position pictured. "Most were pale and thoughtful," he wrote. "Many looked up into my face and smiled."

and finally uncontrollable, not because the men had lost their courage but simply because they had not had enough drill. McDowell saw that nothing more could be done here and passed the word for a retreat to his advanced base at Centreville, four or five miles nearer Washington.

It was after the beaten army had crossed Bull Run that the real trouble came, and the fault lies less with the soldiers than with the reckless Washington civilians who had supposed that the edge of a battlefield would be an ideal place for a picnic.

For hundreds of Washingtonians had come out to see the show that day. They came in carriages, wagons, buggies, and on horseback, they brought hampers of food and drink with them, and they were spread all over the slanting fields east of Bull Run, listening to the clangor of the guns, watching the smoke clouds billowing up to the July sky, and in general making a holiday out of it. Now, as Union wagon trains, ambulances, reserve artillery, and knots of disorganized stragglers began to take the road back to Washington, all of these civilians decided that it was high time for them to get out of there. They got into their

Conrad Chapman's color drawing of Confederate Brigadier General Barnard Bee (above) honors the highest ranking officer to fall in the Battle of Bull Run. Bee is remembered today for something he said, rather than what he did. Bee's rallying cry: "There is Jackson standing like a stone wall," bestowed a timeless sobriquet on that hard-fighting officer, Brigadier General Thomas J. Jackson. Bee's sacrifice and Jackson's indomitable determination helped crack the Union will to fight, bringing on a frenzied retreat to Washington (pictured in an eye-witness sketch, left).

FIRST BULL RUN

July 21, 1861

Sudley
Springs
Ford

②

SUDLEY
CHURCH

MANASSAS-SUDLEY ROAD

MATTHEWS
HOUSE

③

MATTHEWS HILL

STONE
HOUSE

WARRENTON TURNPIKE

⑧

⑦

CHINN
HOUSE

BALD HILL

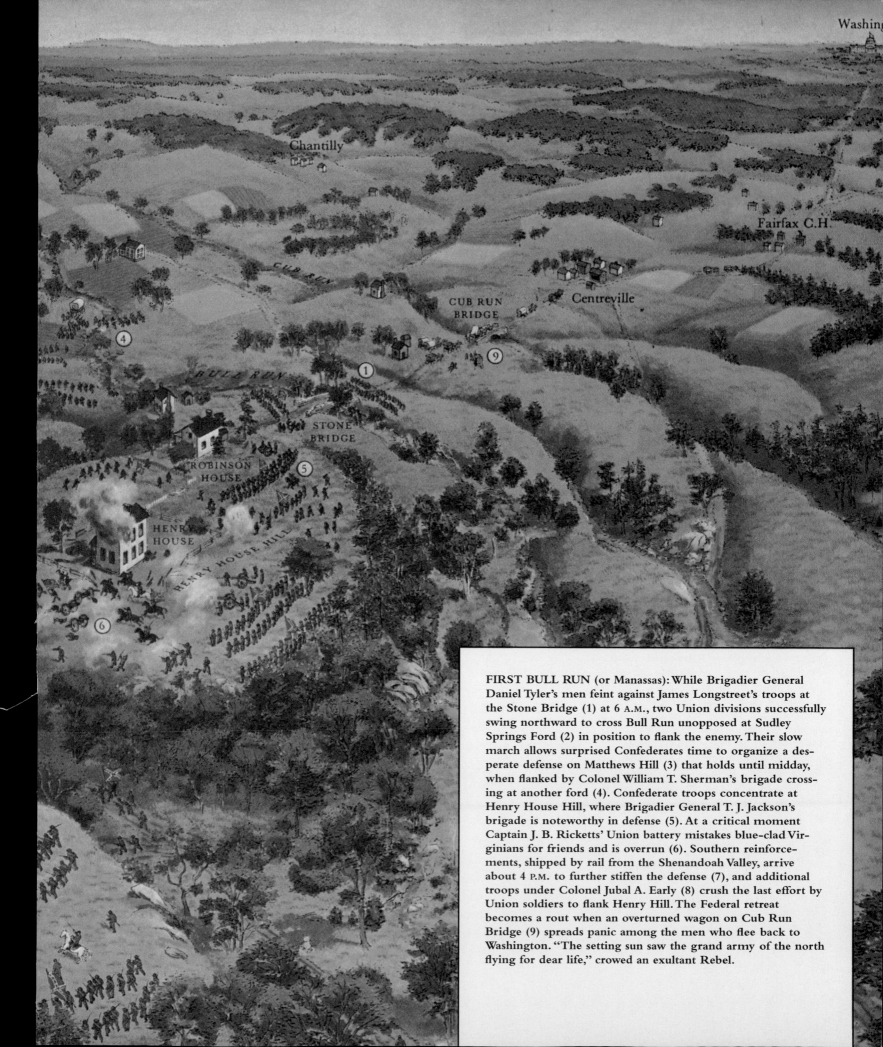

Washing[ton]

Chantilly

Fairfax C.H.

CUB RUN

CUB RUN
BRIDGE

Centreville

BULL RUN

④

①

⑨

STONE
BRIDGE

ROBINSON
HOUSE

⑤

HENRY
HOUSE

HENRY HOUSE HILL

⑥

FIRST BULL RUN (or Manassas): While Brigadier General
Daniel Tyler's men feint against James Longstreet's troops at
the Stone Bridge (1) at 6 A.M., two Union divisions successfully
swing northward to cross Bull Run unopposed at Sudley
Springs Ford (2) in position to flank the enemy. Their slow
march allows surprised Confederates time to organize a desperate defense on Matthews Hill (3) that holds until midday,
when flanked by Colonel William T. Sherman's brigade crossing at another ford (4). Confederate troops concentrate at
Henry House Hill, where Brigadier General T. J. Jackson's
brigade is noteworthy in defense (5). At a critical moment
Captain J. B. Ricketts' Union battery mistakes blue-clad Virginians for friends and is overrun (6). Southern reinforcements, shipped by rail from the Shenandoah Valley, arrive
about 4 P.M. to further stiffen the defense (7), and additional
troops under Colonel Jubal A. Early (8) crush the last effort by
Union soldiers to flank Henry Hill. The Federal retreat
becomes a rout when an overturned wagon on Cub Run
Bridge (9) spreads panic among the men who flee back to
Washington. "The setting sun saw the grand army of the north
flying for dear life," crowed an exultant Rebel.

At first, Northern newspaper accounts erroneously proclaimed a great Union victory at Bull Run. Ironically, when later extra editions correctly reported a major defeat, it was, noted an observer, "regarded as a smart commercial fraud." The pendulum of emotions swung full course and the fight was quickly branded an "overwhelming disgrace." Much of that bitter anger can be seen in the lithographed cartoon (above), titled "The Battle of Bull's Run," that took acid aim at Union follies.

conveyances and went swarming out onto the highway which the army wanted to use, creating the father and mother of all traffic jams; and just as things were at their worst a stray Confederate shell came arching over and upset a wagon on a bridge over a little stream called Cub Run, blocking the road completely.

After this there was unadulterated turmoil, growing worse every moment, with disorganized troops and panicky civilians trying to force their way through a horrible tangle of wheeled vehicles, mounted men riding around and past them, bodies of troops trying in vain to march where they had been told to march; a new surge of fear rising every now and then when someone would shout that Confederate cavalry was coming on the scene. In the weeks before the battle, imaginative newspaper and magazine writers had written extensively about the "black horse cavalry" which the Confederates had developed, and what they said had stuck in men's minds. In the dust and confusion of this disorganized retreat, frightened individuals began to shout that the black horse cavalry was upon them, and outright panic developed, with bewildered thousands dropping their weapons and starting to run, communicating their fears to others by the simple act of running. Before dark there was complete and unregimented chaos spilling all over the landscape, and hardly anyone who could move at all stopped moving until he had reached the Potomac River. For the time being

The London *Times'* William H. Russell Reports Bull Run

When the Englishman William Howard Russell arrived in Washington on March 17, 1861, his celebrated reputation, earned while covering the Crimean War, preceded him. Scenting a battle coming, he left Washington about 9:30 A.M. on July 21 in a rented two-horse carriage, followed closely by a groom carrying ample provisions. Although he never got closer than a long spyglass view of the fighting, Russell wrote a graphic but objective report:

The scene was so peaceful a man might well doubt the evidence of one sense that a great contest was being played out below in bloodshed. . . . But . . . [i]t was no review that was going on beneath us. The shells gave proof enough of that, though the rush of the shot could not be heard at the distance. . . . With the glass I could detect now and then the flash of

arms through the dust clouds in the open. . . . There seemed to be a continuous line, which was held by the enemy, from which came steady solid firing against what might be supposed to be heads of columns stationed at various points or advancing against them. . . . Suddenly up rode an officer, with a crowd of soldiers after him, from the village. "We've whipped them on all points!" he shouted, "We've taken their batteries, and they're all retreating!". . . Soon afterwards . . . I . . . set out to walk towards the front. . . . My attention was . . . called to . . . a tumult in front of me at a small bridge across the road, and then I perceived the drivers of a set of wagons with the horses turned towards me, who were endeavoring to force their way against the stream of vehicles setting in the other direction. . . . At the bridge the currents met in wild disorder. "Turn back! Retreat!" shouted

the men from the front, "We're whipped, we're whipped!". . . Soon I met soldiers who were coming through the corn, mostly without arms. . . . The ambulances were crowded with soldiers, but it did not look as if there were many wounded. . . . Men literally screamed with rage and fright when their way was blocked up. . . . Faces black and dusty, tongues out in the heat, eyes staring— it was a most wonderful sight.

Russell's coverage so highlighted Union mismanagement that, when it was published, it made him (in his own words) "the best abused man in America." Northern papers branded his account "John Bull Russell's Bull Run romance," and the portly correspondent was widely caricatured. When he was subsequently prevented from accompanying another major Federal expedition in 1862, Russell returned to England where he quickly published a book of his experiences titled *My Diary North and South.*

As both sides geared up to win the hearts and minds of their civilian populations, popular printmakers rushed into production with images of the military heroes of the hour. *Defenders of the Union* shows Brevet Lieutenant General Winfield Scott pointing to some strategically important position while a phalanx of other generals (including George B. McClellan, extreme left, and Irvin McDowell, next to him) look on.

most of McDowell's army had simply fallen apart. The bits and pieces of it might be useful later on, but right now they were nothing more than elements in a universal runaway.

The Confederates might have pursued, but did not. Jefferson Davis had reached the scene, and he conferred extensively with Johnston and Beauregard, almost ordered a pursuit, finally did not; and, as a matter of fact, the Confederate army was almost as disorganized by its victory as the Union army was by its defeat. In the end it stayed in camp, sending cavalry patrols to pick up Yankee stragglers and gleaning the field of an immense quantity of military loot, including many stands of small arms which soldiers had thrown away. Stonewall Jackson, it is said, muttered that with 5,000 men he could destroy what remained of the Yankee army, but Stonewall was not yet a man to whom everybody listened. The Confederate high command was content. It had won a shattering victory, and men believed that night that Confederate independence might be a reality before much longer.

It seemed at the time that the casualty lists were fearful, although by the standards of later Civil War battles they would look moderate. The Federals had lost 2,896 men in killed, wounded, and missing, and Confederate losses came to

1,982. For an unmilitary country which had been subconsciously expecting that the war would not really be very costly, these figures were shocking. People began to see that beneath the romance which had been glimpsed in the bright uniforms, the gay flags, and the lilting tunes played by the military bands, there would be a deep and lasting grimness. Holiday time was over. No one was going to play at war any longer. The militia units could go home now; it was time to get ready for the long pull.

For Bull Run was what awakened the North to reality. (It may have had an opposite effect in the South; the victory looked so overwhelming that many Southerners considered the Yankees poor fighters, and expected a speedy final triumph.) Before there could be another campaign, a real army would have to be put together, and expert attention would have to be given to matters of organization, training, and discipline. To attend to this job, President Lincoln plucked victorious George B. McClellan out of the western Virginia mountains and put him in command of the Army of the Potomac.

Uncharacteristically attired in a dress military uniform, Confederate President Jefferson Davis (center) is flanked by his heroes of 1861, including the two commanders at Bull Run, P. G. T. Beauregard (fourth from right) and Joseph E. Johnston (second from right). Before the war was over Davis would have bitter fallings out with both these men. Standing between Davis and Beauregard is Robert E. Lee, who in 1861 seemed destined to play a minor role in the fortunes of the new Confederate nation. When not traveling along the coast, inspecting coastal defenses, he was closely advising Davis, but not otherwise playing an active role in the developing conflict.

CHAPTER 3

Real Warfare Begins

For the time being there was an uneasy breathing space. The victory at Bull Run left the Confederate command feeling that the next move was pretty largely up to the Yankees, and the Yankees would not be ready to make another move for months to come. The Confederate army around Manassas built extensive lines of entrenchments, and in many redoubts General Johnston mounted wooden guns, which looked like the real thing from a distance but which would never kill any Yankees if a fight developed. He also edged patrols forward to the hills on the south bank of the Potomac and erected batteries downstream so that during the summer and fall the water approach to Washington was fairly effectively blockaded. To the Shenandoah Valley, Johnston sent Stonewall Jackson with a division of infantry and a handful of undisciplined but highly effective partisan cavalry led by a minor genius named Turner Ashby.

"In peace I chanted peace," wrote the poet Walt Whitman (above), "but now the drum of war is mine, War, red war is my song. . . ." If nothing else, the brawls of 1861 made it clear that bellicose posturing and scrappy determination would not settle the crisis. Blood had flowed, men had died, but instead of cooling passions, the fighting begat more fighting, which continued to escalate with no end in sight. The year 1862 promised widespread conflict on land and water: the naval battle of Memphis, June 6, 1862, marked by the use of ramming vessels, was a Union victory (left in Alexander Simplot's painting).

"We have undertaken to make war without in the least knowing how," wrote one Northern observer right after Bull Run. "We have made a false start. . . . It only remains to start afresh." As part of that fresh start, Brigadier General McDowell was transferred, his place taken by a charismatic officer with one slight victory in western Virginia to his credit: George B. McClellan. He was a superb organizer but was slow to move and reluctant to share his plans. This attitude soon lent itself to satire, such as the cartoon "Masterly Inactivity" (right), showing McClellan and Beauregard exchanging stares while their men hurl snowballs at each other.

Starting in late September, 1861, Confederate troops began to withdraw from forward positions they held in northern Virginia, near Washington. A small Union demonstration (below, in Alfred Wordsworth Thompson's painting, *Cannonading on the Potomac*) was designed merely to hurry them away from Leesburg, but it blossomed into a bloody fracas when 2,250 Federal troops found themselves pinned against the south bank of the Potomac at Ball's Bluff.

"MASTERLY INACTIVITY," OR SIX MONTHS ON THE POTOMAC.

In Washington glamorous young General McClellan applied himself to the creation of a new army. It would be a national army—the ninety-day militia regiments were sent home and demobilized—and except for a small contingent of regular troops this army would be largely composed of volunteer regiments enlisted for a three-year term. Yet although these were Federal troops, the states' rights tradition was still powerful, and the new volunteer regiments were recruited and officered by the governors of the separate states. In effect, each governor was a

separate and largely independent war department. Washington told him how many regiments he was to provide, but the raising and organizing of these troops were entirely up to him. Only after a regiment was fully up to strength, with its proper complement of officers, was it transferred from state to Federal control. The system was cumbersome, and because the appointment of officers provided a governor with a handy form of political patronage, it made impossible the creation of any effective system of replacements for battle-worn regiments. When new men were needed, it was politically profitable for a governor to raise whole new regiments rather than to recruit men to strengthen outfits that already existed. However, in the summer of 1861 the system worked well enough, and scores of new units came down to the chain of camps around Washington.

McClellan was an exceptionally able organizer. Camps were laid out in formal military pattern, the service of supply was reorganized so that food, munitions, and equipment were properly distributed, and there was an unending program of drill. At frequent intervals there would be reviews, with McClellan himself riding the lines to inspect the newly organized brigades and divisions, and the men were taught to cheer lustily whenever the general appeared. They needed very little urging. McClellan made them feel like soldiers, and they responded by giving him their complete confidence and a deep, undying affection. As summer drew on into fall the Washington scene was completely transformed. The army was beginning to be an army, and the slapdash informality of the old militia days was gone. The capital took heart.

But it was clear that there would be no major campaign in the Virginia area for some time to come. McClellan was going to do what the luckless McDowell had not been allowed to do—get everything ready before he moved—and in addition he was excessively cautious—cautious, his detractors finally would complain, to the point of outright timidity. Through a series of fantastic miscalculations he consistently estimated Confederate numbers at double or treble

Prominent among the U.S. casualties at Ball's Bluff was Colonel Edward D. Baker, a popular Senator from Oregon and a Lincoln confidant. The President wept when he learned of the death of Baker, whose body lay in state for several days (below left). Baker got the glory, posthumously, while his immediate superior, Brigadier General Charles P. Stone (above), lived to receive the blame for the debacle on the Potomac.

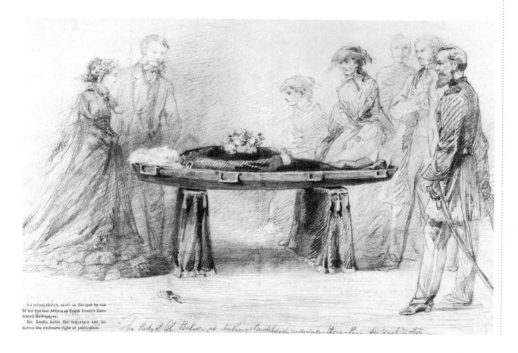

A new phalanx of military and civilian officials began to exert leadership on the Northern war effort. Arthur Lumley's sketch (right) shows Secretary of War Edwin Stanton greeting Brigadier General Daniel E. Sickles, an old political pro, while General McClellan looks on. Among governors, the staunchest supporters of the war were (left to right below) John A. Andrew of Massachusetts, Andrew G. Curtin of Pennsylvania, and Oliver P. Morton of Indiana.

The Joint Committee on the Conduct of the War, 1861-65

Following public outcry over the Federal defeat at Ball's Bluff, and angry over the loss of one of its own, Congress debated a joint resolution calling for a special group "to inquire into the causes of the disasters that have attended the public arms." In the floor debate, the idea was not only applauded, but expanded into an inquiry "into the general conduct of the war." The proposal passed by a substantial majority in both houses and a joint committee was formed under Benjamin F. Wade, a Republican Senator from Ohio. Heartily disliked by military professionals, heavily assailed by Democrats anxious to find an election issue, the committee represented the best and worst of America's political process. When the group delved into purely military matters, its members could be distressingly partisan and opportunistic, but when it tackled corrupt procurement practices or inefficiencies in the war economy, it had a strong, positive effect. Two participants who later chronicled the Lincoln administration concluded that the committee: ". . . was often hasty and unjust in its judgments, but always earnest, patriotic, and honest. . . ."

John A. Andrew

Andrew G. Curtin

Oliver P. Morton

their actual strength, and the man he put in charge of his military intelligence, the famous detective Allan Pinkerton, was so sadly out of his depth that he only abetted McClellan's delusions. On top of all this, the disaster at Ball's Bluff served as a powerful deterrent to hasty action.

Ball's Bluff was a wooded hill on the south bank of the Potomac, thirty-odd miles upstream from Washington. Confederate infantry was camped in the area, and in October McClellan ordered a subordinate to make a reconnaissance in force and see what the Rebels were doing. Several regiments crossed the river, inexpertly led, blundered into a more expertly handled force of Confederates, and were routed with substantial losses. The whole affair had little military significance, but Congress made an issue of it—Colonel Edward D. Baker, a prominent member of the Senate, was among the killed—and the subsequently notorious Joint Committee on the Conduct of the War was set up to look into the doings of the generals. All in all, enough fuss was raised to make it clear that any general who stumbled into defeat might be in for a rough time in Washington.

Still, for the time being McClellan's star was rising. In November Winfield Scott resigned, age and physical infirmities making it impossible for him to continue in active command, and Lincoln made McClellan general in chief of all the armies. McClellan had boundless self-confidence, this fall, and when Lincoln feared that the load of command might be too heavy, McClellan replied jauntily:

Lincoln could see through rhetoric and pettiness to the true quality of a person; it was a skill he demonstrated in putting together his cabinet. For the vital position of Secretary of War, he settled on Edwin M. Stanton (above left), even though that renowned lawyer had, years before, snubbed and humiliated Lincoln, then an inexperienced barrister. One reporter described Stanton as "Force —undaunted Force." Another good selection was that of a Connecticut landlubber to be Secretary of Navy: bushy-bearded, bewigged Gideon Welles (above right). Lincoln's choice had been purely political (it provided New England with a cabinet seat), but it proved fortunate. Welles kept a close rein on his rapidly expanding department; handled vexing problems in a businesslike manner; was open-minded toward innovation, and generally showed excellent judgment in making command assignments.

"I can do it all." He would control military operations all across the board, but he would remain with the Army of the Potomac and would make it his first concern.

Yet the war really began to get into high gear a long way from Virginia. Then and now, what happened in Virginia took the eye. The two capitals were only a hundred miles apart, the armies which defended and attacked them got the biggest headlines, but the war actually took shape in the West. Before McClellan got the Army of the Potomac into action, battles of lasting consequence had been fought in the Mississippi Valley.

To begin with, early in September Kentucky ceased to be neutral and reluctantly but effectively cast its lot with the North. The Federals had a concentration of troops at Cairo, Illinois, where the Ohio River joins the Mississippi, and these troops obviously would invade the Southland sooner or later, either via the Mississippi or up the channels of the Tennessee and the Cumberland. General

W. B. Cox's oil painting *The Heroes of Manassas* (below), celebrates the Confederate States' President, Jefferson Davis (center) who is shown flanked by some of his generals: (left to right) P. G. T. Beauregard, Thomas J. "Stonewall" Jackson, James Ewell Brown "Jeb" Stuart, and Joseph E. Johnston. The image was created before the Seven Days' Battles of 1862 and the rise to prominence of one other Southern military leader, Robert E. Lee.

George W. Randolph

Stephen R. Mallory

John Letcher

Davis Picks His Team

Jefferson Davis' cabinet, which consisted of six positions, was staffed by seventeen incumbents between 1861 and 1865. The problems involved in fashioning an effective central government would haunt Davis throughout his tenure: six different individuals eventually held the all-important post of Secretary of War. The aristocratic George W. Randolph of Virginia (above left)—the son of Thomas Jefferson's oldest daughter—was the third to take the seat, and held it for eight months. The most durable man in the cabinet was Secretary of the Navy Stephen R. Mallory (above middle), an ex-U.S. Senator and a modest expert

on naval affairs: he was the only cabinet member to serve throughout Davis' entire Presidential term. In political opposition to Davis and his cabinet were the eleven governors of the Confederate states, each one with his own agenda. High on the trouble list were Virginia's John Letcher (top right), who had initially opposed his state's secession; North Carolina's Zebulon B. Vance (middle right), forever putting his state's interests before those of the Confederacy, and Georgia's Joseph E. Brown (bottom right), who exempted most of his civil and military officials from national service. Accentuating these problems was the President himself. A reporter wrote of Jefferson Davis at this time: "No public man in our history ever stood closer to his friends, or conceded less to those who had crossed his path or arrayed themselves among his personal or political enemies."

Zebulon B. Vance

Joseph E. Brown

The town of Cairo, Illinois, at the confluence of the Mississippi and Ohio rivers, became a busy staging port for the U.S. military, as shown in Theodore R. Davis' drawing. It was key to the "Anaconda Plan," a strategy by which U.S. military chief Winfield Scott sought to slowly strangle the Confederacy by blockading or otherwise dominating its ocean and river ports. In the meantime, the Union would gain the chance to train its masses of citizen soldiers. Scott's Anaconda Plan was met with impatience by many prominent Northerners, but nonetheless, it held the germ of the eventual Union strategy. Almost from the first, efforts were made to gain control of the vital Mississippi River.

LEVEE CAIRO ILL. 61

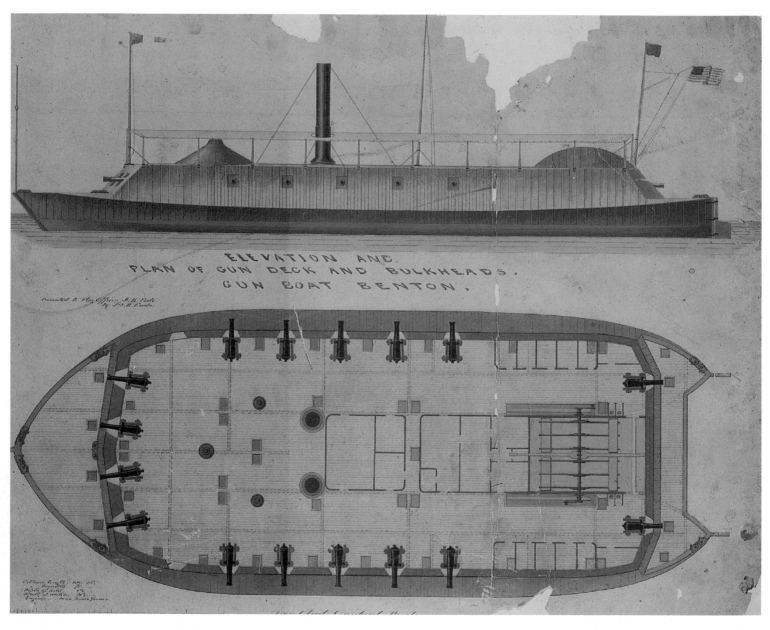

ELEVATION AND
PLAN OF GUN DECK AND BULKHEADS.
GUN BOAT BENTON.

A whole new generation of military machinery was forged to meet the demands of the war. Iron-armored warships, popularly called "ironclads," appeared in naval construction yards during 1861. Until new ships could be built from scratch, existing vessels were converted, as in the case of the snag boat that became the ironclad warship *Benton* (above). Although American designers did not originate the ironclad, the Civil War advanced it markedly: by the time military actions were launched against the Rebel river strongpoints of Fort Henry, the U.S. Navy was able to put a whole fleet of ironclads into action (right).

Frémont, commanding for the Federals in the western area, lacked competence and would presently be replaced, but he had done two things of prime importance: he had started construction of a fleet of gunboats, and he had put a remarkably capable, although then little known, brigadier general named U. S. Grant in command at Cairo.

Top man for the Confederacy in western Tennessee was Major General Leonidas Polk, a classmate of Jefferson Davis' at West Point, who had resigned from the army years ago to take holy orders and had become a bishop in the Episcopal Church. When the war began, he returned to military service, and this fall he rightly concluded that the Yankees would soon be occupying Kentucky. He beat them to it, moving troops up to seize and fortify the bluffs at the town of Columbus, on the Mississippi, northern terminus of the Mobile and Ohio Railroad. Grant countered by seizing Paducah, which controlled the mouths of the Tennessee and Cumberland rivers, and Kentucky was squarely in the war.

. . .

The attack on Fort Henry was an all-navy affair. Located on the Tennessee River, Fort Henry occupied a notably poor site: after river flooding made portions of it indefensible, Flag Officer Andrew Hull Foote's ironclads moved up to capture it. When a similar strategy was attempted at nearby Fort Donelson on the Cumberland River (below), the defenders were in a better position, and it was Foote's boats that took the pounding. Donelson had to be taken by land assault, but the result was an important Union victory. It was the first nationally recognized success for U.S. Brigadier General Ulysses S. Grant, who is seen on the next page watching the Donelson fighting in a painting by Paul Philippoteaux.

Almost a year into the war, the fate of Missouri still hung in the balance; then a Federal force of 10,500 men under Brigadier General Samuel R. Curtis (near right) took to the field to confront 16,000 Rebels, commanded by Major General Earl Van Dorn (far right). On March 6, 1862, Curtis dug in on the bluffs overlooking a wintry field in northwestern Arkansas, not far from Pea Ridge. Van Dorn attacked the next day. After the war, a veteran of the fighting, Hunt P. Wilson, painted the triptych *Battle of Pea Ridge, Arkansas*, the center panel of which (below) shows the final Federal attack from the Confederate point of view. In the picture's lower left, a wounded General Price tells his men to fall back.

DAVIS SENT OUT a new man to take over-all command in the West: a highly regarded regular army officer, General Albert Sidney Johnston, who was thought to be perhaps the ablest of all the professional soldiers who had joined the Confederacy. Johnston was woefully handicapped by a shortage of manpower and equipment, but he did his best with the materials at hand. He made a strong point out of Columbus, mounting heavy guns to control the river and establishing a garrison of some 20,000 troops there. The rest of his line extended eastward through Kentucky, with 25,000 men or more in and around Bowling Green, and with a smaller contingent anchoring the eastern end of the line in the mountainous country along the Tennessee border near the upper reaches of the Cumberland River. Rising in the Kentucky mountains, the Cumberland makes a long loop into Tennessee, passing the state capital, Nashville, and then turning

Van Dorn attacked Curtis in a two-pronged assault. The western wing met defeat, and its popular leader, Brigadier General Ben McCulloch, was killed. The eastern wing, though, had more success, capturing a critical intersection known for a watering place called the Elkhorn Tavern. The right panel of artilleryman Hunt P. Wilson's triptych (left) shows his outfit, Guibor's Missouri Battery, in action on the Telegraph Road near the tavern, late on March 7. Curtis counterattacked the next day; after fierce fighting he forced Van Dorn to withdraw, saving Missouri for the Union. Rebel troops felt betrayed. "By God, nobody was whipped at Pea Ridge but Van Dorn!" exclaimed one.

"If he is not a general," Jefferson Davis said of his friend Albert Sidney Johnston (below), ". . . we have no general." A tall, muscular, handsome man, the highly regarded Johnston, left the union with his adopted state, Texas, to become the highest ranking field officer in the Confederacy. Determined to gain the initiative in the West, Johnston advanced from Corinth, Mississippi, with 44,000 men and attacked the Union army encamped near Pittsburg Landing—otherwise known as Shiloh. Marching with Johnston was the 9th Mississippi, some members of which are pictured above right. Deployed as skirmishers in advance of their brigade, the 9th Mississippi suffered heavy losses in the Peach Orchard; among its dead was its commander, Lieutenant Colonel William A. Rankin.

north to flow into the Ohio. Just below the Kentucky-Tennessee line it flows more or less parallel with the Tennessee, twelve miles to the west.

These two rivers offered a military highway of prime importance. The Cumberland led to Nashville, and the Tennessee led all the way to northern Mississippi and Alabama. With the powerful works at Columbus blocking the way down the Mississippi, a Federal invasion was almost certain to follow the line of these two rivers, and just below the Kentucky line the Confederates had built two forts to bar the way—Fort Henry on the Tennessee and Fort Donelson on the Cumberland. These forts drew Federal attention as the year 1862 began.

Federal command in the West was divided. Frémont had been replaced by Major General Henry Wager Halleck, a professional soldier who possessed vast book knowledge of war, had certain talents as an administrator, and was known, somewhat irreverently, in the old army as Old Brains. Halleck's control, however, extended only to the Cumberland. East of that, Federal forces in Kentucky were commanded by Brigadier General Don Carlos Buell, a close friend of McClellan and a cautious type who shared McClellan's reluctance to move until every preparation had been made. Between them, Halleck and Buell commanded many more men than Johnston could bring to oppose them, but neither man had real driving force, and it seemed to be very hard for them to co-operate effectively. McClellan, who could give orders to both of them, was too far away to enforce real co-ordination, and most of his attention was centered on Virginia.

In any case, as the new year began these armies started to move. The first action came at the eastern end of the line, where Johnston's right wing, under Major General George B. Crittenden, crossed the Cumberland and began an advance toward central Kentucky. Buell's left was led by Virginia-born Brigadier General George H. Thomas, and Thomas fell on Crittenden's little force near the hamlet of Mill Springs and completely routed it. The eastern anchor of Johnston's defensive line was to all intents and purposes annihilated.

Shortly afterward, Halleck ordered Grant to move on Fort Henry. Grant took 15,000 men and a squadron of new ironclad gunboats commanded by Flag Officer Andrew Foote, and by February 6 he got boats and men up to this bastion. Fort Henry proved unexpectedly weak: built on low ground, it was partly under water, the Tennessee being almost at flood stage then, and Foote's gunboats pounded it into surrender before the infantry could get into position to make the attack. Grant promptly turned east, marching his troops cross-country to attack Fort Donelson, on the Cumberland, and sending Foote around to join him by water, and a week after Fort Henry had fallen, the Federals opened their attack.

Donelson was a tougher nut to crack. The fall of Fort Henry made Johnston see that the whole center of his line was in peril, and he evacuated Bowling Green, sending 15,000 men to defend Fort Donelson and taking the rest back to Nashville. Donelson held out for three days, but Grant got strong reinforcements and shelled the place into submission. It surrendered on February 16, and

Johnston's plan depended on catching the Federals by surprise. Unanticipated delays, though, prevented his army from moving into battle position on the day intended for the attack. Although Johnston's subordinates believed that the enemy had been alerted and was being reinforced, the general remained fiercely determined to attack come dawn. "I would fight them if they were a million," he told a staff officer. For a while on April 6, 1862, it seemed as if Johnston's gamble had paid off; by evening, the Federals had been pushed into a chaotic pocket (below) with their backs to the Tennessee River.

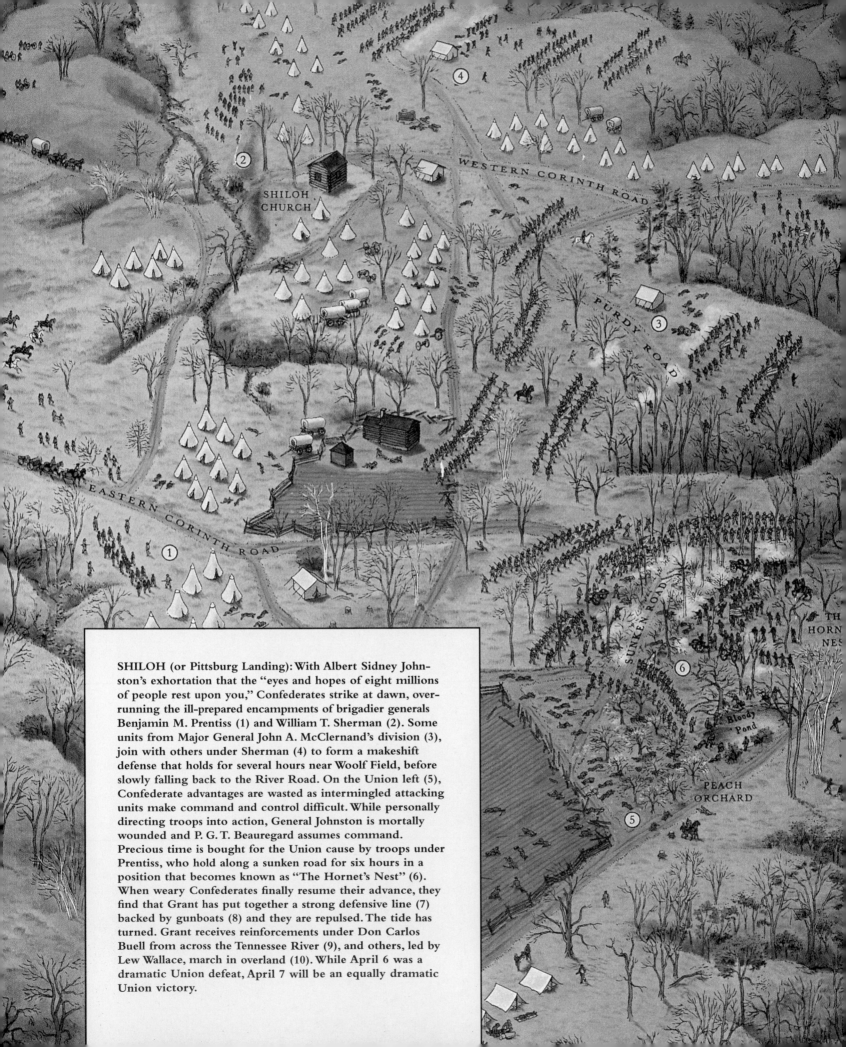

SHILOH CHURCH

WESTERN CORINTH ROAD

PURDY ROAD

EASTERN CORINTH ROAD

SUNKEN ROAD

Bloody Pond

PEACH ORCHARD

TH HORN NES

SHILOH (or Pittsburg Landing): With Albert Sidney Johnston's exhortation that the "eyes and hopes of eight millions of people rest upon you," Confederates strike at dawn, overrunning the ill-prepared encampments of brigadier generals Benjamin M. Prentiss (1) and William T. Sherman (2). Some units from Major General John A. McClernand's division (3), join with others under Sherman (4) to form a makeshift defense that holds for several hours near Woolf Field, before slowly falling back to the River Road. On the Union left (5), Confederate advantages are wasted as intermingled attacking units make command and control difficult. While personally directing troops into action, General Johnston is mortally wounded and P. G. T. Beauregard assumes command. Precious time is bought for the Union cause by troops under Prentiss, who hold along a sunken road for six hours in a position that becomes known as "The Hornet's Nest" (6). When weary Confederates finally resume their advance, they find that Grant has put together a strong defensive line (7) backed by gunboats (8) and they are repulsed. The tide has turned. Grant receives reinforcements under Don Carlos Buell from across the Tennessee River (9), and others, led by Lew Wallace, march in overland (10). While April 6 was a dramatic Union defeat, April 7 will be an equally dramatic Union victory.

SHILOH

First Day: April 6, 1862

RIVER ROAD

Pittsburg
Landing

TENNESSEE RIVER

Fact and Fiction:

One of the youngest celebrities of the Civil War was ten-year-old Johnny Clem (left), who served as a drummer boy in the 22nd Michigan Infantry. His first nickname was "Johnny Shiloh" because of heroic deeds that were much publicized at the time of the battle, but questioned ever since. According to his sister, "He was an expert drummer, and being a bright, cheery child, soon made his way into the affections of the officers and soldiers." By 1863 the press was touting him as the "Drummer Boy of Chickamauga," after he was said to have shot a Rebel colonel in battle. Though it has never been proved that Clem was even on the battlefield at Shiloh, or that he ever picked up a gun at Chickamauga, the myth endured. Clem ended the war wearing sergeant's stripes and sporting a silver medal presented to him by Kate Chase, the beautiful daughter of Treasury Secretary Salmon P. Chase. He remained in the army, retiring at age sixty-five as Major John L. Clem. Interviewed on the occasion of his eightieth birthday, Clem was reported to have insisted that he be referred to as the "'Drummer Boy of Shiloh,' because it was on that field that he first beat a drum in battle."

Grant suddenly found himself famous—not only had he captured some 12,000 Confederates, but his note demanding capitulation had struck a chord that stirred Northern emotions powerfully: "No terms except an immediate and unconditional surrender can be accepted."

Now the Confederates were in serious trouble. Johnston could do nothing but retreat, posthaste, and this he did without delay. Nashville could not be held, and it was evacuated, with substantial military stores falling into Union hands. Even the fortress at Columbus had to be given up. Beauregard, so unhappy in Virginia, had been sent west to be second in command to Johnston, and he led the Columbus garrison south: he and Johnston, if the Federals let them, would reunite their forces at Corinth, Mississippi, just below the Tennessee line. Here the vital railway line which led east from Memphis, connecting the western part of the Confederacy with Virginia, crossed the north-south line of the Mobile and Ohio. Richmond was scraping the seacoast garrisons to provide reinforcements, and if Johnston could reassemble his forces he would have perhaps 50,000 men. Halleck and Buell, between them, could send 70,000 against him if they managed things properly.

Really effective management was not forthcoming. As a reward for victory,

Federal control of the Tennessee River was an inestimable advantage for U. S. Grant at Shiloh. The gunboats *Tyler* and *Lexington,* (in the middle distance of Henri Lovie's drawing at left), were powerful artillery batteries, practically immune from capture, while the steamboat fleet (far left and right in the drawing) successfully conveyed Buell's troops across the river in time to tip the balance to Grant's side.

U. S. Grant (right) seemed outwardly unperturbed as the fighting ended on April 6, despite being victim to a nearly complete tactical surprise and losing almost all the ground he had held that morning. He "appeared as cool and collected as if all were going as he would have planned," noted an amazed staff officer. Speaking to another officer, Grant said: "The enemy has done all he can do today. Tomorrow morning . . . we will soon finish him up." Even after the following day brought the victory he had predicted, the brigadier general was roundly censured by both the press and many of his soldiers for the near disaster on April 6. But it was the victory of April 7 that mattered most to President Lincoln. When a prominent Republican demanded Grant's removal, Lincoln replied: "I can't spare this man; he fights."

Halleck had been given top command in the West and Grant had been made a major general, and under Halleck's orders Grant was moving up the Tennessee with approximately 45,000 men while Buell was marching down from Nashville with 25,000 more. But Halleck had his columns moving slowly; both Grant and Foote wanted to press the beaten foe with vigor, but one delay succeeded another, and Johnston and Beauregard were given just time to regroup and reorganize their troops at Corinth. There Johnston realized that the Federals would before long bring overpowering numbers against him. Grant had put his army on the western bank of the Tennessee at Pittsburg Landing, with most of the men in camp near a country meeting-house known as Shiloh Church, a little more than twenty miles from Corinth. Johnston concluded that his only hope was to strike Grant before Buell could arrive, and in the first days of April the Confederate army marched up from Corinth to give battle.

Gallant charge of Gen: Rousseaus Brig: recapturing our Batt a Louisiana Battery also killing Gen Ruggles — Wounding & the Rebels provisional Governor Johnson who . . . die

The result was the bewildering and bloody Battle of Shiloh, fought on April 6 and 7, 1862. Grant was caught off guard, and in the first day's fight his army was almost pushed into the Tennessee River. It rallied just in time, Johnston was killed in action, and at dark Buell's troops began to arrive and one of Grant's divisions which had been delayed in reaching the field got to the scene. On the second day the Federals reversed the tide, and by midafternoon Beauregard had to admit defeat. He drew his badly battered army back toward Corinth, and the Federals, equally battered, made no more than a gesture at pursuit. The greatest battle ever fought on the American continent, up to that date, was over. The Federals had lost 13,000 men, the Confederates, 10,700. The troops had fought with impressive valor, but they had been poorly handled, especially on the Union side.

Beginning at dawn, April 7, Union troops began to push forth from what had seemed their last stand only a few hours earlier. In a series of brutal combats lasting all day, the Federals steadily drove the Confederates off the battlefield. One of the final attacks came late in the afternoon, when Brigadier General Lovell H. Rousseau's brigade struck an exposed enemy flank (above) along the Corinth Road.

Among the Mississippi River strongholds remaining in Rebel hands after the fall of Forts Henry and Donelson was one located on Island Number Ten—so named because it was the tenth island below the mouth of the Ohio River. Starting on March 17, a flotilla of Union mortar boats opened a concentrated bombardment that failed to overwhelm the defenders. William Torgerson's painting (below) shows the turtle-like mortar boats in action. Not until Federal gunboats successfully ran past Island Number Ten's guns, to threaten the position from below, did the garrison surrender, on April 7.

But although the terrible casualty list and the fact that Grant had let himself be taken unawares stirred violent criticism in the North, the battle nevertheless had been of decisive importance. At Shiloh the Confederacy made its supreme bid to regain western Tennessee. It failed, and after that the Confederate path in the West went downhill all the way. Nor was Shiloh the only disaster that spring. At Pea Ridge, Arkansas, a Union army under Brigadier General Samuel Curtis defeated a Confederate army led by Major General Earl Van Dorn. Other Union forces came down the Mississippi itself, taking New Madrid, Missouri, and capturing a powerful fort at Island Number Ten. Union gunboats came down and destroyed a Confederate river fleet at Memphis, and two months after Shiloh, Memphis itself had to be abandoned. Halleck assembled an army of substantially more than 100,000 men near Pittsburg Landing and moved slowly down to take Corinth—moved with excessive caution, for Beauregard had not half of Halleck's numbers and dared not stay to give battle, but Halleck was the most deliberate of generals. In the end Beauregard left Corinth and retreated toward central Mississippi, the Federals held all of western Tennessee and were in a fair way to reclaim the entire Mississippi Valley, and in the West the Southern cause was well on the way to defeat.

BUT IN VIRGINIA everything was very different.

Like Halleck, McClellan moved with deliberation. He also suffered from a handicap which never afflicted Halleck: he had aroused the active distrust and hostility of the radical Republican leaders in Washington, including the Secretary

On April 13, Union gunboats and army transports arrived to attack the Rebels' Fort Pillow, on the Mississippi River about fifty miles above Memphis. Flag Officer Andrew H. Foote deployed his mortar boats, but this time there was a Confederate "River Defense Fleet" nearby, consisting largely of ramming vessels. On the morning of May 10, this force engaged exposed Union ships in a nautical free-for-all (above), known as the Battle of Plum Run Bend. Before the Rebels drew off, they heavily damaged two of Foote's gunboats; it was a decided Confederate victory.

of War, Edwin M. Stanton. These men had come to distrust McClellan's will to fight. Some of them even believed he was pro-Confederate at heart, and they suggested openly that he was potentially a traitor, willing to let the enemy win the war. What McClellan did in the spring of 1862 cannot be appraised fairly unless this bitter hostility and suspicion are taken into account. If McClellan moved later than he said he would move (which was usually the case), he was certain to be accused of sabotaging the war effort; if a battle went against him, there were sure to be grandstand critics in Washington who would proclaim that he might easily have won if he had really wanted to win.

The first result of all of this was that in the middle of March McClellan lost his job as general in chief of all the armies and was limited to command of the Army of the Potomac. The second result was that when he finally made his move he made it under great difficulties, some of them self-inflicted.

McClellan had given up the idea of moving on Richmond via Manassas. Instead he wanted to go down to Fort Monroe by steamboat and then advance up the Virginia Peninsula, with rivers to protect his flanks and a secure line of communications. President Lincoln and Secretary Stanton agreed to this very reluctantly. A Union army moving overland toward Richmond would always

The Confederate success at Plum Run Bend convinced Union officials of their own need for ramming vessels. When, on June 6, Federal gunboats approached the city of Memphis, the Rebel rams confidently sallied forth, expecting a repeat of May 10. They were met by Yankee ramming vessels under the aggressive command of Charles Ellet, who destroyed the Confederate fleet in less than three hours. "The victory was decisive," declared a Union sailor, "and the [last] that will be fought on the river." Some of the day's battle is shown here in a painting by Frank Schell and Thomas Hogan.

As the summer of 1861 stretched into fall, General Joseph E. Johnston's victorious Confederates built themselves a town of log cabins (right) near Manassas Junction, Virginia, while the Richmond government stockpiled supplies and erected a major meat-curing plant nearby. The following year, though, Johnston felt that his army was exposed at Manassas, leaving the capital too vulnerable, and so on March 8 and 9 he withdrew his troops south to the Rappahannock River, destroying whatever could not be taken along. In addition to burning the meat-curing plant, Johnston's men wrecked the Manassas rail yards and equipment (below). An incredulous Georgia soldier declared the result "the greatest destruction I ever saw in my life."

On the morning of March 10, the Union Army of the Potomac under Major General George B. McClellan marched out of Washington, heading for Manassas. Jubilant Yankee boys found the enemy's impressive lines of earthworks empty and harmless (left). For months, McClellan had been warning that these positions were too heavily protected to take by assault, but curious reporters quickly discovered that many of the Confederate heavy weapons were fakes: "Quaker guns" as they were called (below). "The fortifications are a damnable humbug and McClellan has been completely fooled," wrote one correspondent.

The defense of the lower Virginia Peninsula was the responsibility of Confederate Major General John Bankhead Magruder. Shown in a pre–Civil War photo above, Magruder was a West Point graduate and veteran of the Mexican War. His fondness for high society, coupled with his lordly airs, earned him the nickname, "Prince John." Magruder added to that image with a flair for gaudy uniforms and a peculiar way of talking. According to one Richmond woman, he "lisps and swears at the same time."

Not long after Major General George B. McClellan took over and revitalized McDowell's army following the disaster at Bull Run, he began to think of ways to beat his enemy—without fighting him. The prospect of winning through maneuver was appealing to McClellan, who prided himself on his grasp of the big picture. He first proposed moving the Army of the Potomac from Washington to the lower Chesapeake, which would place it just fifty miles from Richmond.

Johnston's surprise withdrawal upset these plans; under heavy Presidential pressure, McClellan modified his design to target the Virginia Peninsula. He confidently told a friendly reporter: "I believe that we are now on the eve of the success for which we have been so long preparing. . . ." The composite photograph above shows McClellan posing in front of his headquarters prior to the Peninsular Campaign. In the doorway, his wife, Mary Ellen, stands next to his mother-in-law, Mary Marcy. A nurse, holding his infant daughter, Mary, can be seen in the upstairs window.

stand between Washington and the main Confederate army; but it seemed to these men that under McClellan's plan the capital would be dangerously open to capture by a sudden Confederate thrust. As a soldier, McClellan considered this highly unlikely; as politicians, Lincoln and Stanton were bound to realize that if Washington should be captured the Union cause was irretrievably lost, and they refused to take chances. They let McClellan make his move, therefore, on condition that he leave enough troops in Washington (which by now was strongly fortified) to make it safe beyond question. McClellan agreed to this, but apparently he did not take the business very seriously. After he and the army had taken off for the Peninsula, the President and the Secretary of War began counting heads and discovered that the numbers McClellan had promised to leave behind just were not there. Accordingly, they removed an entire army corps from his command—it was commanded by the General McDowell who had had such bad luck at Bull Run—and ordered it to cover the area between Washington and Fredericksburg. Simultaneously, they created a separate command in the Shenandoah Valley, entrusting it to a political major general from Massachusetts, the distinguished, if unmilitary, Nathaniel P. Banks. As a final step they called General Frémont back from retirement and put him in command in western Virginia, with instructions to begin moving east.

So McClellan started up the Peninsula with only 90,000 men instead of the 130,000 he had expected to have. His troubles immediately began to multiply.

Joe Johnston had long since evacuated Manassas, but he had not yet got all of his men down to the Peninsula. At Yorktown he had a chain of earthworks and

By the first week of April, Union troops were pouring ashore near Fortress Monroe (below), a U.S. stronghold about seventy miles southeast of Richmond. Thousands of tramping feet, assisted by a few rain showers, quickly turned the topsoil into a red-clay goo that stuck to everything. A soldier in the 13th Massachusetts declared that "the amount of muscular energy required to lift your feet with ten pounds or more of mud clinging to each foot, can hardly be appreciated except by persons who have a knowledge of the 'sacred soil' of Virginia."

"Forward to Yorktown!!" wrote one eager Union diarist on April 4. There, near the famous Revolutionary War site, the Peninsula neck narrowed, and 15,000 Confederate troops under flamboyant "Prince John" Magruder were waiting. Magruder deftly shifted his few units around to suggest even greater numbers. In addition, he counted upon the psychological effect of such powerful defensive positions as the Water Battery (below, seen after the Union occupation) to give the cautious McClellan pause. After examining Magruder's lines, McClellan concluded: "I must . . . go through the preliminary operations of a siege."

some 15,000 soldiers under Major General John Bankhead Magruder. In the old army Magruder had been famous as a flamboyant play-actor, and he used all of his talents now to bemuse McClellan. As the Yankees approached the Yorktown lines Magruder marched his troops up hill and down dale, safely out of range but plainly visible, and he did it so well that the Unionists concluded that he had a very substantial army. McClellan took alarm, erected works facing the Yorktown lines, and prepared to lay siege. He could certainly have overwhelmed Magruder with one push, and even after Johnston got the rest of his army to the scene the Confederate works could probably have been stormed; but McClellan played it safe, and as a result he lost an entire month. Johnston evacuated Yorktown on May 4—McClellan had his big guns in position, and was going to open a crushing bombardment next day—and the long move up the Peninsula began. The Confederates fought a brisk delaying action at Williamsburg the next day, but

A young combat artist for *Harper's Weekly* named Winslow Homer accompanied McClellan's army. Some of his sketches were published as engravings in the magazine; others were studies later turned into oil paintings. His *In Front of Yorktown* (left), finished in 1871, depicts a Union picket post. In preparation for action, McClellan's engineers were kept busy readying siege batteries for heavy artillery, like the thirteen-inch seacoast mortars (below) that would pulverize Magruder's entrenchments. An officer from Maine would note: "There is scarcely a minute in the day when you cannot hear either the report of a field-piece and the explosion of a shell, or the crack of a rifle."

Never before in U.S. history had such a massive army been in one place under a single command as the force George McClellan amassed for his Peninsular Campaign. Evidence of its size can be seen in the seemingly endless rows of ordnance stockpiled behind the Yorktown lines (right). McClellan's grand build-up was all for naught, though; after nightfall on May 3, the Confederates pulled back, having held him at bay for almost a full month. A Yankee soldier prowling the empty enemy camps found a prophetic piece of graffiti written in charcoal on a tent wall: "He that fights and runs away, will live to fight another day."

The Confederate retreat was a stubborn one; on May 5, there was a day-long clash near Williamsburg that cost Johnston's army 1,700 men and McClellan's 2,300. Johnston controlled the pace, and, once his own supply train was clear of danger, he allowed the slower-moving McClellan to advance unchallenged along the Pamunkey River. Union supply bases were established at various points; James Hope's painting (left) shows McClellan's encampment at Cumberland Landing. Photographer James F. Gibson took a picture at the same location (below left, the actual river landing is only a short distance out of the frame to the right), which suggests something of the awesome power represented by the Federal army.

An Aeronautical Warrior

On days when the wind was slight and the armies were entrenched, soldiers on both sides could count on seeing at least one of the three craft belonging to the U.S. Balloon Corps of Professor Thaddeus Lowe (left). It took a crew of thirty to fifty men about three hours, using special mobile gas generators, to fully inflate each balloon. In the picture below, Lowe himself is ascending to make observations from the basket of his balloon *Intrepid*. Because of the danger of Rebel cannon fire, all such aerial reconnaissance rose a good distance behind the front lines and was limited to long-range perspectives. Often, staff officers or field commanders would accompany Lowe, although on one occasion the mooring line broke and only a fortuitous shift of the wind prevented Brigadier General Fitz John Porter from being carried into Confederate territory.

they did not try to make a real stand until they had reached the very outskirts of Richmond.

Meanwhile, other things had been happening which would have a marked effect on McClellan's campaign. The canny Confederates quickly discovered the extreme sensitivity of Lincoln and Stanton about the safety of Washington and made cruel use of it. In the Shenandoah Valley, Stonewall Jackson with 8,000 men faced Banks, who had nearly twice that number; and Frémont was beginning to edge in through the western mountains with as many more. Jackson was given reinforcements, nearly doubling his numbers; then he set out on one of the war's most dazzling campaigns. A quick march west of Staunton knocked back Frémont's advance; then Jackson swept down the Valley, completely deceiving Banks as to his whereabouts, breaking his supply line and forcing him to retreat, and then striking him viciously while he was retreating and turning his withdrawal

George B. McClellan's Napoleonic ways made him a natural target for cartoonists who did not share his own admiration for his abilities (above). There is no evidence that he initiated comparisons between himself and the great French general; however, there is none either that he would shrink when labeled "The Young Napoleon." Indeed, his self-confidence during the planning and preparation for an operation bordered on supreme egotism. "I seem to have become the power of the land," he told his wife soon after first coming to Washington. He thought of the Army of the Potomac in very personal terms (often referring to it as "my army") and so enjoyed issuing pronouncements and orders directly to his men that his headquarters included a portable printing press. "Let us strike the blow which is to restore peace and union to this distracted land," he intoned before one Peninsula battle.

The 1862 cartoon at left, showing Lincoln trundling McClellan on to Richmond, was not far from the truth. In the months preceding the Peninsular Campaign, Abraham Lincoln stoically endured personal slights and outright insults from the general, who considered his commander in chief a helpless military amateur. If the President held out any hope that McClellan would act with decisiveness and celerity once on the Peninsula, it was quickly dashed by the glacial pace of the Union advance. Soon after the first delays, Lincoln wrote to McClellan: ". . . [I]t is indispensable to you that you strike a blow. I am powerless to help this."

Combat artist Alfred R. Waud's drawing shows a Union corps crossing the Chickahominy River on a military bridge. As McClellan's army drew closer to Richmond, its line of march took it through difficult terrain bordering the river. It was, declared one Federal, "the most damnable bog I ever went through, clear up to our knees in solid mud." Federal engineers were kept constantly busy, constructing so many spans over the Chickahominy that one weary worker mused that postwar traffic would be able to cross anywhere.

By the end of May, Confederate General Joseph E. Johnston had fallen back in Virginia, just as far as was militarily or politically practicable. On May 31, he undertook a complicated movement designed to attack two exposed Union divisions located between Fair Oaks Station and the town of Seven Pines. Only a small number of his troops joined the fight, which raged throughout the day, and finally, a Federal disaster was averted when grizzled Brigadier General Edwin V. "Bull" Sumner (right) managed to bring his corps across the rain-swollen Chickahominy. Union losses were 1,203, some of whom were sketched by Arthur Lumley (above) as they were conveyed by rail to White House Landing.

Union cannoneers at the Battle of Seven Pines (left) unwittingly contributed to the most significant command change in the entire Civil War. General Johnston was watching the fight unfold from a knoll some 200 yards north of Fair Oaks Station, when he was struck: first by a bullet in the shoulder and then, almost immediately, by a spent shell fragment in the chest. Johnston needed six months to recover, and he would never again serve with the Confederacy's eastern army. Just before he was hit, Johnston had gently chided a nervous staff officer who was ducking as bullets hummed by. "Colonel," said Johnston, "there is no use of dodging; when you hear them they have passed." As Johnston's replacement, President Davis settled on General Robert E. Lee.

The Freedom Question

Wilbur Fisk, a young volunteer in the 2nd Vermont Regiment, contributed regular columns to the Montpelier, Vermont, *Green Mountain Freeman*. In a letter written just before Seven Pines he considered a complicated issue that had yet to be fully addressed in the North: *The inevitable Negro question . . . claims preeminence in camp as well as court. . . . The boys think it their duty to put down rebellion and nothing more, and they view the abolition of slavery in the present time as saddling so much additional labor upon them before the present great work is accomplished. Negro prejudice is as strong here as anywhere. . . . The most cordial reception by far that we have received since we left the free states was tendered us by this sable species of human property. . . . They were dirty and ragged . . . but they seemed to understand, as nearly all the Negroes here do, that somehow all this commotion has a connection with them and will bring about their freedom in the end.*

While McClellan battled toward Richmond, a second campaign was taking shape to the west in the Shenandoah Valley. Intent on cutting an important food source from the Confederacy, Major General Nathaniel P. Banks threatened the valley's rich farmland with a 38,000-man Union force. Facing them was an ill-equipped Rebel army, half as big and led by an eccentric former Virginia Military Institute professor: in slightly more than three months of marching and fighting, General Thomas J. "Stonewall" Jackson and his men (some pictured below in D. E. Henderson's *Halt of the Stonewall Brigade*) baffled Banks and beat him in several battles. Hardly had Banks been turned back when three other Federal columns moved against Jackson. At Cross Keys (right) and Port Republic, these Union forces were met and also defeated. On the opposite page, Jackson is portrayed with the lush Shenandoah Valley, which he so ably defended, shown behind his left shoulder.

JACKSON'S VALLEY CAMPAIGN: In a series of operations requiring both steel nerves and strong legs, "Stonewall" Jackson maneuvered his army between rapid marches and sharp engagements. He had two goals: to preserve Confederate control of the Shenandoah region and to tie down Union troops that might otherwise have helped McClellan. Even though Jackson's first fight at Kernstown (March 23) was a tactical defeat for him, it succeeded in forcing the Federals to maintain a strong presence in the Valley. And it was followed by an incredible string of Confederate victories: McDowell (May 8), Front Royal (May 23), Winchester (May 25), Cross Keys (June 8), and Port Republic (June 9). "General," said Jackson to a subordinate following the last victory, "he who does not see the hand of God in this is blind, sir, blind."

ALLEGHENY MOUNTAINS

SHENANDOAH M

Moorefield

Franklin

Mt. Jackson

McDowell

New Market

VALLEY TURNPIKE

Harrisonburg

Cross Keys

VIRGINIA CENTRAL R.R.

Staunton

Port Republic

Swift Run Gap

Brown's Gap

Waynesboro

Rockfish Gap

BLUE RIDGE MOUNTAINS

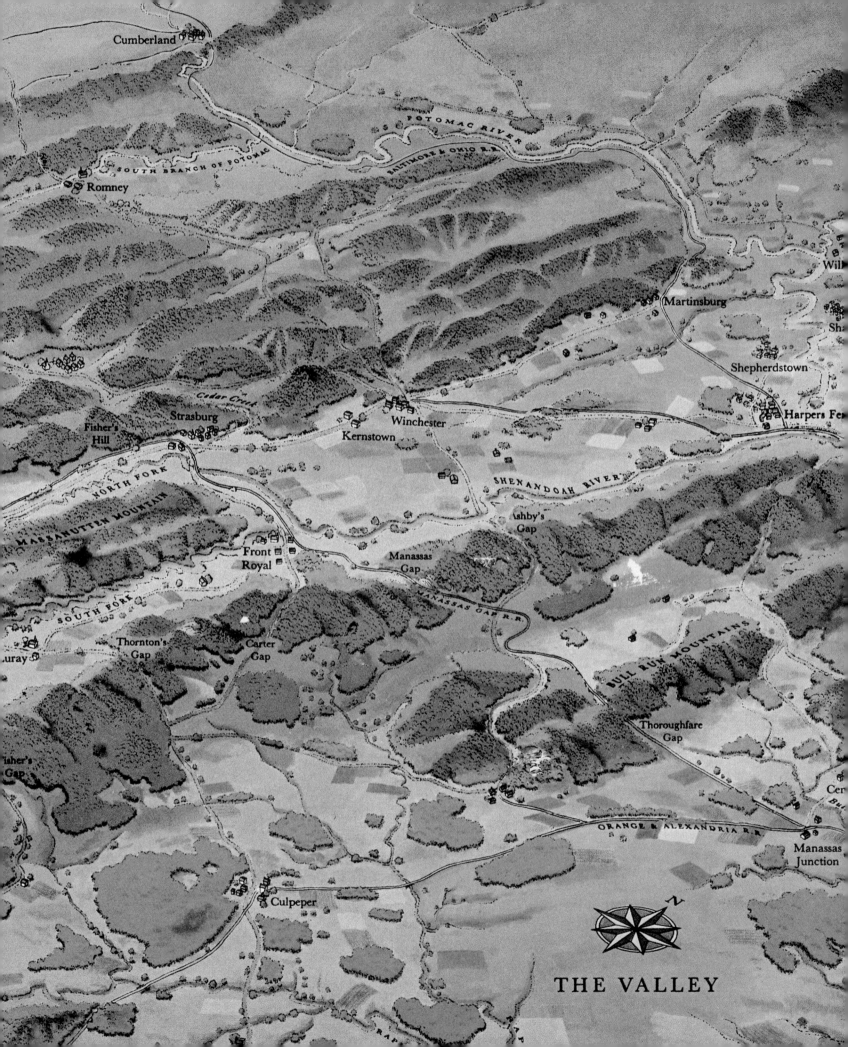

THE VALLEY

into a rout. Banks had to go clear north of the Potomac River, and Jackson's quick movements convinced Secretary Stanton that a major invasion of the North was beginning. McDowell had been under orders to march down and join McClellan, who had drawn his lines astride of the Chickahominy River no more than half a dozen miles from Richmond: these orders were canceled, and McDowell had to send troops posthaste to the Shenandoah to break up Jackson's game. Jackson coolly waited until the Federal panic was at its height, then withdrew up the Valley, bloodied the noses of two pursuing Federal columns—and then slipped swiftly down to Richmond to take a hand in the coming fight with McClellan's Army of the Potomac.

All in all, the Federal government had been utterly bamboozled. By skillful use of his 17,000 men Jackson had immobilized more than 50,000 Yankee troops. When the Confederacy fought to defend its capital, it would not have to face nearly as many men as might easily have been sent against it.

JOE JOHNSTON WOULD NOT BE in command in this fight. At the end of May his troops had fought a hard two-day battle with McClellan's left wing at Fair Oaks—an indecisive struggle that left both sides about where they had been

The marshy ground over which the Army of the Potomac operated in the latter stages of the Peninsular Campaign made life difficult for the soldiers assigned to fatigue duty. A young Minnesotan among those laboring on Grapevine Bridge (below) remembered: "About 3 companys had to work in the water waist deep all day.... The whiskee ration taken on going to bed kept us all rite I guess—at least I kept warm."

Conscription Arrives in the South

An offensive-oriented military strategy, as practiced by Robert E. Lee (left), exacerbated the Confederacy's manpower problems. "'More men,' was the cry from every general in the field," noted one Southern observer in early 1862. "Great as was the need for new blood and new brains, in the council of the nation—still more dire was the need for fresh muscle in its armies." On April 16, 1862, the Confederate Congress enacted the first conscription law in American history, both to meet the need for new men and to prevent short-term volunteers from leaving the service. Targeting able-bodied white men between the ages of eighteen and thirty-five, the law offered preferential treatment for those who volunteered in advance of the draft. It also allowed a wealthy few to pay for substitutes, a provision that proved odious, with one "slacker" callously claiming that since his substitute had been killed in action, he was himself exempt from further service.

On June 1, 1862, General Robert E. Lee took command. Almost at once he began planning an attack on McClellan, ultimately initiating a series of engagements that would be known as the Seven Days' Battles. The clash at Mechanicsville was a tactical defeat for Lee but turned into a strategic victory when the Federals withdrew after the fight. The next combat was at Gaines' Mill on June 27, where the Union V Corps was savagely attacked (above) for five hours and then forced back. It was a clear victory for Lee's men, whose triumphant capture of an abandoned enemy battery (right) was sketched by Alfred Waud.

WOODBURY'S BRIDGE

PORTER'S HQ

LEE'S HQ

New Cold Harbor

Old Cold Harbor

GAINES' MILL
June 27, 1862

GAINES' MILL

MECHANICSVILLE
June 26, 1862

ELLERSON'S MILL

Beaver Dam Creek

MECHANICSVILLE: Snugly posted on high ground east of Beaver Dam Creek, Brigadier General George A. McCall's Pennsylvania division repels frontal attacks by Major General A. P. Hill's division (1 and 2, bottom right). A planned attack on the Union right flank (3) by "Stonewall" Jackson never happens. "I have not been well," Jackson later explained. The Yankees pull back that night.

GAINES' MILL: The entire Federal V Corps, in a formidable defensive position near the Watt House (Porter's headquarters), repel a series of frontal assaults (1 and 2, above) that begin in the afternoon. Follow-up attacks against the Union right by D. H. Hill's and Richard Ewell's divisions (3 and 4) also fail. At 5:30 P.M., Lee's toughest fighters, John B. Hood's Texas Brigade, break the Federal center (5), hold against a mounted counterattack (6), and capture the position. The Federals retreat that night across the Chickahominy (7).

As part of Brigadier General Charles Griffin's brigade, the 4th Michigan was in the thick of it at Gaines' Mill. Its rank and file included the unidentified private pictured on the opposite page, as well as John M. Bancroft, who recalled the retreat as "One of those awful marches—night marches where we move 150 or 100 ft. to rest ten minutes or one-half hour." McClellan was determined to withdraw to the James River, even abandoning his supply depot at Savage's Station (left), where a Union field hospital (above, photographed June 28) was operating. The next day, most of the wounded were captured by Lee's Confederates.

Convinced that he was badly outnumbered by Lee's men (the truth was quite the opposite), General McClellan thought only of retreating to save his grand army from destruction. "I have lost this battle because my force was too small," he rationalized after Gaines' Mill. "I again repeat that I am not responsible for this. . . ." Alfred Waud's sketch (above) shows Union forces falling past the Trent House (roughly midway between Fair Oaks Station and the Chickahominy), site of McClellan's headquarters for much of the operation.

before—and Johnston had been seriously wounded. To replace him, Davis called on Robert E. Lee, who would command the most famous of all Confederate levies, the Army of Northern Virginia, until the end of the war.

Lee's part in the war thus far had been onerous and not particularly happy. He had tried to direct Confederate operations in western Virginia, but the situation there had been hopeless and the area had been lost. He had helped fortify the Southern seacoast, and then he had served Davis as military adviser, in a post which carried heavy responsibility but no genuine authority. (If Jackson had executed the Valley Campaign, the underlying idea was largely Lee's.) Now he was taking an active field command, and within a few weeks he would prove that he was the ideal man for the job.

Because of the success of the Valley Campaign, McClellan's army lay on both sides of the Chickahominy River with substantially less strength than McClellan had expected to have when he took that position. It contained, as June drew to a close, nearly 106,000 soldiers, of whom 25,000 were north of the Chickahominy. Lee, his army reinforced to a strength of over 92,000, left a few divisions to hold the lines immediately in front of Richmond, marched some 65,000 men to the north bank of the Chickahominy, and struck savagely at the exposed Federal flank.

There followed the famous Seven Days' battles—Mechanicsville, Gaines'

General Robert E. Lee pushed hard after McClellan in the hope of bringing on a decisive battle, certain that a major Union defeat before Richmond would ensure Confederate independence. The road system, which favored east-west movement from Richmond (McClellan's retreat path was to the north), helped Lee. Yet even he was bedeviled in places by impassable terrain such as that at White Oak Swamp (left). Time and again, his forward units sparred with McClellan's rear guard (above, an Alfred Waud sketch of a scrap near White Oak Bridge), but were unable to force the Federals to turn and fight.

JAMES RIVER

MALVERN
HOUSE
PORTER'S HQ

MALVERN HILL

July 1, 1862

TO HARRISON'S LANDING

WEST
HOUSE

CREW
HOUSE

FRAYSER'S FARM (or Glendale): In a last effort to intercept McClellan's line of retreat, Lee hurls two divisions (1) against the Union V Corps defending a critical road junction. Although initially successful, a cooperating attack is repulsed (2) and a flank attack assigned to "Stonewall" Jackson is not carried out (3), allowing the hard-pressed Federals to use the Quaker Road (4) to escape.

MALVERN HILL: McClellan has chosen a strong defensive position within supporting range of Union gunboats on the James River. In a series of poorly coordinated assaults (1 and 2), Lee's ranks are blasted apart by massed Federal artillery aided by the gunboats (3). At the end of the day's victory, McClellan continues his retreat (4) to Harrison's Landing.

WILLIS
CHURCH

NELSON
HOUSE

QUAKER ROAD

FRAYSER'S
FARM

FRAYSER'S FARM

June 30, 1862

BRIDGE ROAD

Mill, Savage's Station, Frayser's Farm, Malvern Hill, and a host of lesser fights and skirmishes in between—and at the end of all of this McClellan's army had been roundly beaten and compelled to retreat to Harrison's Landing on the James River, badly shattered and greatly in need of a refit. McClellan's stock at the War Department was lower than ever, his army was effectively out of action as an offensive unit for some time to come, and the way was open for Lee to take the offensive and give some substance to President Lincoln's fears for the safety of Washington. This General Lee would very quickly do; and as he did it the Southern cause would reach its brief, tragic high-water mark for the war.

"The battle [of Malvern Hill] was desperately contested," declared the officer commanding the Union artillery reserve, "and frequently trembled in the balance." Alfred Waud's sketch (above) shows one of the Union guns in action, firing over the Federal battlelines to strike at the charging Confederates. Some Yankee shells landed short, which, said a Federal infantry commander, "did not add to the pleasure of the occasion."

Under Fire at Malvern Hill

Georgia private Edwin Jennison (above) was among those killed at Malvern Hill. M. I. Jones, a Georgia native in the 1st Louisiana, survived, and later recalled: *Our regiment moved from Mechanicsville to Malvern Hill where on July 1, 1862, we went into that bloody charge about 5 o'clock and* *fought till after dark. Forty guns of the enemy threw grape and canister into our ranks with terrible effect. Here we charged across an undulating field of about nine hundred yards, and about half way we encountered a deep ravine. This to some extent shielded us from the enemy's batteries. A hot fire now began. We had the advantage as we fired up* *hill and the enemy down hill. . . . Their killed and wounded were left on the field. We buried their dead on July 2, in a drenching rain. The sight of 2,000 dead men, friends and foes, terribly mangled, and lying in rows, was sickening.*

From Richmond

The Seven Days' Battles cost McClellan 15,855 casualties, 8,066 of them wounded. These maimed heroes (two are depicted in Winslow Homer's watercolor sketch *From Richmond,* above) were, at least, alive. And it was battlefield survivors such as these that Lincoln had in mind when he pledged his administration "to care for him who shall have borne the battle. . . ."

CHAPTER 4

The Navies

While the rival armies swayed back and forth over the landscape, wreathing the countryside in smoke and visiting the dread and sorrow of long casualty lists on people of the North and the South, a profound intangible was slowly beginning to tilt the balance against the Confederacy. On the ocean, in the coastal sounds, and up and down the inland rivers the great force of sea power was making itself felt. By itself it could never decide the issue of the war; taken in conjunction with the work of the Federal armies, it would ultimately be decisive. In no single area of the war was the overwhelming advantage possessed by the Federal government so ruinous to Southern hopes.

The Civil War came while one revolution in naval affairs was under way, and it hastened the commencement of another. The world's navies were in the act of adjusting themselves to the transition from sail to steam when the war began; by the time it ended, the transition from wooden ships to ironclads was well along. Taken together, the two revolutions were far-reaching. The era of what is now thought of as "modern" warfare was foreshadowed by what happened on land; it actually began on the

Charleston Bay and City by John Gadsby Chapman (right), portrays a Rebel ironclad prowess more apparent than real. "Our gunboats are defective," complained General Beauregard in late 1863. "Even in the harbor they are at times considered unsafe in a storm." Nonetheless, the Union had to entice recruits willing to challenge the Confederates on the water. The U.S. Navy poster above pointedly promoted the fact that sailors were eligible for lucrative prize money, a powerful incentive. After recounting the details of his role in the capture of a ship said to be worth $75,000, a young officer, writing to his girlfriend, added, "Pretty good day's work, isn't it?"

John Ericsson (above), a Swedish-born inventor and engineer, responded to the U.S. government's call for ironclad designs with a concept for a turreted warship that was so advanced, it was rejected by the three naval officers charged with reviewing the submissions. Only Ericsson's spirited personal presentation reversed the review board's decision.

water, and by 1865 naval warfare would resemble the twentieth century much more than it resembled anything Lord Nelson or John Paul Jones had known.

At the start of the war the South had no navy at all, and the North had one which, although it was good enough for ordinary combat with an overseas enemy, was almost wholly unadapted for the job which it had to do now. Both sides had to improvise, and in the improvisation the South displayed fully as much ingenuity and resourcefulness as the North. The great difference was that the North had so much more to improvise with. The South was compelled to enter a contest which it had no chance to win.

When the flag came down on Fort Sumter in April, 1861, the Federal government possessed some ninety warships. More than half of these were sailing vessels—models of their class a generation earlier, obsolete now. About forty ships were steam-driven, and a great number of these were tied up at various navy-yard docks, out of commission—"in ordinary," as the expression then went. Some of them were badly in need of repair. Of the steamers that were in commission, many were scattered on foreign stations, and it would take time to get them back into home waters.

Pride of the navy was its set of five steam frigates. They were powerful wooden vessels, ship-rigged, with adequate power plants and exceptionally heavy armament—forty 9-inch rifles on the gun decks, and a few larger weapons mounted on the spar decks. They were probably as powerful as any ships then afloat. All of these were out of commission.

Then there were five first-class screw sloops, smaller and less formidable than the steam frigates but sturdy fighting craft all the same. There were four sidewheelers, dating back to the navy's first experiments with steam power: they were practically obsolete, because machinery and boilers were largely above the water line, but they could still be used. There were eight lighter screw sloops and half a dozen of third-class rating, along with a handful of tugs and assorted harbor craft. That was about the lot.

With this navy the United States had to blockade more than 3,500 miles of Confederate coast line. It had, also, to control such rivers as the Mississippi and the Tennessee, to say nothing of the extensive sounds along the Atlantic coast. Furthermore, it had to be prepared to strike at Southern seaports, most of them substantially fortified, and to join with the army in amphibious offensives all the way from Cape Hatteras to the Rio Grande. To do all of these things it did not have nearly enough ships, and most of the ones it did have were of the wrong kind. The powerful frigates and sloops were designed for combat on the high seas or for commerce raiding, not for blockade duty. They drew too much water to operate in shallow sounds and rivers. For war with a European power they would have been excellent, once they were all repaired and commissioned; for war with the Confederacy they were not quite what the navy needed.

At the very beginning of the war Lincoln proclaimed a blockade of all Southern ports. This, as he soon discovered, was a serious tactical error. A nation "blockaded" the ports of a foreign power; when it dealt with an internal insurrection or rebellion it simply closed its ports. The proclamation of blockade almost amounted to recognition of the Confederacy's independent existence, and European powers promptly recognized the Southland's belligerent rights.

On top of this, foreign nations were not obliged to respect a blockade unless it were genuinely effective. A paper blockade would do no good: unless the navy could make it really dangerous for merchant ships to trade with Confederate ports, the blockade would have no standing in international law. So the navy's first problem was to find, somewhere and somehow, at any expense but in a great hurry, enough ships to make the paper blockade a real one.

The job was done, but it cost a great deal of money and resulted in the creation of one of the most heterogeneous fleets ever seen on the waters of the globe. Anything that would float and carry a gun or two would serve, for most of these blockaders would never have to fight; they were simply cops on the beat, creating most of their effect just by being on the scene. Vessels of every conceivable variety were brought into service, armed, after a fashion, and sent steaming down to take station off Southern harbors: ferryboats, excursion steamers, whalers, tugs, fishing schooners, superannuated clippers—a weird and wonderful collection of maritime oddities, which in the end gave more useful service than

John A. Dahlgren (above) was responsible for the design of one of the most powerful weapons in the U.S. Navy's arsenal: a bottle-shaped, smoothbore "Dahlgren" cannon, one of which is behind him. Known throughout the world for his ordnance expertise, Dahlgren began the war behind a Washington desk. His bureau work so impressed the President that he was promoted two full grades, earning him the unflattering nickname of "Mr. Lincoln's admiral." Dahlgren longed for a combat command, and in 1863, he got his chance. Andrew H. Foote, commander of the western river fleet, had been named to take charge of Union operations against Charleston. But Foote died en route to his post, and Dahlgren was given the command.

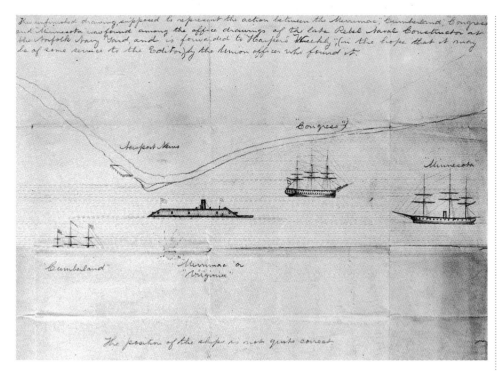

Newport News

"Congress"

"Minnesota"

"Cumberland"

"Merrimac" or "Virginia"

The position of the ships is not quite correct

anyone had a right to expect. They made the blockade legally effective, and their work was aided by the Confederate government's folly in withholding cotton from the overseas market. At the very least they gave the navy time to build some new vessels specially designed for the job.

These included two dozen 500-ton gunboats, steam powered, of shallow draft and moderate armament—"ninety-day gunboats," they were called, because it took just three months from keel-laying to final commissioning. Deep-sea cruisers to run down Confederate commerce destroyers were built, along with forty-seven double-enders—unique, canoe-shaped side-wheelers, with rudders and pilothouses at each end, for use in the narrow rivers that fed into the coastal sounds where there was no room to turn around. The double-enders could change course simply by reversing their engines.

In the end the blockade was made highly effective, and by the final year of the war its effect was fatally constrictive. It was never airtight, and as long as a Southern port remained open, daring merchant skippers would slip in and out with priceless cargoes of contraband; but the measure of its effectiveness was not the percentage of blockade-runners which got through the net, but the increasing quantity of goods which the Confederacy had to do without. Under the blockade the Confederacy was doomed to slow strangulation.

FOR OFFENSIVE OPERATIONS the Federal navy was in much better shape, and the war was not very old before offensive operations got under way. Late in August, 1861, a squadron of warships commanded by Flag Officer Silas Stringham, accompanied by transports bearing infantry under Ben Butler, dropped down the coast for an assault on the Confederate forts which guarded Hatteras Inlet, North Carolina, principal entrance to the vast reaches of Pamlico Sound. Stringham had two of the huge steam frigates with him, and his bombardment pounded the unprepared forts into submission. The government apparently had not

Naval history was made on March 8, 1862, when the first Confederate ironclad steamed down the Elizabeth River into Hampton Roads to attack the wooden-sided U.S. blockading fleet anchored there. Built on the hull of the U.S.S. *Merrimac* (which had been scuttled and burned when the Federals abandoned the Gosport Navy Yard in April, 1861), the new warship had been christened C.S.S. *Virginia,* but in common usage retained its original name. After ramming and sinking the twenty-four-gun wooden-hulled steam-sailing sloop *Cumberland*, the *Merrimac* headed for the fifty-gun frigate *Congress* (above left). An awestruck Union officer watched the one-sided fight as the *Merrimac* fired "shot and shell into her with terrific effect, while the shot from the *Congress* glanced from her iron-plated sloping sides, without doing any apparent injury."

OPPOSITE: When the U.S.S. *Cumberland* died, the age of fighting sail died, too. "The engagement . . . ," wrote Lieutenant John Wood of the *Merrimac*, "was . . . in some respects the most momentous naval conflict ever witnessed. . . . It revolutionized the navies of the world." The cramped condition of the *Merrimac*'s gundeck is suggested by the drawing below of the gun tier on a similar Union vessel.

The results of the first day's fighting at Hampton Roads proved the superiority of iron over wood, but on the next day iron was pitted against iron as the U.S.S. *Monitor* arrived on the scene. It was just in time to challenge the *Merrimac*, which was returning to finish off the U.S. blockading squadron. The Confederate ironclad carried more guns than the Union *Monitor*, but it was slow, clumsy, and prone to engine trouble. The Union prototype, as designed by John Ericsson, was the faster and more maneuverable ironclad, but it lacked the Rebel vessel's brutish size and power. The *Merrimac*'s officers had heard rumors about a Union ironclad, yet, according to Lieutenant Wood: "She could not possibly have made her appearance at a more inopportune time for us. . . ." Lieutenant S. Dana Greene, an officer aboard the *Monitor,* described the first exchange of gunfire: "The turrets and other parts of the ship were heavily struck, but the shots did not penetrate; the tower was intact, and it continued to revolve. A look of confidence passed over the men's faces, and we believed the *Merrimac* would not repeat the work she had accomplished the day before." Neither ironclad seriously damaged the other in their one day of fighting, March 9, 1862 (shown here in a painting by Xanthus Smith), though the *Merrimac* was indeed prevented from attacking any more of the Union's wooden ships. A new age of naval warfare had dawned.

While Southern shipbuilders searched empty cupboards for the material needed to build a new generation of warships, Northern shipyards raced toward full capacity. Using precision parts from forges such as New York's Novelty Iron Works (top), they could quickly execute updated designs for the new vessels, including a second generation of iron-clads, called "monitors" (bottom), which had two gun turrets.

The Naval War

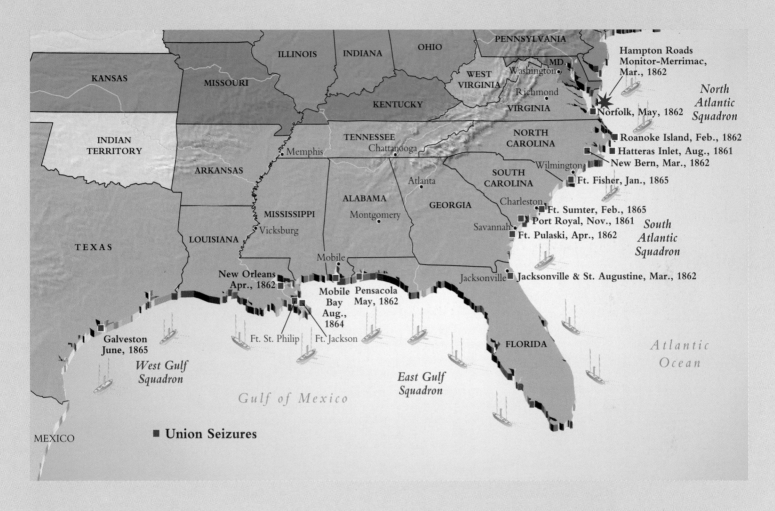

On April 19, 1861, President Lincoln declared a naval blockade of the Confederate coast from South Carolina to Texas; eight days later, he extended that zone to cover Virginia and North Carolina. This, observed an officer in the U.S. Navy, made for a "coast-line of over three thousand miles to be blockaded, greater in extent than the Atlantic coast of Europe—an undertaking without precedent in history...." The map above illustrates the slow, strangling effect of the Northern blockade. The dates indicate Union siezures of various points along the coast line. In January, 1865, when the Union secured Fort Fisher, it closed off the Cape Fear River, the last remaining haven for blockade runners.

The exigencies of war opened opportunities for experimentation and change that had been closed for decades in the tradition-bound U.S. Navy. Designer Samuel M. Pook created a class of paddle-wheeled, armored gun platforms typified by the U.S.S. *Cairo* (above): with a shallow draft, it was suited for service along the nation's western rivers. Not every new idea was the harbinger of the modern age, though. The heavily armored *Dictator* (opposite) cost $1,400,000 dollars to build; it was intended to initiate the war's largest class of monitors but suffered from design problems that kept it out of much of the fighting.

done its advance planning very carefully, and for the time being neither the army nor the navy was prepared to do anything but hold the captured position. However, the operation did set a pattern, and important results would grow from it.

In November a much stronger expedition, the naval part of it commanded by Flag Officer Samuel F. Du Pont, broke into the waters of South Carolina, shelling Forts Walker and Beauregard into surrender and occupying Port Royal, which became a secure base for the blockading fleet. Early in 1862 Flag Officer Louis M. Goldsborough and Brigadier General Ambrose E. Burnside led an amphibious foray into the North Carolina sounds from Hatteras Inlet. Roanoke Island was seized, Elizabeth City and New Bern were captured, and powerful Fort Macon, commanding the approach to Beaufort, was taken. In effect, this action gave the Unionists control of nearly all of the North Carolina coast line and made the task of the blockading fleet much easier; it also added appreciably to Jefferson Davis' problems by posing the constant threat of an invasion between

Blacks in the Union Navy

The U.S. Navy Act of 1813 specifically provided for the enlistment of free "persons of color" in the service, and it is estimated that about 8 per cent of the 118,000 men who entered the Navy during the Civil War were black. One of them, using the pen name "Harry Reeftackle," took the editor of New York's black newspaper *The Weekly Anglo-African* to task for only reporting on the black infantry: *You are aware, probably, that there are about 15,000 colored sailors in the navy, some ships being entirely manned by them excepting officers. I suppose you have no able naval correspondent. I don't think you would disparage one arm to exalt the other. There are just as intelligent men in the navy as in the army. Fully one-quarter of the crew of the U.S.S. Hunchback* (below), part of the James River fleet, were black. Another black sailor, N. W. J. Davis, serving aboard the U.S.S. *Ohio*, related for the same paper a story of lower-deck racial abuse that was reported to the ship's captain: *We soon after heard the boatswain's mate pipe all the colored men in the ship to muster. . . . We met the second officer in command. . . . He said that Capt. Green had received an appeal from the men, and that he had given it to him to peruse, and it met his approval, also that of his superior officer. If we were interfered with, to report the offender, and he would punish him severely. . . . These two officers . . . are gentlemen in every respect. God bless them! May their shadows never grow less! The colored men of our navy should be proud of these gentlemen.*

Over the course of 1861, the manpower of the U.S. Navy grew from 7,600 men in March to not less than 22,000 in December. Unlike infantry regiments, which were raised in specific communities, naval crews were melting pots that threw together men of different nationalities, races, and age groups: it was not unusual for as many as half of a warship's crewmen to be foreign born. Mere boys (above) served as powder monkeys.

Richmond and Charleston. Simultaneously, another army-navy expedition took Fort Pulaski, at the mouth of the Savannah River.

Most important of all was the blow at New Orleans, largest city in the Confederacy. This was entrusted to an elderly but still spry officer named David Glasgow Farragut, who had a strong fleet of fighting craft and a flotilla of mortar vessels—converted schooners, each mounting a tub-shaped mortar that could lob a 13-inch shell high into the air and drop it inside a fort with surprising accuracy. Farragut got his vessels into the mouth of the Mississippi and in mid-April opened a prolonged bombardment of Forts Jackson and St. Philip, which guarded the approach to New Orleans. The mortar boats, commanded by Captain David Dixon Porter, tossed shells into the forts for a week; then, in the blackness of two in the morning on April 24, Farragut's ships went steaming up the river to run past the forts.

Even as shipyards turned out vessels altered or created for war, the search was on for the manpower to operate such a massive fleet. River towns and seaports were scoured for experienced crewmen, while soldiers who signed up for artillery service were sometimes "volunteered" to man naval guns, and thousands of landlubbers learned the language and protocol of ship life. The musically inclined sailors below served aboard an admiral's flagship.

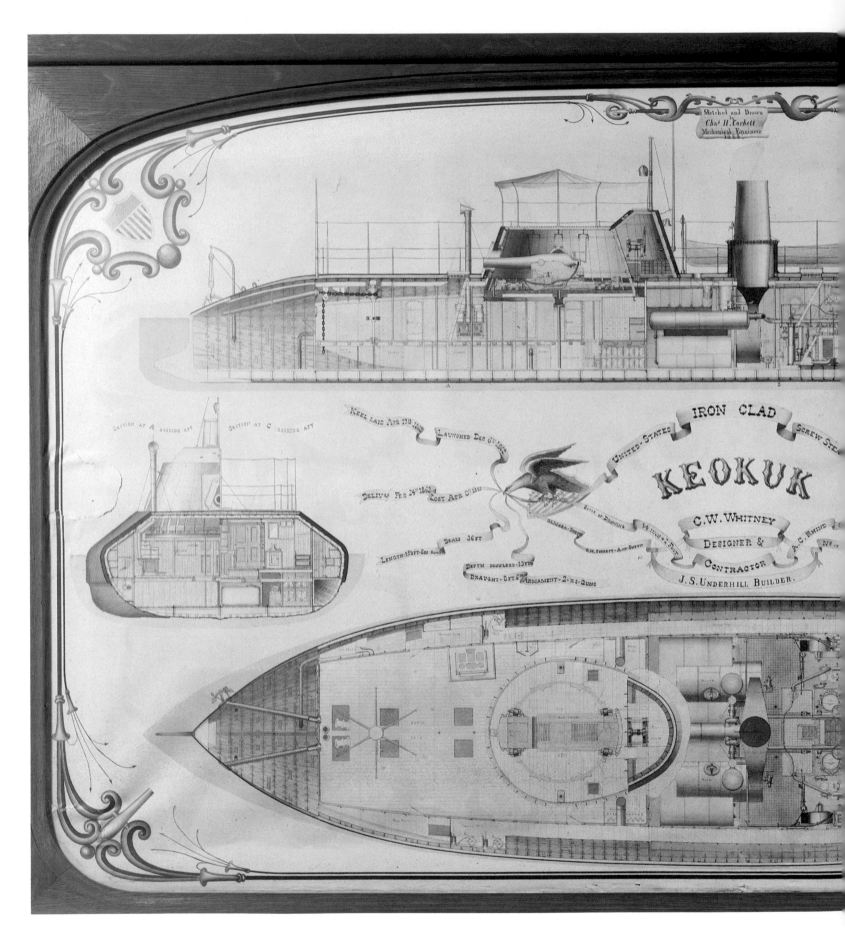

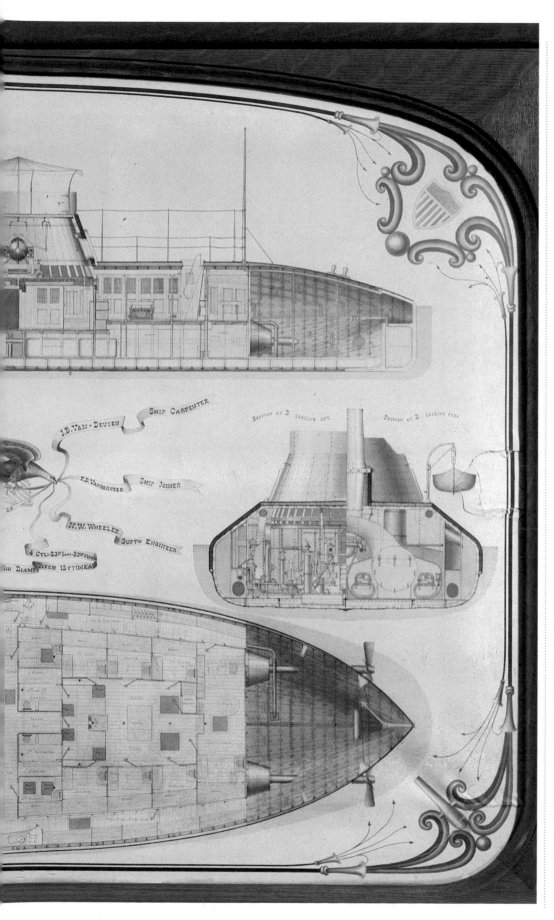

Within the illustration the following labels appear:

SHIP CARPENTER

J.B. VAN-DEUSEN

SECTION AT B LOOKING AFT   SECTION AT B LOOKING FORD

I.B. VANDERVEER   SHIP JOINER

N.W. WHEELER

SUPT'D ENGINEER

4 CYLS 23'F bore 20" stroke

Diamt   Pitch 13 FT (MEA

Civil War monitors represented a triumph of nineteenth-century engineering and design. The plans for the double-turreted U.S.S. *Keokuk* possess a beauty and grace that make them artistic in their own right. Not so pleasing was the fate of the *Keokuk*. It was launched in New York on December 6, 1862, fitted out, and then assigned to service with the U.S. fleet operating against Charleston. On April 7, 1863, it joined in a general bombardment of the harbor's defenses (which included Fort Sumter). The *Keokuk* took an exposed position and was struck nearly a hundred times by enemy ordnance. Badly punctured by this punishment, the ship sank the next day off Rebel-held Morris Island. Jubilant Confederates salvaged the *Keokuk*'s guns and other "substantial trophies of the affair," as General Beauregard later reported.

Throughout the life of the Confederacy, determined engineers worked against overwhelming odds to construct ironclads, finding metal wherever they could, often in recycled railroad tracks and engines salvaged from sunken vessels. Builders began work on the C.S.S. *Albemarle* (above) in a North Carolina cornfield and finally managed to launch it in the spring of 1864. After assisting in the capture of Plymouth and defeating a small Union squadron dedicated to its destruction, the *Albemarle* was sunk in October by a daring torpedo attack.

The Confederates sent fire rafts downstream, but these were dodged. A collection of armed river vessels put up as much of a fight as they could, and the big guns in the forts flailed away in the darkness, Farragut's broadsides replying, the river all covered with heavy smoke lit by the red flares from the burning rafts and the sharp flashes of the guns—and suddenly most of Farragut's ships were past the forts with only moderate damage, the Confederate vessels were sunk or driven ashore, and Farragut went plowing on to occupy New Orleans. Hopelessly cut off, the forts presently surrendered, Ben Butler came in with troops to take possession of the forts and the city, and the mouth of the great river was in Federal hands.

The capture of New Orleans strikingly illustrated the immense value of unchallenged sea power. The Federals could strike when and where they pleased, and all the Southern coast was vulnerable. The Confederates had known that New Orleans was in danger, but they had supposed that the real peril lay upriver, where Shiloh had just been lost and where the Federal gunboats were hammering their way down to Memphis: coming up through the mouth of the river, Farragut had, so to speak, entered by the back door. The loss of New Orleans was one of the genuine disasters to the Southern cause, and it proved irretrievable.

Yet if the Lincoln government had the enormous advantage that goes with control of the sea, the Confederacy made valiant attempts to redress the balance. The South lacked a merchant marine and a seafaring population, and it had very little in the way of shipyards and the industrial plant that could build machinery and armament for warships, but it had vast ingenuity and much energy, and its naval authorities, working with very little, accomplished much more than anyone had a right to expect. Not even the Yankees were any more inventive: the chief difference was that it was easier for the Yankees to turn an invention into a working reality.

THE FAMOUS CASE of the *Merrimac* offers an interesting example.

Merrimac was one of the Federal navy's great steam frigates. Her engines were in bad order, and when the war began she was laid up in the Norfolk navy yard, out of commission. Situated in an ardently pro-Confederate community, the navy yard was quickly lost; and by seizing it on April 20, 1861, the Confederates

Conrad Wise Chapman's painting of the C.S.S. *Hunley* (below) presents a benign image of a singular vessel known as "the peripatetic coffin." Built from a twenty-five-foot-long boiler cylinder, the *Hunley* was a nine-man submarine designed to approach its prey undetected and attach an explosive charge from the end of a long wooden spar. Trial runs killed at least thirty-two volunteer crewmen, and on the night of February 17, 1864, when the *Hunley* sortied to sink a Union sloop in Charleston Harbor, the sub foundered on its return, drowning its entire crew.

In the first amphibious operation of the Civil War, Union army units, closely supported by naval warships, landed at Hatteras Inlet, North Carolina, on August 28, 1861 (right). It was nearly over before it started: heavy surf stranded the first wave of 300 men for twenty-four hours, dangerously isolating them. Fortunately, the Rebel defenders, under heavy fire from the ships, were unable to form a counterattack. After the waters calmed the next day, the full force of the infantry landed and the Federals secured a valuable staging point on the Atlantic coast.

The North's first significant successes in the war came on the water, when its naval forces secured key points on the Confederate coast line. On November 7, 1861, a powerful Federal fleet commanded by Rear Admiral Samuel Francis Du Pont (caricatured above) appeared in Port Royal Sound, off South Carolina. Following a carefully choreographed bombardment (left), two Confederate forts surrendered, and white plantation owners fled, leaving behind hundreds of slaves. It was later written that when one young black asked his mother about the strange thunder they heard, she replied: "Son, dat ain't no t'under, dat Yankee come to gib you Freedom."

acquired not only the physical plant but more than a thousand powerful cannon, which served to arm Confederate forts all along the seacoast.

When the Federals were driven from the yard they set fire to *Merrimac* and scuttled her, but Confederate engineers had little trouble raising the hulk, and on inspection it was found sound, only the upper works having been destroyed by fire. The imaginative Southerners thereupon proceeded to construct a fighting ship the likes of which no one had ever seen.

Merrimac's hull was cut down to the berth deck, and a citadel with slanting sides was built on the midships section, with ports for ten guns. The walls of this citadel were made of pitch pine and oak two feet thick, and on this was laid an iron sheathing four inches thick. An open grating covered the top of this citadel, admitting light and air to the gun deck. An armored pilothouse was forward, and a four-foot iron beak was fastened to the bow. When she left the dry dock, *Merrimac*, rechristened *Virginia*, looked like nothing so much as a barn gone adrift and submerged to the eaves. The decks forward and aft of the citadel were just awash. *Merrimac*'s engines, defective to begin with, had not been improved by the

In early 1862, Union forces moved to expand their foothold on the North Carolina coast: the city of New Bern on the Neuse River was targeted. On March 13, troops landed ashore while naval vessels challenged the nearby Rebel forts, one of which, Fort Thompson, was a thirteen-gun, sod fortification located about six miles below the town. Frank H. Schell's drawing shows the fort's gunners responding to the approaching Yankee gunboats. Only three of Fort Thompson's guns faced away from the river; it was from that direction that Federal infantry successfully stormed the position.

Frank H. Schell
MARCH 14th '62

Confederate officials expected that the sturdy stone and masonry walls of Fort Pulaski, at the mouth of the Savannah River, could withstand any Yankee artillery fire. They failed to reckon with the determined skill of a Federal officer named Quincy Gillmore, who, in February and March of 1862, deployed thirty-six heavy guns (many of them the new type of powerful rifled cannon) for his attack. On April 10, Gillmore opened a devastating bombardment. After thirty hours, Pulaski's impregnable walls had been breached and the garrison was forced to surrender. Theodore R. Davis' drawings (this page) show scenes from this operation, including the effect of the bombardment.

fact that they had spent weeks under water, but somehow the engineers got them into running order, and the ship could move. She could not move very fast, and she was one of the unhandiest brutes to steer that was ever put afloat; but in all the navies of the world there were not more than two ships that could have given her a fight. (The French had one ironclad frigate, and the British had another; all the rest of the world's warships were of wood.)

It should be pointed out that since warships had never worn armor, no one had ever bothered to create an armor-piercing shell, and *Merrimac*'s iron sides—very thinly armored, by later standards—were impervious to anything the ordinary warship would fire at her. It developed, as the war wore along, that the only way to deal with an ironclad was to fire solid shot from the largest smoothbore cannon available—15-inch, if possible—at the closest possible range. These would not exactly pierce good iron sheathing, but repeated blows might crack it so that other projectiles could pierce it. This worked sometimes, and sometimes it did not; but when *Merrimac* left the Elizabeth River, on

March 8, 1862, and chugged laboriously out into the open waters of Hampton Roads, none of the Federal warships in sight mounted guns that could do her any particular damage.

On her first day in action *Merrimac* created a sensation and put the Lincoln administration—especially Secretary of War Stanton—into something like a panic. She destroyed two of the navy's wooden warships, *Congress* and *Cumberland*, drove the big steam frigate *Minnesota* aground, and was herself so little damaged by the shot which the Union warships threw at her that it almost looked as if she could whip the entire Federal navy. When evening came *Merrimac* went back into her harbor, planning to return in the morning, destroy *Minnesota*, and sink any other ships that cared to stick around and fight.

While off-duty soldiers enjoy a game of baseball, members of the 48th New York snap to attention in a photograph (below) taken several months after the occupation—and refurbishment—of Fort Pulaski by Union forces. However uneventful this garrison duty may have been for the Yankee boys, Federal control of Pulaski meant that Rebel blockade-runners would have to look elsewhere for a friendly coastal port.

The Man Who Captured New Orleans

It was a personal dilemma too often posed by the Civil War: one of the Union navy's best fighting commanders was a Tennessee native with family ties to Louisiana and deep roots in Virginia. As a young midshipman, David Glasgow Farragut had served on the U.S.S. *Essex* in the War of 1812. During the Mexican War, he proposed a daring amphibious operation that older officers ultimately deemed too risky. At the outset of the Civil War, Farragut vowed allegiance to the U.S. flag; even so, his loyalty was thought suspect, and so he began the war assigned to a desk in Washington. Through the intervention of David Dixon Porter and Secretary of the Navy Gideon Welles, though, he was chosen to direct the assault on New Orleans. Welles asserted that Farragut "will more willingly take great risks to obtain great results than any officer in either army or navy." In addition to overseeing the victory at New Orleans, Farragut successfully led Union naval forces at Port Hudson and Mobile Bay.

For the Union blockaders, the grand prize of 1862 was New Orleans; its capture would close a major Rebel outlet to foreign markets. The attempt on it would be another combined navy-army operation, and the command belonged to Flag Officer David G. Farragut (above). The peculiar confines of the Mississippi River delta posed special problems for deep-water officers like Farragut; not the least was the prospect of sailors trying to fight shoreline snipers, as depicted in Allen C. Redwood's postwar drawing (right).

An actual sketch, made on the spot by one of the Special Artists of Frank Leslie's Illustrated Newspaper.

Mr. Leslie holds the copyright and reserves the exclusive right of publication.

Downstream from New Orleans, two powerful bastions protected the Mississippi River at its mouth: Fort St. Philip and Fort Jackson. Farragut first tried to reduce them by heavy mortar bombardment, using a flotilla of partially camouflaged ships (left); when that failed, he decided to run his fleet past the enemy guns. The attempt, made on April 24, was a success, despite a vigorous Confederate response (below). Farragut directed the movement from the mizzenmast of his flagship, the *Hartford*, which was near the vanguard of the procession. To him it seemed "as if the artillery of heaven were playing upon the earth."

Mauritz F. H. Dehaas' 1867 painting, *The Battle of New Orleans—Farragut's Fleet Passing the Forts below New Orleans*, gently mutes the horrors and chaos of that night. After running a gauntlet of cannon fire from both shores, Farragut's ships met and defeated a small Rebel defense fleet waiting upriver. The commander of the Union warship *Pensacola* saw men killed on either side of him. "At daylight," he marveled, "I found the right leg of my pantaloons and drawers cut away by the knee, and the skirt of my coat cut in a strip; yet my body was untouched."

The next day, March 9, brought what was certainly the most dramatic naval battle of the war—the famous engagement between *Merrimac* and *Monitor*.

It had taken the Confederates many months to design and construct their pioneer ironclad, and word of what they were doing quickly got North—very few military secrets were really kept, in that war—and the Federal Navy Department had to get an ironclad of its own. It went to the redoubtable Swedish-American inventor John Ericsson for a design, getting a craft which in its own way was every bit as odd-looking as the rebuilt *Merrimac*. Ericsson built a long, flat hull with no more than a foot or two of freeboard, putting amidships a revolving iron turret mounting two 11-inch guns. A smoke pipe came up aft of this, and forward there was a stubby iron pilothouse; people who saw *Monitor* afloat said she looked like a tin can on a shingle. This craft was finished just in the nick of time,

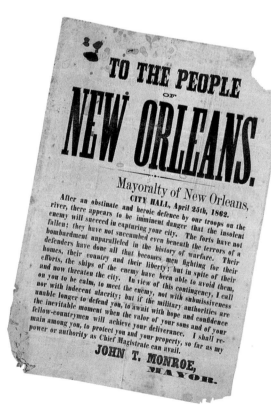

Residents and officials of New Orleans reacted with supreme self-confidence when word first came that a Union fleet had gathered off the mouth of the Mississippi. But Farragut's successful run past the two forts representing the Crescent City's only practical line of defense sent waves of panic that Mayor John T. Monroe's proclamation (below) attempted to calm.

TO THE PEOPLE
OF
NEW ORLEANS.

Mayoralty of New Orleans,
CITY HALL, April 25th, 1862.

After an obstinate and heroic defence by our troops on the river, there appears to be imminent danger that the insolent enemy will succeed in capturing your city. The forts have not fallen: they have not succumbed even beneath the terrors of a bombardment unparalleled in the history of warfare. Their defenders have done all that becomes men fighting for their homes, their country and their liberty; but in spite of their efforts, the ships of the enemy have been able to avoid them, and now threaten the city. In view of this contingency, I call on you to be calm, to meet the enemy, not with submissiveness nor with indecent alacrity; but if the military authorities are unable longer to defend you, to await with hope and confidence the inevitable moment when the valor of your sons and of your fellow-countrymen will achieve your deliverance. I shall remain among you, to protect you and your property, so far as my power or authority as Chief Magistrate can avail.

JOHN T. MONROE,
MAYOR.

came down to the Chesapeake from New York in tow of a tug, almost foundering en route—neither of these great ironclads was very seaworthy—and steamed in past the Virginia capes late in the afternoon of March 8, just as *Merrimac* was completing her day's chores. Next day the two ships met in open combat.

The fight was singularly indecisive. Each ship took a sound hammering, but neither one was badly damaged. Although *Merrimac*, in the end, retired to a safe spot in the Elizabeth River, *Monitor* did not try to follow her, nor did the Federal craft ever attempt to force a finish fight. *Merrimac* destroyed no more Union warships, but she remained afloat until May 10, effectively keeping the Federals out of the James River; indeed, her continued existence was one of the reasons why McClellan was so very slow in moving up the Virginia Peninsula. She was lost, finally, when the Federals occupied Norfolk, which left her without

Once past Forts St. Philip and Jackson and the Rebel defense fleet, Farragut took his warships upriver to New Orleans, leaving behind the infantry to secure the two bastions. At 1:00 P.M., April 25, the Union ships anchored midriver with their guns trained on the defenseless city. While patriotic citizens openly displayed their defiance (above), negotiations dragged on for four days. Not until the city administration verified that Forts St. Philip and Jackson had surrendered did it haul down all Confederate flags. Major General Benjamin F. Butler (below) soon arrived as the military governor.

a home port. She drew too much water to go up the James to Richmond, and she was far too unseaworthy to go out into the open ocean, and her crew had no recourse but to scuttle her. But by any standard she had been a success, she had helped to create a revolution in naval warfare, and her design and construction proved that Southern engineers were quite as ready as Yankees to move into the new mechanical age.

If the South had had Northern industrial facilities, the story of the war at sea might have been very different. A number of ironclads on the *Merrimac* pattern were built, and most of them were highly serviceable. There was *Arkansas,* built in Memphis, Tennessee, which ran straight through a fleet of Yankee gunboats above Vicksburg, outfought the best the Yankees could send against her, and was destroyed by her own crew when her engines failed and sent her hopelessly aground near Baton Rouge. There was *Albemarle,* which shook Federal control of the North Carolina sounds until young Lieutenant William Cushing sank her with a torpedo; and there was *Tennessee,* which singlehanded fought Farragut's entire fleet at Mobile Bay in the summer of 1864, surrendering only after having survived one of the most one-sided contests in naval history. As a matter of fact, a Confederate ironclad almost saved the day at New Orleans. A very heavily armored vessel named *Louisiana* was built to hold the lower river, but Farragut came along before she was quite ready: her engines were not serviceable, and her gun ports needed to be enlarged so that her guns could train properly, and she was tied to the bank, virtually useless, when the Federal fleet steamed by. When the forts surrendered, *Louisiana* was blown up.

THE MARVEL IN ALL OF THIS is not that the Confederacy did so poorly with its navy, but that it did so well. Almost uniformly, her ironclads gave the Federal navy much trouble, and it is worth recording that most of them finally failed not because they were poorly designed, but because the industrial facilities that could put them into first-class shape and keep them there did not exist. The South was painfully short of mechanics, short of metal, short of fabricating plants; there was never any chance that she could create a fleet solid enough to go out and challenge the Federal navy, and what was done had to be done on a bits-and-pieces basis. All things considered, the Confederate Navy Department acquitted itself very well.

Confederate commerce raiders drew a great deal of attention during the war and in the generations that followed, but although they were a most expensive nuisance to

Never a man for half measures, Benjamin Butler acted quickly to enforce the will of the Union over the citizens of New Orleans. Known Confederate officials or activists were rounded up: some were jailed, others banished. When one resident publicly desecrated the U.S. flag, Butler had him arrested, tried, and hanged. In response to a campaign of verbal harassment by some of the city's upper-class women, Butler issued the infamous General Orders, No. 28 (above right), an action that quickly became the object of Southern satire (below).

Head-Quarters, Department of the Gulf, New Orleans, May 15, 1862.

General Orders, No. 28.

As the Officers and Soldiers of the United States have been subject to repeated insults from the women calling themselves ladies of New Orleans, in return for the most scrupulous non-interference and courtesy on our part, it is ordered that hereafter when any Female shall, by word, gesture, or movement, insult or show contempt for any officer or soldier of the United States, she shall be regarded and held liable to be treated as a woman of the town plying her avocation.

By command of Maj.-Gen. BUTLER,

GEORGE C. STRONG,
A. A. G. Chief of Staff.

Union forces occupied the Texas port of Galveston in October, 1862; within two months, Confederates mounted an operation by land and sea to recapture it. J. O. Davidson's drawing shows a climactic moment in the bitter fight: on New Year's Day, Rebels boarded and captured the U.S. revenue cutter *Harriet Lane*. When a Confederate major involved in the action arrived on the deck of the ship, he found his son, a lieutenant in the Union navy, lying mortally wounded.

The U.S.S. *Galena* (above) was a hastily armored wooden gunboat that one observer likened to "a great fish with scales." It served on Virginia's James River, where, on May 15, 1862, it took part in the attempt by Union vessels to bludgeon their way past the defenses guarding Richmond at Drewry's Bluff. Alert Rebel gunners pounded the Yankee ships: the *Galena* alone was hit forty-four times. As the battered Union flotilla withdrew, a Confederate defender called out derisively, "Tell the captain that is not the way to Richmond!"

Under pressure since early in the war, the proud city of Charleston withstood all Federal attacks from the seaward side. In addition to Fort Sumter (whose gun tier is shown above), Charleston Harbor depended on a ring of fortified positions, including the Laurens Street Battery (opposite top), in Charleston and Battery Simkins (opposite bottom), on the south shore near the harbor's mouth.

OVERLEAF: Conrad Chapman's painting shows a torn but defiant Rebel flag still flying over Fort Sumter despite the presence of Union guns in the near distance on Morris Island and a massive Federal fleet blockading the harbor entrance. A soldier in the 54th Massachusetts noted in November, 1863, that "the bombardment at Sumter is still kept up night and day, and still the gallant rebels are masters of the situation. . . ."

It required iron nerves, tremendous skill, and a healthy dollop of luck to succeed as a blockade-runner. If nothing else kept the trade thriving, the prospect of enormous profits did, even as a combination of Union warships and natural hazards whittled at the pugnacious little fleet plying in and out of Southern ports. The blockade-runner pictured in D. J. Kennedy's watercolor (above) has been driven ashore by Union vessels visible in the distance; the cause of the grounding of the blockade-running side-wheeler on Sullivan's Island, South Carolina (right) is unknown.

THE BLOCKADE ON THE "CONNECTICUT PLAN".

Respectfully dedicated to the Secretary of the Navy.

the North, they could never have had a decisive effect on the course of the war. The best of them, like *Alabama* and *Shenandoah,* were built in England: ably commanded, they roamed the seven seas almost at will, helping to drive the American merchant fleet out from under the American flag but ultimately having only a minor bearing on the war itself. Toward the close of the war English yards did undertake the construction of a number of ironclad rams for the Confederacy, ships meant for close combat rather than for commerce destroying, and if these had been delivered they might have changed everything. But their construction and intended destination became known, the United States government plainly meant to go to war with Great Britain if they were actually delivered, and in the end the British government saw to it that they were kept at home.

Far more important to the Southern cause than the commerce destroyers were the blockade-runners. Most of these were built abroad for private account—long, lean, shallow-draft side-wheelers, for the most part, capable of high speeds, painted slate gray to decrease their visibility, and burning anthracite coal so that smoke from their funnels would not betray them to the blockading

Lincoln's announcement of a blockade of Southern ports had been greeted with derision, as the possibility of a Union fleet of thirty-two ships effectively closing down the coast line from Virginia to Texas seemed remote. Indeed, the bumbling initial Federal efforts inspired satiric responses such as the lithograph above. By mid-1862, however, increasingly desperate Southerners found that the Union blockade was no longer a laughing matter.

The North's great mercantile and whaling fleets were an economic strength and yet a point of weakness. These merchantmen were prime targets for fast, heavily armed raiding vessels; in its brief history, the Confederacy spawned some of the most memorable raiders in the annals of naval warfare. Rebel captains needed grit and bravado to sail alone, where every funnel cloud might signify an enemy warship. One of the most feared and successful was Raphael Semmes (in the foreground above), captain of the C.S.S. *Alabama*. In all, the *Alabama* captured or sank sixty-four Union merchantmen.

fleets. In the usual course of things, goods meant for the Confederacy were shipped from England (or from a port on the Continent) to Nassau, in the Bahamas—a little port that enjoyed a regular Klondike boom while the war lasted. There the cargoes were transferred to the blockade-runners, which would make a dash for it through the Federal cruisers to some such Southern seaport as Wilmington, North Carolina. Many of these were caught, to be sure, but many of them got through, and profits were so remarkable that if a ship made one or two successful voyages her owners were money ahead, even if thereafter she were captured. On the return trip, of course, the blockade-runners took out cotton.

Not all of the material imported via these vessels was for military use. It paid to bring in luxuries, and so luxuries were brought in, to be sold at fantastic prices; and eventually the Confederate government took a hand, outlawing the importation of some luxuries entirely and stipulating that one-half of the space on every ship must be reserved for government goods. Tightly as the Federal squadrons might draw their patrols, they were never able to stop blockade-running

entirely; it ceased, at last, only when the last of the Confederate ports was occupied. But if the traffic could not be entirely stopped, it was increasingly restricted, and the very fact that the blockade-runners could make such outlandish profits testified to the Southland's desperate shortage of goods from the outside world.

"Please proceed with all dispatch to Bermuda in pursuit of the rebel steamer *Nashville,* which vessel on Saturday last ran the blockade from Charleston." That U.S. naval communication referred to one of the Confederacy's first raiding ships, which had a short but destructive career. A trim side-wheeler, the *Nashville* (above) eluded the Federal search and reached England. On its departure, the British navy enforced neutrality laws mandating a twenty-four-hour spacing between belligerents by anchoring one of its war-ships alongside a shadowing Union sloop until the *Nashville* had gained the requisite head start.

Many of the blockade-runners operated
out of ports in Cuba, the Bahamas, or
Bermuda (which is the subject of this
painting by William Torgerson). Such ports
offered the official safety of foreign waters
with proximity to the U.S. coast. Despite
the best efforts of the Union navy, resulting
in a respectable rate of capture, fast ships
remained more than willing to undertake
the risks. On average, a blockade-runner
needed just two successful trips to recoup
its cost; several of them finished forty
runs, amply rewarding their owners and
their crews.

The end of the C.S.S. *Alabama* was the most dramatic of any commerce raider. Chased and finally bottled up in France's Cherbourg harbor by the U.S.S. *Kearsarge* (whose officers are shown on deck above), Captain Raphael Semmes opted to fight rather than surrender. On a bright, clear, and cool Sunday, under the gaze of some 15,000 spectators on shore, the raider and the U.S. warship circled in a deadly dance, trading broadsides for more than an hour. The Union ship, protected by chain mail, was impervious to the guns of the *Alabama*, which sank after taking hard hits at close range. Semmes and most of his crew were rescued by sympathetic onlookers, some of which were in a little French vessel, as shown in the foreground of the painting *The Battle of the* Kearsarge *and the* Alabama (opposite) by the great French artist, Edouard Manet. Semmes ended the war in command of a land battalion, with a rank of brigadier general.

OPPOSITE: By the end of 1864, the Confederacy's viable seaports had been reduced in number to one: Wilmington, North Carolina. Located up the Cape Fear River, Wilmington was protected at the river's mouth by a series of batteries and forts, the most formidable of which was Fort Fisher. This painting gives some idea of the sheer weight of firepower that the Union navy assigned to the task of reducing the fort.

ABOVE: Rear Admiral David Dixon Porter's bombardment fleet (shown in the photograph) included the iron-plated warship *New Ironsides*. This vessel was awarded the honor of opening the bombardment against Fort Fisher on December 24, 1864. The initial expedition proved a failure; a second was quickly organized, and on Friday, January 13, the *New Ironsides* again fired on Fort Fisher, which fell to a land assault mounted two days later. A Union soldier watched in awe as the ironclads unleashed their broadsides on the Rebel bastion. "To me it seemed like meteors were being fired out of a volcano," he said.

CHAPTER 5

Confederate High-Water Mark

"The dust-cover'd men...with artillery interspers'd — the wheels rumble, the horses sweat, as the army corps advances." Those were some of the images of 1862, as observed by the poet Walt Whitman. It was a year of combat, with the two armies, no longer innocent, caught in death grapples across gently rolling country-sides, often watched over by symbols of peaceful religion. James Hope's postwar painting (right) depicts Dunker Church on the battlefield known as Antietam. Regiments came to Antietam from near and far; the lively little watercolor created by a Massachusetts soldier (above) includes a Confederate St. Andrew's Cross battle flag with a distinctive Palmetto insignia, as carried by South Carolina troops. These men may have been part of Brigidier General Maxcy Gregg's South Carolina Brigade, which suffered one hundred sixty-five casualties at Antietam.

Toward the end of the summer of 1862 the mirage of final Southern independence looked briefly and dazzlingly like an imminent reality. In April the Confederacy had been on the defensive everywhere—New Orleans lost, McClellan approaching the gates of Richmond, Halleck coming in on Corinth as slowly and as irresistibly as a glacier, Missouri gone and the whole Mississippi Valley apparently about to follow it. But by August the Southern nation had gone on the offensive, and for a few weeks it looked as if the gates were about to open. Never before or afterward was the Confederacy so near to victory as it was in the middle of September, 1862.

There was a tremendous vitality to the Southern cause, and it was aided this summer by fumbling military leadership on the part of the North. For a time the Federals had no over-all military commander except for the President and the

Perhaps the most vexing problem Abraham Lincoln faced was finding generals who would bring him victories. When informed that one of his military appointees had been captured along with some army animals, Lincoln reportedly replied: "I don't care so much for brigadiers; I can make them. But horses and mules cost money." Lincoln's jest suggested a military problem that threatened public confidence. The cartoon below lampoons the commander in chief and his "toy" soldiers, including generals Butler, McClellan, and Scott. In an effort to bolster his military expertise, Lincoln brought in a western general, Henry Wager Halleck (far right), to serve as his adviser. Harsh in manner and lacking in tact, Halleck was considered a brilliant military theoretician. That reputation, abetted by a balding pate, brought him the nickname "Old Brains." Lincoln also made note of a string of small victories in the West, won by a general named John Pope (near right). Pope had directed the capture of New Madrid and Island Number Ten on the Mississippi River early in 1862; those achievements, and powerful political connections, moved Pope's name to the top of the list when Lincoln sought a general to take charge in northern Virginia.

GREAT AMERICAN TRAGEDIANS, COMEDIANS, CLOWNS AND ROPE DANZERS IN THEIR FAVORITE CHARACTERS.

Your honours players...are come to play a pleasant comedy.... Is it a comedy....a Christmas Gambol or a tumbling trick....No my Lord it is more pleasing stuff...it is a kind of history.

Secretary of War, who were men who knew exactly what they wanted but who did not quite know how to get it. Then, in July, Lincoln called General Halleck to Washington and made him general in chief of the Union armies.

On form, the choice looked good. The great successes had been won in Halleck's territory, the West, and as far as anyone in Washington could tell, he was fully entitled to take the credit. Except for continuing guerrilla activity, Kentucky and Missouri had been swept clear of armed Confederates, western Tennessee had been reclaimed, there was a Yankee army in Cumberland Gap, another one was approaching Chattanooga, and a third was sprawled out from Memphis to Corinth, preparing to slice down through Mississippi and touch hands with the Union occupation forces in Baton Rouge and New Orleans. If any Northern general was entitled to promotion, that general certainly appeared to be Halleck.

Halleck was a bookish sort of soldier, a headquarters operator who could handle all of the routine chores of military housekeeping with competence, but who somehow lacked the vital quality which such Confederates as Lee and Jackson possessed in abundance—the driving, restless spirit of war. The impulse to crowd a failing foe into a corner and compel submission simply was not in him, nor did he have the knack of evoking that spirit in his subordinates. His grasp of the theories of strategy was excellent, but at heart he was a shuffler of papers.

He came east to repair disaster. McClellan had been beaten in front of Richmond, and his army was in camp on the bank of the James River—still close enough to the Confederate capital, and still strong enough to resume the offensive on short notice, yet temporarily out of circulation for all that. (Like Halleck, McClellan was not especially aggressive.) In northern Virginia the Federal government had put together a new army, 50,000 men or thereabouts, troops who might have gone down to help McClellan in the spring, but who had been held back because of Jackson's game in the Shenandoah Valley. This army had been entrusted to one of Halleck's old subordinates, John Pope, who had taken Island Number Ten and New Madrid, and who seemed to have a good deal of energy and a desire to fight. Pope was moving down toward Richmond along the line of the Orange and Alexandria Railroad, and the general notion was that Robert E. Lee could not possibly fend off both Pope and McClellan.

The general notion was good enough, but Lee had accurately appraised the generals he was fighting. He suspected that McClellan would be inactive for

In the words of a poem popular in 1862: "We are coming, Father Abraam, three hundred thousand more. From Mississippi's winding stream and from New England's shore." Among those who were coming were the soldiers of the 73rd Ohio Infantry (below), shown leaving Chillicothe for the East, where they would be baptized in battle on Chinn Ridge at the Second Battle of Bull Run.

After driving McClellan's Peninsula army into a defensive pocket on the James River, Robert E. Lee turned his attention north, where Union forces again threatened the Shenandoah Valley. He quickly dispatched some 20,000 men under Stonewall Jackson, a man known for keeping his plans to himself. "If silence be golden," grumbled one Southern officer, "he was a bonanza." Determined to tackle the numerically superior Federal army in smaller parts, rather than facing the whole, Jackson confronted a single corps in the shadow of Cedar Mountain (left side in Edwin Forbes' drawing, above).

some time to come, so while he held the bulk of his own army in the defensive lines around Richmond, he detached Stonewall Jackson with 25,000 men and sent him north to deal with Pope. (Pope was given to bluster and loud talk, and Lee held him in contempt: he told Jackson he wanted Pope "suppressed," as if the man were a brawling disturber of the peace rather than a general commanding an army of invasion.)

Arriving in Washington, Halleck could see that the Union military situation in Virginia was potentially dangerous. Pope and McClellan together outnumbered Lee substantially, but they were far apart, and communication between them was slow and imperfect. Lee was squarely between them, and unless both armies advanced resolutely he might easily concentrate on one, put it out of action, and then deal with the other at his leisure. Halleck went down to the James to see McClellan and find out if he could immediately move on Richmond.

This McClellan could not quite do. He needed reinforcements, material, time, and he had no confidence that Pope was going to do anything important anyway. Convinced that the Army of the Potomac would not advance, Halleck ordered it to leave the Peninsula and come back to Washington. It seemed to him that the sensible thing was to unite both armies and then resume the drive on the Confederate capital. Protesting bitterly, McClellan prepared to obey. But it would take a long time to get all of his troops back to the Washington area, and the move presented Lee with a free gift of time to attend to General Pope. Of this gift Lee took immediate advantage.

It began on August 9, when Jackson advanced, met a detachment of Pope's army at Cedar Mountain, not far from Culpeper, and drove it in retreat after a

Charge of Union troops of the left flank of Army Commanded by Genl Stonewall Jackson at Cedar Mountain
Augst 9th

sharp battle. This Confederate victory gained very little, since Pope's main body was not far away and Jackson soon had to withdraw, but it was a forecast of things to come. Concentrating his troops in front of Pope, and leaving only detachments to see McClellan off, Lee began a series of maneuvers which caused Pope to retreat to the north side of the upper Rappahannock River. Pope held the river crossings and, for the time at least, seemed quite secure. McClellan's troops were coming north, some of them marching west from Fredericksburg and others going by boat to Alexandria, across the Potomac from Washington; with Halleck's blessing, Pope proposed to stay where he was until these troops joined him. Then the Federal offensive could begin in earnest.

Lee could see as clearly as anyone that time was on the side of the Federals. If McClellan and Pope finally got together, their strength would be overwhelming; Lee's only hope was to beat Pope before this happened. With consummate skill he set about this task, although he was compelled to take some hair-raising risks in the process.

ACCORDING TO THE MILITARY textbooks, no general should ever divide his forces in the presence of the enemy. This is a very sound rule in most cases, but it is a rule that was made to be broken now and then, and Lee was the man to break it. He was in the immediate presence of John Pope's army, with the shallow Rappahannock River between; and now he divided his army, sending half of it, under Stonewall Jackson, on a long hike to the northwest, and holding the remainder, with Major General James Longstreet in immediate command, to keep Pope occupied. Jackson swung off behind the Bull Run Mountains, came swiftly east through Thoroughfare Gap, and pounced suddenly on the Federal army's base of supplies at Manassas Junction, twenty miles or more in Pope's rear. Pope turned to

The Battle of Cedar Mountain was fought on a day of blistering heat, August 9, 1862, and lasted from about 3:00 P.M. until nearly 9:00 P.M. An artillery duel lasted perhaps ninety minutes, while Confederate and Union infantry troops hurried to the scene. The Federals attacked first; for a while it seemed as if Jackson's army would be rolled up and routed by the much smaller force. Edwin Forbes' drawing (above) shows exultant Yankees overwhelming the Virginia boys who were holding Jackson's left flank. Jackson personally led the counterattack that turned the tide, resulting in a Confederate victory. Jackson, marveled one subordinate, "was in the thickest of the combat, at very short range."

An Iron Man for an Iron Job

The importance of trains to the Union war effort was confirmed on January 31, 1862, when Abraham Lincoln signed a bill that gave him unprecedented authority to control and even to operate the nation's railroads. The system was massive, but it consisted of many small networks that had grown without any central plan: track gauges varied from one locality to the next and there were no standards for either roadbeds or equipment. Making order out of this chaos seemed impossible, but Lincoln found the right man for the job, Herman Haupt (left, paddling a small pontoon boat of his own design, used for inspecting bridges), a brilliant, though abrasive, civil engineer of prodigious energy. With profound insight into the mechanics of railroading and a seemingly limitless inventive genius, Haupt stepped on toes—he continually violated every aspect of military protocol—but he also brought order and efficiency to the nation's rail network. After Stonewall Jackson's "Foot Cavalry" moved along the Orange and Alexandria Railroad, wrecking it as they went along, Haupt and his work crews had their hands full repairing the damage (above).

attend to Jackson, and Lee and Longstreet then followed Jackson's route, to join him somewhere east of the Bull Run Mountains.

Seldom has a general been more completely confused than Pope was now. He had vast energy, and he set his troops to marching back and forth to surround and destroy Jackson, but he could not quite find where Jackson was. With his 25,000 men, Stonewall had left Manassas Junction before the Federals got there—destroying such Federal supplies as could not be carried away—and took position, concealed by woods and hills, on the old battlefield of Bull Run. Pope wore out his infantry and his cavalry looking for him, blundered into him at last, and gathered his men for a headlong assault. There was a hard, wearing fight on August 29, in which Jackson's men held their ground with great difficulty; on the morning of August 30 Pope believed he had won a great victory, and he sent word to Washington that the enemy was in retreat and that he was about to pursue.

No general ever tripped over his own words more ingloriously than Pope did. Unknown to him, Lee and Longstreet had regained contact with Jackson on

Haupt's men became so adept, it was said, "the Yankees can build bridges quicker than the Rebs can burn them down." Crews came prepared, using prefabricated materials and well-choreographed construction techniques. In one celebrated instance, a bridge several hundred feet long over Potomac Creek was rebuilt in forty hours. To brace a wrecked bridge on the Orange and Alexandria Railroad (above) took less than a day. At first, Major General John Pope, newly arrived for his command in the East, sent Haupt home. He thought he could do without him, but Stonewall Jackson's depredations changed his mind. "Come back immediately," Haupt was informed, "cannot get along without you; not a wheel moving on any of the roads."

When Robert E. Lee learned that portions of McClellan's army had boarded river transports heading down the James River, he decided to shift operations to northern Virginia, where Stonewall Jackson was maneuvering against Pope's army. On August 13, Major General James Longstreet's corps (constituting nearly half of Lee's army) took trains to Gordonsville. After two weeks of operations in the Gordonsville area, Longstreet marched his corps through Thoroughfare Gap (above right) toward Manassas. Unaware of how the odds were changing against him, Pope continued to pursue the elusive Jackson. Edwin Forbes' sketch (below) shows some of Pope's men caught in a late August rainstorm.

the afternoon of August 29, and on August 30, when Pope was beginning what he considered his victorious pursuit, they struck him furiously in the flank while Jackson kept him busy in front. Pope's army was crushed, driven north of Bull Run in disorder, and by twilight of August 30 the Confederates had won a sensational victory. Pope had lost the field, his reputation, and about 16,000 men. The Confederate casualty list had been heavy, but in every other respect they had won decisively.

Lee had acted just in time. Some of McClellan's divisions had joined Pope and had taken part in the battle, and the rest of McClellan's army was not far off.

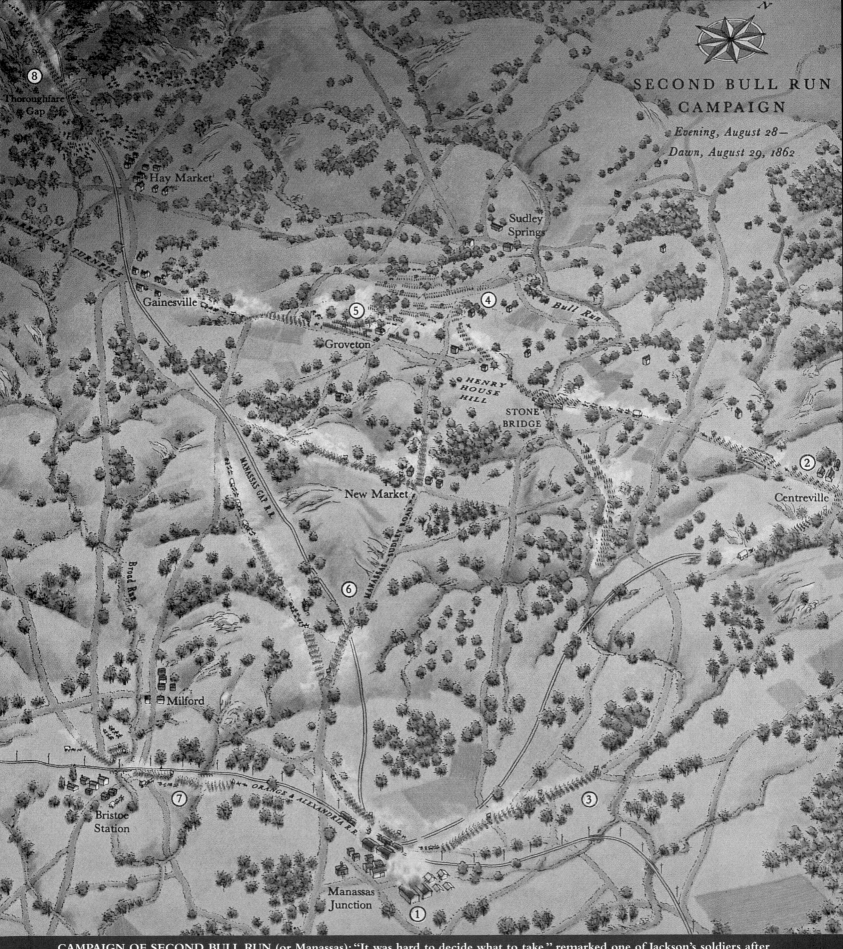

CAMPAIGN OF SECOND BULL RUN (or Manassas): "It was hard to decide what to take," remarked one of Jackson's soldiers after the battle: they first pillage, and then burn, the Yankee supplies at Manassas Junction on August 26, 1862 (1). Jackson moves on to Centreville (2) with Union columns (3) dogging him. Expecting reinforcements under Longstreet, sent by Lee, Jackson stands his ground outside of Groveton (4) near the Bull Run battlefield. On August 28, in a brutal stand-up fight at Brawner's Farm (5), he attacks a Union force marching east from Gainesville. Union columns under Sigel (6) and Porter (7) converge on him, even as Longstreet draws near (8). John Pope believes he has at last cornered Jackson's corps. The battle will begin the next day.

The combat artist Edwin Forbes preferred the big picture—and usually observed it from a safe distance. This panoramic view (above), looking west from Bald Hill on August 28, shows the Confederate lines (2) behind which lies Thoroughfare Gap (1). At Brawner's Farm (8) opposing battle-lines stood toe to toe for hours. "If I had held up an iron hat I could have caught it full of bullets in a short time," wrote one Rebel.

One or two days more would have made the Union force safe: the big point about Lee was that he was always mindful of the difference that one or two days might make.

By any standard, Lee's achievements this summer had been remarkable. He had taken command of the Army of Northern Virginia in June, almost in the suburbs of Richmond, badly outnumbered by an enemy which had thousands upon thousands of additional troops not far away. By the end of August he had whipped the army that faced him, had whipped the army that came to its relief, and had transferred the war from the neighborhood of Richmond to the neighborhood of Washington. (After the Bull Run defeat the Federals withdrew to the fortifications of Washington, leaving practically all of Virginia to the Confederates.) Now Lee was about to invade the North.

In the spring the Federal War Department had been so confident that it had closed the recruiting stations. Now Secretary Stanton was frantically appealing to the Northern governors for more troops, and President Lincoln—to the great joy of the soldiers—was reinstating McClellan in command of the Army of the Potomac, with which Pope's troops were incorporated.

Technically, McClellan had never actually been removed from that command. His army had simply been taken away from him, division by division, and

Stonewall Jackson (top) became an even greater Southern hero after Second Bull Run. "Jackson, second to Lee, is the favorite here," wrote a Confederate following the battle. Controversy dogged James Longstreet (above), whose battlefield management was questioned afterward. Critics claimed that Longstreet delayed his entry into the fight for "an interminable period," thereby undermining Lee's battle plan. Also stained by his actions on August 29 was the Union general Fitz John Porter (shown at left with his staff), a strong McClellan supporter. John Pope blamed him outright for the Union disaster, and Porter eventually lost his command. It would take a widely publicized postwar court of inquiry to restore his reputation.

America's fascination with the Civil War joined forces with its love of grand spectacle to popularize a genre of painting that flourished in the last thirty years of the nineteenth century. Known as cycloramas, the works were circular paintings of epic scope, designed to overwhelm viewers with vivid detail of historic events. Cycloramas celebrated what one exhibition catalogue called "the romantic and picturesque in warfare." A large number of Civil War battles were depicted in cycloramas, though just two have survived. Theophile Poilpot's canvas of Second Bull Run is known today only through photographs of it: the section shown here depicts one of the Federal attacks made against Jackson's men along the railroad embankment.

SECOND BULL RUN

Second Day: August 30, 1862

SUDLEY CHURCH

JACKSON'S HQ

GROVETON–SUDLEY ROAD

UNFINISHED RAILROAD

① ⑥

Groveton

③

WARRENTON TURNPIKE

MANASSAS–SUDLEY ROAD

MATTHEWS HILL

MATTHEWS HOUSE

POPE'S HQ

STONE HOUSE

② YOUNG'S BRANCH

④

BALD HILL

HENRY HOUSE

HENRY HOUSE HILL

⑤

ROBINSON HOUSE

TO CENTREV...

SECOND BULL RUN (or Manassas): After stumbling into an unplanned battle on August 28, John Pope begins the next day by attacking Jackson's men, who successfully defend themselves along an unfinished railroad line (1). Unknown to Pope, a second Confederate corps led by James Longstreet has arrived on the field. While the Federals continue to assail Jackson, Longstreet takes a position against the weak Federal left. Announced by a hard-hitting artillery barrage (2), Longstreet's men (3 and 4) advance in the late afternoon of August 30, overwhelming the Yankees who oppose them, including the 73rd Ohio. When the Federals try to hold on Henry House Hill (5), Jackson strikes them hard on their right (6). At 8:00 P.M. Pope orders a retreat to Centreville. "It's another Bull Run, sir, it's another Bull Run!" declares one Federal general.

Like an irresistible wave, Brigadier General John B. Hood's Texas Brigade crashed into the Union left flank, inaugurating Longstreet's attack on August 30. The Edwin Forbes' sketch above shows the view from the Federal side as the enemy battlelines emerge from the woods. "It was a magnificent sight," said one of the Texans. Despite the desperate valor of Union artillery (left), Hood's men were triumphant. One Union gunner, shot as he tried to fire a last canister round, gasped to advancing Rebels: "I have promised to drive you back, or die under my guns, and I have kept my word."

"The present seems to be the most propitious time since the commencement of the war for the Confederate army to enter Maryland," Robert E. Lee informed Jefferson Davis on September 3. The very next night, advance elements of his army began crossing the Potomac River into Maryland (right). Stonewall Jackson's troops led the way, the vanguard reaching the Maryland town of Frederick on September 6. It is probable that this unique image (below) of Rebel troops in enemy territory was taken in 1862 by a local Frederick merchant and amateur photographer named J. Rosenstock.

when the Second Battle of Bull Run was fought, McClellan was in Alexandria, forwarding his men to Manassas but unable to go with them. After the battle, speedy reorganization was imperative, and Lincoln could see what Stanton and the Republican radicals could not see—that the only man who could do the job was McClellan. Such men as Stanton, Secretary of the Treasury Salmon P. Chase, and Senators Ben Wade and Zachariah Chandler believed that McClellan had sent his men forward slowly, hoping that Pope would be beaten; Lincoln had his own doubts, but he knew that the dispirited soldiers had full confidence in McClellan and that it was above all things necessary to get those soldiers back into a fighting mood. So Pope was relieved and sent off to Minnesota to fight the Indians, a task which was well within his capacities; and McClellan sorted out the broken fragments of what had been two separate armies, reconstituted the Army of the Potomac, manned the Washington fortifications, and early in September marched northwest from Washington with 85,000 men to find General Lee, who had taken the Army of Northern Virginia across the Potomac into western Maryland on September 5.

After the Second Battle of Bull Run, the capable and colorful Major General J. E. B. Stuart led a pair of fast-moving divisions in a raid behind enemy lines and almost into Pope's headquarters, near Catlett's Station, Virginia. Undetected by Federal scouts, Stuart made the most of his overnight foray, capturing some of Pope's belongings and about 300 of his men. Some civilians were also detained, among them the *Harper's Weekly* artist–correspondent Alfred Waud. Waud was only briefly delayed, just long enough to make a sketch of his dashing "hosts" from the 1st Virginia (below). He also noted that most were armed with weapons taken from Union cavalrymen "for whom they expressed utter contempt."

A major obstacle to Lee's movement into Maryland was the large Union garrison at Harpers Ferry, posted there to guard the Baltimore and Ohio Railroad. As William MacLeod's painting (below) makes only too clear, the fate of Harpers Ferry depended on control of the heights surrounding it. A soldier who served there declared the town was "no more defensible than a well bottom." Commanding the post was Colonel Dixon S. Miles, who had been found by a court of inquiry to have been drunk while leading a division at First Bull Run. Instead of reinforcements, his department commander sent encouragement. "Be energetic and active, and defend all places to the last extremity," Miles was told.

Lee seemed bent on getting into Pennsylvania. He had gone to Frederick, Maryland, forty miles from Washington, and then he went off on the old National Road in the direction of Hagerstown, vanishing from sight behind the long barrier of South Mountain, whose gaps he held with Jeb Stuart's cavalry. Following him, McClellan did not know where Lee was or what he was up to, and until he found out, he was in trouble: to lunge straight through the gaps with his massed force would be to risk letting Lee slip past him on either flank and seize Washington itself. A real advance was impossible until he had better information, the news that was coming out of western Maryland was confused, contradictory, and of no value to anyone . . . and if Lee was not quickly caught, fought, and driven below the Potomac, the Northern cause was lost forever.

It was not only in Maryland that the Federals were in trouble. In the western area, where everything had looked so prosperous, there had been a similar reversal of fortune. At the beginning of the summer a sweeping Federal triumph west of the Alleghenies looked inevitable; by mid-September the situation there looked almost as bad as it did in the East, one measure of the crisis being the fact

that Cincinnati had called out the home guard lest the city be seized by invading Rebels.

SEVERAL THINGS HAD GONE WRONG in the West, but the root of the trouble was General Halleck's fondness for making war by the book. The book said that in a war it was advisable to occupy enemy territory, and after the capture of Corinth, Halleck had set out to do that. He had had, in front of Corinth, well over 100,000 men, and with that army he could have gone anywhere in the South and beaten anything the Davis government could have sent against him. But instead of continuing with the offensive under circumstances which guaranteed victory, Halleck had split his army into detachments. Grant was given the task of holding Memphis and western Tennessee. Buell was sent eastward to occupy Chattanooga, rebuilding and protecting railway lines as he moved—a task that took so much of his time and energy that he never did get to Chattanooga. Other troops were sent to other duties, and by August the war had come to a standstill. Halleck was in Washington by now, and Grant and Buell were independent commanders.

Above is a photo of Harpers Ferry as it looked in 1862, when Jackson's men gazed down on it from the commanding heights they'd captured: the wreckage of the Baltimore and Ohio Railroad bridge (destroyed by the Confederates when they abandoned the town in June, 1861) is in the foreground. Knowing the Union position was hopeless, Colonel Miles resolved to surrender. "We have done our duty," he said, seconds before he was struck by one of the last shots fired by the Rebel artillery. He died the next day.

Lee's high-risk strategy depended on the continuing passivity of the opposing commander, Major General George B. McClellan, who had been restored to field command following John Pope's defeat at Second Bull Run. What Lee could not have anticipated in his planning was a stroke of bad luck, incredible to this day. On the morning of September 13, two Union soldiers camped near Frederick found an envelope containing three cigars wrapped in a piece of paper. They smoked the cigars, but the paper proved to be a copy of one of Lee's operational orders to his subordinates. This "lost order" provided McClellan with critical details regarding the scattered dispositions of the Confederate forces. When he started moving with uncharacteristic determination, Lee began to gather his army at Sharpsburg (above), a peaceful Maryland crossroads. Its houses of religion, including St. Paul's Lutheran Church (right), would soon be filled with Rebel wounded.

B-7198

The principal Confederate army in the West, the Army of Tennessee, was commanded now by General Braxton Bragg—a dour, pessimistic martinet of a man, who had an excellent grasp of strategy and a seemingly incurable habit of losing his grip on things in the moment of climax. (Beauregard, this army's former commander, had been relieved, the victim of ill health and inability to get along with President Davis.) Bragg had his men, 30,000 strong, in Chattanooga; Major General Edmund Kirby Smith was in Knoxville with 20,000 more; and in August these generals moved northward in a campaign that anticipated nothing less than the reoccupation of western Tennessee and the conquest—or liberation, depending on the point of view—of all of Kentucky.

The small Union force at Cumberland Gap beat a hasty retreat all the way to the Ohio River. Buell, outmaneuvered, gave up railroad-building and turned to follow Bragg, who had slipped clear past him. Grant was obliged to send all the troops he could spare to join Buell; and to keep him additionally occupied, the Confederates brought troops from across the Mississippi and formed an army of between 20,000 and 25,000 men in northern Mississippi under Earl Van Dorn. By late September, Bragg had swept aside the hastily assembled levies with which the Federals tried to bar his path and was heading straight for the Ohio River, Buell marching desperately to overtake him, Smith near at hand. It looked very

One of the sights to see in Sharpsburg had always been the sturdy stone bridge across Antietam Creek (above), carrying the road to Rohrersville. Located a short distance from the farm owned by H. Rohrbach, the span was known thereabouts as Rohrbach's Bridge. Sharp fighting there on September 17 would change the name forever to Burnside's Bridge.

John B. Gordon

Lee's army at Antietam included a number of officers who would serve with distinction throughout the war. Colonel John B. Gordon (pictured above as a brigadier general) was a courageous man and a natural leader. Gordon, recalled one of his soldiers, "had a way of putting things to the men that was irresistible, and he showed them at all times that he shrank from nothing in battle." Major General Ambrose P. Hill, a feisty Virginian who liked to wear a bright red shirt in battle, feuded with Stonewall Jackson throughout the campaign. Relegated by Jackson to the rear of his column, Hill was seen by one soldier "looking as mad as a bull." Actually, the perceived slight was a misinterpretation of marching orders.

much as if Bragg's ambitious plan might succeed, and if Van Dorn could defeat or evade Grant and reach Kentucky too the Union situation in the West would be almost hopeless.

Never had military events better illustrated the folly of surrendering the initiative in war. In both the East and West the Federals had a strong advantage in numbers; but in each area an inability to make use of that advantage in a vigorous, unceasing offensive, and a desire to protect territory rather than to compel the enemy's army to fight, had caused the Federals to lose control of the situation. Now, in Maryland, in Kentucky, and in Tennessee, the North was fighting a defensive war, and the Confederates were calling the tune. (To use an analogy from football, the North had lost the ball and was deep in its own territory.)

This was the authentic high-water mark of the Confederacy. Never again was the South so near victory; never again did the South hold the initiative in every major theater of war. Overseas, the British were on the verge of granting outright recognition—which, as things stood then, would almost automatically have meant Southern independence. Cautious British statesmen would wait just a little longer, to see how this General Lee made out with his invasion of the North. If he made out well, recognition would come, and there would be a new member in the world's family of nations.

THEN, WITHIN WEEKS, the tide began to ebb.

Preparing to move into Pennsylvania, Lee wanted to maintain some sort of

One of the toughest fighters to serve under Longstreet was Brigadier General John B. Hood. Stonewall Jackson, never an easy man to please, wrote of Hood: "I regard him one of the most promising officers of the army."

Despite suffering from chronic back pain, Major General Daniel H. Hill earned what one subordinate called a "high and well-deserved reputation as a hard fighter." He also was Stonewall Jackson's brother-in-law.

Ambrose P. Hill

John B. Hood

Daniel H. Hill

line of communications with Virginia. At Harpers Ferry the Federals had a garrison of 12,000 men, and these soldiers were almost on Lee's communications. It seemed to the Confederate commander that it would be well to capture Harpers Ferry and its garrison before he went on into the Northern heartland. He knew that McClellan was very cautious and deliberate, and he believed the man would be even more so now because he had to reorganize his army. So it looked as if the Army of Northern Virginia could safely pause to sweep up Harpers Ferry: with the South Mountain gaps held, McClellan could be kept in the dark until it was too late for him to do anything about it.

So Lee once more divided his army. The advance, under Longstreet, was at Hagerstown, Maryland, not far from the Pennsylvania border. One division, under Major General D. H. Hill, was holding Turner's Gap in South Mountain, to make certain that no inquisitive Federals got through. The rest, split into three wings but all under the general control of Jackson, went down to surround and capture Harpers Ferry.

Now sheer, unadulterated chance took a hand, and changed the course of American history.

Some Confederate courier lost a copy of the orders which prescribed all of

Two of McClellan's generals who marched to their deaths at Antietam are shown here. Major General Joseph K. F. Mansfield (above left), nearly sixty years old, led the XII Corps. An officer with forty years in the regular army, Mansfield had been performing administrative duties near Washington when he received orders for his first combat command. He reached his men on September 15; on September 17, while personally leading them forward into the East Woods, he was shot in the chest and mortally wounded. Major General Israel B. Richardson (above right) commanded a division in the II Corps that included the rowdy fighters of the Irish Brigade. Richardson was called "Fighting Dick" in the brigade, made up mostly of soldiers from New York and Massachusetts. Soon after his men overran the Rebels defending Bloody Lane, Richardson was mortally wounded by an exploding artillery shell.

Walton Taber's postwar drawing (right) depicts Union troops charging across David R. Miller's cornfield during the first phase of the Battle of Antietam. Attacks by the Federal I and XII Corps were met by vicious Confederate counterattacks that left the corn rows littered with bodies. "Everybody tears cartridges, loads, passes guns, or shoots," recalled a New York soldier. "Men are falling in their places or running back into the corn. . . . Many of the recruits who are killed or wounded only left home ten days ago."

these movements. A Union enlisted man found the order, and it got to McClellan's headquarters, where there was an officer who could identify the handwriting of Lee's assistant adjutant general and so convince McClellan that the thing was genuine. Now McClellan had the game in his hands: Lee's army was split into separate fragments, and McClellan was closer to the fragments than they were to each other. If he moved fast, McClellan could destroy the Army of Northern Virginia.

McClellan moved, although not quite fast enough. He broke through the gap in South Mountain, compelling Lee to concentrate his scattered forces. Lee ordered his troops to assemble at Sharpsburg, on Antietam Creek, near the Potomac. At that point Jackson, who had had just time to capture Harpers Ferry, rejoined him; and there, on September 17, McClellan and Lee fought the great Battle of Antietam.

Tactically, the battle was a draw. The Federals attacked savagely all day long, forcing the Confederates to give ground but never quite compelling the army to retreat, and when Lee's battered army held its position next day, McClellan did not renew the attack. But on the night of September 18 Lee took his worn-out

While the fighting in Miller's cornfield represented the beginning of the battle, the charge by the 9th New York Zouaves (left) across the fields overlooking Rohrbach Bridge occurred near the end of the fight. When the 9th began its attack, private David Thompson, a member of the regiment, was reminded of the writer Goethe's description of a similar incident when, "the whole landscape for an instant turned slightly red."

ANTIETAM

September 17, 1862

TO POTOMAC RIVER

LEE'S HQ

Sharpsburg

TO HARPERS FERRY

ANTIETAM CREEK

BURNSIDE'S
BRIDGE

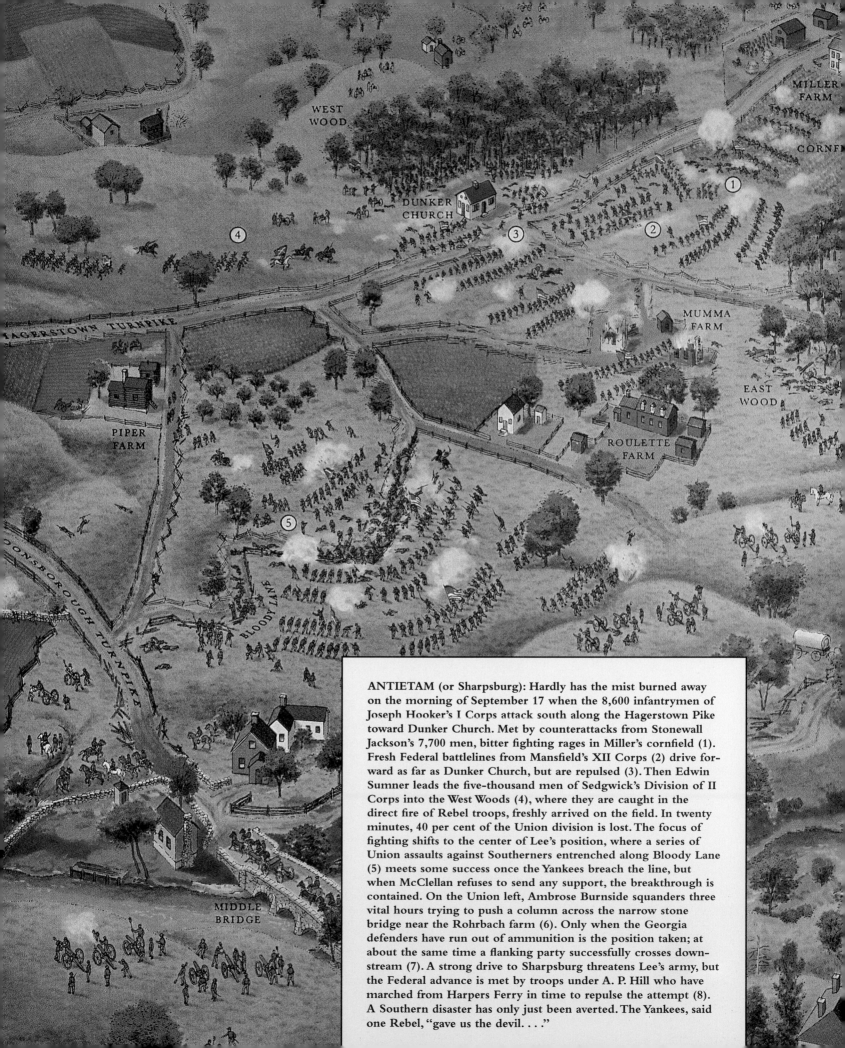

ANTIETAM (or Sharpsburg): Hardly has the mist burned away on the morning of September 17 when the 8,600 infantrymen of Joseph Hooker's I Corps attack south along the Hagerstown Pike toward Dunker Church. Met by counterattacks from Stonewall Jackson's 7,700 men, bitter fighting rages in Miller's cornfield (1). Fresh Federal battlelines from Mansfield's XII Corps (2) drive forward as far as Dunker Church, but are repulsed (3). Then Edwin Sumner leads the five-thousand men of Sedgwick's Division of II Corps into the West Woods (4), where they are caught in the direct fire of Rebel troops, freshly arrived on the field. In twenty minutes, 40 per cent of the Union division is lost. The focus of fighting shifts to the center of Lee's position, where a series of Union assaults against Southerners entrenched along Bloody Lane (5) meets some success once the Yankees breach the line, but when McClellan refuses to send any support, the breakthrough is contained. On the Union left, Ambrose Burnside squanders three vital hours trying to push a column across the narrow stone bridge near the Rohrbach farm (6). Only when the Georgia defenders have run out of ammunition is the position taken; at about the same time a flanking party successfully crosses downstream (7). A strong drive to Sharpsburg threatens Lee's army, but the Federal advance is met by troops under A. P. Hill who have marched from Harpers Ferry in time to repulse the attempt (8). A Southern disaster has only just been averted. The Yankees, said one Rebel, "gave us the devil. . . ."

James Hope's painting (right) depicts incidents spread over several hours, including the moment when two Federal regiments, the 51st New York and 51st Pennsylvania, accomplished what others had not: a charge across Rohrbach's Bridge. The Pennsylvanians, who had lost their liquor privileges, were promised them back if they succeeded. The men were waved across by their colonel, who had shouted himself hoarse. "Come on, boys," he croaked, "for I can't halloo anymore!"

army back to Virginia. Strategically, the battle had been a Northern victory of surpassing importance. The Southern campaign of invasion had failed. The Federals had regained the initiative. Europe's statesmen, watching, relaxed: the time to extend recognition had not arrived, after all.

ANTIETAM WAS NOT ONLY strategically decisive: it has the melancholy distinction of having seen the bloodiest single day's fighting in the entire Civil War. The Union army lost over 12,400 men, and the Confederate loss was over 10,300. Never before or after in all the war were so many men shot on one day.

In the West, too, the Confederate offensive collapsed.

Until he actually arrived in Kentucky, Bragg had handled his campaign with vast skill. Now, however, he became irresolute, and his grasp of strategic principles weakened. It had been supposed that the people of Kentucky, crushed under the heel of Northern despots, would rise in welcome once they were liberated by Confederate armies, and whole wagon-loads of weapons were carried along by the Confederates to arm the new recruits. The anticipated welcome did not develop, however, recruits were very few in number, and Bragg's swift drive became slower. He lost time by going to Frankfort to see that a secessionist state government was formally installed—it would fall apart, once his troops left—and

Sunken Lane, a wagon-worn old road, was the site of some of the fiercest fighting at Antietam. Wave after wave of men from the Union II Corps tried and finally succeeded in wresting it from Southerners commanded by D. H. Hill. Approximately 3,000 Union soldiers and 2,500 Confederate soldiers were killed, wounded, or missing once the fighting over the Sunken Lane and the adjacent Piper Farm was over. The postwar painting (below) by Union veteran James Hope shows the ghastly human debris of this vital corner of the larger battle, which became known afterward as "Bloody Lane."

Antietam was the first Civil War battle to be photographed immediately afterward. Right after the fighting, Alexander Gardner took a series of pictures that conveyed the horrors of combat for those at home. The Rebel dead (above) are laid out for burial near Dunker Church.

These Confederate bodies (right) lay along the Hagerstown Pike. "Let him who wish to know what war is look at this series of illustrations," said Dr. Oliver Wendell Holmes, Sr., whose son, a Union captain, was badly wounded in the battle.

"The dead and dying lay as thick . . . as harvest sheaves," remembered a Confederate officer who served under Jackson. The dead men pictured above also served under Jackson.

A Union burial detail tends to its business (left). "We seen among the rebels Boys of Sixteen and Fifteen and old Gray headed men," wrote a soldier assigned to that thankless task. "There was not to the best of my knowledge in all that was buried two dressed alike."

An Alexander Gardner photograph (above) shows Battery E of the Pennsylvania Light Artillery, Captain Joseph M. Knap commanding. The gunners had fought near Dunker Church alongside other artillery units. "These batteries were bravely and excellently served from morning till late in the afternoon," reported their corps commander. "The enemy repeatedly attempted to seize them, but always met with bloody punishment."

Buell was just able to get his own army between Bragg's Confederates and the Ohio River.

Buell managed to bring Bragg to battle at Perryville, Kentucky, on October 8. Only parts of the two armies were engaged, and the fight was pretty much a standoff; but afterward the mercurial Bragg concluded, for some reason, that his whole campaign had been a failure, and he and Smith drew off into eastern Tennessee. Buell pursued with such lack of spirit that the administration removed him and put William S. Rosecrans in his place, and Rosecrans got his army into camp just below Nashville, Tennessee, and awaited further developments. Meanwhile, in northern Mississippi, a part of Grant's army, then led by Rosecrans, had beaten a detachment from Van Dorn's at Iuka on September 19 and 20, and early in October defeated the entire force in a hard-fought engagement at Corinth. Van Dorn retreated toward central Mississippi, and Grant began to make plans for a campaign against Vicksburg.

So by the middle of October the situation had changed once more. The one

great, co-ordinated counteroffensive which the Confederacy was ever able to mount had been beaten back. In the East the Federals would begin a new campaign aimed at Richmond; in the West they would resume the advance on Chattanooga and would continue with the drive to open the whole Mississippi Valley. They would have many troubles with all of these campaigns, but they had at least got away from the defensive. The danger of immediate and final Northern defeat was gone.

During the fighting on September 17, Major General McClellan held back nearly two full corps, at least 20,300 men, as a reserve against a possible Confederate counterattack. Among the regiments not engaged was the 93rd New York (above), which, as McClellan's headquarters guard, remained in the rear of the action. Organized at the state capital in January, 1862, the 93rd (sometimes called "Morgan Rifles") first saw action at the siege of Yorktown and was present when Lee surrendered at Appomattox Court House.

The General and the President

When Lee withdrew his army from Sharpsburg on the night of September 18, McClellan let it go without any serious challenge. Over the next few weeks, Lincoln waited for him to make some aggressive move in pursuit of the enemy, or at least to give some indication that he had plans to do so. Dissatisfied with McClellan's inaction, Lincoln came calling on October 1 (above), determined to see the situation for himself. The troops cheered the President, but reporters present thought he looked weary and care-worn. Lincoln had a series of long talks with McClellan (opposite) during which he urged the general to strike a blow. McClellan's tepid response angered Lincoln, who gave vent to his feelings when he pointed to the endless

rows of army tents and asked a colleague if he knew what they were looking at. When the surprised man answered that they were viewing the Army of the Potomac, Lincoln replied: "So it is called, but that is a mistake; it is only McClellan's bodyguard." Finally, after much complaining, McClellan put the army in motion on October 26. By then it was too late: on November 5, Lincoln relieved McClellan of his command. "He is an admirable engineer," Lincoln supposedly said of McClellan, "but he seems to have a special talent for a stationary engine."

There was a cocky roughness about the Federal troops raised in the West. The 44th Indiana (its Company H is shown above) displays the rough-and-ready qualities typical of Western units; the regiment fought at Fort Donelson, Shiloh, and Corinth. In September, 1862, it marched from western Tennessee into central Kentucky under Major General Don Carlos Buell to intercept enemy columns intent on reclaiming that border state for the Confederacy. Other Federals taking part in Buell's campaign were photographed crossing the Big Barren River, near Bowling Green, Kentucky (right).

Don Carlos Buell (left), in command of the Union forces defending Kentucky, was a hot-tempered West Pointer who deeply distrusted the state volunteers he led into battle. Buell faced a combined invasion by two Rebel armies, one led by General Braxton Bragg, the other by Major General Edmund Kirby Smith (below left). It was Smith who designed the Kentucky invasion and who persuaded the authorities in Richmond to commit Bragg's forces to the operation.

On October 8, Braxton Bragg's forces surged across the shallow, twisting Chaplin River to strike at Buell's army near the town of Perryville. Although his troops gained ground at almost every point attacked, Bragg retreated at day's end when he realized that the Federals outnumbered him. This lithograph shows a Wisconsin regiment holding back an assault by Brigadier General George E. Maney's Tennessee Brigade, an action that preserved the Union left flank. The two sides suffered more than 7,500 casualties; both claimed Perryville as a victory.

While Bragg and Buell were moving toward their bloody confrontation at Perryville, Confederates in northern Mississippi were making a bold bid to recapture the strategically important rail center at Corinth. On October 3 and 4, Rebel troops attacked it in the midst of a ninety-degree heat wave; the heaviest blows fell on Battery Robinett in the Union center where the Confederates were repulsed with terrible slaughter. "Our boys were shot down like hogs," declared one bitter Rebel. These pictures, taken on October 5, show the carnage.

High Tides of 1862

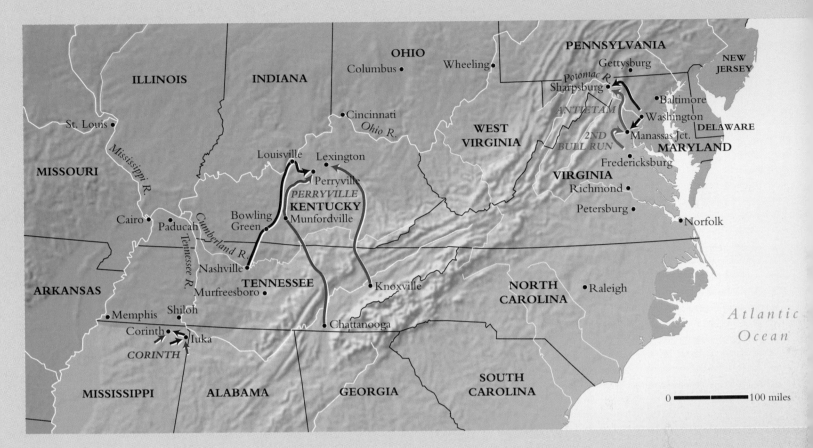

The map above shows three of the Confederate army's efforts to gain the initiative in the fall of 1862. The red arrows indicate the Rebel invasion routes in the East and West; the Union pursuit is in black. The high tide of the Confederacy is shown in the portion shaded gray.

Following the Rebel defeat at Shiloh, Federal forces advance into northwestern Mississippi (lower left of map), and occupy the vital Rebel rail junction at Corinth on May 28. In mid-September, the Confederates initiate an effort to recapture it, with a short-lived occupation of the U.S. supply depot at nearby Iuka. This is followed by a fierce, but unsuccessful, assault on Corinth in early October. In eastern Tennessee (center), Confederate columns under generals Braxton Bragg and Edmund Kirby Smith make a strong northward advance in an attempt to reclaim Kentucky. While Kirby Smith's columns reach Lexington with little opposition, Bragg's are met by Union general Don Carlos Buell's forces at Perryville in early October; and when Bragg is forced to retreat, Kirby Smith also has to withdraw. In the East (upper right), Robert E. Lee, buoyed by his victory at Second Bull Run, promptly invades Maryland, hoping to rally support there and encourage foreign recognition of the Confederacy. He is defeated at the horrific Battle of Antietam on September 17.

CHAPTER 6

Stalemate at Home and Abroad

In spite of all of its material handicaps, the South during the first eighteen months of the war did have one great advantage which probably would have proved decisive if it had continued. Its war aims were perfectly clear and definite, and every Southerner could understand them both with his mind and with his heart. The South wanted its independence: its people, struggling for their freedom, were fighting off invaders. The ordinary Confederate soldier might understand little and care less about the intricacies of the states' rights argument, but he did feel that he was protecting the home place against people who wanted to despoil it, and that was enough for him.

By contrast, the Federal government seemed to be fighting for an abstraction. The call to make war for the Union did indeed arouse deep feelings of patriotism, but as the hard months passed and the casualty lists grew longer and longer this rallying call did not seem quite adequate. Much blood was being shed for it, but by itself it seemed bloodless. The deep principle that was involved in it became hard to see through the thick layers of battle smoke. Simply to defend the *status quo* against a revolutionary upheaval offers little nourishment for the blood and muscles and spirit when war weariness sets in. In plain terms, the Union cause was not quite broad enough to support a war of this magnitude.

"A march in the ranks hard-prest, and the road unknown,"
wrote Walt Whitman. "A route through a heavy wood with muf-
fled steps in the darkness." An unknown artist painted this scene
(left) near Fredericksburg, Virginia, but it could have been almost anywhere in the
country in the bitter winter of 1862. Young men in blue and gray fought the elements
and one another, seeking a victory that seemed increasingly elusive and unattainable to
both sides.

On November 8, 1861, the U.S. warship *San Jacinto* stopped the British mail steamer *Trent* in the Bahama Channel. Union sailors removed two passengers, James M. Mason (near right) and John Slidell (far right), who were traveling to Europe as diplomats, representing the Confederacy. Mason, who carried credentials as the Davis government's commissioner to England, and Slidell, its commissioner to France, expected to build upon Southern battlefield successes to persuade Europe's most powerful nations to recognize the Confederate States of America. The British government strongly protested the U.S. action, calling it a serious breach of international law. For the moment it seemed as if the *Punch* cartoon (below) accurately depicted the Lincoln administration, caught up a tree by an armed and ready England, symbolized by the figure of John Bull.

PUNCH, OR THE LONDON CHARIVARI—JANUARY 11, 1862.

"UP A TREE."
Colonel Bull and the Yankee 'Coon.
'Coon. "AIR YOU IN ARNEST, COLONEL?"
Colonel Bull. "I AM."
'Coon. "DON'T FIRE—I'LL COME DOWN."

All of this had a direct bearing on the United States' foreign relations.

The relations that were most important were those with the two dominant powers of Europe, England and France. Each country was a monarchy, and a monarchy does not ordinarily like to see a rebellion succeed in any land. (The example may prove contagious.) Yet the war had not progressed very far before it was clear that the ruling classes in each of these two countries sympathized strongly with the Confederacy—so strongly that with just a little prodding they might be moved to intervene and bring about Southern independence by force of arms. The South was, after all, an aristocracy, and the fact that it had a broad democratic base was easily overlooked at a distance of three thousand miles. Europe's aristocracies had never been happy about the prodigious success of the Yankee democracy. If the nation now broke into halves, proving that democracy did not contain the stuff of survival, the rulers of Europe would be well pleased.

To be sure, the Southern nation was based on the institution of chattel slavery—a completely repugnant anachronism by the middle of the nineteenth century. Neither the British nor the French people would go along with any policy that involved fighting to preserve slavery. But up to the fall of 1862 slavery was not an issue in the war. The Federal government had explicitly declared that it was fighting solely to save the Union. If a Southern emissary wanted to convince Europeans that they could aid the South without thereby aiding slavery, he could prove his case by citing the words of the Federal President and Congress. As far as Europe was concerned, no moral issue was involved; the game of power politics could be played with a clear conscience.

So it *was* played, and the threat of European intervention was real and immediate. Outright war with England nearly took place in the fall of 1861, when a hot-headed U.S. naval officer, Captain Charles Wilkes, undertook to twist the lion's tail and got more of a reaction than anyone was prepared for.

Jefferson Davis had named two distinguished Southerners, James M. Mason of Virginia and John Slidell of Louisiana, as commissioners to represent Confederate interests abroad, Mason in England and Slidell in France. They got out of Charleston, South Carolina, on a blockade-runner at the beginning of October and went via Nassau to Havana, where they took passage for England on the British mail steamer *Trent*.

Precisely at this time U.S.S. *San Jacinto* was returning to the United States from a long tour of duty along the African coast. She put in at a Cuban port, looking for news of Confederate commerce raiders which were reported to be active in that vicinity, and there her commander, Captain Wilkes, heard about Mason and Slidell. He now worked out a novel interpretation of international law. A nation at war (it was generally agreed) had a right to stop and search a neutral merchant ship if it suspected that ship of carrying the enemy's dispatches. Mason and Slidell, Wilkes reasoned, were in effect Confederate dispatches, and he had a right to remove them. So on November 8, 1861, he steamed out into the Bahama Channel, fired twice across *Trent*'s bows, sent a boat's crew aboard, collared the Confederate commissioners, and bore them off in triumph to the United States, where they were lodged in Fort Warren, in Boston Harbor. Wilkes was hailed as a national hero. Congress voted him its thanks, and Secretary of the Navy Gideon Welles, ordinarily a most cautious mortal, warmly commended him.

BUT IN ENGLAND there was an uproar which almost brought on a war. The mere notion that Americans could halt a British ship on the high seas and remove lawful passengers was intolerable. Eleven thousand regular troops were sent to Canada, the British fleet was put on a war footing, and a sharp note was dispatched to the United States, demanding surrender of the prisoners and a prompt apology.

If the general tempo of things had not been so feverish just then, experts on international law might have amused themselves by pointing out that the American and British governments had precisely reversed their traditional policies. In the Napoleonic wars British warships had exercised the right of search and seizure without restraint, stopping American merchant ships on the high seas to remove persons whom they suspected of being British subjects—doing, in fact, exactly what Wilkes had done with a slightly different object. The United States government had protested that this was improper and illegal, and the whole business had helped bring on the War of 1812. Now an American naval officer had done what British naval officers had done half a century earlier, and the British government was protesting in the same way the earlier American government had done. If anyone cared to make anything of it, the situation was somewhat ironic.

It was touch and go for a while, because a good many brash Yankees were quite willing to fight the British, and the seizure of the Confederate commissioners had somehow seemed like a great victory. But Lincoln stuck to the policy of one war at a time, and after due deliberation the apology was made and the prisoners were released. The *Trent* incident was forgotten, and the final note was strangely anticlimactic. The transports bearing the British troops to Canada arrived off the American coast just after the release and apology. Secretary of State Seward offered, a little too graciously, to let the soldiers disembark on American soil for rapid transportation across Maine, but the British coldly rejected this unnecessary courtesy.

The *Trent* affair had been symptomatic. The war had put a heavy strain on relations between the United States and Great Britain, and there would always be

"War with America is such a calamity that we must do all we can to avoid it," said William E. Gladstone, the English Chancellor of the Exchequer at the time of the *Trent* affair. And when the Lincoln administration agreed to release Mason and Slidell, the *Trent* affair subsided almost as quickly as it had flared up. The men promptly continued their journey, confident that Europe's governments would be sympathetic to their cause. In London and Paris, the two found themselves well-fêted guests; however, when they attempted to present their credentials as representatives of the Confederate States of America, no official doors opened. Europe, as shown in the *Punch* cartoon below, was content to watch and wait. A frustrated James M. Mason recorded that when he approached the British foreign secretary, Earl Russell, about establishing a Confederate embassy, "[Russell's] only reply was he hoped I might find my residence in London agreeable."

PUNCH, OR THE LONDON CHARIVARI—August 27, 1864.

AMERICA ANOTHER FEDERAL DEFEAT

VERY PROBABLE.

LORD PUNCH. "THAT WAS JEFF DAVIS, PAM! DON'T YOU RECOGNISE HIM?"
LORD PAM. "HM! WELL, NOT EXACTLY—MAY HAVE TO DO SO SOME OF THESE DAYS."

JOHN BULL MAKES A DISCOVERY.

America's Civil War posed a serious dilemma for England, whose textile mills depended on Southern cotton, but whose laws and public sentiment rejected slavery. The choice that England's rulers seemed to face between these two interests is represented in the 1862 lithograph above right. In the midst of the quandary, Confederate agents could operate in England under the flimsiest of subterfuges, and easily obtain war matériel. In a move certain to rile the Lincoln administration, Southern representatives contracted with an English shipbuilding firm, Laird Brothers, for construction of a pair of powerful ironclad rams (below).

danger that some unexpected occurrence would bring on a war. Yet the two countries were fortunate in the character of their diplomats. The American Minister in London was Charles Francis Adams, and the British Minister in Washington was Lord Lyons, and these two had done all they could, in the absence of instructions from their governments, to keep the *Trent* business from getting out of hand. Even Secretary of State Seward, who earlier had shown a politician's weakness for making votes in America by defying the British, proved supple enough to retreat with good grace from an untenable position; and Earl Russell, the British Foreign Secretary, who had sent a very stiff note, nevertheless phrased it carefully so that Seward could make his retreat without too great difficulty.

MUCH MORE SERIOUS WAS the situation that developed late in the summer of 1862. At that time, as far as any European could see, the Confederacy was beginning to

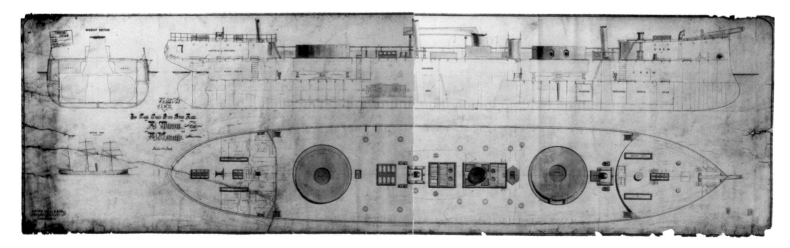

YE CONFERENCE.

"NOT ANY. WE THANK YOU MR DAVIS."

In France, Confederate hopes for recognition focused on the emperor Napoleon III, who seemed more disposed to intervene than did any of England's leaders. It quickly became clear, however, that Napoleon III was not prepared to act unilaterally on behalf of the South; he offered only to mediate the conflict, and only if England and Russia would back him. The emperor thus spurned the inducements offered by Jefferson Davis' government to acknowledge its legitimacy (left).

look very much like a winner—a point which James Mason insistently pressed home with British officialdom. The Northern attempt to capture the Confederate capital had failed, Virginia's soil had been cleared of invaders, and in the East and West alike the Confederates were on the offensive. Minister Adams warned Seward that the British government might very soon offer to mediate the difficulty between North and South, which would be a polite but effective way of intimating that in the opinion of Great Britain the quarrel had gone on long enough and ought to be ended—by giving the South what it wanted. Adams knew what he was talking about. Earl Russell had given Mason no encouragement whatever, but after news of the Second Battle of Bull Run reached London, he and Lord Palmerston, the Prime Minister, agreed that along in late September or thereabouts there should be a cabinet meeting at which Prime Minister and Foreign Secretary would ask approval of the mediation proposal. (Implicit in all of this was the idea that if the Northern government should refuse to accept mediation, Britain would go ahead and recognize the Confederacy.) With a saving note of caution, Russell and Palmerston concluded not to bring the plan before the cabinet until they got further word about Lee's invasion of the North. If the Federals were beaten, then the proposal would go through; if Lee failed, then it might be well to wait a little longer before taking any action.

On October 7 the Chancellor of the Exchequer, William E. Gladstone, made a notable speech at Newcastle in which he remarked that no matter what one's opinion of slavery might be, facts had to be faced: "There is no doubt that Jefferson Davis and other leaders of the South have made an army; they are making, it appears, a navy; and they have made what is more than either—they have made a nation." He added, "We may anticipate with certainty the success of the Southern States so far as regards their separation from the North."

Naturally enough, this raised a sensation. Gladstone explained that he had simply been expressing his own opinion rather than that of the government, and

Besides contracting for new warships, Confederate agents in England also located vessels that could be re-outfitted as commerce raiders or blockade-runners. The enormous profits reaped by the blockade-runners, transporting munitions, medicines, and other commodities, were such that many British firms considered the risks worth taking. This activity became so widespread that underwriters in London and Liverpool openly offered insurance policies for shippers involved in the business. Recognizing that the situation would not soon change, the U.S. ambassador to England, Charles Francis Adams, quietly amassed evidence for a future tribunal. The image (right) of the steamship *Old Dominion* undergoing transformation into a blockade-runner was among the damning exhibits he gathered.

when Earl Russell saw the speech, he wrote Gladstone that he "went beyond the latitude which all speakers must be allowed." His lordship went on to say that he did not think the cabinet was prepared for recognition, but that it would meet very soon to discuss the project.

In all of this there was less of actual hostility toward the North than is usually supposed. Palmerston and Russell were prepared to accept an accomplished fact, when and if such a fact became visible; if the Confederacy was definitely going to win, the fact ought to be admitted and the war ought to be ended. But they were not prepared to go further than that. Gladstone might commit his calculated indiscretion, the upper class might continue to hold the Confederates as sentimental favorites, and the London *Times* might thunder at intervals against the Northern government; but the British government itself tried to be scrupulously correct, and long before the war ended, ardent Southerners were complaining that the government's attitude had been consistently hostile to the Confederacy. Even the business of the British-built cruisers and ironclad rams did not alter this situation. Legally, vessels like the *Alabama* were simply fast merchant ships, given arms and a warlike character only after they had left English waters, and the government had no legal ground to prevent their construction and delivery. The famous rams themselves were technically built for French purchasers, and even though it was an open secret that they would ultimately go into the Confederate navy, there was never anything solid for the British authorities to put their teeth into. When the British government finally halted the deal and forced the builders to sell the rams to the British navy, it actually stretched the law very substantially. That it did this under a plain threat of war from the United States did not alter the fact that in the end the Confederacy could not get what it desperately wanted from Great Britain.

Nor was the United States without active friends in England. Such reformers as John Bright and Richard Cobden spoke up vigorously in support of the Lincoln government, and even when the cotton shortage threw thousands of textile workers out of employment, the British working class remained consistently opposed to the Confederacy. But the decisive factor, in the fall of 1862 and increasingly thereafter, was the Battle of Antietam and what grew out of it.

Antietam by itself showed that Lee's invasion was not going to bring that final, conclusive Confederate triumph which had been anticipated. The swift

The Price of Neutrality

Soon after the end of the Civil War, the United States filed formal grievances against the British government for knowingly permitting the construction on its soil of Confederate commerce raiders, most notably the C.S.S. *Alabama,* whose commander, Raphael Semmes, was caricatured by Thomas Nast (right). In legal actions that became known as the "Alabama Claims," the Americans started out simply seeking compensation for the damage done by the ships that the British officials had allowed to be built. Then some elected officials in Washington turned it into a saber-rattling campaign and even tried to use it to evict Great Britain from dominion in Canada. As the claims escalated, Massachusetts Senator Charles Sumner, Chairman of the Foreign Relations Committee, declared that England was responsible not only for fifteen million dollars in direct damages but also for one hundred and ten million in lost revenues. An international tribunal had to be convened to adjudicate the matter. In 1872, it ruled that Great Britain had acted improperly and was liable for a total of fifteen million dollars. Although the British representative at the tribunal refused to sign the final settlement, the crown's ambassador paid a call on the U.S. Secretary of State a year later and said, "I believe my government owes the United States a sum of money which it is my purpose to pay today." With that, he presented gold certificates for the full amount.

Semmes Motto "I am here"

While some nationalistic British cartoonists suggested that the upstart Yankees deserved a good drubbing (left), U.S. diplomats worked hard to keep London from taking an official stand. "People [here] . . . think this is a hasty quarrel. . . ," wrote Ambassador Adams, "which will be arranged as soon as the cause of it shall pass off. They do not comprehend the connection which slavery has with it. . . . With the commercial men the wish is father to the thought. . . . [T]heir sole panacea is settlement, somehow, no matter how. If it be by a recognition of two governments, that is as good a way as any other."

PUNCH, OR THE LONDON CHARIVARI.—December 7, 1861.

LOOK OUT FOR SQUALLS.

Jack Bull. "YOU DO WHAT'S RIGHT, MY SON, OR I'LL BLOW YOU OUT OF THE WATER."

While many in the North and in Europe viewed the Emancipation Proclamation as a noble, praiseworthy step, Southern leaders saw it as opening doorways to social chaos. Adalbert Volck's drawing (right) shows Lincoln composing the document surrounded by satanic symbols, images of slave revolts, and sheer desolation. An early draft of one page of the Emancipation Proclamation is shown below.

recession of the high Confederate tide was as visible in England as in America, and as the autumn wore away Palmerston and Russell concluded that it would not be advisable to bring the mediation-recognition program before the cabinet.

Far more significant than Antietam, however, was the Emancipation Proclamation, which turned out to be one of the strangest and most important state papers ever issued by an American President.

During the late spring and early summer of 1862 Lincoln had come to see that he must broaden the base of the war. Union itself was not enough; the undying vitality and drive of Northern antislavery men must be brought into full, vigorous support of the war effort, and to bring this about the Northern government must officially declare itself against slavery. Lincoln was preparing such a declaration even before McClellan's army left the Virginia Peninsula, but he could not issue it until the North had won a victory. (Seward pointed out that to issue it on the heels of a string of Northern defeats would make it look as if the government were despairingly crying for help rather than making a statement of principle.) Antietam gave Lincoln the victory he had to have, and on September 22 he issued the famous proclamation, the gist of which was that on January 1, 1863, all slaves held in a state or a part of a state which was in rebellion should be "then, thenceforward and forever free."

Technically, the proclamation was almost absurd. It proclaimed freedom for all slaves in precisely those areas where the United States could not make its authority effective, and allowed slavery to continue in slave states which remained under Federal control. It was a statement of intent rather than a valid statute, and it was of doubtful legality; Lincoln had issued it as a war measure, basing it on his belief that the President's undefined "war powers" permitted him to do just about anything he chose to do in order to win the war, but the courts might not agree with him. Abolitionists felt that it did not go nearly far enough, and border-state people and many Northern Democrats felt that it went altogether too far. But in the end it changed the whole character of the war and, more than any other single thing, doomed the Confederacy to defeat.

THE NORTHERN GOVERNMENT now was committed to a broader cause, with deep, mystic overtones; it was fighting for union and for human freedom as well, and the very nature of the Union for which it was fighting would be permanently deepened and enriched. A new meaning was given to Daniel Webster's famous "Liberty *and* Union, now and forever, one and inseparable"; the great Battle Hymn now rang out as an American Marseillaise, and Northerners who had wondered whether the war was quite worth its terrible cost heard, at last, the notes of the bugle that would never call retreat. A war goal with emotional power as direct and enduring as the Confederacy's own had at last been erected for all men to see.

And in Europe the American Civil War had become something in which no western government dared to intervene. The government of Britain, France, or

A popular image of Lincoln at work on the Emancipation Proclamation (below) shows him in a lonely struggle surrounded by the precedents of history. In fact, he composed much of the first draft over a period of weeks, carefully working out and then reworking some of its passages as he waited in the military telegraph office for war news. Each time Lincoln visited that office, he would retrieve the papers from a locked drawer and read over and revise what he had previously written. Only then would he begin to add to the document. After Lincoln finished the first draft, he finally told the understandably curious superintendent of the office what he had been writing.

In popular literature and art, the Emancipation Proclamation was invested with profound symbolism, as in A. A. Lamb's allegorical painting (above). In reality, the document was pragmatic and carefully circumscribed. It freed only slaves in areas under Confederate control, not those in loyal border states or in areas occupied by Union forces. It was still a great breakthrough to Northern black leaders, however; jubilation erupted everywhere. At one celebration, remembered Frederick Douglass, "we got into such a state of enthusiasm that almost everything seemed to be witty and appropriate to the occasion."

any other nation could play power politics as it chose, as long as the war meant nothing more than a government's attempt to put down a rebellion; but no government that had to pay the least attention to the sentiment of its own people could take sides against a government which was trying to destroy slavery. The British cabinet was never asked to consider the proposition which Palmerston and Russell had been talking about, and after 1862 the chance that Great Britain would decide in favor of the Confederacy became smaller and smaller and presently vanished entirely. The Emancipation Proclamation had locked the Confederates in an anachronism which could not survive in the modern world.

Along with this there went a much more prosaic material factor. Europe had had several years of short grain crops, and during the Civil War the North exported thousands of tons of grain—grain which could be produced in increasing quantities, despite the wartime manpower shortage, because the new reapers and binders were boosting farm productivity so sharply. Much as Great Britain needed American cotton, just now she needed American wheat even more. In a showdown she was not likely to do anything that would cut off that source of food.

All of this did not mean that Secretary Seward had no more problems in his dealings with the world abroad. The recurring headache growing out of the British habit of building ships for the Confederate navy has already been noted. There was also Napoleon III, Emperor of the French, who was a problem all by himself.

Napoleon's government in many ways was quite cordial to the Confederates, and in the fall of 1862 Napoleon talked with Slidell and then proposed that France, England, and Russia join in trying to bring about a six-month armistice. To Slidell the Emperor remarked that if the Northern government rejected this proposal, that might give good reason for recognition and perhaps even for active intervention. Neither Britain nor Russia would go along with him, but early in 1863 Napoleon had the French Minister at Washington suggest to Seward that there ought to be a meeting of Northern and Southern representatives to see whether the war might not be brought to a close. Seward politely but firmly rejected this suggestion, and the Congress, much less politely, formally resolved that any foreign government which made such proposals was thereby committing an unfriendly act. Whether Napoleon really expected anything to come of his suggestion is a question; probably he strongly wanted a Southern victory but was afraid to do anything definite without British support. His real interest was in Mexico, where he took advantage of the war to create a French puppet state, installing the Hapsburg Maximilian as Emperor of Mexico in direct violation of the Monroe Doctrine. Propped up by French troops, Maximilian managed to hang on to his shaky throne for several years, and if his control over the country had been firmer, Napoleon would probably have given the Confederacy, from that base, more active support. Shortly after Appomattox the Federal government sent Phil Sheridan and 50,000 veterans to the Mexican border in blunt warning, Seward filed a formal protest against the occupation, and Napoleon withdrew his

Despite one cartoonist's cynical portrayal of a desperate U.S. President forced by circumstances to resort to emancipation (above), when 1863 arrived and Lincoln's proclamation went into effect, black Americans throughout the South knew that their lives had been changed forever. William Tolman Carlton's painting *Waiting for the Hour* (below left) depicts the anxious minutes before midnight for one group of slaves. A Missouri field hand named Andrew Evans never forgot the day his boss gathered the workers to tell them of the Emancipation Proclamation. "We didn't quite understand what it was all about until he informed us that it meant we were slaves no longer, that we were free to go as we liked, to work for anyone who would hire us and be responsible to no one but ourselves."

soldiers. When the French troops left, the Mexicans regained control, and Maximilian was deposed and executed.

Singularly enough, the one European country which showed a definite friendship for the Northern government was Czarist Russia. In the fall of 1863 two Russian fleets entered American waters, one in the Atlantic and one in the Pacific. They put into New York and San Francisco harbors and spent the winter there, and the average Northerner expressed both surprise and delight over the visit, assuming that the Russian Czar was taking this means of warning England and France that if they made war in support of the South, he would help the North. Since pure altruism is seldom or never visible in any country's foreign relations, the business was not quite that simple. Russia at the time was in some danger of getting into a war with England and France, for reasons totally unconnected with the Civil War in America; to avoid the risk of having his fleets icebound in Russian ports, the Czar simply had them winter in American harbors. If war should come, they would be admirably placed to raid British and French commerce. For many years most Americans believed that for some inexplicable reason of his own the Czar had sent the fleets simply to show his friendship for America.

Considering the course of the war as a whole, it must be said that Northern

The year 1862 marked a high point for the fortunes and élan of the Confederate cavalry in the East, commanded by Major General J. E. B. Stuart. Though often outnumbered and not as well-armed as their Yankee counterparts, the tough Rebel horsemen (depicted by Walton Taber, below) usually rode circles around their hapless opponents. Things became so bad for the Union troopers that Federal infantrymen took to jeering their own cavalry as they passed them on the march: "Who ever saw a dead cavalryman?"

Major General Ambrose E. Burnside stands outside his headquarters tent: his outwardly rakish demeanor suggested a self-satisfaction he did not possess. "He was pre-eminently a manly man," wrote an officer who served with him. "His large, fine eyes, his winning smile and cordial manners bespoke a frank, sincere and honorable character. . . . " Burnside, appointed to command the Army of the Potomac after Lincoln sacked McClellan, was honest to the point of frankly admitting to anyone who would listen that he lacked the talent to succeed Little Mac. "He remarked in my presence that he had concluded to take the command of the army," a subordinate wrote after the offer had been made, "but did not regard the subject as one for congratulation."

The pontoon bridge (one near Berlin, Maryland, on the Potomac, is shown at right) was an important element in the engineering arsenal of Civil War armies. In simple terms, a pontoon bridge consisted of a step-like series of small, interlocking boats, covered with planking so that men, animals, and even wagons could cross on them. An efficient, well-equipped detachment of pontooneers made it possible for an army to keep moving even where regular bridges had been destroyed by the enemy. A veteran of the Army of the Potomac declared that "the crowning work of this corps . . . was that of pontoon-bridge laying."

diplomacy was highly successful and that Southern diplomacy was a flat failure. At the time, most Northerners bitterly resented what they considered the unfriendly attitude of Britain and France, but neither country did much that would give the South any real nourishment. The British commerce raiders were indeed expensive nuisances to the North, and the famous "*Alabama* claims" after the war were prosecuted with vigor; but cruisers like the *Alabama* might have ranged the seas for a generation without ever compelling the North to give up the struggle. The open recognition, the active aid, the material and financial support which the South needed so greatly were never forthcoming. Europe refused to take a hand in America's quarrel. North and South were left to fight it out between themselves.

AFTER THE FAILURE OF the great Southern counteroffensive in the fall of 1862, the North tried to pick up the lost threads afresh. Its problem, then as always, was deceptively simple: to use its immense preponderance of physical strength in a sustained, increasing pressure that would collapse the Confederate defenses and destroy the Confederate armies and the government which they supported. In the spring it had seemed that success was very near; by autumn the vast difficulties that lay across the path were much more clearly visible. Momentum, so important to military success, had been lost, and in the East and in the West a new start would have to be made.

In this effort three armies would be chiefly involved—the Army of the Potomac in Virginia, the Army of the Cumberland in central Tennessee, and the Army of the Tennessee along the Mississippi River. The Army of the Potomac was led now by Major General Ambrose E. Burnside, a handsome, likable, unassuming West Pointer with a legendary growth of side whiskers, a man whose sincere desire to do the right thing was a good deal stronger than his ability to discern

Building Pontoon bridge at Fredericksburg Dec. — [?]

When Burnside took over the Army of the Potomac, its headquarters was near Warrenton, Virginia, while Robert E. Lee's troops were posted at Winchester and Culpeper. Under intense pressure from Washington to act, Burnside decided to quietly move his army out of its encampment and march south to Fredericksburg, where he would quickly cross the Rappahannock River via pontoon bridges and place himself between Lee's army and Richmond. Everything went wrong; the first problem was that pontoon materials failed to reach Fredericksburg before Lee's men did. Alfred Waud's sketch (left) shows Union engineers trying to construct the pontoon bridge while under deadly fire from Confederate snipers on the opposite shore.

what that right thing might be. McClellan had at last been removed. He had let six weeks pass after Antietam before he crossed the Potomac and began a new offensive, and then he moved, as always, with much deliberation; Lincoln had lost patience, McClellan was in retirement, and Burnside now had the army.

It lay in the neighborhood of Warrenton, Virginia, east of the Blue Ridge. Burnside did not like the advance down the Orange and Alexandria Railroad which McClellan seemed to have projected, and he devised a new plan: go east to Fredericksburg, cross the Rappahannock there and force Lee to give battle somewhere between Fredericksburg and Richmond, and then drive on toward the Confederate capital. By the middle of November, Burnside had the army on the move.

The Army of the Cumberland was just below Nashville, Tennessee. Like the Army of the Potomac, this army had a new commander: bluff, red-faced William S. Rosecrans, who had taken Buell's place when that officer proved unable to overtake Bragg on the retreat from Kentucky. Rosecrans was well-liked by his troops, and he was a stout fighter. He had commanded the portion of Grant's force which won the bloody battle at Corinth, and although Grant had been critical of the way he pursued Van Dorn's beaten army after the battle (it seemed to Grant that that army should have been destroyed outright), Rosecrans' general record of performance was good. He devoted some weeks now to refitting and reorganization, and late in December he began to move south from Nashville with 45,000 men. The Confederate army under Braxton Bragg lay in camp at Murfreesboro, behind Stones River, thirty miles away. At the moment it numbered some 37,000 soldiers.

The third army, Grant's, held western Tennessee, and it had two principal

The Irish Brigade at Fredericksburg

Few units in the Union army enjoyed as colorful a reputation as that of the Second Brigade of the II Corps' 1st Division. The Irish Brigade, as it was known, consisted of regiments from Massachusetts, New York, and Pennsylvania, marching into battle under emerald flags sporting gold shamrocks and harps. The unit was commanded at Fredericksburg by Brigadier General Thomas F. Meagher, who had escaped to the United States from Tasmania, to which he had been banished for conducting revolutionary activities in Ireland. As part of Winfield Scott Hancock's corps, Meagher's men attacked at the Stone Wall in front of Marye's Heights, perhaps the toughest task of this battle. "The brilliant assault on Marye's Heights of their Irish Brigade was beyond description," wrote a Confederate officer on the scene. A Rebel infantryman in the ranks remembered how the cannon fire "tore great gaps in their ranks," followed by "the blinding flash, the deafening roar, the murderous destruction of two thousand well-aimed rifles. . . ." Though the Irish Brigade advanced closer to the enemy lines than almost any other unit on their part of the battlefield, the attack failed, and cost the 1,300-man Irish Brigade 50 killed, 421 wounded, and 74 captured or missing. "As for the Brigade," wrote an officer, "may the Lord pity and protect the widows and orphans of nearly all those belonging to it! It will be a sad, sad Christmas by many an Irish hearthstone in New York, Pennsylvania, and Massachusetts." Alfred Waud's sketch (below) depicts the December 13 Union assaults against Marye's Heights.

Late in the day, December 11, Union troops finally succeeded in crossing the Rappahannock River to take possession of battered Fredericksburg. The next day, while most of the Union army was transferred across the river, the troops already in the town engaged in an orgy of looting and random destruction. Arthur Lumley's drawing (left) is based on eyewitness testimony. A Massachusetts man recalled a lighter moment when soldiers clothed "in the costumes of Virginia that were in fashion in the days of Mary Washington" paraded through the streets "with all the fun and frolic of Harlequin in his happiest mood."

On December 11, the streets of Fredericksburg reverberated with gunfire, as Confederate sharpshooters (such as those depicted above) were driven out of the town by Federal soldiers. After a day was squandered in maneuvering and pondering lost opportunities, Burnside finally issued his attack orders for the following day. At about 4:30 P.M., December 13, the two brigades of Brigadier General Andrew A. Humphreys' division moved to join the Union assault, a moment sketched by Alfred Waud (right). As their advance began, Confederate batteries in front were replaced by fresh units, bringing full ammunition chests. Thinking that the enemy was withdrawing, Humphreys' men let out a cheer and rushed forward, only to be savagely raked by artillery fire. "[W]e gave them our choicest varieties," remembered one of the Rebel gunners, "canister and shrapnel, just as fast as we could put it in."

functions: to occupy the western third of the state, holding Memphis and the important network of railroads that ran east and northeast from that city and north from the Mississippi border to the upper Mississippi River; and to move down the great river, capture the Confederate stronghold at Vicksburg, join hands with the Union forces which held New Orleans and Baton Rouge, and so open the river from headwaters to gulf. Grant had 80,000 men in his department, but half of them were needed for occupation duties. When he moved against Vicksburg he would be able to put fewer than 40,000 in his field army. He would follow the north-and-south railroad that ran to the Mississippi capital, Jackson, forty miles east of Vicksburg, and then he would swing west. Opposing him was an undetermined number of Confederates led by Lieutenant General John C. Pemberton, a Pennsylvania-born West Pointer who had cast his lot with the South.

THESE THREE FEDERAL ARMIES, then, would move more or less in concert, and if all went well, the Confederacy would be pressed beyond endurance. If all did not go well, the Lincoln administration might be in serious trouble. The Emancipation Proclamation was meeting with a mixed reception in the North, and the fall elections had gone badly. The Democrats had sharply reduced the Republican majority in Congress and had elected Horatio Seymour governor of New York; and to the Republican radicals, Seymour, lukewarm about the war at best, looked no better than an arrant Copperhead. In the Northwest war weariness was clearly visible, and Lincoln was being warned that if the Mississippi were not soon opened, there would be an increasing demand for a negotiated peace with the South. For political reasons he needed new military successes.

For the immediate present he did not get them. Instead he got one disaster and a series of checks which looked almost as bad.

First there was Burnside. He got his army to the Rappahannock, opposite Fredericksburg, and if he could have crossed the river at once, he might have

made serious trouble for Lee, who did not have all of his men on hand just yet. But the pontoon trains which Burnside needed to bridge the river had gone astray somewhere, and Burnside could think of nothing better to do than wait quietly where he was until they arrived. They reached him, eventually, but a fortnight had been lost, and by the end of it Lee had both Jackson and Longstreet in position on the opposite shore—75,000 veteran fighters of high morale, ably led, ready for the kind of defensive battle in which they were all but unbeatable.

Burnside lacked the mental agility to change his plan, and he tried to go through with it even though the conditions essential for success had gone. He built his bridges, crossed the Rappahannock, and on December 13 assailed Lee's army in its prepared positions. As made, the attack had no chance to succeed. Solidly established on high ground with a clear field of fire, the Confederates beat off a succession of doomed assaults in which the Federals displayed great valor but an almost total lack of military acumen. At the end of the day the Army of the Potomac had lost more than 12,000 men, most of them in front of a stone wall and a sunken road that ran along the base of Marye's Heights. The Confederates had lost fewer than half that many men, and at no time had they been in any serious danger of being dislodged. Burnside called for new assaults the next day—he proposed to lead them in person, there being nothing wrong with his personal courage—but his subordinates managed to talk him out of it, and the Army of the Potomac sullenly withdrew to the north side of the river, its morale all but ruined. The two armies glowered at each other from opposite banks of the

Confederate artilleryman William Sheppard's drawing (above) shows a Rebel battery in action. Said one artillery officer: "Fredericksburg was the easiest battle we ever fought." Both on the Confederate left flank, spread along Marye's Heights, and the right flank, posted at Prospect Hill, Rebel gunners played an important role in securing victory for Robert E. Lee. When they were not blasting cannister rounds into massed ranks at close range, the cannon were pummeling units waiting to move forward. A Pennsylvania soldier wrote afterwards that "to remain quiet under such a fire was more trying than active conflict."

FREDERICKSBURG

December 13, 1862

BURNSIDE'S HQ

STAFFORD HEIGHTS

RAPPAHANNOCK

Fredericksburg

HANOVER STREET

CANAL

Ditch

PLANK ROAD

STONE WALL

SUNKEN ROAD

MARYE'S HOUSE

MARYE'S HEIGHTS

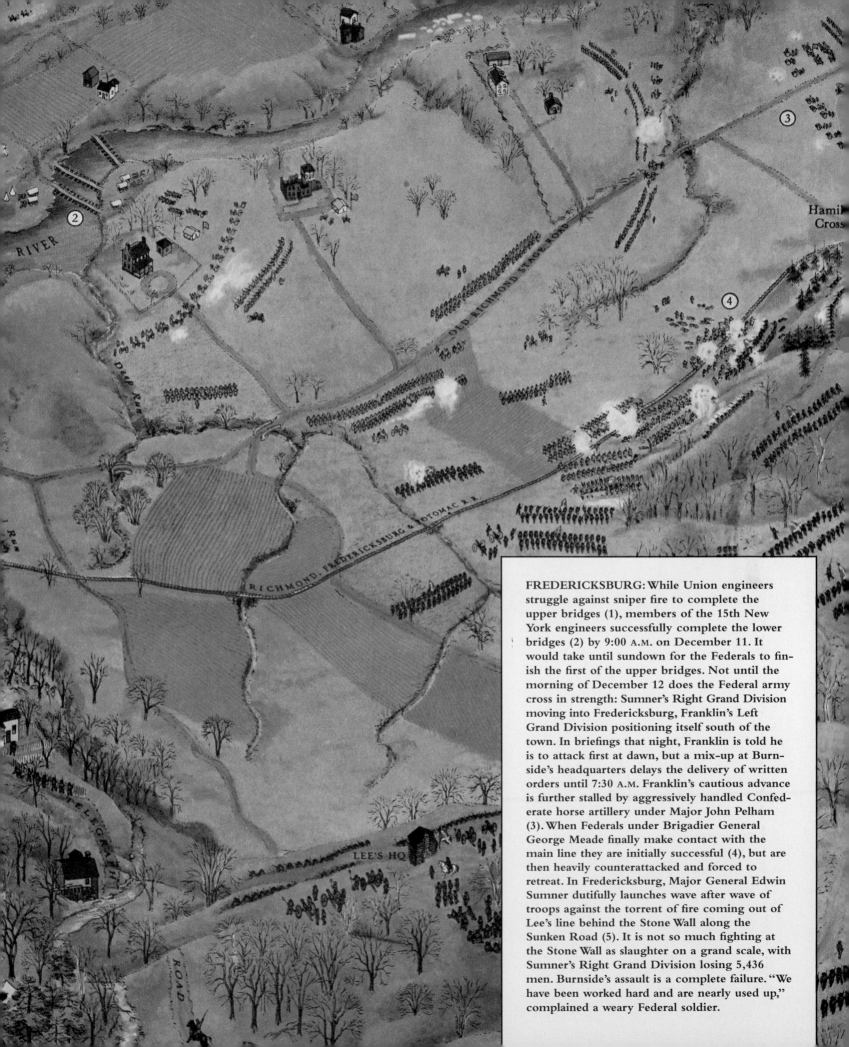

Hami
Cross

RIVER

② ③ ④

OLD RICHMOND STAGE ROAD

Deep Run

RICHMOND, FREDERICKSBURG & POTOMAC R.R.

TELEGRAPH

LEE'S HQ

ROAD

FREDERICKSBURG: While Union engineers struggle against sniper fire to complete the upper bridges (1), members of the 15th New York engineers successfully complete the lower bridges (2) by 9:00 A.M. on December 11. It would take until sundown for the Federals to finish the first of the upper bridges. Not until the morning of December 12 does the Federal army cross in strength: Sumner's Right Grand Division moving into Fredericksburg, Franklin's Left Grand Division positioning itself south of the town. In briefings that night, Franklin is told he is to attack first at dawn, but a mix-up at Burnside's headquarters delays the delivery of written orders until 7:30 A.M. Franklin's cautious advance is further stalled by aggressively handled Confederate horse artillery under Major John Pelham (3). When Federals under Brigadier General George Meade finally make contact with the main line they are initially successful (4), but are then heavily counterattacked and forced to retreat. In Fredericksburg, Major General Edwin Sumner dutifully launches wave after wave of troops against the torrent of fire coming out of Lee's line behind the Stone Wall along the Sunken Road (5). It is not so much fighting at the Stone Wall as slaughter on a grand scale, with Sumner's Right Grand Division losing 5,436 men. Burnside's assault is a complete failure. "We have been worked hard and are nearly used up," complained a weary Federal soldier.

John Richards' painting *The Battle of Fredericksburg* (above) provides a sweeping view of the fighting on Marye's Heights as seen from the edge of town, where Union surgeons are already at work. One reserve regiment in this battle came across blocks of ribbon in town, which were soon put to use in the hospital, in a manner unanticipated by those who made the material. "Generous hands quickly unwound the blocks, and tenderly, it may be awkwardly, applied the ribbon to wounds gaping, exposed and yet untreated, and bandaged hurts, possibly nearing fatality from want of care," remembered a soldier in the regiment. "But whether life was saved or not, it was a comfort and consolation for kindly hands to minister to those pressing needs."

river for several weeks; then Burnside tried to move upstream, to cross beyond Lee's left flank and fight a new battle, but three days of steady, icy rain turned the unpaved roads into bottomless mud and left his army completely bogged down. In the end the soldiers managed to pull themselves, their wagons, and their artillery out of the mire and came slogging back to camp, utterly dispirited. This fiasco was too much for everybody, and Burnside was removed from command. To all intents and purposes the Army of the Potomac was out of action for the winter.

In central Tennessee things went better, although what was gained cost a good deal more than it was worth. Rosecrans moved down to Murfreesboro, and Bragg waited for him, and on December 31 their armies fought a desperate, inconclusive battle on a desolate frozen field. Tactically, the fight presented an interesting oddity; each general prepared to hold with his right and attack with his left, and if the two plans had been carried out simultaneously the armies would have swung around like a huge revolving door. As it happened, however, Bragg's men struck first, crushing the Federal right wing and compelling Rosecrans to abandon all thought of an advance with his left. For a time it appeared that the Union army would be completely routed, but Rosecrans' center was commanded by George Thomas, and that stolid Virginian was very hard to dislodge. His corps hung on while the shattered right was re-formed far to the rear, and the sound of musket fire rose to such a deafening pitch that Confederates charging across a weedy cotton field stopped and plucked raw cotton from the open bolls and stuffed it in their ears before going on with the advance.

When night came, Rosecrans' line, which had been more or less straight at dawn, was doubled back like a jackknife with a partly opened blade, but it had not been driven from the field. Bragg notified Richmond that he had won a signal victory—and then, unaccountably, failed to renew the attack the next day. Through all of January 1 the armies faced each other, inactive; late in the afternoon of January 2 Bragg finally assailed the Union left, but his columns were broken up by Federal artillery, and at nightfall the armies were right where they had been at dawn. On January 3, again, they remained in contact, with sporadic firing along the picket lines but no real activity. Then, after dark, the unpredictable Bragg drew off in retreat, marching thirty-six miles south to Tullahoma. Rosecrans moved on into Murfreesboro, but his army was too badly mangled to go any farther. Six months would pass before it could resume the offensive.

NO ONE QUITE KNEW who had won this battle, or what its military significance was, if indeed it had any. The Federals did occupy the field, and the Confederates had retreated, so the North accepted it as a victory; but nothing of any consequence had been gained, Bragg's army was still in position squarely across the road to Chattanooga, the key city which the Federals wanted to possess, and the only concrete result seemed to be that both armies had been immobilized for some time to come. Since the North could not possibly win the war if armies were immobilized, this victory was not quite worth the price.

The casualties had been shocking. The Federals had lost 13,000 men and the Confederates 11,700 or more—in each case, about a third of the army's total strength. Few Civil War battles ever cost more or meant less.

If the Federals were to get anything at all out of the winter's operations,

they would have to get it from Grant, and for a long time it did not seem that his luck was going to be any better than anybody else's.

He started out brightly enough, beginning in November to advance down the line of the railroad. He established a base of supplies at the town of Holly Springs, two dozen miles south of the Tennessee-Mississippi border, and went on with a methodical advance toward the town of Grenada. His progress, however, was first delayed and then brought to a complete halt by two unexpected developments—a strange case of military-political maneuvering among the Federals, and a display of highly effective aggressiveness by Confederate cavalry led by Van Dorn and Forrest.

Grant had hardly begun his advance before he began to realize that something odd was going on in the rear. He was moving so as to approach Vicksburg from the east—the only point from which that riverside stronghold could really be attacked with much hope of success. But as he moved he got persistent reports that there was also going to be an expedition straight down the river, some sort of combined army-navy operation apparently intended to break the river defenses by direct assault. He had planned no such operation, but it was going to take place in his department, and although he could get no clear information about it from Halleck, it seemed that the business would be more or less under his command if he played his cards carefully. It took him a long time to find out what was really in the wind, and when he did find out he was obliged to revise his plans.

What was in the wind was an ambitious attempt by one Major General John A. McClernand to find and to use a new route to victory. McClernand had been

"It seems very strange to see a deserted town, with nothing but corpses of dead men and horses for inhabitants," wrote one of the first Confederates to enter Fredericksburg after the Federals pulled back across the Rappahannock River. This photograph (below right) captures the extent of the desolation. On January 20, in an effort to regain the initiative, Major General Burnside ordered his men on a march to outflank Lee. A winter storm turned what had been a difficult movement into a nightmare of mired wagons and dispirited men (above). After the exhausted soldiers returned to camp, their pickets saw a new sign erected by scoffing Rebels across the river: "Burnside's stuck in the mud. Why don't you come over?"

prominent in Democratic politics in Illinois before the war, and as a prominent "War Democrat" his standing with the administration was very high; he had been given a brigadier general's commission and then he had been made major general, and he had led troops under Grant at Fort Donelson and at Shiloh. He was not a West Pointer, and Grant considered him too erratic and opinionated for independent command, but he was a good fighter and leader of men, and on the whole his combat record was good. He had taken leave of absence late in September and had gone to Washington to see Lincoln and Stanton, and he had persuaded them that unless a conclusive victory were won soon in the Mississippi Valley, the whole Northwest might fall out of the war. Since this jibed with what they already had been told, the President and the Secretary of War listened attentively.

McClernand's proposal was unorthodox but direct. He had a solid following among the Democrats of the Northwest. He believed that he could organize enough fresh troops in that area to form a new army. With such an army, he believed, he could go straight down the Mississippi, and while Grant and the others were threshing about inland he could capture Vicksburg, opening the waterway to the sea and providing the victory which would inspire the Northwest and make possible a final Federal triumph. Lincoln and Stanton liked the idea and gave McClernand top-secret orders to go ahead. In these orders, however, they wrote an escape clause which McClernand seems not to have noticed; what McClernand did was to be done in Grant's department, and if Halleck and Grant

The mood of the young men far from home on Christmas Eve, 1862, is the subject of an unknown artist's painting (below), based on a Thomas Nast engraving in *Harper's Weekly*. Much the same sentiment could also be heard in the verses of a song written that year: "Many are the hearts that are weary tonight/Wishing for the war to cease/Many are the hearts looking for the right/To see the dawn of peace/Tenting tonight, tenting tonight/Tenting on the old Camp ground."

This cartoon, showing Columbia, symbol of America, accusing Lincoln of lacking in concern for the dead at Fredericksburg, seriously misjudged its subject. A clerk in the Department of the Interior wrote in his diary that he had heard Lincoln say, right after the battle: "If there is a worse place than Hell, then I am in it." A newspaperman who was familiar with the President confided to his editor: "He is awfully shaken." To the men of the Army of the Potomac, Lincoln said: "The courage with which you, in an open field, maintained the contest against an entrenched foe . . . show[s] that you possess all the qualities of a great army, which will yet give victory to the cause of the country and of popular government."

saw fit, Grant could at any time assume over-all command over McClernand, McClernand's troops, and the entire venture.

McClernand went back to Illinois and began to raise troops, and rumors of the project trickled out. Halleck could not tell Grant just what was up, but he did his best to warn him by indirection: also, he saw to it that as McClernand's recruits were formed into regiments the regiments were sent downstream to Grant's department. In one way and another, Grant finally came to see what was going on. There was going to be an advance on Vicksburg by water, and Halleck wanted him to assume control of it; wanted him, apparently, to get it moving at once, before McClernand (for whose abilities Halleck had an abiding distrust) could himself reach the scene and take charge.

THE UPSHOT OF ALL THIS was that in December Grant recast his plans. He sent his most trusted subordinate, William T. Sherman, back to Memphis, with orders to organize a striking force out of Sherman's own troops and the new levies that were coming downstream from Illinois, and to proceed down the river with it at the earliest possible date and put his men ashore a few miles north of Vicksburg. Grant, meanwhile, would bring his own army down the line of the railroad, and Pemberton could not possibly meet both threats; if he concentrated against one Federal force, the other would strike him in the rear, and since he would be out-numbered he could not possibly meet both threats at once. Sherman hurried to get things in motion, and Grant went on with his own advance.

At this point the Confederates took a hand. The General Van Dorn who had been beaten at Corinth took a cavalry force, swung in behind Grant, and captured the vast Federal supply base at Holly Springs; and at the same time Bedford Forrest rode up into western Tennessee, cutting railroads and telegraph lines, seizing enough Federal weapons, horses, and equipment to outfit the new recruits who joined him in that stoutly secessionist area, and creating vast confusion and disorganization deep in the Federal rear. In consequence, Grant was brought to a standstill, and he could not get word of this to Sherman, who by now was en route to Vicksburg with 30,000 men, many of whom belonged to the absent McClernand.

So Sherman ran into trouble, because Pemberton was able to ignore Grant and give Sherman all of his attention. The Federals attacked on December 29 and were decisively repulsed, losing more than 1,700 men. Sherman withdrew to the Mississippi River, and on January 2 he was joined there by the indignant McClernand, who was beginning to realize that things were not working out quite as he had hoped. McClernand assumed command, and—for want of anything better to do—he and Sherman, with the help of the navy's gunboats, went up the Arkansas River to capture Confederate Fort Hindman: a nice little triumph, but not precisely what had been contemplated earlier. From Fort Hindman they returned to make camp on the west shore of the Mississippi at Young's Point and Milliken's Bend, some dozen miles above Vicksburg.

There, at the end of the month, Grant showed up, bringing with him most of the men with whom he had attempted the advance down the railroad. His arrival reduced McClernand to the position of a corps commander—a demotion which McClernand protested bitterly but in vain—and gave Grant a field force which numbered between 40,000 and 50,000 men. It also gave Grant a position from which it was all but impossible even to get at the Confederate stronghold, let alone capture it.

Grant's move to the river had been inevitable. There was going to be a Federal column operating on the river, whether Grant liked it or not—Washington had settled that, and the decision was irreversible—and it was clearly unsound to try to co-ordinate that column's movements with the movements of a separate army operating in the interior of the state of Mississippi. The only sensible thing to do was concentrate everything along the river and make the best of it. But in this area geography was on the side of the Confederates.

Vicksburg occupied high ground on the east bank of the Mississippi, and it could be attacked with any chance of success only from the east or southeast. The Yazoo River entered the Mississippi a short distance north of Vicksburg, with steep bluffs along its left bank, and Pemberton had entrenched these bluffs and put troops in them; Sherman's December experience had shown the futility of trying an assault in that area. North of there, the fertile low country of the Yazoo delta ran for two hundred miles, cut by innumerable rivers, creeks, and bayous—fine land for farming, almost impossible land for an army of invasion to cross with all of its guns and supplies.

To the south things looked little better. The Louisiana shore of the Mississippi was low, swampy, intersected like the Yazoo delta by many streams, and if the army did go south it could not cross the river without many steamboats, and there did not seem to be any good way to get these past the Vicksburg batteries. Even if steamboats were available, Confederates had mounted batteries to cover most of the downstream places where a crossing might be made.

What all of this meant was that the army must somehow get east of Vicksburg in order to assault the place, and there did not seem to be any way to get east without going all the way back to Memphis and starting out again on the overland route which Grant had tried in December. This was out of the question because it would be an obvious, unmitigated confession of defeat, and an unhappy Northern

Two Kentuckians who followed very different paths are pictured here. John Alexander McClernand (above) grew up in Illinois, where he became a popular congressman. Since McClernand represented a Democratic constituency necessary for the war effort, Lincoln made him a brigadier general, soon promoting him to major general. A dedicated schemer and self-promoter, McClernand spent much of 1862 trying to get the job held by U. S. Grant. John Hunt Morgan (below) was a successful businessman with a flair for the military, who led his 2nd Kentucky Cavalry Regiment on a series of spectacular raids behind enemy lines. Shortly before Christmas he got married, then left his bride to go on a raid that resulted in the dramatic destruction of two large railroad trestles— a sweet victory for Morgan in that it further crippled Union supply lines.

Major General William S. Rosecrans (above) had his work cut out for him when he succeeded Don Carlos Buell as commander of Union forces in Kentucky. Nearly 6,500 men had deserted, the cavalry was next to useless, and supplies had to be hauled in by wagon because Rebel raiders had wrecked most of the railroad routes. Rosecrans was the man for this task. He was a tireless worker who often kept busy until dawn. Under his leadership, the Army of the Cumberland began to take shape. It included the 21st Michigan (below), a regiment that had already seen combat at Perryville.

public which was trying to digest the bad news from Fredericksburg and Murfreesboro probably could not swallow one more defeat.

Apparently, then, the Northern war machine was stalled, on dead center. It was perfectly possible that the Federals had broken the great Confederate counteroffensive in the fall only to let their hopes of victory die of sheer inanition during the winter. The Army of the Potomac had a new commander—Major General Joseph Hooker, handsome, cocky, a hard drinker and a hard fighter—and Hooker was doing his best to get the army back into shape. By reorganizing his supply and hospital services, shaking up the chain of command, overhauling his cavalry, and instituting a program of constant drills, Hooker was restoring morale, but it would be the middle of the spring before the army could be expected to do anything. (No one except Hooker himself was really prepared to bet that it would then fare any better against Lee than McClellan, Pope, and Burnside had fared.) At Murfreesboro lay the Army of the Cumberland, licking its wounds and recuperating. It had suffered no decline in morale, but it had been cruelly racked at Stones River, and Rosecrans was going to take his time about resuming the offensive.

IT WAS UP TO GRANT, EVEN THOUGH he did seem to be stymied. He had hardly reached the Mississippi before he began to try every possible means to solve the problem which faced him. There seemed to be four possibilities. He would try them all.

Opposite Vicksburg the Mississippi made a hairpin turn. If a canal could be cut across the base of the narrow finger of land that pointed north on the Louisiana side, the Mississippi might pour through it, bypassing the city entirely. Then gunboats, transports, and everything else could float downstream unhindered, and

The panorama was a form of epic painting like the cyclorama, except that its extremely long canvas was coiled on rollers: the story unfolded as the drawing unwound. While the subject matter of William Travis' 528-foot painting covers the history of the Union Army of the Cumberland, the portions shown here are devoted to the Battle of Murfreesboro. Above, Union troops cheer as Rosecrans (at far right) comes forward to view the action. Few soldiers among the rank and file had cared for his predecessor. "However good a military man General Buell may have been . . . he never won the love, and entirely lost the confidence, of the army he commanded," said one soldier. "There was silent rejoicing everywhere when Rosecrans took his place." The panel below shows Federal troops retreating before a Rebel charge during the fight on December 31. A Union captain described some of the battlefield this day: "The whole area in rear between our right and left was a scene of strife and confusion that beggars description. Stragglers from the front, teamsters, couriers, negro servants, hospital attendants, ambulances added to the turmoil. Wounded and riderless horses and cattle wild with fright rushed frantically over the field."

MURFREESBORO

December 31, 1862
January 2, 1863

FIELD OF JANUARY 2ND

BRAGG'S JAN.

STONES RIVER

NASHVILLE & CHATTANOOGA R.R.

ROSECRANS HQ

FIELD OF

PIKE

Murfreesboro

G'S HQ
C. 31

WILKINSON TURNPIKE

WIDOW
SMITH
HOUSE

...EMBER 31ST

GRISCOM
HOUSE

①

MURFREESBORO (or Stones River): At dawn on December 31, the Confederates launch a devastating attack against the Federal right flank that overruns the Union encampments (1) and pushes five Union brigades back some three miles to the Nashville Turnpike. The Rebel tidal wave crashes against Philip H. Sheridan and his men, who hold for a while in the rocky, cedar woods (2) but are eventually forced to retire. Under stubborn Major General Thomas, a new defensive line takes shape (3) alongside Colonel William B. Hazen's artillery, which has held its position throughout the day (4). In a council of war that night at his headquarters (5), Rosecrans, hearing Thomas say, "I know of no better place to die than right here," resolves not to retreat. On the Confederate side, Bragg loses a day, and does not attack until January 2; his effort to turn the Union flank is met by forewarned defenders (6) who receive timely reinforcements (7), enabling them to hold their position. That evening Bragg begins his retreat.

Vicksburg would be a problem no longer. Dredges were brought down, and Sherman's corps was put to work with pick and shovel, and the canal was dug. (In the end it did not work; perversely, the Mississippi refused to enter it in any volume, and Sherman's men had their work for nothing.)

Fifty miles upstream from Vicksburg, on the Louisiana side, a backwater known as Lake Providence lay near the river. It might be possible to cut a channel from river to lake and to deepen the chain of streams that led south from Lake Providence. If that worked, steamers could go all the way down to the Red River, coming back to the Mississippi 150 miles below Vicksburg. Using this route, the army could get east of the river, roundabout but unhindered; it also could draw supplies and substantial reinforcements from New Orleans. So this too was tried; after two months it could be seen that this was not quite going to work, partly because the shallow-draft steamers needed could not be obtained in quantity.

A good 300 miles north of Vicksburg, streams tributary to the Yazoo flowed from a deep-water slough just over the levee from the Mississippi. Cut the levee, send transports and gunboats through, get into the Yazoo, and cruise down to a landing point just above the fortified chain of bluffs; put troops ashore there, take the fortifications in flank—and Vicksburg is taken. Engineer troops cut the levee, gunboats and transports steamed through: and where the Tallahatchie and Yalobusha rivers unite to form the Yazoo, they ran into Confederate Fort Pemberton, which was not particularly strong but was situated in a place that made it practically impregnable. It was surrounded by water, or by half-flooded bottom land, and could be attacked only from the river, and the river just here came up to

the fort in a straight, narrow reach which was fully controlled by the fort's guns. The gunboats moved in to bombard, got the worst of it—and the whole expedition had to go ignominiously back to the Mississippi. The Yazoo venture was out.

A fourth possibility involved a fearfully complicated network of little streams and backwaters which could be entered from the Mississippi near the mouth of the Yazoo. Gunboats and transports might go up this chain for a hundred miles or more and, if their luck was in, safely below Fort Pemberton go on over to the Yazoo, coming down thereafter to the same place which the other expedition had tried to reach. This too was tried, with troops under Sherman and gunboats under the David Porter who had commanded Farragut's mortar boats below New Orleans. This move was a total fiasco. Porter's gunboats got hung up in streams no wider than the boats were, with an infernal tangle of willows growing up ahead to block further progress, and with busy Confederates felling trees in the rear to cut off escape. The whole fleet narrowly escaped destruction. It finally got back to the Mississippi, but it had demonstrated once and for all that this route to Vicksburg was no good.

Four chances, and four failures: and as spring came on Grant sat in the cabin of his headquarters steamer at Milliken's Bend, stared into the wreaths of cigar smoke which surrounded him, and worked out the means by which he would finally be enabled to attack Vicksburg. If he failed, his army would probably be lost, and with it the war; if he succeeded, the North would at last be on the road to victory. Either way, everything was up to him.

General Braxton Bragg's Army of Tennessee, organized into two corps, fought at Stones River. One was led by Lieutenant General William J. Hardee (above left), a West Point graduate and author of a standard work on military tactics. Following Bragg's performance at Perryville, Hardee was one of two senior officers who urged President Jefferson Davis to replace him. The other, Lieutenant General Leonidas Polk (above), commanded the II Corps under Bragg at Stones River; he had forsaken his clerical robes as an Episcopal bishop when the war began. Their combined experience could not save Bragg's army when the January 2 Federal counterattack (left) shattered the last hope for a Confederate victory at Stones River.

CHAPTER 7

The South's Last Opportunity

In the spring of 1863 the Northern grip on the Confederacy was slowly tightening; yet there was still a chance for the South to upset everything, and for a few unendurably tense weeks that chance looked very good. With Rosecrans inactive in Tennessee, and with Grant seemingly bogged down hopelessly in the steaming low country north of Vicksburg, attention shifted to the East, and it appeared that a Southern victory here might restore the bright prospects that had gone so dim in the preceding September. Robert E. Lee set out to provide that victory; winning it, he then made his supreme effort to win the one final, unattainable triumph that would bring the new nation to independence. He never came quite as close to success as men supposed at the time, but he did give the war its most memorable hour of drama.

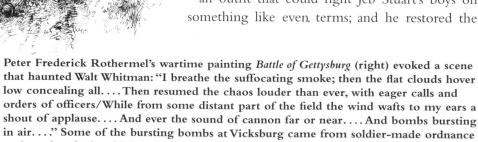

Joe Hooker had done admirably in repairing the Army of the Potomac. He displayed genuine talents as an organizer and an executive, which was something of a surprise, for he was believed to be a dashing heads-down fighter and nothing more. He saw to it that the routine chores of military housekeeping were performed properly, so that the men got enough to eat and lived in decent camps; he turned his cavalry corps into an outfit that could fight Jeb Stuart's boys on something like even terms; and he restored the

Peter Frederick Rothermel's wartime painting *Battle of Gettysburg* (right) evoked a scene that haunted Walt Whitman: "I breathe the suffocating smoke; then the flat clouds hover low concealing all.... Then resumed the chaos louder than ever, with eager calls and orders of officers/While from some distant part of the field the wind wafts to my ears a shout of applause.... And ever the sound of cannon far or near.... And bombs bursting in air...." Some of the bursting bombs at Vicksburg came from soldier-made ordnance such as that depicted in Theodore R. Davis' *Wooden Mortar, Vicksburg* (above).

At the beginning of 1863, the volunteer regiments that had enlisted for three years at the outset were just halfway through their service. Many had already seen hard fighting; the 110th Pennsylvania (above, organized at Harrisburg and Philadelphia in August, 1861) fought against Jackson in the Shenandoah Valley and served under Burnside at Fredericksburg. Ahead lay combat at Chancellorsville, Gettysburg, and Mine Run.

OPPOSITE: This photograph shows a railroad bridge across Bull Run, back in service after having been destroyed by Rebels, thanks to the use of prefabricated segments known as "shad-belly" trusses. It took constant ingenuity to keep the supply routes open.

weary army's confidence in itself. He himself had abundant confidence—too much, Mr. Lincoln suspected, for Hooker's jaunty remark that the question was not whether he could take Richmond, but simply when he would take it, struck the President as a little too optimistic. But when April came, and the spring winds dried the unpaved roads so that the armies could use them, Hooker led his troops off on a new offensive with the highest hopes.

Hooker had a greater advantage in numbers than McClellan had ever had. The manpower shortage was beginning to handicap the Confederacy. Union troops were moving about the Virginia landscape on the south side of the lower James River, apparently with aggressive intent; to hold them in check, and to keep that part of the country open so that its bacon and forage could be used, Lee had had to detach James Longstreet and most of Longstreet's army corps early that spring, and when Hooker began to move, Lee's army in and around Fredericksburg numbered hardly more than 65,000 men of all arms. Hooker had more than twice that many, and he was handling them with strategic insight.

He would not repeat Burnside's mistake, butting head-on against the stout Confederate defenses at Fredericksburg. Instead, he left a third of his army at

In A. J. Russell's photograph (above), Yankees from Major General John Sedgwick's corps remained entrenched along the west bank of the Rappahannock River early in 1863. With the coming of spring dirt roads began to dry, allowing the great armies with their winding wagon trains to go on the move again seeking battle. In the East, Lee's Army of Northern Virginia still confronted the Army of the Potomac (now under Major General Joseph Hooker) at Fredericksburg. As part of a major campaign launched in May, Union troops, like those shown here, managed to cross the Rappahannock briefly to occupy the town.

Fredericksburg to hold Lee's attention, and took the rest on a long swing up the Rappahannock, planning to cross that river and the Rapidan twenty-five miles away, and then march in on Lee's unprotected left and rear. He made the move competently and swiftly, and he sent his cavalry on ahead to make a sweep across Lee's lines of communication near Richmond. He would compel Lee to retreat, his own army would lie on Lee's flank when the retreat began, Lee would have to attack this army on ground of Hooker's choice—and, all in all, this might be the recipe for a resounding Union victory.

It might have worked, except for two things. At the critical moment Hooker seemingly lost his nerve—and Lee refused to act by the script which Hooker had written. What followed was one more dismal Union defeat, and the end of another of those "on to Richmond" drives that never seemed to get anywhere.

The first part of Hooker's plan went very smoothly. Hooker got more than 70,000 men established around Chancellorsville, a crossroads a dozen miles back of Lee's left flank, and his cavalry went swooping down to cut the Richmond, Fredericksburg, and Potomac Railroad farther south. But Lee ignored the cavalry raid and used Stuart's cavalry to control all of the roads around Chancellorsville, so that

In the early months of 1863, the stalemate at Fredericksburg had become so pre-dictable that bored Confederate soldiers willingly posed (above) for a Northern cameraman on the other side of the ruined railroad bridge. Union pickets recovered a small model boat launched from the opposite side of the river. Filled with tobacco to be traded for Yankee coffee, it carried a signature on its side: "Run the blockade off Fredericksburg, Va., . . . sent by . . . 1st Texas Regiment, C.S.A."

A. J. Russell's photograph shows an abandoned Rebel encampment (left): it may have looked more empty than it was. "Pestiferous vermin swarmed in every camp," declared one Confederate soldier, ". . . an indescribable annoyance to every well-raised man yet seemingly uneradicable. Nothing would destroy the little pests but *hours of steady boiling*, and of course, we had neither kettles, nor the time to boil them, if we had been provided with ample means."

With 75,000 Union troops tied down by a much smaller Confederate army near Chancellorsville, Federal forces at Fredericksburg were urgently ordered across the Rappahannock, May 3, 1863. "Everything in the world depends on the rapidity and promptness of your movement," read the orders. "Push everything." The 5th U.S. Artillery, Battery D (above), depicted in a posed shot taken by Timothy O'Sullivan, helped to provide a protective artillery curtain for the crossing. Heavily outnumbered, Confederate troops were driven back off the once-impregnable Mayre's Heights, allowing the Yankees to occupy it. A. J. Russell's picture (right) shows the Stone Wall, abandoned not thirty minutes before the Yankees and the cameraman arrived.

Hooker could not find out where the Confederates were. Worried and somewhat bewildered, Hooker called a halt and put his troops in sketchy field-works near Chancellorsville, instead of pushing on to the more open country half a dozen miles to the east, which was where he had originally planned to take position. Then Lee, in the most daring move of his whole career, split his army into three pieces and gave Joe Hooker an expensive lesson in tactics.

Lee left part of his men at Fredericksburg to make sure that the massed Federals there did not do anything damaging. With 45,000 men he went to Chancellorsville to face Hooker; and after making a quick size-up of the situation he gave Stonewall Jackson 26,000 of these and sent him on a long swing around Hooker's exposed right. Two hours before dusk on May 2 Jackson hit that right flank with pile-driver force, shattering it to pieces, driving a whole Yankee army corps in wild rout, and knocking Hooker's army completely loose from its prepared position. Two or three days of confused and desperate fighting ensued—around Chancellorsville clearing and back at Fredericksburg, where the Federals forced a crossing and then found they could accomplish nothing in particular—and in the end Hooker beat an ignominious retreat, pulling all of his troops north of the Rappahannock. He had lost 17,000 men, he had let an army half the size of his own cut him to pieces, and he had handled his men so poorly that a very substantial part

While the best-known photographers of the Civil War were civilians, Andrew J. Russell was an official army photographer, on special assignment with the Construction Corps of the U.S. Military Railroads. His position allowed him an unusual degree of access to the front. Crossing the Rappahannock with the first Union units, Russell took this powerful image (above) of a Rebel caisson that had been struck a short time earlier by a Federal shell fired from the east bank. Brigadier General Herman Haupt (leaning against the stump) and W. W. Wright (next to him), a military railroad superintendent, posed amid the debris.

On April 30, 1863, General Joe Hooker led nearly 90,000 Union soldiers on a march from Fredericksburg, bringing them around and behind Lee's army entrenched across the Rappahannock River. Two Alfred Waud drawings give different perspectives on this aggregation; the one above concentrates on a small portion of the force on the march, while the one below shows the massed troops waiting for orders on May 1. "No doubt General Hooker intends and expects to do all he advertises," wrote a Maine soldier in his journal. "[However] [t]here are many things the rebels insist on doing, to our disgust, that frequently upset our calculations and plans."

of his immense host had never been put into action at all. Chancellorsville was Lee's most brilliant victory. It had been bought at a heavy cost, however, for Stonewall Jackson was mortally wounded, shot down by his own troops in the confused fighting in the thickets on the night of May 2.

Once more, Lee had taken the initiative away from his Federal opponent. The next move would be his, and after conferences with President Davis and his cabinet in Richmond, that move was prepared: Lee would invade Pennsylvania, trying in the early summer of 1863 the move that had failed in the fall of 1862.

This decision may have been a mistake: a thing which is more easily seen now than at the time it was made. It would be a gamble, at best—a bet that the magnificent Army of Northern Virginia could somehow win, on Northern soil, an offensive victory decisive enough to bring the war to a close. The army was certain

Stoneman's Raid

In a bold move to disrupt the flow of supplies to Robert E. Lee's army, Hooker directed Stoneman's cavalry corps on a wide sweep north, west, and then south of Lee, with orders to wreck the railroads near Richmond. The raid got underway on April 13, but was stymied when heavy rains closed the fords that Stoneman intended to use. Not until April 28 did the waters recede enough for him to proceed. Even then, wrote a Rhode Island cavalryman, Stoneman's "progress was so slow that the Confederate cavalry came up with him, and, though not able to defeat him, yet stopped him and prevented the accomplishment of his plan." Thus, units that might have provided Hooker with invaluable scouting intelligence at Chancellorsville were instead wasted on a soggy ride through the Virginia countryside.

Hooker wanted the Union cavalry to dominate its dashing Rebel counterpart, and so he put Major General George Stoneman (above) in command. Stoneman was a West Point graduate (one of his classmates was Stonewall Jackson) who had commanded a division of infantry during both the Peninsular Campaign and the Battle of Fredericksburg. Under his leadership, Union riders operated for the first time as a single corps; previously the various regiments had been parceled out to serve under infantry control. "[T]he cavalry had greatly improved," declared a Rhode Island trooper, "and wanted but a dashing general to win laurels."

to be outnumbered. The thrust into the Northern heartland was certain to stir the Federals to a new effort. The business would have to be a quick, one-punch affair—a raid, rather than a regular invasion—for Confederate resources just were not adequate to maintain a sustained campaign in Northern territory. If it failed, the Confederacy might lose its army and the war along with it. When he marched for Pennsylvania, Lee would be marching against long odds. He would have Longstreet and Longstreet's soldiers, which he had not had at Chancellorsville, but he would greatly miss Stonewall Jackson.

BUT THE FACT IS THAT NO REALLY good move was available to him. If he stayed in Virginia, holding his ground, the North would inevitably refit the Army of the Potomac and in a month or so would come down with another ponderous offensive. That offensive might indeed be beaten back, but the process would be expensive, and the campaign would further consume the resources of war-racked Virginia. European recognition and intervention—that will-o'-the-wisp which still flickered across the Confederate horizon—could never be won by defensive warfare. A good Confederate victory in Pennsylvania might, just possibly, bring it about.

Perhaps the most successful command partnership of the war was that of Robert E. Lee and Stonewall Jackson (opposite). Their bond was born of mutual respect and complementary skills. Lee was the bold strategizer, Jackson the equally fearless executor of his plans. Although initially out-maneuvered and heavily out-numbered at Chancellorsville, Lee and Jackson nimbly responded with a high-risk operation that in the end led to a decisive victory. Their opponent was Joseph Hooker (above), who, while effective on some levels of command, was a tireless self-promoter and schemer. His grandiose pronouncements led one soldier to describe him as "a veritable Bombastes Furioso."

CHANCELLORSVILLE: On the evening of May 1, Confederate troops hold a ridge line east of Chancellorsville, blocking the Orange Turnpike (upper right). When Lee's cavalry discovers that Hooker's western flank is vulnerable, he sends Jackson on a march (lower right) across the Union front. An aggressive Union corps commander, Daniel Sickles attacks the tail of Jackson's column (1) but does not stray Jackson from his course. While Hooker is distracted by probing attacks launched by Lee from the east (2), Jackson completes his march (lower left) and positions his men across the Orange Turnpike. At 6:00 P.M. he orders an advance that routs the Union corps commanded by O. O. Howard (3 and 4) who is heard crying, "I'm ruined!" A desperate last stand by Union troops near Wilderness Church and Dowdall's Tavern (5) buys valuable time. Troops under Sickles hold firm at Hazel Grove (6) and, aided by Federal batteries massed at Fairview Cemetery (7), stopped the Southern advance. At about 9:30 P.M., returning from a scouting patrol of the Union lines (8), Stonewall Jackson and his staff are mistaken for Yankee cavalry and fired at by nervous pickets. Jackson is fatally wounded.

A total Union disaster was averted on May 2, thanks in part to the hurried defense of the collapsed Federal right flank by Major General Darius N. Couch's II Corps (above). At one point in the fighting, General Couch led his mounted staff and escort into the open to draw enemy fire. "This entire forgetfulness or disregard of self," said one in that party, "characteristic of that pure-minded officer, was not, I fear, appreciated fully by some of his staff, who had not yet arrived at the pitch of magnanimity which would make them desirous of stopping shots intended for others."

Furthermore, the Confederacy was beginning to feel the pressure which Grant was applying in the Vicksburg area. An invasion of the North might very well compel the Federals to pull troops away from the Mississippi Valley; certainly, a Southern victory in Pennsylvania would offset anything that might be lost in the West . . . for it was beginning to be obvious that a great deal was likely to be lost in the West, and fairly soon at that.

For Grant, having tried all of the schemes that could not work, had finally hit upon one that would work, and he was following it with an energy and a daring fully equal to Lee's own.

To get east of the river, where he could force his enemy to give battle, Grant had followed the simplest but riskiest plan of all. He would march his troops downstream on the Louisiana side of the river; he would use gunboats and transports—which first must run the gantlet of the powerful Vicksburg batteries—to get the soldiers over to the eastern shore; and then he could march to the northeast, destroying any field army that might come to face him, cutting Pemberton's lines of communication with the rest of the Confederacy, herding Pemberton's troops back inside of the Vicksburg entrenchments, and then laying siege to the place and capturing army, fortress, and all. Like Lee's move at Chancellorsville, this would be a dazzling trick if it worked. If it did not work, the North would lose much more than it could afford to lose.

"Let us cross over the river . . ."

Suffering from three different wounds, Stonewall Jackson was carried to a field hospital near Wilderness Tavern, where his mangled left arm was amputated. He was then transported eastward over rocky Virginia roads to Guinea Station, located on a direct rail line to Richmond. When his doctor determined that he was too weak to move any further, Jackson was placed in a small outbuilding on property owned by the Chandler family. Although the amputated stump had begun to heal, Jackson contracted pneumonia and it did what bullets had failed to do. On May 10, with his wife at his side, the feverish Jackson mumbled, "Let us cross over the river, and rest under the shade of the trees," and then died. A Richmond newspaper editor asked: "Oh, who can take his place in our armies? Who can fill his place in our hearts?" This sentiment matched the solemn gazes of the women (below) paying their respects at Jackson's grave.

The U.S.S. *Hartford*, and the smaller gunboat *Albatross* lashed to it, dodge a barrage on the Mississippi (below). As great armies battled in Virginia, the Civil War in the West centered on control of the Mississippi River. In March, 1863, Union naval forces, moving steadily upriver, found their way blocked by the Rebel bastion on the high banks at Port Hudson, twenty-five miles north of Baton Rouge. On the night of March 14, a flotilla under Rear Admiral David G. Farragut tried to run past Port Hudson's powerful guns. Only his flagship, the *Hartford*, and the *Albatross*, made it. A jubilant Confederate officer gloated that it was a "beautiful sight to see the enemy's fleet on fire before our eyes."

As the month of May wore along Grant was making it work.

The area which his army would have to traverse on the Louisiana side was swampy, with a tangle of bayous and lakes in the way. The western pioneers in Grant's army were handy with the axe and the spade, and they built roads and bridges with an untaught competence that left the engineer officers talking to themselves. Downstream the army went; and downstream, too, came Admiral Porter's gunboats and enough transports to serve as ferries, after a hair-raising midnight dash past the thundering guns along the Vicksburg waterfront. The navy proved unable to beat down the Confederate defenses at Grand Gulf, twenty-five miles below Vicksburg, but Grant got his troops across a few miles farther down, flanked the Grand Gulf defenses, beat an inadequate force which Pemberton had sent down to check him, and then started out for the Mississippi state capital, Jackson, fifty miles east of Vicksburg. Jackson was a supply base and railroad center; if the Richmond government sent help to Vicksburg, the help would come through Jackson, and Grant's first move was to take that piece off the board before it could be used.

· · ·

GRANT MADE HIS RIVER CROSSING with some 33,000 men. (He had more soldiers in the general area, and would have many more than 33,000 before long, but that was what he had when he started moving across the state of Mississippi.) At this time the Confederates had more troops in the vicinity than Grant had, but they never could make proper use of them; Grant's swift move had bewildered Pemberton much as Lee's had bewildered Hooker. Just before he marched downstream, Grant had ordered a brigade of cavalry to come down from the Tennessee border, riding

Determined to eliminate Port Hudson, Major General Nathaniel P. Banks ordered his columns to surround the Rebel fortress. Frank H. Schell's drawing (left) shows the kind of terrain that made the march an enduring misery for Union soldiers. On the evening of May 26, Banks met with his senior officers to plan an all-out offensive. Major General Christopher C. Augur (below, seated in the rocking chair) was among those who opposed Banks' plan. Nevertheless, Augur obeyed orders and directed the attack in his sector the next day. The heavy assaults launched on May 27 were bloody failures, leading to a siege that soon forced the defenders into near starvation. "Rats," reported one Southerner in Port Hudson, "which are very numerous in our camps, are considered a dainty dish, and are being considerably sought after. . . ." Port Hudson did not surrender until July 9, ending the longest true siege in American military history.

between the parallel north-south lines of the Mississippi Central and the Mobile and Ohio railroads. This brigade was led by Colonel Benjamin H. Grierson, and it was eminently successful; it went slicing the length of the state, cutting railroads, fighting detachments of Confederate cavalry, and reaching Union lines finally at Baton Rouge. For the few days that counted most, it drew Pemberton's attention away from Grant and kept him from figuring out what the Yankees were driving at.

From Port Gibson, a town in the rear of Grand Gulf, Grant moved on Jackson. Joe Johnston was at Jackson. He had recovered from his wounds, and Davis had sent him out to take general command in the West—an assignment which Johnston did not care for, because Pemberton's and Bragg's armies, for which he now had responsibility, were widely separated, and Johnston did not see how he could control both of them at once. He was trying now to assemble enough of a force to stave Grant off and then, with Pemberton, to defeat him outright, but Grant did not give him time enough. On May 14, having driven off a Confederate detachment at the town of Raymond, Grant occupied Jackson, and Johnston, moving north, sent word to Pemberton to come east and join him. (It was clear enough to Johnston that Pemberton would lose both his army and Vicksburg if he were ever driven into his entrenchments and compelled to stand siege.)

Pemberton was in a fix. From Richmond, Davis was ordering him to hold Vicksburg at any cost; Johnston, meanwhile, was telling him to leave the place and save his army; and Pemberton, trying to do a little of both, came quickly to grief. He marched east to find Grant, heeded Johnston's orders too late and tried to swing to the northeast, and on May 16 he was brought to battle on the rolling, wooded plateau known as Champion's Hill, halfway between Vicksburg and Jackson. Grant beat him and drove him back to the west, followed hard and routed his rear guard the next day at the crossing of the Big Black River, and sent him headlong into his Vicksburg lines. Grant's army followed fast, occupying the high

The capture of Vicksburg loomed large in the plans of Major General Ulysses S. Grant (opposite), as commander of the Department of the Tennessee. Vicksburg was vital because it both closed the Mississippi to Union traffic and maintained Confederate access to the Western states of the Trans-Mississippi Department. In a series of operations beginning in November, 1862, Grant groped to find the key that would bring Vicksburg to him. He was already marked by Abraham Lincoln as a rising star, but he was something of a mystery man to the national press. All through 1862, one New York newspaper ran a picture that was supposed to be of U. S. Grant; it turned out to be that of a beef contractor named William Grant.

By the spring of 1863, Confederates had erected a series of formidable batteries at Vicksburg (one is depicted at left) that allowed the South to command the Mississippi River. Jefferson Davis considered the citadel city the "Gibraltar of the West." The man entrusted with its defense was Major General John C. Pemberton (above), a Pennsylvanian by birth who had married into a prominent Norfolk family. When he first arrived at Vicksburg in October, 1862, a local newspaper assured its readers that "No officer ever devoted himself with greater assiduity to his duties."

VICKSBURG CAMPAIGN: Grant's first grab for Vicksburg is a disaster. In December, 1862, at Chickasaw Bluffs (1) William T. Sherman loses 1,800 men and fails to break the Rebel line. Hoping to develop an easy way to move troops past Vicksburg's guns, Grant authorizes work on what becomes known as the Williams Canal (2), only to eventually cancel the digging. Another bypass is attempted via Lake Providence (3), the Tensas River, and the Red River, but this route proves impractical. An effort to flank Vicksburg using the Yazoo River also fails when Union transports attempting to descend it are blocked at Fort Pemberton (4). Yet one more attempt to penetrate the northern approaches to the city through Steele's Bayou (5) is a near catastrophe when Federal gunboats are ensnared in narrow waterways and nearly captured by Confederate land forces. Beginning in April, 1863, Grant takes an entirely new tack. Marching his army south from Milliken's Bend (6), he makes a rendezvous at Hard Times Landing (7) with military transports that have run Vicksburg's gantlet, and uses them to cross to the east bank. He pushes his units forward, meeting and defeating Rebel defenders at Port Gibson (8) and outflanking them at Grand Gulf (9). He then strikes for Jackson to prevent Joseph E. Johnston from reinforcing Pemberton. Grant wins a small fight at Raymond (10) on May 12 and enters Jackson (11) two days later. He throws back Pemberton's best effort to stop him at Champion's Hill (12), forces a crossing of the Big Black River (13), and first attacks Vicksburg (14) on May 19. Pemberton is trapped, and on July 4 surrenders.

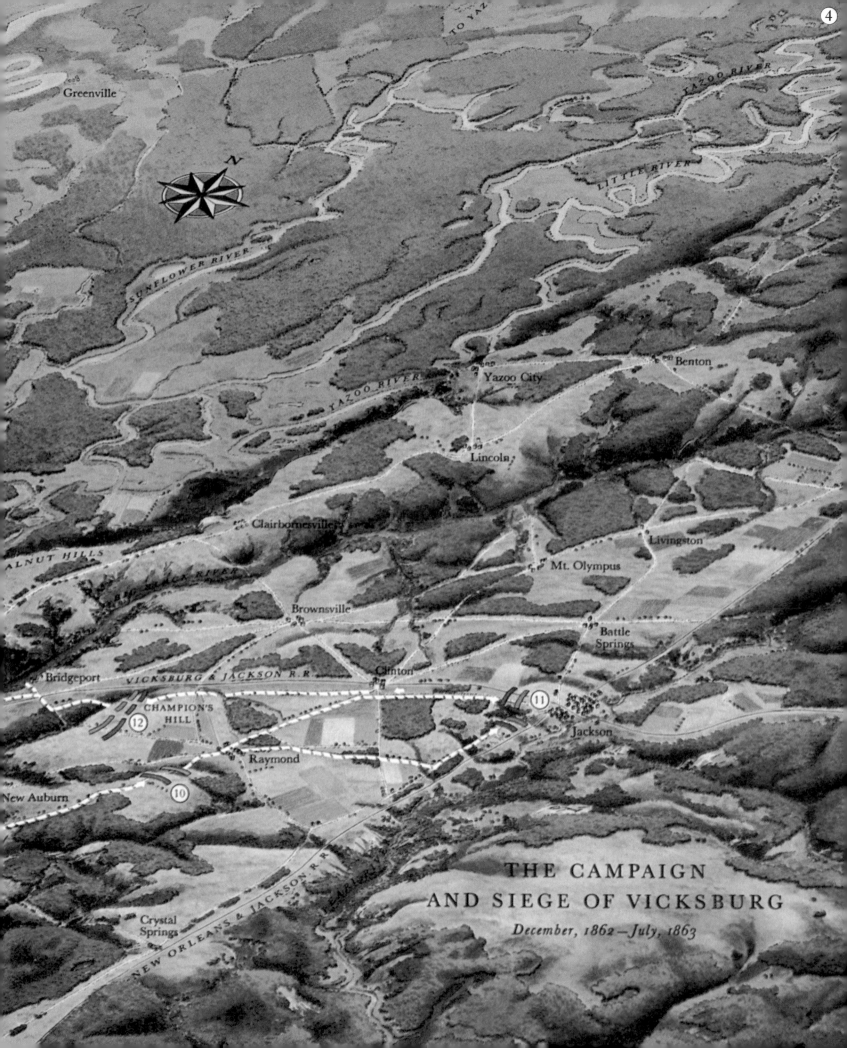

THE CAMPAIGN
AND SIEGE OF VICKSBURG

December, 1862 – July, 1863

The Union's Mississippi River fleet was a mix of specially designed warships and civilian vessels pressed into military use. In addition to the armed steamer *Blackhawk* (at center in Fred B. Schell's drawing), the naval forces operating against Vicksburg included the triple-casemated armored ram *Choctaw* (lower left) and the *Osage* (upper right), the first of a new class of river ironclads modeled after the *Monitor* of Hampton Roads fame.

ground along the Yazoo River—the ground that had been the goal of all the winter's fruitless campaigning—and establishing there a secure base, where steamboats from the North could reach it with all the supplies and reinforcements it might need. On May 19 and again on May 22 Grant made an attempt to take Vicksburg by storm. He was repulsed both times, with heavy loss, so he resorted to siege warfare. He drew lines of trenches and redoubts to face the entire length of the Confederate lines—all in all, Grant's entrenched line was fifteen miles long by the time it was finished—he detached a sufficient force eastward to hold Joe Johnston at bay, and then he settled down grimly to starve the place into submission. Johnston was building up his relieving army, but he never could make it strong enough. He had perhaps 25,000 men, and Pemberton had 30,000, but Grant was reinforced until he had 75,000, and he could handle both Pemberton and Johnston without difficulty. By the first of June, Pemberton was locked up, Johnston was helpless, and it seemed likely that Vicksburg's fall would only be a question of time.

. . .

Although at times he could be quite full of himself, Rear Admiral David Dixon Porter (left) was also full of what one observer called "vim, dash—recklessness perhaps is the word. . . ." His determination to win, whatever the cost, made him the perfect naval complement to the army's U. S. Grant. Porter jumped over eighty senior officers when he was promoted to command the Mississippi squadron. That decision was validated on the night of April 16 when he successfully led his ships past Vicksburg's blazing guns (below left) to link up with Grant's troops further downstream. Grant and his family watched the action from a transport anchored safely upstream. An officer present recalled that "the whole scene was grand and awe-inspiring. One of the Grant children sat on my knees with its arms around my neck, and as each crash [of gunfire] came, it nervously clasped me closer. . . ."

ABOVE: Maintaining supply lines during the advance from Port Gibson to Vicksburg was difficult for Grant, so he permitted his soldiers to forage from the surrounding areas. This painting by Owen J. Hopkins shows some Federals helping themselves during the Vicksburg Campaign. "Let a foraging party go to one [Southern plantation] . . . and they'll find themselves reduced from the pinnacle of affluence to the absolute necessity of studying up the next meal," declared a Union officer, who also noted that he had "seen more silver cups in use by the soldiers here than tin ones."

OPPOSITE: The Union victory at the Big Black River not only turned the railroad stop into a busy supply depot (top) for General Grant, but it marked the beginning of the end of Confederate Vicksburg. "O, how proud we felt as we marched, up to the muzzles of the abandoned guns that had been planted to stay our program," said a Federal soldier of Big Black River. Further west, U.S. cannon were trained on the once-bustling commercial town of Vicksburg (bottom).

James Shirley's house stood in the heart of the north end of the Union earthworks facing Vicksburg. As shown in a picture taken during the siege (above), the gentle hillside around the house was soon honeycombed with "bomb proofs"—individual shelters that protected soldiers from Rebel artillery. The members of the Shirley family were from New England and they were strong supporters of the Union cause. Because their home was within range of Confederate cannon, Grant had them moved to a plantation well in the rear of the battlelines.

SO WHEN LEE PREPARED FOR HIS own campaign, the inexorable pressure of Grant's grip on Vicksburg was an important factor in his plans. It may be that his best move then would have been to stay on the defensive in Virginia and send troops west so that Johnston could beat Grant and raise the siege of Vicksburg, but to argue so is to indulge in the second-guessing that is so simple long after the event. The move would have been very chancy, at best, and there was no guarantee that the Federals in Virginia would permit it. The Army of the Potomac had been disgracefully beaten at Chancellorsville, but it had not been disorganized, and the battle somehow had not left the depression and low morale which had followed Second Bull Run and Fredericksburg. The army would be ready for action very soon, and if it began a new campaign of invasion, Lee would need every man he could get. To send west enough troops to turn the tables on Grant might be to invite a disastrous defeat in Virginia . . . and so, in the end, the idea was dropped, and Lee prepared to head north.

Lee began his move on June 3, shifting his troops northwest from Fredericksburg behind the line of the Rappahannock River, aiming to reach the Shenandoah Valley and cross the Potomac west of the Blue Ridge. His army was divided into

On May 19, flushed from a string of open field victories, Grant ordered a direct assault against Vicksburg's earthwork defenses (shown above in an unknown artist's painting). Pemberton's men, anything but demoralized, met the Federal advances with devastating fire. "The heads of [infantry] columns have been swept away as chaff thrown from the hand on a windy day," said William T. Sherman. The operation turned into a siege, in which tunneling was part of the strategy. Grant's miners drove one shaft under a Rebel strongpoint and packed the head of the passageway with 2,200 pounds of gunpowder. The mine was exploded at 3:30 P.M., June 25 (left). Twenty-six hours of savage fighting followed with the Yankees repulsed at every point.

Civilians Under Fire

In addition to the 30,000 soldiers manning the earthen ramparts, some 2,500 civilian residents still lived in Vicksburg at the time of the siege. "We would be out of danger, so we thought," said one woman present, "for we felt that now, indeed, the whole country was unsafe, and that our only hope of safety lay in Vicksburg." However, as shown in the oil painting *Siege of Vicksburg* (above, artist unknown), the city became a very dangerous place to be once Grant's industrious soldiers tightened their lines. Confederate forces destroyed outlying houses in an effort to deny the enemy cover and to open up fields of fire. Cannon ranged over the whole city, so no one was safe from the terror of a random shell. One civilian survived the same blast that killed a soldier who had ducked into a small shelter directly in the projectile's path. "I was covered with earth," the man recalled, "and it gave me a considerable shock." Vicksburg residents began to burrow into the hillsides near the river and soon a small underground community sprang into existence (opposite). A young boy remembered that the cave his family occupied "was shaped like the prongs of a garden rake, the five excavations from the street or road, all terminating in a long central gallery, so that in case any one of them should collapse

escape could be made through the inner cave and its other branches. The entrance galleries at either end were reserved for servants and cooking purposes, and the intervening galleries and inner central gallery were occupied as family dormitories, separated from each other by such flimsy partition of boards, screens, and hanging as could be devised."

Food shortages, untended family pets, and unchecked vermin added to Vicksburg's misery. "Dogs howled through the streets at night; cats screamed forth their hideous cries; an army of rats, seeking food, would scamper around your very feet, and across the streets and over the pavements," recalled a Confederate sergeant. "Lice and filth covered the bodies of the soldiers. Delicate women and little children, with pale, care-worn, and hunger-pinched features, peered at the passerby with wistful eyes from the caves."

One of Vicksburg's women was standing at the opening of her cave when she learned that the city had surrendered. An old Rebel soldier who was passing stopped and touched his hat. "It's a sad day this, madam," he said, "I little thought we'd come to it, when we first stopped in the intrenchments. I hope you'll yet be happy, madam, after all the trouble you've seen." To which the woman could only answer: "Amen."

Theodore R. Davis' sketch (right) shows U. S. Grant and John C. Pemberton meeting under a flag of truce to discuss Vicksburg's capitulation. "A thousand conjectures and rumors afloat as to the meaning of the flag," noted a Confederate officer. For a while, the discussions only prolonged the stalemate, with Pemberton insisting on concessions and Grant on unconditional surrender. When the two parted, Grant promised to reconsider; that night, he decided to parole the garrison: that is, release them on their word they would not take up arms. Pemberton accepted the offer, with the provision that his men be allowed to march out of Vicksburg in military formation. Grant agreed. The Vicksburg campaign was over.

three corps, now: one led by the redoubtable Longstreet (who took a very dim view, incidentally, of this invasion of Pennsylvania), and the others commanded by two new lieutenant generals, Richard S. Ewell and A. P. Hill. Longstreet's corps led off, pausing at Culpeper Court House while Ewell's corps leapfrogged it and went on to drive scattered Federal detachments out of the lower Valley. Hill stayed in Fredericksburg to watch the Yankees.

The movement was made with skill, and Hooker was given no real opening for an attack on the separated segments of Lee's army. Hooker did propose, once he saw what was going on, that he himself simply march toward Richmond, in the belief that that would force Lee to return quickly enough. But Washington did not approve. Hooker's mishandling of the army at Chancellorsville had aroused the gravest distrust of his abilities; and although the administration could not quite nerve itself to remove him (he enjoyed the powerful backing of Secretary of the Treasury Salmon P. Chase), it apparently was unwilling to let him try a new offensive. Hooker was told to act strictly on the defensive, and to follow Lee wherever Lee might go.

By June 14 Lee had pulled Hill out of Fredericksburg, and the whole army was on the move, with Longstreet holding the gaps in the Blue Ridge, and Ewell, behind him, moving toward the Potomac crossings. Hooker's army was sidling toward the northwest, determined, whatever happened, to keep between Lee and Washington. Between the two armies the rival cavalry sparred and skirmished, each commander trying to get news of the enemy's army and deny to the enemy

Logans Division Entering

Logans Division Entering by The Jackson Road
July 4th '63

Arrival of Grant

May 3 1

Vicksburg July 4th 63
Arrival of genl. Grant at genl Pemberton's
Vicks House

To the accompaniment of bands playing "Yankee Doodle," Major General John A. Logan's division (above) was the first to march into Vicksburg. Grant selected tha division for the honor because it "had approached nearest the Rebel works" during the siege. Grant soon followed Logan's men (left) and was amazed at the instant reconciliation between the opposing rank and file. "The men of the two armies fraternized as if they had been fighting for the same cause," he reflected. "Really, I believe there was a feeling of sadness just then in the breasts of most of the Union soldiers at seeing the dejection of their late antagonists."

Francis Millet's 1904 painting, *Fourth Minnesota Regiment Entering Vicksburg* (right), shows the tall columns and layered cupola of the town's courthouse in the background. Shortly after they occupied Vicksburg, Federal troops celebrated by displaying the Stars and Stripes from that cupola, an incident sketched (above) by an artist-correspondent on the scene. Grant later wrote: "The capture of Vicksburg, with its garrison, ordnance and ordnance stores, and the successful battles fought in reaching them, gave new spirit to the loyal people of the North. New hopes for the final success of the cause of the Union were inspired."

A crisis in the West at Vicksburg, a glorious victory in the East at Chancellorsville: when Robert E. Lee (right) pondered these matters, he saw a solution to the South's dilemma. Instead of reinforcing Western armies from those in the East, Lee argued for a vigorous counteroffensive that would take the war into the Northern states. He did so with the confidence that his soldiers were capable of great things. "There never were such men in an army before," he declared. "They will go anywhere and do anything if properly led." Increasingly, in the weeks following Chancellorsville, Lee's gaze turned north toward the fertile fields and rich towns of Pennsylvania.

news of his own. Out of all of this sparring came a moment of inspiration to Jeb Stuart. He acted on it, and thereby helped Lee lose the campaign.

As Lee's army crossed the Potomac and wheeled eastward, Stuart and his cavalry were to move on its right flank and front, keeping Lee informed about the Union army's movements. It occurred to Stuart that he could best get his horsemen across the Potomac by riding all the way around Hooker's army—a feat which would bring Stuart much acclaim—and so Stuart, with Lee's permission, undertook to do it that way. But the Federal army occupied more ground and was much more active than Stuart had supposed, and Stuart, driven far to the east, was completely out of touch with Lee for ten days. Lacking Stuart, Lee during those ten days was completely out of touch with Hooker. Invading the enemy's country, Lee was in effect moving blindfolded.

THE ENEMY
IS APPROACHING!

I MUST RELY UPON THE PEOPLE FOR THE

DEFENCE of the STATE!

AND HAVE Called THE MILITIA for that PURPOSE!

A. G. CURTIN, Governor of Pennsylvania.

THE TERM OF SERVICE WILL ONLY BE WHILE THE DANGER OF THE STATE IS IMMINENT.

Warnings of a coming military storm began to appear throughout Pennsylvania (left), as emergency militia, like the minutemen of old, formed units. They were instigated by the specter of a Confederate army riding on momentum. In early June, the first of Lee's men began to march quietly away from Fredericksburg on a route that would take them through the Blue Ridge Mountains into the Shenandoah Valley. "The morale of the army was superb," remembered a young Virginia soldier, "officers and men alike inspired with confidence in the ability of the army to beat its old antagonist anywhere he chose to meet us. . . . We [were] . . . marching unobstructed . . . through an enemy's country, whose people had scarcely known that war was in progress. . . ." The 26th Pennsylvania Militia included a company raised in the prosperous town of Gettysburg (below).

As Lee progressed, ripples of wild alarm spread as far east as Baltimore, Maryland (right), where many black residents were forcibly pressed into work gangs digging earthworks. Amid the panic, rumors lent larger-than-life status to the Rebel cavalry campaigning under the flamboyant Major General J. E. B. Stuart (opposite page). In the first phase of Lee's grand invasion, Stuart's troopers kept busy blocking gaps in the Blue Ridge Mountains to prevent Union cavalry from scouting the Confederate movement. Mounted soldiers battled at Aldie, Middleburg, and Upperville (below). A soldier who took part in the latter fight remembered it as "one of the liveliest and most exciting times we have ever yet experienced. . . ."

OPPOSITE: Union pursuit of Lee was slow to develop. Major General Joseph Hooker wanted to strike for Richmond once he was sure that the Confederates had left his front at Fredericksburg. After the strong admonition from President Lincoln that Lee's army, and not the Rebel capital, was Hooker's "sure objective point," Federal columns started north. David Gilmour Blythe's painting (top) shows Federals belonging to the army's I Corps crossing the Potomac. On June 25, in a move still considered controversial, J. E. B. Stuart diverted most of Lee's cavalry on an independent raid, far to the east of the main force of the Confederate army and out of touch with it. On July 1, Stuart struck at the Pennsylvania town of Carlisle, stoutly defended by two militia brigades. After angrily shelling the place (as shown in Charles B. Cox's painting *Carlisle, Pa., July 7, 1863,* bottom), he belatedly learned that Lee's army was battling at Gettysburg.

ABOVE: The closer the two armies drew to a full battle, the more Lincoln became convinced that Joseph Hooker was the wrong man to have in command. Early on the morning of June 28, a staff officer informed Major General George Gordon Meade (shown in a painting by Daniel Ridgway Knight), then directing Hooker's V Corps, that he was to take charge. To assume control of a grand army on the eve of a desperate battle was a daunting task for the Pennsylvania native, whose career had been solid if unspectacular. According to one source, Meade's first comment upon being informed of his promotion was, "Well, I've been tried and convicted without a hearing. I suppose I shall have to go to execution."

Lieutenant General Richard S. Ewell (above) was considered by many to possess qualities of leadership similar to those of Stonewall Jackson. A nervous, fidgety man, Ewell was found by one observer to bear a "striking resemblance to a woodcock." His troops would play a critical role in the smashing Confederate victory in the first day's fighting at Gettysburg, July 1, though afterward some suggested that Ewell did not follow through as Jackson would have. A famous scene in the bitter combat of July 1 is depicted below in an unknown artist's painting: *Attack at Seminary Ridge, Gettysburg.*

Lee got his army into Pennsylvania, its three corps widely separated—the advance of the army, as June neared its end, was at York, and the rear was at Chambersburg—and he believed that this dispersion was proper, since, as far as he knew, Hooker had not yet come north of the Potomac. (Stuart surely would have notified Lee if the Federals had moved.) But the Army of the Potomac had actually crossed the river on June 25 and 26, and on June 28 Lee learned that the whole Yankee army was concentrated around Frederick, Maryland, squarely on his flank. He also learned that it was Hooker's army no longer. Hooker had at last been relieved, and the command had gone to the short-tempered, grizzled, and competent Major General George Gordon Meade.

Lee hastened to concentrate, and the handiest place was the town of Gettysburg. Moving north to bring him to battle, Meade collided with him there, and on July 1, 2, and 3 there was fought the greatest single battle of the war—Gettysburg, a terrible and spectacular drama which, properly or not, is usually looked upon as the great moment of decision.

In the fighting on July 1 the Federals were badly outnumbered, only a fraction of their army being present, and they were soundly beaten. On the next two days Lee attacked, striking at both flanks and at the center in an all-out effort to crush the Army of the Potomac once and for all. Nothing quite worked. The climactic moment came in the afternoon of July 3, when 15,000 men led by a division under Major General George Pickett made a gallant but doomed assault on the central Federal position on Cemetery Ridge. The assault almost succeeded, but "almost" was not good enough. Broken apart and staggered by enormous losses, the assaulting column fell back to the Confederate lines, and the Battle of

The great battle was inevitable, but that it took place at Gettysburg was largely due to the determination of two lesser-known men. Brigadier General John Buford (above, sitting, with his staff) commanded a division in the Army of the Potomac's cavalry corps. Operating within a liberal interpretation of his orders, Buford opted to contest the Rebel occupation of Gettysburg on July 1. He was fully backed in his decision by Major General John F. Reynolds, a Pennsylvanian, who led his I Corps forward to support Buford's defiant stand. Reynolds paid with his life for his decision; he was shot and killed early in the battle (left).

The End of the Line

On the afternoon of July 2, Colonel Joshua Lawrence Chamberlain (above) and the 20th Maine Volunteer Infantry (360 strong) were placed on the lower slope of a hill called Little Round Top, with orders to hold their position at all costs. The 20th Maine had been formed in the summer of 1862 with the leftovers of other units, previously mustered. Its numbers included fishermen from the coast, farmers from the south-central and western parts of the state, and woodsmen from big-timber country. They marched to Gettysburg under the command of Chamberlain, a language teacher from Bowdoin College who had enlisted after telling the deans he was going on a leave of absence. At Gettysburg, positioned on Little Round Top, the 20th Maine was the end of the line, the last unit in the whole Federal formation. Beginning around 5:00 P.M. Chamberlain and his regiment were furiously assaulted by two Alabama regiments, perhaps 644 men, nearly twice their number. The combat was desperate at times, with the Rebels heavily pressing Chamberlain's left flank, forcing him to bend back or "refuse" it. After several hours, with his ammunition nearly exhausted, Chamberlain ordered a bayonet charge that cleared the hill of the enemy. "Ours was an important position," declared a Maine man, "and had we been driven from it, the tide of battle would have been turned against us."

On July 2, Lee attacked both Federal flanks. Moving against Meade's left, Lieutenant General James Longstreet's corps first struck the Federal III Corps, which was commanded by a politician-turned-general named Daniel E. Sickles (above). Without orders to do so, Sickles had moved his men forward to higher ground in his front; the resulting combat destroyed the III Corps and cost Sickles his right leg. The Confederate attack against Meade's right flank, made by Ewell's corps, was slow to develop and did not begin until Longstreet's attack was virtually ended. Facing a line of Union cannon atop Cemetery Hill (top left), Louisiana and North Carolina troops made a determined charge that briefly captured some of the Yankee guns (bottom left). Colonel Isaac E. Avery, who commanded one of the North Carolina brigades in the attack, was mortally wounded in the action; he had time only to scribble a last message for his family: "Tell my father I died with my face to the enemy."

Gettysburg was over. The Federals had lost 23,000 men, and the Confederates at least that many—which meant that Lee had lost nearly a third of his whole army. He could do nothing now but retreat. Meade followed, but his own army was too mangled, and Meade was too cautious to try to force another battle on Lee north of the Potomac. Lee got his army back into Virginia, and the campaign was over.

Stuart's absence had been expensive. (He finally reached Lee on the evening of the second day of the battle.) Lee had been forced to fight before he was ready for it, and when the fighting began he had not felt free to maneuver because, with Stuart away, he could never be sure where the Yankees were. At the close of the first day's fighting Longstreet had urged Lee to move around the Federal left flank and assume a position somewhere in the Federal rear that would force Meade to do the attacking, but with the knowledge he then had

GETTYSBURG (July 2): At about 3:00 P.M., Sickles moves the Union army's III Corps forward from an area between the Weikert House and Little Round Top to occupy Devil's Den and the Peach Orchard along the Emmitsburg Road. At the same time, Longstreet's Confederates are completing a roundabout flank march from Gettysburg (upper left) to a spot near the Rose Farm (lower left). His artillery opens at 4:00 P.M., followed by an infantry attack that seizes Devil's Den (1) and pushes toward Little Round Top. Desperate fighting, including a valiant stand by the 20th Maine, saves the position for the Union (2). Longstreet's attack, by design, moves northward to smash Sickles' salient (3), embracing the Peach Orchard and the Wheat Field. Sickles loses his leg to a cannon ball near the Trostle Farm. The Federals hastily patch together a defensive line, which is savagely assailed (4 and 5), but not breached. Longstreet presses the Federal center (6), where his men are stopped by stiff resistance, including a suicidal counterattack by the 1st Minnesota. Late off the mark, Ewell attacks Culp's Hill at dark (7), managing only to secure some abandoned trenches. Two Rebel brigades overrun some Federal batteries on Cemetery Hill (8), but are driven off by sharp counterattacks.

In Thure de Thulstrup's painting *Hancock at Gettysburg* (above), the mounted and pointing Union II Corps commander directs the defense of Cemetery Ridge in the face of the Pickett–Pettigrew charge. Major General Winfield S. Hancock was both a seasoned military veteran and a charismatic leader. During the heavy artillery bombardment that preceded Lee's attack, Hancock rode calmly along his lines, ignoring the cannon balls that hissed through the air around him. When a subordinate ventured the opinion that a corps commander should not risk his life that way, Hancock replied, "There are times when a corps commander's life does not count." Another officer present on Cemetery Ridge, after observing this inspiring performance, declared, "I had never seen him when he looked every inch the magnificent, ideal soldier so truly as on this occasion." Hancock, who exposed himself to enemy fire throughout the action, was wounded near the end of the fighting by a Rebel bullet in his groin. Nevertheless, as he proudly informed General Meade afterward, he "did not leave the field till the victory was entirely secured and the enemy no longer in sight."

An Immortal Charge

Still believing that a decisive victory was possible, General Lee ordered a massed assault for July 3 on the Union center. Major General George E. Pickett (right), a thirty-eight-year-old Virginian, commanded the division that led the attack. Although the entire action is popularly known as "Pickett's Charge," Pickett commanded just one of the three divisions involved. Longstreet was in overall command of the assault which included divisions led by Brigadier General James Johnston Pettigrew and Major General Isaac R. Trimble. Approximately 12,500 strong, they faced nearly a mile of open ground, forcing them to pass through both long- and short-range fire. The sketch below shows the effects of the Union cannon firing from as far away as Little Round Top. "We could not help hitting them at every shot," said a Federal artillerist. Afterward, a Confederate report acknowledged that Yankee guns enfiladed entire ranks, "with fearful effect, sometimes as many as ten men being killed and wounded by the bursting of a single shell."

In 1884, the French artist Paul Philippoteaux created a 400-foot cyclorama painting of the battle of Gettysburg, focusing on Pickett's Charge. Philippoteaux undertook an impressive amount of primary research before beginning his work. In addition to interviewing battle survivors, he and his assistants visited the actual site, where they made a series of photographs from the point of view they had selected. This portion of the resulting canvas shows Major Winfield S. Hancock (upper right side of painting, riding a black horse), urging forward a portion of the 7th Michigan (center of the picture) that has scrambled up from a section of the Union line slightly south of where the Confederates have broken through. The colonel commanding the 7th Michigan was killed in the action depicted. According to his successor, "The field was soon won and the enemy fleeing in great disorder."

Cycloramas were painted by teams of painters who had different specialties; some did animals, others landscapes, while still others created the hundreds of individuals featured. From interviews with survivors and published recollections of the battle, the cyclorama team filled the canvas with authentic vignettes that added human detail to the epic sweep of the painting. In the center of this panel from the Philippoteaux Gettysburg cyclorama, a Union caisson disintegrates in a fiery explosion. In the foreground, Union infantrymen use their bayonets to hurry Confederate prisoners to the rear, while a few of their comrades jubilantly flout the red and white colors they have captured.

The first photographers reached Gettysburg just two days after the battle ended. Timothy O'Sullivan's picture (opposite page top) shows Confederate dead scattered across the lower slope of Big Round Top, an area known for a time as the "Slaughter Pen" because of the bitter fighting there. More Rebel casualties were photographed by Alexander Gardner (opposite page bottom right). Perhaps the best-known of all Gettysburg images shows a dead Confederate sniper in Devil's Den (opposite page bottom left). However, evidence suggests that O'Sullivan composed the scene, using a "prop" rifle he carried along and a body he had just photographed. No faking was needed when O'Sullivan set up in front of the Trostle House to show the numerous dead artillery horses there (above), or at the nearby Rose Farm, south of the Peach Orchard, where Confederate bodies awaited burial (left).

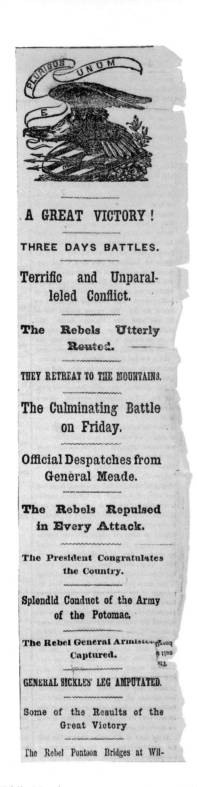
Lee could not be sure that such a move would not take him straight to destruction. He had felt compelled to fight where he was, and when the fighting came he desperately missed Stonewall Jackson: Ewell, leading Jackson's old troops, proved irresolute and let opportunities slip, while Longstreet was sulky and moved with less than his usual speed. All in all, Lee was poorly served by his lieutenants in the greatest battle of his career.

BUT IF GETTYSBURG WAS WHAT TOOK the eye, Vicksburg was probably more important; and the climax came at Vicksburg, by odd chance, at almost exactly the same time that it came at Gettysburg. Grant's lines had grown tighter and tighter, and Pemberton's army was strained to the breaking point; and on July 3, just about the time when Pickett's men were forming for their hopeless charge, Pemberton sent a white flag through the lines and asked for terms. Grant followed the old "unconditional surrender" line, but receded from it quickly enough when Pemberton refused to go for it; and on July 4 Pemberton surrendered the city and the army, on terms which permitted his men to give their paroles and go to their homes. Halleck, back in Washington, complained that Grant should have insisted on sending the whole army north as prisoners of war, but Grant believed that this was not really necessary. The 30,000 soldiers whom Pemberton had surrendered were effectively out of the war. Vicksburg itself was taken, within a week the Confederates would surrender the downstream fortress at Port Hudson—and, as Lincoln put it, the Father of Waters would roll unvexed to the sea.

Gettysburg ruined a Confederate offensive and demonstrated that the great triumph on Northern soil which the South had to win if it was to gain recognition abroad could not be won. But Vicksburg broke the Confederacy into halves, gave the Mississippi Valley to the Union, and inflicted a wound that would ultimately prove mortal. Losing at Gettysburg, the Confederates had lost more than they could well afford to lose; at Vicksburg, they lost what they could not afford at all.

While Northern newspapers trumpeted the Union success at Gettysburg (above), Abraham Lincoln was still less than satisfied with George Meade's cautious pursuit (at right in an Edwin Forbes painting) of Lee's defeated army. Lincoln wanted nothing less than the complete destruction of the Rebel fighting force. Informed by Meade that he intended to "drive from our soil every vestige of the presence of the invader," Lincoln reacted with anger. "Drive the invader from our soil!" he exclaimed. "My God! Is that all?"

The image above, probably taken on July 15 by photographers working for Mathew Brady, shows a trio of Confederate soldiers standing on Seminary Ridge.

Since most of the Rebels captured during the actual fighting had been shipped off to prison camps soon afterward, these men were probably taken from one of Lee's retreating columns, possibly as

stragglers. In the fighting and pursuit that followed, Meade's army scooped up more than 12,000 prisoners, better than half of them walking wounded.

On November 19, 1863, dignitaries joined citizens from around the country for the dedication of the National Cemetery in Gettysburg. The dramatic importance of the battle and the large number of Union soldiers who died there made this occasion an event of national interest. Following a ceremonial parade (above), hundreds of spectators gathered at the seventeen-acre cemetery site (right) to hear a speech by the noted orator Edward Everett, followed by a "few appropriate remarks" delivered by President Lincoln.

Four score and seven years ago our fathers brought forth, upon this continent, a new nation, conceived in Liberty, and dedicated to the proposition that all men are created equal.

Now we are engaged in a great civil war, testing whether that nation, or any nation, so conceived, and so dedicated, can long endure. We are met here on a great battle-field of that war. We have come to dedicate a portion of it, as a final resting place for those who here gave their lives that that nation might live. It is altogether fitting and proper that we should do this.

But in a larger sense we can not dedicate—we can not consecrate—we can not hallow this ground. The brave men, living and dead, who struggled here, have consecrated it, far above our poor power to add or detract. The world will little note, nor long remember, what we say here, but can never forget what they did here. It is for us, the living, rather to be dedicated here to the unfinished work which they have, thus far, so nobly carried on. It is rather

for us to be here dedicated to the great task remaining before us—that from these honored dead we take increased devotion to that cause for which they here gave the last full measure of devotion—that we here highly resolve that these dead shall not have died in vain; that this nation shall have a new birth of freedom; and that this government of the people, by the people, for the people, shall not perish from the earth.

In the custom of the day, Everett spoke for a long time, at least two hours. Next, the "music ran on a bit," wrote a reporter on the scene, "and then the President arose." Lincoln held in his hand the text of a short speech (above) which he had carefully crafted over several weeks. No printed version was distributed, so the newspapermen had to rely on their own notes to report its content, resulting in a number of discrepancies, including "The world will little know and nothing remember what we see here. . . ." For those present, Lincoln's words had a powerful effect. When he proclaimed that "The world will little note nor long remember what we say here, but it can never forget what they did here," a wounded Union officer in the crowd broke down in tears and buried his face in his handkerchief.

CHAPTER 8

Men at Arms

The statesmen and the diplomats did their best to control and direct the war, but the real load was carried from first to last by the ordinary soldier. Poorly trained and cared for, often very poorly led, he was unmilitary but exceedingly warlike. A citizen in arms, incurably individualistic even under the rod of discipline, combining frontier irreverence with the devout piety of an unsophisticated society, he was an arrant sentimentalist with an inner core as tough as the heart of a hickory stump. He had to learn the business of war as he went along because there was hardly anyone on hand qualified to teach him, and he had to pay for the education of his generals, some of whom were all but total-ly ineducable. In many ways he was just like the G.I. Joe of modern days, but he lived in a simpler era, and when he went off to war he had more illusions to lose. He lost them with all proper speed, and when the fainthearts and weaklings had been winnowed out, he became one of the stoutest fighting men the world has ever seen. In his own person he finally embodied what the war was all about.

The first thing to remember about him is that, at least in the beginning, he went off to war because he wanted to go. In the spring of 1861 hardly any Americans in either section had any understanding of what war really was like. The Revolution was a legend, and the War of 1812 had been no more than an episode, and the war with Mexico had never

The soldiers of the Civil War faced the ultimate test of courage and manhood in battle, but they spent most of their time in camp or on the march, accompanied by the sounds of the fife, drum, and bugle (above). A Massachusetts chaplain would declare that the music played by these instruments "scatters the dismal part of camp life; gives new spirit to the men jaded by or on a march; wakes up their enthusiasm."

Conrad Wise Chapman's painting *Camp, 59th Virginia Infantry at Diascund Bridge* (above), shows the orderly way of life of a soldier society. "A favorite arrangement for two men consisted of a bed of clean straw between the halves of a large oak log, covered, in the event of rain, with a rubber blanket," remembered a Virginia veteran. "The more ambitious builders made straw pens, several logs high, and pitched over these a fly tent, adding sometimes a chimney."

Millions of men donned Union uniforms in the Civil War; two of them are pictured above. "Speaking for myself, I had *no* inclination for the business," said one such citizen-soldier, "but once committed in a momentary spasm of enthusiasm to serve under certain circumstances, which I never expected to occur, I found myself face to face with the alternative of going, or showing a white liver by backing out. I decided to do as I had agreed and enlisted for 'three years, unless sooner discharged.' Shot or starved should have been added to the contract."

At right, a forage cap as worn by the 119th Pennsylvania.

gone to the heart. Right after Fort Sumter war looked like a great adventure, and the waving flags and the brass bands and the chest-thumping orators put a gloss of romance over everything; thousands upon thousands of young Northerners and Southerners hastened to enlist, feeling that they were very lucky to have the chance. Neither government was able to use all of the men who crowded the recruiting stations in those first glittering weeks, and boys who were rejected went back home with bitter complaints. Men who went off to camp were consumed with a fear that the war might actually be over before they got into action—an emotion which, a year later, they recalled with wry grins.

In the early part of the war the camps which received these recruits were strikingly unlike the grimly efficient training camps of the twentieth century. There were militia regiments which hired civilian cooks and raised mess funds to buy better foods than the government provided. In the South a young aristocrat would as likely as not enlist as a private and enter the army with a body servant and a full trunk of spare clothing; and in the North there were volunteer regiments which were organized somewhat like private clubs—a recruit could

be admitted only if the men who were already in voted to accept him. In both sections the early regiments were loaded down with baggage, as well as with many strange notions. These sons of a rawboned democracy considered it degrading to give immediate and unquestioning obedience to orders, and they had a way of wanting to debate things, or at least to have them explained, before they acted. In the South a hot-blooded young private might challenge a company officer to a duel if he felt that such a course was called for, and if the Northern regiments saw no duels, they at least saw plenty of fist fights between officers and men. The whole concept of taut, impersonal discipline was foreign to the recruits of 1861, and many of them never did get the idea.

The free and easy ways of the first few months were substantially toned down, of course, as time went on, and in both armies it presently dawned on the effervescent young volunteer that his commanders quite literally possessed the power of life and death over him. Yet the Civil War armies never acquired the automatic habit of immediate, unquestioning obedience which is drilled into modern soldiers. There was always a quaint touch of informality to those regiments; the men did what they were told to do, they saluted and said "Sir" and adjusted themselves to the army's eternal routine, but they kept a loose-jointed quality right down to the end, and they never got or wanted to get the snap and

Many young men of the South (above) were eager to enter the fray against their Northern counterparts. A Virginia college student who answered the call to arms remembered: "Recitation-bells no longer sounded; our books were left to gather dust, and forgotten, save only to recall those scenes that filled our minds with the mighty deeds and prowess of such characters as the 'Ruling Agamemnon' and his warlike cohorts, and we could almost hear 'the terrible clang of striking spears against shields, as it resounded throughout the army.'"

Colonel Elmer E. Ellsworth established a fad (below) at the beginning of the war for uniforms patterned after the colorful garb of Zouaves, French-North African soldiers. Units formed both in the North and in the South followed the fashion, at least at first. "The full dress. . . ," declared a Southern Zouave, "made a very brilliant effect on street parade but was totally unsuitable for any active service."

OPPOSITE: Louisiana's Washington Artillery (top left) came into existence in 1838 and was still in combat up to World War II. Its crest showed a tiger's head superimposed on crossed cannon above the motto: "Try us." An unidentified Union soldier models the uniforms of a cavalry corporal (top), an ordnance sergeant (middle), and an infantry private (bottom).

precision which European soldiers considered essential. The Prussian General von Moltke remarked in the 1870's that he saw no point in studying the American Civil War, because it had been fought by armed mobs, and in a way—but only in a way—he was quite right. These American armies simply did not follow the European military tradition.

One reason why discipline was imperfect was the fact that company and regimental officers were mostly either elected by the soldiers or appointed by the state governor for reasons of politics: they either were, or wanted to be, personally liked by the men they commanded, and an officer with political ambitions could see a postwar constituent in everybody in the ranks. Such men were not likely to bear down very hard, and if they did the privates were not likely to take it very well. On top of this, neither North nor South had anything resembling the officer-candidate schools of the present day. Most officers had to learn their jobs while they were performing them, and there is something pathetic in the way in which these neophytes in shoulder straps bought military textbooks and sat up nights to study them. They might be unqualified for military command, but as a

ELLSWORTH'S CAMPAIGN & BARRACK OR DRESS UNIFORMS.
PLATE I.

general thing they were painfully conscientious, and they did their best. A regiment which happened to have a West Pointer for a colonel, or was assigned to a brigade commanded by a West Pointer, was in luck; such an officer was likely to devote a good deal of time to the instruction of his subordinates.

THERE IS ONE THING TO REMEMBER about Civil War discipline. In camp it was imperfect, and on the march it was seldom tight enough to prevent a good deal of straggling, but in battle it was often very good. (The discipline that will take soldiers through an Antietam, for instance, has much to be said for it, even though it is not recognizable to a Prussian martinet.) The one thing which both Northern and Southern privates demanded from their officers was the leadership and the physical courage that will stand up under fire, and the officers who proved lacking in either quality did not last very long.

The training which a Civil War soldier got included, of course, the age-old fundamentals—how to stand at attention, how to pick up and shoulder a musket, how to do a right face, and so on—but beyond this it was designed largely to teach him how to get from a formation in which he could march into a formation in which he could fight. A division moving along a country road would go, generally, in column of fours; moving thus, it would be a spraddled-out organism eight feet wide and a mile long. When it reached the battlefield, this organism had to change its shape completely, transforming length into width, becoming, on occasion, six feet long and a mile wide. It might form a series of lines, each line one or more regiments in width; it might temporarily throw its regiments into boxlike shapes, two companies marching abreast, while it moved from road to fighting field; if the ground was rough and badly wooded, the ten companies of a regiment might go forward in ten parallel columns, each column two men wide and forty or fifty men deep; and the fighting line into which any of these formations finally brought itself might lie at any conceivable angle to the original line

Charles W. Reed entered the war by sketching a picture of Boston's recruiting office (above right), where thoughtful citizens discussed matters of the day, while prospective candidates considered the advantages of serving with the artillery. During his enlistment as a gunner with the 9th Massachusetts Battery, he kept sketching, filling a notebook with scenes of the service. Young warriors became familiar with all the amenities of camp life, including the services of a military dentist (below right). One day Reed's unit enjoyed a visit from the Commander in Chief himself (below). The comical caption reads: "Good God, you [are] goin' to shake [hands] with ol' 'Uncle Abe.'"

of march, with underbrush and gullies and fences and swamps to interfere with its formation. Once put into action, the fighting line might have to shift to the right or left, to swing on a pivot like an immense gate, to advance or to retreat, to toss a swarm of skirmishers out in its front or on either flank—to do, in short, any one or all of a dozen different things, doing them usually under fire, and with an infernal racket making it almost impossible to hear the words of command.

A regiment which could not do these things could not fight efficiently, as the First Battle of Bull Run had abundantly proved. To do them, the men had to master a whole series of movements as intricate as the movements of a ballet; had to master them so that doing them became second nature, because they might have to be done in the dark or in a wilderness and almost certainly would have to be done under great difficulties of one sort or another. As a result an immense amount of drill was called for, and few generals ever considered that their men had had enough.

Oddly enough, the average regiment did not get a great deal of target practice. The old theory was that the ordinary American was a backwoodsman to whom the use of a rifle was second nature, but that had never really been true, and by 1861 it was very full of holes. (Here the Confederacy tended to have an advantage. A higher proportion of its men had lived under frontier conditions

When winter came, the armies of both sides settled into more permanent camps; log huts were home for both Johnny Reb (left) and Billy Yank (below). During one especially severe cold spell a Union soldier observed, "The boys, if they had to venture into the open air, invariably clapped their hands to their noses, and whatever it was necessary for them to do, they did as quickly as possible. Dilatory traveling was unknown, almost every one by mutual consent adopting the double quick." Every camp had its pranksters, such as these who thought it was fun to tip over chimneys (above, sketched by Charles Reed).

Some Southern military units spent their service close to home. South Carolina's Palmetto Battalion Light Artillery (above, photographed in 1861) played an active role in the defense of Charleston Harbor throughout the war.

PREVIOUS SPREAD: The neat ranks of the 96th Pennsylvania reflect many hours engaged in what one soldier called "the mysteries of battalion drill. . . . Now it was 'Left foot, right foot,' which the giddy novices soon termed 'Hay foot, straw foot'; then 'Now step off with your left foot, all together,' until the recruits were sick of the whole business, and protested that they did not come to tramp, but to fight."

and really did know something about firearms before they entered the army.) In some cases—notably at Shiloh—green troops were actually sent into action without ever having been shown how to load their muskets; and although this was an exceptional case, very few regiments ever spent much time on a rifle range. As late as the summer of 1863 General George Gordon Meade, commanding the Army of the Potomac, felt compelled to call regimental officers' attention to the fact that the army contained many soldiers who apparently had never fired their weapons in action. On the field at Gettysburg his ordnance officers had collected thousands of muskets loaded with two, three, or even ten charges; in the excitement of the fight many men had feverishly loaded and reloaded without discharging the pieces.

This musket was one great source of woe for the Civil War soldier. It looked like the old weapon of infantry tradition, but in actual fact it was a new piece, and it compelled a radical change in infantry tactics. The change was made late and slowly, and thousands of lives were lost as a result.

Infantry tactics at that time were based on the use of the smoothbore musket, a weapon of limited range and accuracy. Firing lines that were much more than a hundred yards apart could not inflict very much damage on each other, and so troops which were to make an attack would be massed together, elbow to elbow, and would make a run for it; if there were enough of them, and they ran fast enough, the defensive line could not hurt them seriously, and when they got to close quarters the advantage of numbers and the use of the bayonet would settle things. But the Civil War musket was rifled, which made an enormous difference. It was still a muzzle-loader, but it had much more accuracy and a far longer range than the old smoothbore, and it completely changed the conditions under which soldiers fought. An advancing line could be brought under killing fire at a distance of half a mile, now, and the massed charge of Napoleonic tradition was miserably out of date. When a defensive line occupied field entrenchments—which the soldiers learned to dig fairly early in the game—a direct frontal assault became almost impossible. The hideous casualty lists of Civil War battles owed much of their size to the fact that soldiers were fighting with rifles but were using tactics suited to smoothbores. It took the generals a long time to learn that a new approach was needed.

MUCH THE SAME DEVELOPMENT was taking place in the artillery, although the full effect was not yet evident. The Civil War cannon, almost without exception, was a muzzle-loader, but the rifled gun was coming into service. It could reach farther

Alfred Waud's sketch (above) depicts a Napoleon, one of the standard artillery pieces of the war. A 12-pound, smoothbore, muzzle-loading gun, it was developed during the reign of France's Napoleon III and was used by both sides in the Civil War. Allen C. Redwood's drawing (left) captures something of the cocky self-confidence of the men who served the guns. One such artillerist on the Confederate side wrote, "Hurrah! Hurrah! our bulldogs bark,/And the enemy's line is a glorious mark;/Hundreds fall like grain on the lea,/Mowed down by the light artillery."

Pennsylvania's Keystone Independent Battery Light Artillery (above) posed in firing position: guns to the front, horses behind them, and ammunition well to the rear. It is an example of one of the two types of artillery units found in each army. This type used mobile, horse-drawn cannon that accompanied armies to the field. They were called "light" artillery units because of the low weight of the ordnance pieces and small-caliber shells they used. The other principal type of cannon were large-caliber guns placed in fixed positions or fortifications. Conrad Wise Chapman's sketch (right) shows one of these "heavy" artillery weapons, a British-made Armstrong rifle. The sling and pulley helped raise the big shell to the muzzle mouth.

and hit harder than the smoothbore, and for counterbattery fire it was highly effective—a rifled battery could hit a battery of smoothbores without being hit in return, and the new 3-inch iron rifles, firing a 10-pound conoidal shot, had a flat trajectory and immense penetrating power. But the old smoothbore—a brass gun of 4.62-inch caliber, firing a 12-pound spherical shot—remained popular to the end of the war; in the wooded, hilly country where so many Civil War battles were fought, its range of slightly less than a mile was about all that was needed, and for close-range work against infantry the smoothbore was better than the rifle. For such work the artillerist fired canister—a tin can full of iron balls, with a propellant at one end and a wooden disk at the other—and the can disintegrated when the gun was fired, letting the iron balls be sprayed all over the landscape. In effect, the cannon became a huge sawed-off shotgun, and at ranges of 250 yards or less it was in the highest degree murderous.

The rifled cannon had a little more range than was ordinarily needed. No one yet had worked out any system for indirect fire; the gunner had to see his target with his own eyes, and a gun that would shoot two miles was of no especial

Fort Slemmer (below) was one of the forts spaced throughout the city of Washington for defense during the war. Only Fort Stevens, located with Fort Slemmer in the northeast quadrant, actually came under enemy fire. The units manning the large-caliber guns in these fortifications were heavy artillery regiments; the one pictured marching out of the Fort Slemmer is the 2nd Pennsylvania Heavy Artillery. In 1862 and 1863 the artillerists guarding Washington had a comfortable life, a surprise inspection representing just about their most stressful occasion. By 1864, however, the Union army needed manpower and transferred many of these regiments to the front, where they served as infantry.

advantage if the target was less than a mile away. Shell fuzes were often defective, and most gunners followed a simple rule: never fire over your own infantry, except in an extreme emergency. (The things were likely to go off too soon, killing friends instead of enemies.) Against fixed fortifications, or carefully prepared fieldworks, the gunners liked to use mortars, which gave them a highangle fire they could not get from fieldpieces. They would also bring up siege guns—ponderous rifled pieces, too heavy to be used in ordinary battles, but powerful enough to flatten parapets or to knock down masonry walls. These large guns were somewhat dangerous to the user. They tended to be weak in the breech, and every now and then one of them would explode when fired.

The Federals had a big advantage in artillery, partly because of their superior industrial plant and partly because, having larger armies, they could afford to use more batteries. On most fields they had many more guns than the Confederates, with a much higher percentage of rifled pieces. (An important factor at Antietam was that Federal artillery could overpower the Confederate guns, and Southern gunners for the rest of the war referred to that fight as "artillery hell.") It appears too that Northern recruits by and large had a little more aptitude for artillery service, just as Southerners outclassed Northerners in the cavalry.

For at least the first half of the war Confederate cavalry was so much better than that of the Federals that there was no real comparison. Here the South was helped both by background and tradition. Most of its recruits came from rural areas and were used to horses; and the legends of chivalry were powerful, so that it seemed much more knightly and gallant to go off to war on horseback than in

OPPOSITE: *Fight for the Standard,* an 1865 painting by an unknown artist, depicts a scene repeated with countless variations throughout the war, as soldiers either struggled to protect their regimental flag from capture or fought to capture an enemy's standard. The honor of carrying the regiment's flag into battle was usually given to the best-trained company, and that company could expect to suffer the highest casualties in the battle.

Winslow Homer's drawing (below) shows the 6th Pennsylvania Cavalry, a regiment that was experimentally armed (at the suggestion of Major General McClellan) with nine-foot-long lances. While the colonel commanding the regiment had nothing but praise for the weapon, the men were glad when the spears were replaced with carbines. "The officers like it," said a Pennsylvania trooper, "but the men do not, and the officers wouldn't if they had to use [it]."

A painting (by an unknown artist) of the 4th Pennsylvania Cavalry on review displays the colorful pageantry of the horse soldier. "[T]here hung about the cavalry service," said a trooper, "a dash and an excitement which attracted those men who had read and remembered the glorious achievements of 'Light Horse Harry' . . . and of 'Morgan's Men' in the Revolutionary War."

348

Quartermasters of a Union regiment (above right, by an unidentified artist) wait to distribute rations sent from a central supply depot. Army depots like the one at right established to service the Federal V Corps, could assume enormous proportions. Among the basic foods on the military menu was a plain flour-and-water biscuit known as hardtack. A typical soldier received nine or ten of them each time rations were distributed. "While hardtack was nutritious," said one soldier, "yet a hungry man could eat his ten in a short time and still be hungry." Occasionally the biscuits would arrive infested with maggots or weevils. "Eaten in the dark," a Union veteran assured his readers, "no one could tell the difference between it and hardtack that was untenanted."

the infantry. Quite literally, the Confederate trooper rode to the wars on his own charger, cavalry horses not being government issue with the Richmond administration. In the beginning this was an advantage, for many Confederate squadrons were mounted on blooded stock that could run rings around the nags which sharpshooting traders were selling to the Yankee government. In the long run, though, the system was most harmful. A trooper who lost his horse had to provide another one all by himself, and he usually could get a furlough so that he might go home and obtain one. Toward the end of the war replacements were hard to come by.

In any case, both horses and riders in the Confederate cavalry were infinitely superior to anything the Yankees could show for at least two years. There were plenty of farm boys in the Federal armies, but they did not come from a horseback country; most horses on Northern farms were draft animals, and it never occurred to a Northern farm boy that he could acquire social prestige simply by getting on a horse's back. Being well aware that it takes a lot of work to care for a horse, the Northern country boy generally enlisted in the infantry. The Union

Military telegraphic crews such as the one in Walton Taber's engraving (above) connected widely scattered army headquarters in a matter of hours, using rubber-coated wires that could be laid out and did not require grounded poles. Innovations in telegraph technology helped to make field communications in camp or battle quick and efficient. A well-equipped mobile telegraph station (below) was standard equipment later in the war for armies on the march.

cavalry got its recruits mostly from city boys or from nonagricultural groups; and before this cavalry could do anything at all, its members had first to be taught how to stay in the saddle. Since Jeb Stuart's troopers could have taught circus riders tricks, the Yankees were hopelessly outclassed. Not until 1863 was the Army of the Potomac's cavalry able to meet Stuart on anything like even terms.

In the West matters were a little different. Here the Confederacy had a very dashing cavalry raider in the person of John Hunt Morgan, who made a number of headlines without particularly affecting the course of the war, and it had the youthful Joe Wheeler, who performed competently; but most of all it had Nathan Bedford Forrest, an untaught genius who had had no military training and who never possessed an ounce of social status, but who was probably the best cavalry leader in the entire war. Forrest simply used his horsemen as a modern general would use motorized infantry. He liked horses because he liked fast movement, and his mounted men could get from here to there much faster than any infantry could; but when they reached the field they usually tied their horses to trees and fought on foot, and they were as good as the very best infantry. Not for nothing did Forrest say that the essence of strategy was "to git thar fust with the most men." The Yankees never came up with anybody to match Forrest, and tough William T. Sherman once paid him a grim compliment: there would never be peace in western Tennessee, said Sherman, until Forrest was dead.

Aside from what a man like Forrest could do, cavalry in the Civil War was actually of secondary importance as far as fighting was concerned. It was essential for scouting and for screening an army, but as a combat arm it was declining.

Getting the Message Through

Union veteran Henry Bacon painted *All Quiet on the Potomac* of an old chestnut tree that became one link in a communications chain manned by the U.S. Army Signal Corps. The flagman atop the platform is shown signaling to the next post in the chain, using a wigwag system developed before the war by an army officer named Albert J. Myer. Starting from a straight-up central position (as depicted in Bacon's painting), the signalman dipped the flag to the left or right, each combination of wigwags denoting a letter of the alphabet. In this way, even fairly long messages could be passed along a chain of many miles in much less time than it took a mounted courier to cover the same distance. At night, signalmen used special torches to pass their messages.

The photograph at right was taken of Sunday morning Mass in the camp of the 69th New York, the "Fighting Irish." Formal religious services were rare when armies were on the move. After attending camp services in 1863, a Vermonter wrote, "The boys went back to their tents to digest thoughts of no inferior consequence, though too often forgotten in the hurly burly of a soldier's life." Alfred Waud made a sketch (below) of an even more unusual event: a military wedding in the field. They were generally reserved for officers and could be impressive. Noted Waud: "After the wedding was a dinner, a ball, fireworks, etc.; and on the whole it eclipsed entirely an opera at the Academy of Music in dramatic effect and reality."

Sunday morning Mass in Camp of 69th N.Y.S.M.

7 NJV

Cavalry skirmished frequently with other cavalry, and the skirmishes at times rose to the level of pitched battles, but it fought infantry only very rarely. It enjoyed vast prestige with the press and with back-home civilians, but neither infantry nor artillery admired it. The commonest infantry wisecrack of the war was the bitter question: "Who ever saw a dead cavalryman?"

Infantry, artillery, cavalry—these were the three major subdivisions of a Civil War army. Numerically very small, but of considerable value, were the engineer troops. They built bridges, opened roads, laid out fortifications, and performed other technical chores; pontoon trains were in their care, and they were supposed to do any mining or countermining that was done, although in actual practice this was frequently done by troops of the line. Indeed, it was the engineer officer rather than the engineer battalion that was really important. In the Northern armies the average regiment contained men of so many different skills that with proper direction they could do almost anything an engineer out-fit could do; it was the special skill and ability of the trained officer that really counted. The Confederate regiments contained fewer jacks-of-all-trades, but this shortage never proved a serious handicap. At the top the South had the best engineer officer of the lot in the person of Robert E. Lee.

. . .

"I see before me now a traveling army halting," wrote Walt Whitman. "The numerous camp-fires scatter'd near and far . . . ,/The shadowy forms of men and horses, looming, large-sized, flickering,/ And over all the sky—the sky! far, far out of reach, studded, breaking out, the eternal stars." Sanford Robinson Gifford's painting is titled *Night Bivouac of the Seventh Regiment New York at Arlington Heights, Virginia.*

Members of one of the best bands in the Confederate army, the 26th North Carolina Regimental Band, posed for this photograph in 1862. The players came from Moravian communities around the town of Salem, a social culture that placed a high value on musical literacy and expression. In addition to playing music, bandsmen served as stretcher-bearers and helped care for the wounded. During the first day's fight at Gettysburg the 26th North Carolina itself suffered many casualties; the remaining musicians labored well into the night to succor the injured. The next day the band still turned out to play for their fellow troops. "We accordingly went to the regiment and found the men much more cheerful than we were ourselves," remembered a band member. "We played for some time . . . and the men cheered us lustily."

IT IS HARD TO GET AN ACCURATE count on the numbers who served in the Civil War armies. The books show total enlistments in the Union armies of 2,900,000 and in the Confederate armies of 1,300,000, but these figures do not mean what they appear to mean. They are fuzzed up by a large number of short-term enlistments and by a good deal of duplication, and the one certainty is that neither side ever actually put that many individuals under arms. One of the best students of the matter has concluded that the Union had the equivalent of about 1,500,000 three-year enlistments, from first to last, and that the Confederates had the equivalent of about 1,000,000. Anyone who chooses may quarrel with these figures. Nobody will ever get an exact count, because the records are very confusing, and some figures are missing altogether. In any case, approximately 360,000 Federal soldiers and 258,000 Confederate soldiers lost their lives in the course of the war. These figures, to be sure, include deaths from disease as well as battle casualties, but a young man who died of dysentery is just as dead as the one who stopped a bullet, and when these figures are matched against the total possible enrollment, they are appalling.

For the unfortunate Civil War soldier, whether he came from the North or from the South, not only got into the army just when the killing power of weapons was being brought to a brand-new peak of efficiency; he enlisted in the closing years of an era when the science of medicine was woefully, incredibly imperfect, so that he got the worst of it in two ways. When he fought, he was

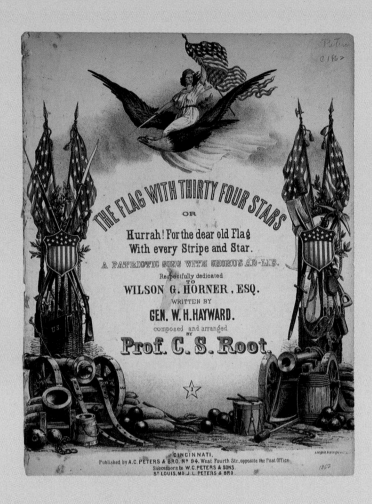

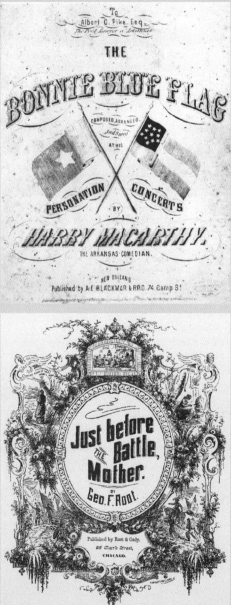

The Musical Accompaniment to a Conflict

The same passions that propelled the nation to civil war also helped to generate a huge outpouring of music, encompassing the hopes and fears of the soldiers and their families, along with the propaganda churned out on both sides in the conflict. Most sheet music was targeted for the home market, and was often scored for solo voice and piano (or sometimes guitar). Shown above is "The Flag with Thirty-Four Stars" by "Gen. W. H. Hayward" (there was no Civil War general with that name) which longs for the Union to be a union unmarred by secession. Walter Kittredge's sentimental reverie, "Tenting on the Old Camp Ground" (top right), was a phenomenal success, selling a hundred thousand copies by war's end. Harry Macarthy's tribute to the South, "The Bonnie Blue Flag"

(middle right), attached his patriotic words to an old Irish tune called "The Irish Jaunting Car." George F. Root was a longtime songwriter who produced and published his very first Civil War piece as early as April 18, 1861. He went on to compose a string of tunes known to this day, including "The Battle Cry of Freedom," "Tramp, Tramp, the Boys are Marching" and "Just Before the Battle, Mother" (bottom right). More than anyone else, Root recognized the maudlin sentimentality that lay near a soldier's heart or near that of his piano-playing folks back home. One of the lyrics of "Just Before the Battle, Mother" reads, "Comrades brave are round me lying,/Filled with thoughts of home and God;/For well they know that on the morrow,/Some will sleep beneath the sod."

Sketched by Jasper Green

Drawings by Jasper Green (right) and Arthur Lumley (below) show how armies moved on their stomachs when in enemy territory, subsisting on the local produce. "The means employed to accomplish this end was known as *Foraging*," explained a Union soldier, "which is generally understood to mean a seeking after food, . . . and appropriating to one's own use whatsoever is found . . . in an enemy's country." A righteous Yankee defended the right to forage, at least when practiced by his side: "The view which the average soldier took . . . was . . . that the people of the South were in a state of rebellion against the Government . . . and . . . that they had therefore forfeited all claim to whatever property the soldier chose to appropriate. . . ."

likely to be hurt pretty badly; when he stayed in camp, he lived under conditions that were very likely to make him sick; and in either case he had almost no chance to get the kind of medical treatment which a generation or so later would be routine.

Both the Federal and Confederate governments did their best to provide proper medical care for their soldiers, but even the best was not very good. This was nobody's fault. There simply was no such thing as good medical care in that age—not as the modern era understands the expression.

Few medical men then knew why wounds become infected or what causes disease; the treatment of wounds and disease, consequently, ranged from the inadequate through the useless to the downright harmful. When a man was wounded and the wound was dressed, doctors expected it to suppurate; they spoke of "laudable pus" and supposed that its appearance was a good sign. The idea that a surgical dressing ought to be sterilized never entered anyone's head; for that matter, no physician would have known what the word "sterilized" meant in such a connection. If a surgeon's instruments were so much as rinsed off between operations at a field hospital, the case was an exception.

In camp, diseases like typhoid, dysentery, and pneumonia were dreaded killers. No one knew what caused them, and no one could do much for them when they appeared. Doctors had discovered that there was some connection between the cleanliness of a camp and the number of men on sick call, but sanitation was still a rudimentary science, and if a water supply was not visibly befouled or odorous, it was thought to be perfectly safe. The intestinal maladies

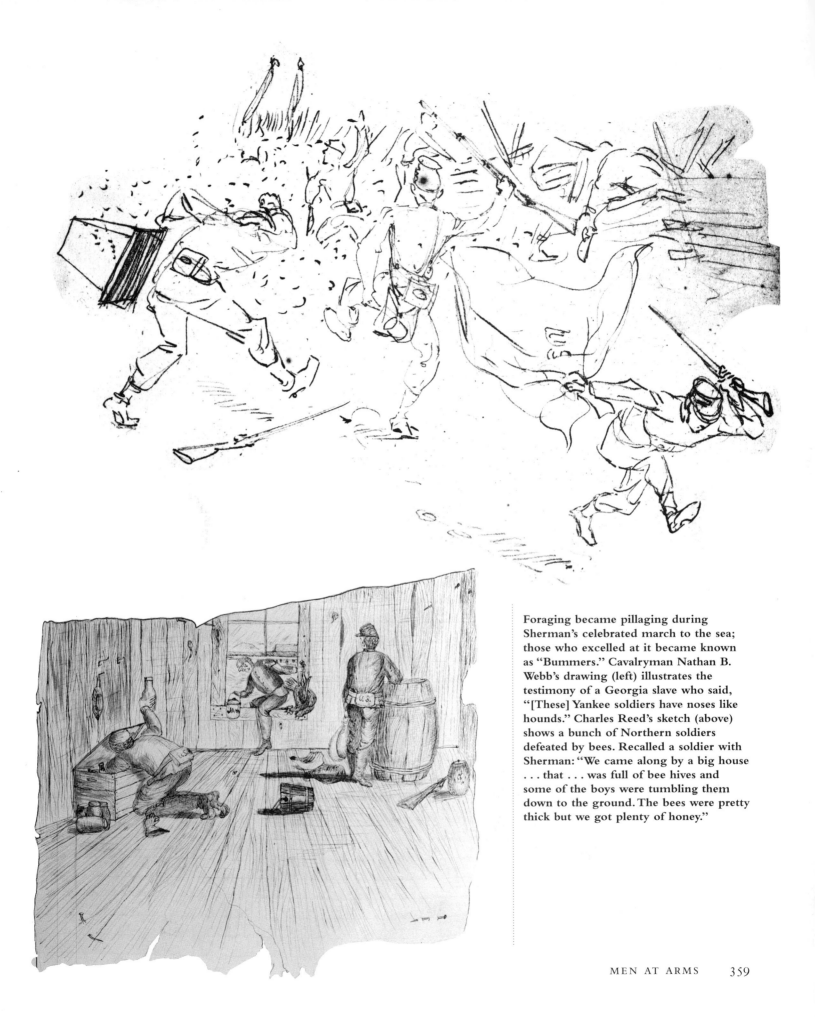

Foraging became pillaging during Sherman's celebrated march to the sea; those who excelled at it became known as "Bummers." Cavalryman Nathan B. Webb's drawing (left) illustrates the testimony of a Georgia slave who said, "[These] Yankee soldiers have noses like hounds." Charles Reed's sketch (above) shows a bunch of Northern soldiers defeated by bees. Recalled a soldier with Sherman: "We came along by a big house . . . that . . . was full of bee hives and some of the boys were tumbling them down to the ground. The bees were pretty thick but we got plenty of honey."

In 1862 Major General George B. McClellan stated, "Drunkenness is the cause of by far the greater part of the disorders which are examined by the courts-martial." Winslow Homer's *Punishment for Intoxication* shows the typical fate of a soldier convicted of the crime. Under this sentence, the guilty man had to stand on a box in public view with a small log on his shoulder for one or more days, defined as "from Reveille to Retreat."

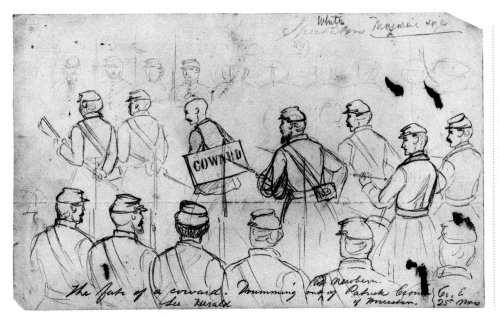

Even veteran soldiers experienced fear in battle; but to show it by running or hiding was an offense punishable at the very least by public humiliation (top left). Cowardice, declared a Rebel soldier, "is the one sin which may not be pardoned either in this world or the next." Other breaches of discipline called for harsher penalties, such as being bound and gagged (top right). For those convicted of desertion, the price could be death (above). Although intended as a deterrent, these executions often left veteran soldiers more angry than intimidated. "I have seen men shot down by scores and hundreds in the field of battle, and have stood within an arm's reach of comrades that were shot dead," said one, "but I believe I never have witnessed that from which any soul shrunk with such horror, as to see those . . . soldiers shot dead in cold blood at the iron decree of military law."

that took so heavy a toll were believed due to "miasmic odors" or to even more subtle emanations in the air.

So the soldier of the 1860's had everything working against him. In his favor there was a great deal of native toughness, and a sardonic humor that came to his rescue when things were darkest; these, and an intense devotion to the cause he was serving. Neither Yank nor Reb ever talked very much about the cause; to listen to eloquence on the issues of the war, one had to visit cities behind the lines, read newspapers, or drop in on Congress, either in Washington or in Richmond, because very little along that line was ever heard in camp. The soldier had ribald mockery for high-flown language, and he cared very little for the patriotic war songs which had piped him down to the recruiting office in the first place. In his off hours, at camp or in bivouac, he was a sentimentalist, and one of the most typical of all Civil War scenes is the campfire group of an evening, supper finished, chores done, darkness coming on, with dim lights flickering and homesick young men singing sad little

OPPOSITE: By war's end, Richmond was filled with hospitals like the one at Howard's Grove (top), where women were the primary caregivers. "The women of the South . . . [felt] a passion of interest in every man in the gray uniform," declared a female volunteer. For Northern families anxious to retrieve the bodies of loved ones fallen in war, a Philadelphia mortician offered a service well suited to the times (bottom).

Immediately following a battle, hospital attendants, bandsmen, and friends would help collect the wounded for treatment (left). Those who survived being carried to the field hospital might be sent to larger medical facilities in ambulance wagons (above), a trip that extended the patient's ordeal. Noted one medical man, ". . . each jarring of the ambulance is enough to make the sympathetic brain burst with agony."

Angels of Mercy

William Ludwell Sheppard's watercolor *In the Hospital, 1861* (above) pays tribute to those women of the South who labored ceaselessly to care for the war's wounded. "I have never worked so hard in all my life and I would rather do that than anything else in the world," declared one weary attendant.

A devoted nurse later praised her female colleagues: *Would that I could do more than thank the dear friends who made my life for four years so happy and contented; who never made me feel by word or act, that my self-imposed occupation was otherwise than one which would ennoble any woman. If ever any aid was given through my own exertions, or any labor*

rendered effective by me for the good of the South—if any sick soldier ever benefited by my happy face or pleasant smiles at his bedside, or death was ever soothed by gentle words of hope and tender care, such results were only owing to the cheering encouragement I received from them. They were gentlewomen in every sense of the

word, and though they might not have remembered that "noblesse oblige," they felt and acted up to the motto in every act of their lives. My only wish was to live and die among them, growing each day better from contact with their gentle, kindly sympathies and heroic hearts.

Eastman Johnson's painting *The Letter Home* (above) depicts a scene repeated countless times in hospital wards north and south. Walt Whitman, who spent much of the war assisting the sick in Washington's hospitals, wrote: *When I go into a new ward, I always carry two or three quires of paper and a good lot of envelopes and walk up and*

down and circulate them around to those who desire them. . . . He who goes among the soldiers with gifts, etc. must beware how he proceeds. . . . They are not charity patients but American young men of pride and independence.

Even when the wounded could be transported via ambulances (below), U.S. army medical facilities often proved understaffed and overwhelmed. The U.S. Sanitary Commission, the biggest private relief organization created during the Civil War, was formed in June, 1861, to address the problem. The commission raised enough funds to field a small army of physicians and volunteer assistants who tended to the soldiers' medical, personal, and other needs. The picture above shows a Sanitary Commission office near Petersburg in 1864.

songs like "Lorena" or "Tenting Tonight." No matter which army is looked at, the picture is the same. On each side the soldier realized that he personally was getting the worst of it, and when he had time he felt very sorry for himself. . . . But mostly he did not have the time, and his predominant mood was never one of self-pity. Mostly he was ready for whatever came to him.

Angels of the Battlefield

Dorothea Dix (above left) and Clara Barton (above right) were the leaders of a national effort to organize a nursing corps to care for the war's wounded and sick. Dix was already recognized for her work in improving the treatment received by the insane when she began to recruit women to serve as nurses in the Army Medical Bureau. Military traditionalists opposed her, but she prevailed, armed with an indomitable will and a singleness of purpose. One of the standards that Dix established for her nurses was that they be "plain-looking" and middle-aged. "In those days it was considered indecorous for angels of mercy to appear otherwise than gray-haired and spectacled," explained one young lady rejected by Dix. "Such a thing as a hospital corps of comely young maiden nurses, possessing grace and good looks, was then unknown." Recruits nicknamed her "Dragon Dix," but it was a badge of honor if it indicated what it took to succeed in creating the army's first professional nursing corps. Clara Barton worked on parallel lines, but outside the official military system. A Massachusetts schoolteacher, Barton had come to Washington in 1854 to work at the U.S. Patent Office. Determined to play a role in the events of 1861, she cared for wounded soldiers who had returned to Washington. Thanks to financial support garnered throughout New England, Barton had the means, along with the resolve, to overcome the military bureaucracy and travel to the front lines. "I went in while the battle raged," she recalled with pride. After the war, she was instrumental in the creation of an American branch of the International Red Cross.

Conrad Wise Chapman painted scenes he had witnessed himself during the Civil War. Sketches like those below of cavalrymen practicing their fencing became the basis of a series of thirty-one oil paintings. *Picket Post* (right), completed after the war, was also based on one of his wartime sketches. Virginia-born Chapman was the son of the noted portrait-and-landscape artist, John Gadsby Chapman. He was in Italy with his family when the Civil War began; despite his father's wish that he remain overseas, he sold enough of his own paintings to book passage back to the South he deeply loved, enlisting in the 3rd Kentucky Infantry (C.S.A.). Wounded at Shiloh, Chapman later returned to duty with a Virginia regiment. At the end of the war, he went back to Italy and produced the paintings that established him as one of the foremost soldier–artists of the Confederacy.

Winslow Homer sketched scenes of camp life throughout the Civil War; some were engraved onto woodblocks for use in *Harper's Weekly*, others served as studies for his own paintings. *Playing Old Soldier* (left) portrays a malingerer, a bad sort described by a veteran as one of the "few individuals . . . who to escape guard or fatigue duty would feign illness, and if possible delude the surgeon into believing them proper subjects for his tenderest care. . . ." Sometimes Homer was close enough to the fighting to capture vivid images of combat, like that of soldiers furiously loading and reloading on the firing line (below left). Boston-born Homer was an aspiring painter living in New York when the war broke out in 1861. He turned down a staff position with *Harper's Weekly* so as not to be tied to the life of a commercial artist but toured the war's front lines as one of the magazine's free-lance "special artists." Homer continued to create major works from his Civil War sketch portfolio years after the fighting was over.

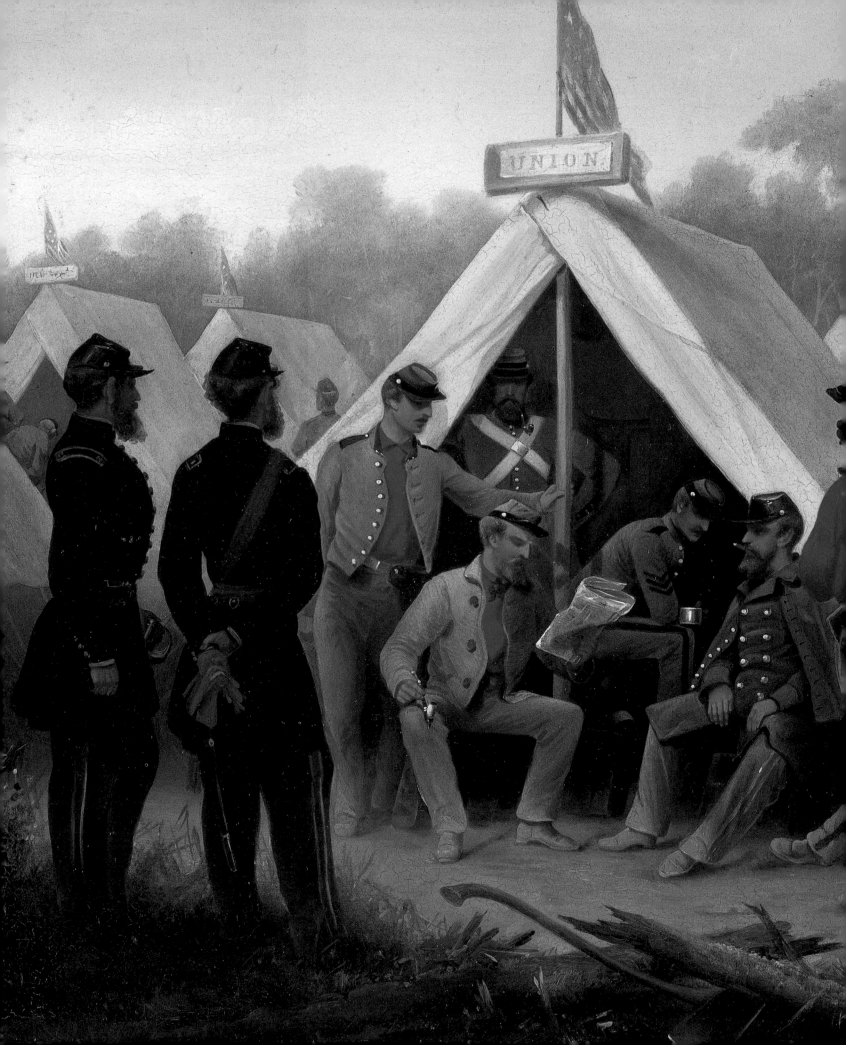

Letters from Home was painted by James Walker, an English-born artist who knew Civil War camp life first hand. The painting captures the moment in the routine of the army that most strongly reminded the lonely soldiers of their ties to home. "We can only pity the man who goes empty away from the little group assembled about the mail bag," wrote one veteran, "and rejoice with him who strolls away with a letter near his heart." Walker's vignette is set in a Federal bivouac early in the war, before blue became the standard color for Union uniforms. In the words of one critic, obviously impressed, Walker "made careful studies on the march."

OVERLEAF: "I think I would rather fight three battles a week and be in the field than thus rot and rust in camp," wrote a young Massachusetts officer, echoing the general theme of Winslow Homer's *Rainy Day in Camp*. ". . . [H]ere I am, attending daily to the needs of my men and horses, duly seeing that hair is short and clothes are clean, paying great attention to belts and sabres, inspecting pistols and policing quarters and so, not very intellectually and indeed with some sense of fatigue, playing my part in the struggle."

CHAPTER 9

The Destruction of Slavery

A singular fact about modern war is that it takes charge. Once begun it has to be carried to its conclusion, and carrying it there sets in motion events that may be beyond men's control. Doing what has to be done to win, men perform acts that alter the very soil in which society's roots are nourished. They bring about infinite change, not because anyone especially wants it, but because all-out warfare destroys so much that things can never again be as they used to be.

In the 1860's the overwhelming mass of the people, in the North and in the South, were conservatives who hated the very notion of change. Life in America had been good and it had been fairly simple, and most people wanted to keep it that way. The Northerner wanted to preserve the old Union, and the Southerner wanted to preserve the semifeudal society in which he lived; and the unspoken aim in each section was to win a victory which would let people go back to what they had had in a less turbulent day. But after a war which cuts as deeply and goes on as long as the Civil War,

Ending slavery was *not* a Union goal when the war began. At first, most slaves who escaped to Federal lines were returned to their masters under the Fugitive Slave Act. Later, at the discretion of Union officers they might be considered legitimate property of war or "contrabands." Most contrabands were kept in refugee camps, while some were appended to the army as laborers or teamsters (the latter of which are depicted in Winslow Homer's *The Bright Side*, left). With the Emancipation Proclamation, the Lincoln administration endorsed a controversial policy of recruiting blacks (former slaves and free born) into the U.S. army (poster, above).

It took resourcefulness, courage, and luck for a slave to escape from the South before the war. Thomas Moran's 1863 painting *Slaves Escaping Through the Swamp* (above) provides a dramatic depiction of the tragic end of one such attempt, as the slave catcher's hounds corner a desperate family. With the war, the approach of the Union army meant freedom for thousands of seemingly docile, contented slaves who fled their plantations en masse. By Southern standards the slaves of the Mississippi River plantations of Jefferson and Joseph Davis were well treated and allowed privileges enjoyed by few others. Yet, as Frank Schell sketched it (right), when Grant's army closed on Vicksburg, the Davis slaves packed up and entered the Union lines.

no one "goes back" to anything at all. Everybody goes on to something new, and the process is guided and accelerated by the mere act of fighting.

One trouble was that once this war was well begun there was no way, humanly speaking, to work out a compromise peace. The thing had to end in total victory for one side or the other: in a completely independent Confederacy, or in a completely restored Union and the final evaporation of the theory of the right of secession. The longer the war went on and the more it cost, the less willing were patriots on either side to recede from this position. The heroic dead, who were so tragically numerous and who had died for such diametrically opposite causes, must not have died in vain, and only total victory would justify what had been done. And because total victory was the only thinkable outcome, men came to feel that it was right to do anything at all that might bring victory nearer. It was right to destroy railroads, to burn factories and confiscate supplies of food or other raw materials, to seize or ruin any kind of property which was helpful to the enemy.

This feeling rested with especial weight on the North because the North was of necessity the aggressor. The Confederacy existed and it had to be destroyed—not merely brought to the point where its leaders were willing to talk about peace, but destroyed outright. It had to be made incapable of carrying on the fight; both its armies and the industrial and economic muscle which supported them must be made helpless. And so the North at last undertook to wipe out the institution of human slavery.

The photograph below shows a group of contrabands who worked for the U.S. Army Quartermaster Department at Alexandria, Virginia. Under the special status of contraband, blacks were neither free men nor slaves, yet the concept opened a route toward ending slavery entirely. "When at last the truth began to dawn upon the [Lincoln] administration that the Negro might be made useful to loyalty, as well as to treason, to the Union as well as to the Confederacy," wrote Frederick Douglass, "it then considered in what way it could employ him, which would in the least shock and offend the popular prejudice against him."

Although some black military units were organized in Kansas, South Carolina, and Louisiana in 1862, wholesale recruitment did not begin until 1863, after the Emancipation Proclamation. This print was created to help raise black Pennsylvania regiments at Camp William Penn, outside Philadelphia. The unit depicted is commanded by a white officer, a policy that the U.S. government followed until 1865, and even then the color barrier was broken in only rare circumstances.

Lincoln had made this official with the Emancipation Proclamation, but that strange document had to be ratified by the tacit consent of the people at home and by the active endorsement of the soldiers in the field. And most of the soldiers had not, in the beginning, felt very strongly about slavery. There were, to be sure, many regiments of solid antislavery sentiment: New Englanders, many of the German levies, and certain regiments from abolitionist areas in the Middle West. But these were in a minority. The average Federal soldier began his term of service either quite willing to tolerate slavery in the South or definitely in sympathy with it. He was fighting for the Union and for nothing more. Lincoln's proclamation was not enthusiastically accepted by all of the troops. A few regiments, from border states or from places like southern Illinois and Indiana where there were close ties of sentiment and understanding with the South, came close to mutiny when the document was published, and a good many more grew morose with discontent.

Yet in the end all of the army went along with the new program; became, indeed, the sharp cutting edge that cut slavery down. This happened, quite simply, because the Federal armies that were being taught to lay their hands on any property which might be of service to the Confederate nation realized that the most accessible and most useful property of all was the Negro slave. They had little sympathy with the slave as a person, and they had no particular objection to the fact that he was property; indeed, it was his very status as property which led them to take him away from his owners and to refer to him as "contraband." As property, he supported the Southern war effort. As property, therefore, he was to be taken away from his owners, and when he was taken away, the only logical thing to do with him was to set him free.

THE WAR, IN OTHER WORDS, was taking charge. To save the Union the North had to destroy the Confederacy, and to destroy the Confederacy it had to destroy slavery. The Federal armies got the point and behaved accordingly. Slavery was doomed, not so much by any proclamation from Washington as by the necessities of war. The soldiers killed it because it got in their way. Perhaps the most profound miscalculation the Southern leaders ever made was that slavery could be defended by force of arms. By the middle of the nineteenth century slavery was too fragile for that. It could exist only by the tolerance of people who did not like it, and war destroyed that tolerance.

So where the Northern armies went, slavery went out of existence. In Virginia this meant little, partly because in Virginia the Federal armies did not go very far, and partly because in the fought-over country most Southerners got their slaves off to safety as fast as they could. But in the West, in Tennessee and northern Mississippi and Alabama, Federal armies ranged far, destroying the substance of the land as they ranged. They burned barns, consuming or wasting the contents. They burned unoccupied homes, and sometimes rowdy stragglers on the fringes of the armies burned occupied homes as well; they seized any cotton that they found, they broke bridges and tore up railway tracks and ruined mills and ironworks and similar installations . . . and they killed slavery. Grim General Sherman, the author of so much of this destruction, remarked not long after the victory at Vicksburg that all the powers of the earth could no more restore slaves to the bereaved Southerners than they could restore their dead grandfathers. Wherever

Martin R. Delany (above), an able recruiter of black soldiers, was mustered with the rank of major on February 26, 1865, making him the first black staff officer in the U.S. military. He never exercised his rank with a field command. In a speech given in late 1865, Delany told the audience: "Do you know that if it was not for the black men this war never would have been brought to a close with success to the Union, and the liberty of your race if it had not been for the Negro? I want you to understand that." The photograph below left shows a guard detail from the 107th U.S.C.T. (United States Colored Troops), a unit that was organized in Kentucky in late 1864. By war's end, approximately 180,000 black men had donned blue uniforms to shoulder arms for the Union, representing about 8.5 per cent of the army's infantry, cavalry, and artillery forces.

A Black Soldier's Creed

The determination of the corporal in the photo above was echoed in the words of Joseph E. Williams, a black man from Pennsylvania, who helped recruit freed slaves in North Carolina. Writing from that post in 1863, Williams said: *An instinctive love for liberty is the real principle of the first N[orth] C[arolina] C[olored] V[olunteers] of General [Edward A.] Wild's Brigade. Is the negro not a man? Is he not capable of bearing arms? Has he not talent? Has he not courage? . . . How preposterous, therefore, how absurd it is, that people should think . . . no submissions too much in order to purchase such a temporary and uncertain happiness as the joys of this sort of life can give. It is beneath the greatness of their soul to respect and elevate the downtrodden from the level of the brute creation. Nevertheless, in spite of their prejudice, and jealousies and schemes, they are compelled to acknowledge us as men in the defense of the Republic, which is our redemption. For this cause we will fight, for the cause of freedom. I will draw my sword against my oppressor and the oppressors of my race. I must avenge my debasement. I will ask no quarter, nor will I give any. With me there is but one question, which is life or death. And I will sacrifice everything in order to save the gift of freedom for my race.*

Union armies moved, they were followed by long lines of fugitive slaves—unlettered folk who did not know what the war was about and could not imagine what the future held, but who dimly sensed that the road trodden by the men in blue was the road to freedom.

Neither the soldiers nor the generals were entirely happy about this increasing flood of refugees. In a clumsy, makeshift manner camps were set up for them; thousands of the refugees died, of hunger or disease or simple neglect, but most of them survived—survived in such numbers that the Federals had to do something about them. Negro labor could be used to build roads or fortifications, to harvest cotton in plantations that lay inside the Union lines, to perform all manner of useful military chores about the camps.

The refugee camps needed guards, to keep intruders out and to police the activities of the refugees themselves, and the Federal soldiers almost unanimously objected to performing such service. (They had enlisted to save the Union, not to guard a milling herd of bewildered blacks.) It seemed logical, after a time, to raise guard detachments from among the blacks themselves, outfitting them with castoff army uniforms. Then it appeared that the immense reserve of manpower represented by the newly freed slaves might be put to more direct use, and at last the government authorized, and even encouraged, the organization of black regiments, to be officered by whites but to be regarded as troops of the line, available for combat duty if needed.

To this move the soldiers made a good deal of objection—at first. Then they began to change their minds. They did not like Negroes, for race prejudice of a malignity rarely seen today was very prevalent in the North at that time, and they

Edward Lamson Henry's painting (above) shows the March 5, 1864, ceremonial presentation of flags to the 20th U.S.C.T., New York's first black regiment. "You are in arms, not for the freedom and law of the white race alone," the soldiers were told, "but for universal law and freedom." Even after the Emancipation Proclamation, raising black regiments was sometimes difficult in the North, especially when powerful political figures such as New York's governor, Horatio Seymour, rejected the whole idea. When New York City's Union League Club (made up of "500 of the [city's] wealthiest and most respectable citizens") threw its weight behind the effort, though, opposition wilted and recruitment began.

The Great Locomotive Chase

Shortly after 6:00 A.M., April 12, 1862, a band of bold Union army raiders in civilian clothing hijacked a railroad train at Big Shanty (above), outside Atlanta. Under the leadership of Federal spy James J. Andrews, they planned to disrupt the vital Rebel supply line connecting Atlanta and Chattanooga by burning the railroad bridges between the two. Within minutes, Andrews and his sixteen men had control of the train, pulled by a locomotive named the *General*. Moving toward the all-important Oostanaula

River Bridge near Resaca, the saboteurs pulled down telegraph wires as they went. There were unexpected delays, especially at busy Kingston Junction, where suspicious station attendants demanded explanations that delayed the raiders for more than an hour. Four minutes after the *General* left Kingston, a small locomotive named the *Yonah* arrived at the station, bearing William A. Fuller, the conductor of the seized train, in hot pursuit. Fuller had given chase on foot, then on a handcar, finally on the *Yonah*. Finding his way blocked at Kingston by other traffic, Fuller abandoned the *Yonah*, next commandeering the *William R. Smith*, then taking over the *Texas*, which continued the pursuit by running in reverse. By the time Andrews and his men had reached Resaca, Fuller was so close behind

that the raiders were unable to set the rain-soaked covered bridge on fire. The chase was really on now, until finally, a short distance past Ringgold, with the *General* almost out of fuel, Andrews ordered his men to jump off the train and scatter. Within a week, the entire raiding force had been captured; eventually Andrews and seven of them, randomly chosen, were hanged. While the operation had failed to knock out the Chattanooga supply line objectives, it became the stuff of legend and the inspiration for several modern films.

did not want to associate with them on anything remotely like terms of equality, but they came to see that much might be said for Negro regiments. For one thing, a great many enlisted men in the Northern armies could win officers' commissions in these regiments, and a high private who saw a chance to become a lieutenant or a captain was likely to lose a great deal of his antagonism to the notion of black soldiers. More important than this was the dawning realization that the black soldier could stop a Rebel bullet just as well as a white soldier could, and when he did so, some white soldier who would otherwise have died would go on living. . . . And so by the middle of 1863 the North was raising numbers of black regiments, and the white soldiers who had been so bitter about the idea adjusted themselves rapidly.

All told, the Federals put more than 180,000 Negroes into uniform. Many of these regiments were used only for garrison duty, and in many other cases the army saw to it that the black regiments became little more than permanent fatigue details to relieve white soldiers of hard work, but some units saw actual combat service and in a number of instances acquitted themselves well. And there was an importance to this that went far beyond any concrete achievements on the field of battle, for this was the seed of further change. The war had freed the slave, the war had put freed slaves into army uniforms—and a permanent alteration in the colored man's status would have to come out of that fact. A man who had worn the country's uniform and faced death in its service could not, ultimately, be

Following Gettysburg and Vicksburg, the focus of the war turned to central Tennessee. In early September the adroit maneuvering of the Union Army of the Cumberland under Major General William S. Rosecrans forced Confederate forces to abandon the city of Chattanooga. Overconfident after this bloodless success, Rosecrans spread out his army south of the city, unaware that the Confederates were planning a massive counterstroke. Among the veteran units serving under Rosecrans was the 9th Indiana (below), which had already done its share of fighting in Tennessee, at Shiloh, Perryville, and Stones River.

The Battle of Chickamauga on September 19 and 20, 1863, was fought on a steep, thickly wooded terrain. The John Ross House (right), nucleus for the tiny village of Rossville just inside the Georgia border, became a temporary headquarters for Major General Gordon Granger of the Union army. Ross himself was long gone, having followed the members of his beloved Cherokee Nation when they were driven west in 1838. The second day of the battle opened with fighting along the banks of Chickamauga Creek, near Lee & Gordon's Mills (below).

anything less than a full-fledged citizen, and it was going to be very hard to make citizens out of some Negroes without making citizens out of all.

The armies moved across the sun-baked American landscape in the summer of 1863, trying to preserve the cherished past and actually breaking a way into the unpredictable future; and after Gettysburg and Vicksburg the center of attention became central Tennessee and northern Georgia, where the chance of war gave the South one more opportunity to restore the balance.

NOTHING OF MUCH CONSEQUENCE would happen just now in Virginia. Both armies had been badly mangled at Gettysburg, and the rival commanders were being very circumspect. Lee had not the strength to make a real offensive campaign, and Meade was little better off; the two maneuvered up and down around the Orange and Alexandria Railroad, sparring for position, neither one willing to bring on a stand-up fight unless he could do so to real advantage, each one careful to give the other no opening. There were skirmishes, cavalry engagements, and now and then sharp actions between parts of the armies, but nothing really important took place, and as the summer gave way to fall it became apparent that there would not be a really big campaign in Virginia before 1864.

In Mississippi there was a similar lull. After the capture of Vicksburg, Grant wanted to go driving on. There was nothing in the South that could stop his army, and he believed that he could sweep through southern Mississippi and Alabama, taking Mobile and compelling Bragg to hurry back from in front of Chattanooga. The authorities in Washington, however, clung to the notion that

Alfred Waud's drawing (above) shows some of Confederate General James Longstreet's men driving Federal cavalry away from a Chickamauga Creek bridge before the battle. Longstreet's men were also among those who tried and failed to break the Union rear guard on Snodgrass Hill (below). Using interior lines of communication and rail links, the Confederates successfully transferred Longstreet's entire corps from Virginia to join General Braxton Bragg's Army of Tennessee at Chickamauga. They arrived in time to turn the tide of the battle.

Although admired for his personal courage during the Mexican War, General Braxton Bragg (right), commander of the Army of Tennessee, had become a dour, contentious man, constantly at odds with subordinate officers and thoroughly disliked by the rank and file, whom he disciplined without compassion. "None of General Bragg's soldiers ever loved him," declared a Tennessee infantryman. "They had no faith in his ability as a general. He was looked upon as a merciless tyrant." Nevertheless, when called upon by their commander, Bragg's soldiers would fight, and fight hard. Walton Taber's drawing (below) shows a Confederate line of battle at Chickamauga.

the important thing in this war was to occupy Southern territory, and Grant was compelled to scatter his troops. Some of them he had to send to Louisiana, where Major General Nathaniel P. Banks was preparing to invade Texas. Others went to Missouri and to Arkansas, and those that were left were engaged in garrison duty in western Tennessee and Mississippi, occupying cities and guarding railroad lines, effectively immobilized.

Virginia and Mississippi were, so to speak, the wings of the war front. The center was in middle Tennessee, where Rosecrans with the Army of the Cumberland faced Bragg with the Army of Tennessee; and at the end of June Rosecrans at last began to move, hoping to seize Chattanooga and thus to make possible Federal occupation of Knoxville and eastern Tennessee—a point in which President Lincoln was greatly interested, because eastern Tennessee was a stronghold of Unionist sentiment.

Rosecrans made his move late, but when

he did so he moved with much skill. Bragg, covering Chattanooga, had weakened his force sending troops to Joe Johnston, and in his position around the town of Tullahoma he had perhaps 47,000 men, of which a disproportionate number were cavalry. (Forrest's cavalry though, mostly, and hence of value against infantry.) The Confederates held good defensive ground, and considering everything Rosecrans' field force of 60,000 was none too large for the job at hand.

Old Rosy, as his troops called him, feinted smartly and moved with speed. He made as if to swing around Bragg's left flank, then sliced off in the opposite direction, and despite seventeen consecutive days of rain his troops got into the rear of Bragg's right before Bragg realized what was going on. Rosecrans bluffed an attack and then slipped off on another flanking movement, and Bragg found himself compelled to retreat. By July 4 the Confederate army was back in Chattanooga, and Rosecrans, calling in vain for reinforcements (the government was sending pieces of Grant's army off in all directions, but somehow it could not spare any for Rosecrans), was trying to find a line of advance that would force Bragg to retreat still farther. He presently found it, and in August he made an unexpected crossing of the Tennessee River thirty miles west of Chattanooga. Establishing a base of supplies at Bridgeport, Alabama, on the Tennessee, Rosecrans moved over into a mountain valley with nothing between him and Chattanooga

CHICKAMAUGA

Second Day: September 20, 1863

BROTHERTON
HOUSE

POE
HOUSE

①

KELLY
HOUSE

④

THOMAS'
HQ

SNODGRASS HILL

SNODGRASS
HOUSE

⑤

BRAGG'S
HQ

LAFAYETTE ROAD

OSBU[...]
HOUS[...]

VINIARD
HOUSE

JACKSON
HOUSE

ROSECRANS
HQ

WITHERS
HOUSE

DYER
HOUSE

DRY VALLEY ROAD

VILLETOE
HOUSE

③

CHICKAMAUGA: The two armies fought to a standstill on September 19, with the Federals holding a line that generally followed the Lafayette Road (lower left to upper right). Bragg's battle plan for September 20 called for Leonidas Polk's wing to first attack the Union left, followed by successive actions moving along the line toward the Federal right. Polk's fierce assaults (1) fail to break General Thomas' position, but a division holding a critical place in the Federal center is hastily sent to support the right flank leaving a fatal gap. Into that gap, General Longstreet advances at midday, breaking through the Union line between the Brotherton and Viniard houses (2). Panic sweeps the Union right and many of its commanders flee, General Rosecrans included (3). Total destruction of the Union army is avoided when the left flank, under George H. Thomas, stands firm on Snodgrass Hill (4), a defense prevented from becoming sacrificial when, without orders, Major General Granger, commanding the Federal reserve, sends troops forward to check a Confederate effort to surround Thomas (5). Weary Rebels, having fought to the point of exhaustion, let Thomas and his men retreat in good order at sundown.

Harry J. Kellogg's postwar painting *Battle of Kelly's Field, Chickamauga*, shows the bitter fighting that took place throughout the early part of September 20 on the Union left flank, positioned at the Kelly House and across its fields. "The enemy were driving the skirmishers in swiftly, firing as they came," recalled a Federal soldier who fought there. "When within two or three rods of our brigade line the regimental flags were raised suddenly, a sheet of flame went from the muzzles of our guns, and a windrow of dead and wounded Confederate lay on the ground."

Following Chickamauga, the Army of the Cumberland fell back to Chattanooga, where the Federals dug in and reorganized under siege. Confederate troops under General Bragg seized Lookout Mountain which overlooked Chattanooga and the Tennessee River (below), while mounted raiders spread out to disrupt Union supply trains trying to get foodstuffs and munitions into the city (right). As commander of the Army of the Cumberland, Major General Rosecrans was replaced by Major General Thomas, lauded throughout the land as the "Rock of Chickamauga" for his valiant stand on Snodgrass Hill. Lincoln turned to Major General U. S. Grant, who left to take charge in Chattanooga. In the meantime, Grant instructed Thomas to hold Chattanooga at all hazards. Replied Thomas: "We will hold the town until we starve."

but the long rampart of Lookout Mountain. Refusing to make a frontal assault on Bragg's defensive position, he then went southeast, going through a series of gaps in Lookout Mountain and heading for the Western and Atlantic Railroad, which ran from Chattanooga to Atlanta and was Bragg's supply line. Bragg had to evacuate Chattanooga, Union troops entered the place, and Old Rosy had completed a brilliant and virtually bloodless campaign.

The only trouble was that Rosecrans did not know that he had completed it. He might have concentrated in Chattanooga, paused to renew his supplies and let his hard-marching army catch its breath, and then he could have advanced down the railroad line to good effect. Instead, he tried to keep on going, and as he moved through the mountain passes his three army corps became widely separated. Furthermore, Bragg had stopped retreating and was making a stand at La Fayette, Georgia, about twenty-five miles from Chattanooga, awaiting reinforcements. These he was getting; troops from Knoxville, from Mississippi, and two divisions from the Army of Northern Virginia itself, led by James Longstreet. (The move the Richmond government had refused to make in June was being made now, with troops from Lee going to fight in the West.) Thus reinforced, Bragg moved in for a counterattack, and Rosecrans, waking up in the nick of time, hastily pulled his troops together to meet him. On the banks of Chickamauga Creek, about twelve miles below Chattanooga, Bragg made his attack, and on September 19 and 20 he fought and won the great Battle of Chickamauga. Part of Rosecrans' army was driven from the field in wild rout, and only a last-ditch stand by George Thomas saved the whole army from destruction. The Union troops retreated to Chattanooga, Bragg advanced and entrenched his men on high ground in a vast crescent, and the Army of the Cumberland found itself besieged.

The name Chickamauga was an old Cherokee word, men said, meaning "river of death," and there was an awful literalness to its meaning now. Each army had lost nearly a third of its numbers, Bragg's casualty list running to 18,000 or

For many weeks in late autumn, supplies trickled into Chattanooga by way of a hastily improvised "cracker line" of steamships. The stern-wheeled *Chattanooga* (below), piled high with bags of grain, was cobbled together by army builders to shuttle goods from the nearest railhead. Theodore R. Davis' drawing (above left) shows Union troops landing at Brown's Ferry, where they soon built a bridge over the Tennessee River to help convey more supplies into besieged Chattanooga.

more, and Rosecrans' to 16,000. Rosecrans' campaign was wrecked, and his own career as a field commander was ended; he was relieved and assigned to duty in St. Louis, and Rock-of-Chickamauga Thomas took his place. Bragg, the victor, had not added greatly to his reputation. He had made the Federals retreat, but if he had handled his army with more energy he might have destroyed the whole Army of the Cumberland, and his subordinates complained bitterly about his inability to make use of the triumph the troops had won. Their complaints echoed

No sooner had U. S. Grant taken charge at Chattanooga than he started planning to renew the offensive. As soon as the supply problem had been resolved in late October, Grant moved ahead with his objective of driving the enemy away from the high ground. The long Confederate line was spread out along the ridge east and south of the city, anchored on the right at Tunnel Hill and on the left on Lookout Mountain. After Grant opened his offensive, Major General Sherman's men maneuvered against Tunnel Hill while Major General Joseph Hooker ordered his troops to attack Lookout Mountain. Hooker's soldiers fought the terrain (right) as well as the enemy.

The emphasis is on vivid spectacle in James Walker's painting *Battle of Lookout Mountain* (left). In fact, a heavy mist blanketed much of the landscape, and the rugged terrain would have precluded the massed deployment depicted by the artist. Union soldiers were hungry for a victory to avenge Chickamauga; when some of Hooker's leading troops finally stopped from sheer exhaustion, they called to those coming up behind them: "Go to it, boys. We've chased them up for you. Pour it into them! Give 'em hell!"

in Richmond, and President Davis came to Tennessee to see whether Bragg ought to be replaced; concluded, finally, that he should remain, and went back to Richmond without ordering any change.

Chickamauga was a Union disaster, but at least it jarred the Federal campaign in the West back onto the rails. It forced the government to drop the ruinous policy of dispersion and concentrate its forces, and in the end this was all to the good. Additionally, it gave new powers and a new opportunity to U. S. Grant, who knew what to do with both. Thus it may have been worth what it cost, although the soldiers of the Army of the Cumberland probably would have had trouble seeing it that way.

As September ended these soldiers were in serious trouble. They held Chattanooga, but they seemed very likely to be starved into surrender there. The Confederate line, unassailable by any force George Thomas could muster, ran in a vast semicircle, touching the Tennessee River upstream from Chattanooga, following the high parapet of Missionary Ridge to the east and south, anchoring itself in the west on the precipitous sides of Lookout Mountain, and touching the Tennessee again just west of Lookout. The Confederates had no troops north of the river, nor did they need any there; that country was wild, mountainous, and all but uninhabited, and no military supply train could cross it. Supplies could reach Thomas only by the river itself, by the railroad which ran along the river's southern bank, or by the roads which similarly lay south of the river, and all of these were firmly controlled by Bragg. The Union army could not even retreat. (No army under Thomas was likely to retreat, but physical inability to get out of a trap is a handicap any way you look at it.) As far as Bragg could see, he need only keep

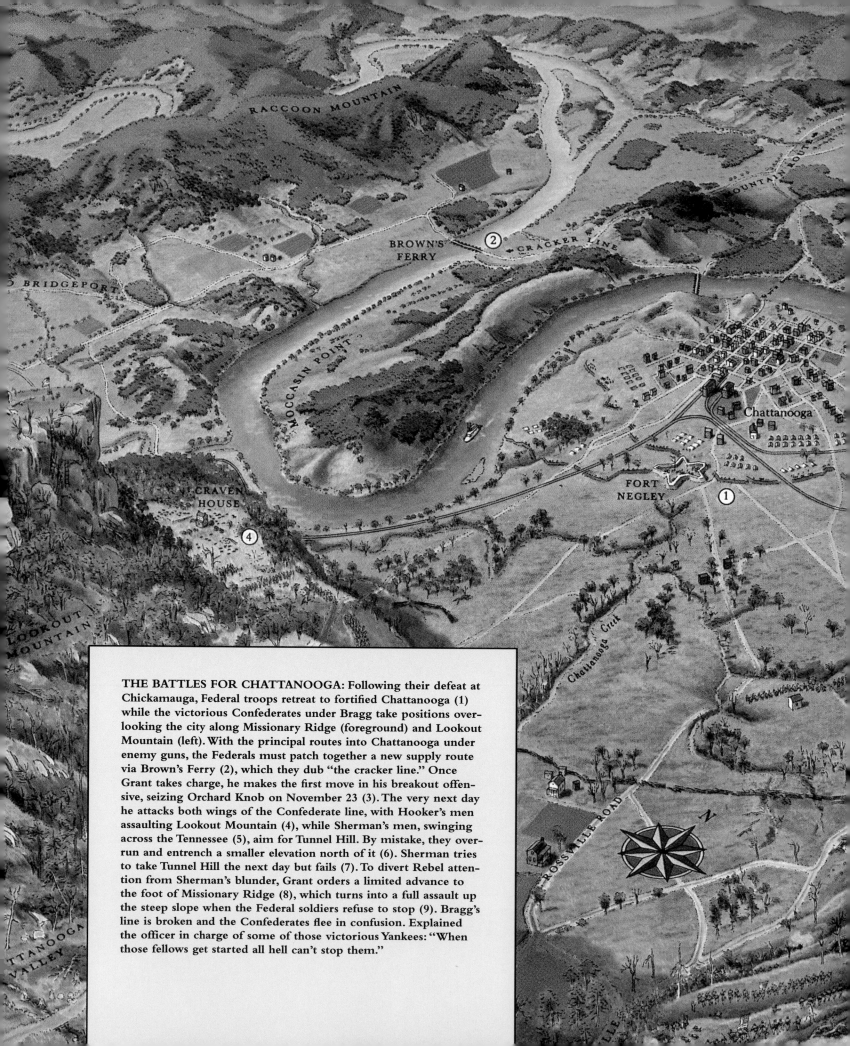

THE BATTLES FOR CHATTANOOGA: Following their defeat at Chickamauga, Federal troops retreat to fortified Chattanooga (1) while the victorious Confederates under Bragg take positions overlooking the city along Missionary Ridge (foreground) and Lookout Mountain (left). With the principal routes into Chattanooga under enemy guns, the Federals must patch together a new supply route via Brown's Ferry (2), which they dub "the cracker line." Once Grant takes charge, he makes the first move in his breakout offensive, seizing Orchard Knob on November 23 (3). The very next day he attacks both wings of the Confederate line, with Hooker's men assaulting Lookout Mountain (4), while Sherman's men, swinging across the Tennessee (5), aim for Tunnel Hill. By mistake, they overrun and entrench a smaller elevation north of it (6). Sherman tries to take Tunnel Hill the next day but fails (7). To divert Rebel attention from Sherman's blunder, Grant orders a limited advance to the foot of Missionary Ridge (8), which turns into a full assault up the steep slope when the Federal soldiers refuse to stop (9). Bragg's line is broken and the Confederates flee in confusion. Explained the officer in charge of some of those victorious Yankees: "When those fellows get started all hell can't stop them."

RAISING THE SIEGE OF CHATTANOOGA

Orchard Knob: November 23, 1863
Lookout Mountain: November 24, 1863
Missionary Ridge: November 25, 1863

TENNESSEE RIVER

Chickamauga Creek

TO KNOXVILLE

FORT GROSE

WESTERN & ATLANTIC R.R.

CHATTANOOGA & CLEVELAND R.R.

THE TUNNEL

GRANT'S HQ

ORCHARD KNOB

BRAGG'S HQ

MISSIONARY RIDGE

RETREAT TO

5

6

7

3

8

9

The extent of the Union victory at Missionary Ridge, Tennessee, is evident in this photograph (right) of fifty-two Confederate cannon captured by Union forces. So suddenly and unexpectedly did General Thomas' men scramble up the steep slope that Rebel artillerymen had little chance to hitch up their guns and escape. The smoothbore Napoleon cannon visible in the foreground had a range of 1,700 yards, but in this action they proved less effective, having barrels that could not be depressed far enough to fire at the Yankees as they came up Missionary Ridge.

his army in position for a month or two longer, and the Unionists would have to give up.

Neither by a military nor a political calculation could the Federal cause afford a catastrophe like the outright loss of the Army of the Cumberland, and the crisis at Chattanooga had a galvanic effect on the Federal nerve center in Washington. Two army corps were detached from Meade, placed under the command of Joe Hooker, and sent west by rail. This was the most effective military use of railroads yet made anywhere, and the soldiers were moved with surprising speed; leaving the banks of the Rappahannock on September 24, they reached Bridgeport, Alabama, just eight days later. Sherman was ordered to move east from Memphis with part of the Army of the Tennessee, and Grant was put in command of all military operations west of the Alleghenies (except for Banks' venture in the New Orleans-Texas area) and was ordered over to Chattanooga to set things straight.

This Grant proceeded to do, his contribution being chiefly the unflagging energy with which he tackled the job. Plans for loosening the Confederate strangle hold had already been made, and what Grant did was to make certain that they were put into effect speedily. He brought Hooker east from Bridgeport, used a brigade of Thomas' men in a sudden thrust at the Confederate outpost on the Tennessee River west of Lookout Mountain, and presently opened a route through which supplies could be brought to Chattanooga. The route combined the use of steamboats, scows, a pontoon bridge, and army wagons, and it could not begin to supply the army with everything it needed, but at least it warded off starvation. Thomas' men dubbed it "the cracker line" and began to feel that life might be worth living after all.

Sherman, leaving Memphis, had about three hundred miles to march, and for some reason Halleck had given him orders to repair the line of the Memphis and Charleston Railroad as he moved, so his progress was glacial. Grant told him to

Mission Impossible

Charles A. Dana, a newspaperman, had been sent west by Lincoln to keep an eye on Grant, but he wound up becoming his friend and confidant. After viewing the unexpected Union assault of November 25 as depicted in Thure de Thulstrup's *Grant at Missionary Ridge*, Dana wrote: *It was a bright, sunny afternoon, and, as the forces marched across the valley in front of us as regularly as if on parade, it was a great spectacle. They took with ease the first rifle-pits at the foot of the ridge as they had been ordered, and then, to the amazement of all of us who watched on Orchard Knob, they moved out and up the steep [slope] ahead of them, and before we realized it they were at the top of Missionary Ridge. . . . As soon as Grant saw the ridge was ours, he started for the front. As he rode the length of the lines, the men, who were frantic with joy and enthusiasm over the victory, received him with tumultuous shouts. The storming of the ridge by our troops was one of the greatest miracles in military history. No man who climbs the ascent by any of the roads that wind along its front can believe that eighteen thousand men were moved in tolerably good order up its broken and crumbling face unless it was his fortune to witness the deed. It seemed as awful as a visible interposition of God.*

forget about the track-gang job and to come as fast as he could; and by early November the Federal force in Chattanooga, no longer half-starved, had powerful reinforcements at hand and was ready to try to break the ring that was around it. Bragg, meanwhile, acted with incredible obtuseness. A Federal force under General Burnside had come down through the Kentucky-Tennessee mountain country to occupy Knoxville, and although it had got into the place it was not, for the moment, doing any particular harm there; but Bragg sent Longstreet and 12,000 men away to try to dislodge this force, and he detached his cavalry and still more infantry to help—so that when it came time for the big fight Bragg would be badly outnumbered, facing the best generals the Federals could muster, Grant, Sherman, and Thomas.

The big fight came on November 24 and 25. Hooker with his men from the Army of the Potomac drove the Confederate left from Lookout Mountain—less of an achievement than it looked, since Bragg had only a skeleton force there, which was dug in along the slopes rather than on the crest, but it was one of the war's spectacular scenes for all that. There had been low-lying clouds all day, and when these finally lifted and the sun broke through, the Northern flag was on the top of Lookout, and war correspondents wrote enthusiastically about the "battle above the clouds." Sherman took his Army of the Tennessee units upstream and attacked the Confederate right. He made some progress but not enough, and was getting

U. S. Grant (far left in the photo below), complete with his trademark cigar, visited Lookout Mountain after the fighting ended. Long after the war, Grant wrote with typical understatement, "The victory at Chattanooga was won against great odds, considering the advantage the enemy had of position, and was accomplished more easily than was expected. . . ."

not much more than a bloody nose for his pains; and on the afternoon of November 25 Grant told Thomas to push his Army of the Cumberland forward and take the Rebel rifle pits at the base of Missionary Ridge. This pressure might force Bragg to recall troops from Sherman's front.

At this point Thomas' soldiers took things into their own hands. They had been suffering a slow burn for a month; both Hooker's and Sherman's men had jeered at them for the Chickamauga defeat and had reminded them that other armies had to come to their rescue, and the Cumberlands had had all they cared to take. Now they moved forward, took the Confederate rifle pits as ordered—and then, after a brief pause for breath, went straight on up the steep mountain slope without orders from either Grant or Thomas, broke Bragg's line right where it was strongest, drove the Confederate army off in complete retreat, and won the Battle of Chattanooga in one spontaneous explosion of pent-up energy and fury.

Chattanooga was decisive. The beaten Confederates withdrew into Georgia. Burnside's position in Knoxville was secure. Grant, with new laurels on his unassuming head, was very clearly going to become general in chief of the Union armies, the South had definitely lost the war in the West—and, when spring came, the Federals would have a chance to apply more pressure than the Confederacy could hope to resist.

Under a rainbow bestowing benediction, victorious Union troops relax, as painted by an unknown artist in the watercolor *Blue in Bivouac, on Lookout Mountain, Tennessee* (above). Popular writers of the time celebrated the Union victory, including one poet who believed that Major General Joseph Hooker, through his victory at Lookout Mountain, regained the honor he had lost at Chancellorsville: "Oh, glorious courage that inspires the hero and runs through all his men!/The heart that failed beside the Rappahannock, it was itself again!/The star that circumstance and jealous faction shrouded in envious night/Here shone with all the splendor of its nature, and with a freer light!"

CHAPTER 10

The Northern Vise Tightens

On the ninth of March, 1864, U. S. Grant was made lieutenant general and given command of all the Union armies, and the hitherto insoluble military problem of the Federal government was at last on its way to solution. President Lincoln had learned that it took a soldier to do a soldier's job, and he had at last found the soldier who was capable of it: a direct, straightforward man who would leave high policy to the civilian government and devote himself with unflagging energy to the task of putting Confederate armies out of action. There would be no more side shows: from now on the whole weight of Northern power would be applied remorselessly, with concentrated force.

There had been a number of side shows during the last year, and the net result of all of them had been to detract from the general effectiveness of the Union war effort. An army and navy expedition had tried throughout the preceding summer to hammer its way into Charleston, South Carolina. It had

At the beginning of 1864 the Confederate flag still waved defiantly over Charleston, despite the aggressive efforts of Federal engineers, who had pressed their cannon close enough to pound Fort Sumter into rubble and even to drop shells into the city itself. One of the heaviest Union bombardments is the subject of John Ross Key's 1865 painting *The Bombardment of Fort Sumter*. In Virginia, Robert E. Lee's army remained entrenched just south of the Rapidan River, while in Georgia Joseph E. Johnston's army watched over the forces Sherman was assembling around Chattanooga. The Confederacy appeared to be holding its own, though the warm spring of 1864 would bring new dangers.

The first months of 1864 were jarred by attacks on the Confederate periphery. On February 20 a Union expedition into north-central Florida ended in defeat at Olustee, a battle depicted in a lithograph of a Thure de Thulstrup painting (right). "I fear the rebels . . . have out-generaled us," wrote a sergeant in the 54th Massachusetts. "They chose the battle-ground, . . . and managed it so adroitly that no man in the Union army knew anything about it."

In the West a two-pronged effort that began in March cut through the heart of the Confederate Trans-Mississippi Department. While one Union infantry column pushed south through Arkansas, another pressed into northwest Louisiana for a planned link-up along the Red River. Lieutenant General Richard Taylor (below) commanded the Confederate troops posted to meet them along the Red River. "This is Genl. Taylor's Country," wrote one of his soldiers. "He has set his heart to defend it."

reduced Fort Sumter to a shapeless heap of rubble, but it had cost the North a number of ships and soldiers and had accomplished nothing except to prove that Charleston could not be taken by direct assault. In Louisiana, General Banks was trying to move into Texas, partly for the sake of the cotton that could be picked up along the way and partly because the government believed that Napoleon III would give up his Mexican adventure if a Northern army occupied Texas and went to the Rio Grande. The belief may have been justified, but Banks never came close, and his campaign was coming to grief this spring. Early in April he was beaten at Mansfield and Pleasant Hill, Louisiana, far up the Red River, and he retreated with such panicky haste that Admiral Porter's accompanying fleet of gunboats narrowly escaped complete destruction. (The water level in the Red River was falling, and for a time it seemed that the gunboats could never get out; they were saved at the last when a backwoods colonel in the Union army took a regiment of lumbermen and built dams that temporarily made the water deep enough for escape.) In Florida a Union expedition in which white and black troops were brigaded together attempted a conquest that would have had no important results even if it had succeeded; it had failed dismally, meeting defeat at Olustee late in February. Union cavalry under William Sooy Smith had tried to sweep across Mississippi during the winter and had been ignominiously routed by Bedford Forrest.

All of these ventures had dissipated energy and manpower that might have been used elsewhere. (Banks' Texas expedition had been the chief reason why Grant had not been allowed to exploit the great opportunity opened by the capture of Vicksburg.) They had won nothing, and they would not have won the war even if all of them had succeeded. Now, it was hoped, there would be no more of them. Grant had intense singleness of purpose, and the government was giving him a free hand. He would either win the war or be the man on the spot when the Union confessed that victory was unattainable.

Grant considered the military problem to be basically quite simple. The principal Confederate armies had to be destroyed. The capture of cities and

The Red River Campaign unfolded as a succession of Union mishaps and missed opportunities. The confident advance directed by Major General Nathaniel P. Banks (above), a politician turned soldier, was frustrated both by a lack of co-ordination and the stubborn resistance of the smaller Confederate force commanded by General Taylor. The Red River itself also played a role, as falling water levels trapped Rear Admiral David Dixon Porter's powerful naval flotilla (left), which was to accompany Banks' expedition. On the river above Alexandria, Louisiana, engineers improvised with temporary dams, raising the water level so Porter's boats could escape (below).

Federal supply centers like the one at Corinth, Mississippi (right), closed in the wake of the war's progress. Finally co-ordinating nationally, the Union army began a series of moves against vulnerable points in the Confederacy. When Major General William T. Sherman assembled a powerful striking force near Chattanooga, with Atlanta as his goal, he required great quantities of matériel: food and accoutrements for the soldiers, ammunition for their weapons, forage for their animals. Sherman ordered that non-essential depots, such as the one at Corinth, be closed, so that personnel could be reassigned to more closely support an army on the move.

"strategic points" and the occupation of Southern territory meant very little; as long as the main Confederate armies were in the field the Confederacy lived, and as soon as they vanished the Confederacy ceased to be. His objectives, therefore, would be the opposing armies, and his goal would be to put them out of action as quickly as possible.

There were two armies that concerned him: the incomparable Army of Northern Virginia, led by Robert E. Lee, and the Army of Tennessee, commanded now by Joseph E. Johnston. Bragg's inability to win had at last become manifest even to Jefferson Davis, who had an inexplicable confidence in the man. Bragg had made a hash of his Kentucky invasion in the late summer of 1862, he had let victory slip through his grasp at Murfreesboro, and he had utterly failed to make proper use of his great victory at Chickamauga. After Chattanooga, Davis removed him—bringing him to Richmond and installing him as chief military adviser to the President—and Johnston was put in his place.

Davis had scant confidence in Johnston and had grown to dislike the man personally, and Johnston felt precisely the same way about Davis. But the much-abused Army of Tennessee, which had fought as well as any army could fight but which had never had adequate leadership, revered and trusted Johnston profoundly, and his appointment had been inevitable. His army had recovered its morale,

To provide Sherman with a clear supply route, Union engineers worked miracles, completely rebuilding the Tennessee River bridge at Chattanooga using abutments of fresh-hewn logs and prefabricated "shad-belly" trusses (opposite bottom and below). Sherman's first priority was to accumulate enough supplies to maintain 100,000 soldiers and 35,000 animals (mostly mules and horses) for seventy days. When he limited the train space available for civilian travel in and out of Chattanooga, Christian charity organizations, concerned that their access to the soldiers would be limited, protested. "Show me that your presence at the front is more valuable than two hundred pounds of powder, bread, or oats," Sherman told them.

"Have you ever seen Sherman?" asked Walt Whitman. "Try to picture Sherman —seamy, sinewy, in style—a bit of stern open air made up in the image of a man." U. S. Grant, in his grand plan for 1864, assigned the critical task of taking Atlanta to his friend William Tecumseh Sherman (opposite page). Opposing him was one of the South's best strategists, General Joseph E. Johnston (left). Though Confederate officials in Richmond constantly differed with Johnston, he was much loved by his men: they recognized him as an officer who would risk their lives sparingly.

and it was strongly entrenched on the low mountain ridges northwest of Dalton, Georgia, a few miles from the bloodstained field of Chickamauga. It contained about 60,000 men, and Lee's army, which lay just below the Rapidan River in central Virginia, was about the same size.

These armies were all that mattered. The Confederacy had sizable forces west of the Mississippi, under the over-all command of Edmund Kirby Smith, but the trans-Mississippi region was effectively cut off now that the Federals controlled the great river, and what happened there was of minor importance. The Southern nation would live or die depending on the fate of Lee's and Johnston's armies. Grant saw it so, and his entire plan for 1864 centered on the attempt to destroy those two armies.

IN THE WEST EVERYTHING would be up to Sherman. Grant had put him in control of the whole Western theater of the war, with the exception of the Banks expedition, which was flickering out in expensive futility. Sherman was what would now be called an army group commander. In and around Chattanooga he had his own Army of the Tennessee, under Major General James B. McPherson; the

Well-constructed earthworks (below) enabled Johnston's men to hold off many times their number at New Hope Church, Georgia. After avoiding an encirclement by Sherman's armies at Resaca, and failing to spring his own trap on a portion of the Union force near Cassville, General Johnston fell back along the railroad to a strong line of works at Allatoona Pass. Opting against a frontal attack on that position, Sherman moved his entire force to the west in a grand flanking maneuver. Johnston took a new blocking position and fought Sherman on May 25 at New Hope Church, where the South depended on the spade as well as the gun.

redoubtable Army of the Cumberland, under Thomas; and a small force called the Army of the Ohio—hardly more than an army corps in actual size—commanded by a capable regular with pink cheeks and a flowing beard, Major General John M. Schofield. All in all, Sherman had upwards of 100,000 combat men with him. When he moved, he would go down the Western and Atlantic Railroad toward Atlanta; but Atlanta, important as it was to the Confederacy, was not his real objective. His objective was the Confederate army in his front. As he himself described his mission after the war, "I was to go for Joe Johnston."

Grant, meanwhile, would go for Lee.

Although he was general in chief, Grant would not operate from headquarters in Washington. The demoted Halleck was retained as chief of staff, and he would stay in Washington to handle the paper work; but Grant's operating headquarters would be in the field, moving with the Army of the Potomac. General Meade was kept in command of that army. With a fine spirit of abnegation, Meade had offered to resign, suggesting that Grant might want some Westerner in

whom he had full confidence to command the army; but Grant had told him to stay where he was, and he endorsed an army-reorganization plan which Meade was just then putting into effect. Grant made no change in the army's interior chain of command, except that he brought a tough infantry officer, Phil Sheridan, from the Army of the Cumberland and put him in charge of the Army of the Potomac's cavalry corps. But if Grant considered Meade a capable officer who deserved to retain his command, he himself would nevertheless move with Meade's army, and he would exercise so much control over it that before long people would be speaking of it as Grant's army.

Grant's reasons were simple enough. The Army of the Potomac had much the sort of record the Confederate Army of Tennessee had—magnificent combat performance, brought to nothing by repeated failures in leadership. It had been unlucky, and its officer corps was badly clique-ridden, obsessed by the memory of the departed McClellan, so deeply impressed by Lee's superior abilities that its talk at times almost had a defeatist quality. The War Department had been second-guessing this army's commanders so long that it probably would go on doing it unless the general in chief himself were present. All in all, the Army of the Potomac needed a powerful hand on the controls. Grant would supply that hand, although his presence with the army would create an extremely difficult command situation.

This army was in camp in the general vicinity of Culpeper Court House, on the northern side of the upper Rapidan. (A measure of its lack of success thus far is the fact that after three years of warfare it was camped only a few miles farther south than it had been camped when the war began.) Facing it, beyond the river, was the Army of Northern Virginia. Longstreet and his corps were returning from an unhappy winter in eastern Tennessee. When the spring campaign opened, Lee would have rather more than 60,000 fighting men. The Unionists, who had called up Burnside and his old IX Corps to work with the Army of the Potomac, would be moving with nearly twice that number.

The mission of the Army of the Potomac was as simple as Sherman's: it was to head for the Confederate army and fight until something broke. It would move toward Richmond, just as Sherman was moving toward Atlanta, but its real assignment would be less to capture the Confederate capital than to destroy the army that was bound to defend that capital.

Grant was missing no bets. The irrepressible Ben Butler commanded a force of some 33,000 men around Fort Monroe, denominated the Army of the James, and when the Army of the Potomac advanced, Butler was to move up the south bank of the James River toward Richmond. At the very least his advance would occupy the attention of Confederate troops who would otherwise reinforce Lee; and if everything went well (which, considering Butler's defects as a strategist, was not really very likely), Lee would be compelled to retreat. On top of this there was a Union army in the Shenandoah, commanded by the German-born Franz Sigel, and this army was to move down to the town of Staunton, whence it might go east through the Blue Ridge in the direction of Richmond. All in all, three Federal armies would be converging on the Confederate capital, each one with a powerful numerical advantage over any force that could be brought against it.

Everybody would move together. Sherman would march when Grant and

Theodore Davis' drawing *An Incident at New Hope Church* (above) shows a Rebel sharpshooter trapped at his post in a tree. One of Sherman's corps commanders described the route from Chattanooga to Atlanta as a "bloody road." Although it was largely a campaign of maneuver, there were sharp fights all along the way; at Resaca (May 14 and 15), Cassville (May 19), New Hope Church (May 25), Pickett's Mill (May 27), Dallas (May 28), Kolb's Farm (June 22), and Kennesaw Mountain (June 27). By early July, though, Sherman was close enough to see the church spires of Atlanta. An officer present recalled that occasion, seeing the Union general "stepping nervously about, his eyes sparkling and his face all aglow."

A Master Plan for Victory

→ **Union Troop movements**

----► **Ultimate Courses of Sherman and Grant**

After three years of war the Union strategy changed under Ulysses S. Grant. In the spring of 1864 the primary objectives were the Confederacy's armies rather than its cities. The solid lines on the map above show the progress of Sherman's march against Johnston in Georgia and Meade's against Lee in Virginia. The dotted lines reflect the campaigns as they unfolded through the rest of the year. The two campaigns developed differently: much of the action in the southern theater was a general's game of constant maneuvering, while the northern theater inched along as a war of attrition. Grant kept his eye on the end result: *I was determined, first, to use the greatest number of troops practicable against the armed force of the enemy . . . second, to hammer continuously against the armed force of the enemy and his resources, until by mere attrition, if no other way, there should be nothing left to him. . . .*

Throughout May and into June, Johnston continually gave up ground before Sherman's advance, often backing off without a fight, a policy that did not endear him to the war-room generals in Richmond. It was not a bloodless period—when the armies met they clashed violently—but Sherman repeatedly executed a flank movement that compelled Johnston to fall back. This slow dance ended along a line of hills before Marietta, Georgia, where Johnston held firm. Sherman probed this line for several days, seeking a weak point. While observing the skirmishing on June 14, the Confederate Lieutenant General Leonidas Polk (below) was killed by an artillery shell; an ordained bishop in the Episcopal church, Polk was carrying copies of a newly published tract, "Balm for the Weary and Wounded," when he died. Within a few days Johnston fell back again and Sherman began to lose patience with maneuvering. Thure de Thulstrup's painting *Behind the Union Line* (above left) shows Sherman watching as his men prepare for an all-out assault at Kennesaw Mountain. At every point the Federals were repulsed with great loss. "I tell you the men were mowed down like grass," a young Yankee told his parents.

Meade marched, and Butler and Sigel would advance at the same time. For the first time in the war the Union would put on a really co-ordinated campaign under central control, with all of its armies acting as a team.

ON MAY 4, 1864, the machine began to roll.

Public attention on both sides was always centered on the fighting in Virginia. The opposing capitals were no more than a hundred miles apart, and they were the supremely sensitive nerve centers. What happened in Virginia took the eye first, and this spring it almost seemed as if all of the fury and desperation of the war were concentrated there.

The Army of the Potomac crossed the Rapidan and started to march down through a junglelike stretch of second-growth timber and isolated farms known as the Wilderness, with the hope that it could bring Lee to battle in the open country farther south. But one of Lee's distinguishing characteristics was a deep unwillingness to fight where his opponent wanted to fight. He liked to choose his own field, and he did so now. Undismayed by the great disparity in numbers, he marched straight into the Wilderness and jumped the Federal columns before they could get across. Grant immediately concluded that if Lee wanted to fight here, he might as well get what he wanted, and on May 5 an enormous two-day battle got under way.

The Wilderness was a bad place for a fight. The roads were few, narrow, and bad, and the farm clearings were scarce; most of the country was densely wooded, with underbrush so thick that nobody could see fifty yards in any direction, cut up by ravines and little watercourses, with brambles and creepers that made movement almost impossible. The Federal advantage in numbers meant little here, and its advantage in artillery meant nothing at all, since few guns could be used. Because a much higher percentage of its men came from the country and were used to the woods, the Confederate army was probably less handicapped by all of this than the Army of the Potomac.

The Battle of the Wilderness was blind and vicious. The woods caught fire, and many wounded men were burned to death, and the smoke of this fire together with the battle smoke made a choking fog that intensified the almost impenetrable gloom of the woods. At the end of two days the Federals had lost more than 17,000 men and had gained not one foot. Both flanks had been broken in, and outright disaster had been staved off by a narrow margin. By any indicator one could use, the Army of the Potomac had been beaten just as badly as Hooker had been beaten at Chancellorsville a year earlier. On May 7 the rival armies glowered at each other in the smoldering forest, and the Federal soldiers assumed that the old game would be repeated: they would retreat north of the Rapidan,

Theodore R. Davis' drawing (right) shows General Sherman watching the Federal attack at Kennesaw Mountain. He is accompanied by General George Thomas, whose troops had been selected for the action. A comparison between the two senior officers was made by a soldier who wrote that Thomas was "quite the reverse of Sherman, both in manners and appearance. . . . He is . . . calm and cautious; does everything by rule; leaves nothing to chance."

reorganize and refit and get reinforcements, and then they would make a new campaign somewhere else.

That night, at dusk, the Army of the Potomac was pulled back from its firing lines and put in motion. But when it moved, it moved south, not north. Grant was not Hooker. Beaten here, he would sideslip to the left and fight again; his immediate objective was a crossroads at Spotsylvania Court House, eleven miles southwest of Fredericksburg. It was on Lee's road to Richmond, and if Grant got there first, Lee would have to do the attacking. So the army moved all night, and as the exhausted soldiers realized that they were not retreating but were actually advancing they set up a cheer.

GRANT HAD MADE ONE of the crucial decisions of the war, and in retrospect the Battle of the Wilderness became almost a Federal victory. This army was not going to retreat, it was not even going to pause to lick its wounds; it was simply

Sherman's goal was Atlanta: transportation hub, industrial center, and unofficial capital for the entire lower South. This photograph (below) of the Western and Atlantic Railroad's Atlanta "car shed" suggests something of the scale of the city's commercial activity. In an effort to rouse the citizenry's fighting spirit, the Atlanta *Southern Confederacy* proclaimed: "We are fighting the good fight of home and family, of hearthstone and sepulchre, not only against the hosts marshaled at the North, but the refuse of European prisons, of men who hire themselves to cut the throats of innocent men, women, and children."

Edward Lamson Henry's painting (above) shows a New Jersey regiment, one of many units that brought fresh recruits to army training camps along the Potomac River near Brady Station, Virginia. On the night of May 3 nearly 100,000 of the new men began a march south into a region of Virginia known as the Wilderness.

going to force the fighting, and in the end Lee's outnumbered army was going to be compelled to play the sort of game which it could not win.

It was not going to be automatic, however. Lee saw what Grant was up to and made a night march of his own. His men got to Spotsylvania Court House just ahead of the Federals, and the first hot skirmish for the crossroads swelled into a rolling battle that went on for twelve days, from May 8 to May 19. No bitterer fighting than the fighting that took place here was ever seen on the American continent. The Federals broke the Southern line once, on May 12, at a spot known ever after as "Bloody Angle," and there was a solid day of hand-to-hand combat while the Federals tried unsuccessfully to enlarge the break and split Lee's army into halves. There was fighting every day, and Grant kept shifting his troops to the left in an attempt to crumple Lee's flank, so that Federal soldiers who were facing east when the battle began were facing due west when it closed. Phil Sheridan took the cavalry off on a driving raid toward Richmond, and Jeb Stuart galloped to meet him. The Unionists were driven off in a hard fight at Yellow Tavern, in the Richmond suburbs, but Stuart himself was killed.

Elsewhere in Virginia things went badly for the Federals. Sigel moved up the Shenandoah Valley, was met by a scratch Confederate force at New Market, and was routed in a battle in which the corps of cadets from Virginia Military Institute greatly distinguished itself. Ben Butler made his advance up the James River most ineptly and was beaten at Bermuda Hundred. He made camp on the Bermuda Hundred peninsula, the Confederates drew a fortified line across the base of the peninsula, and in Grant's expressive phrase Butler was as much out of action as if he had been put in a tightly corked bottle. He would cause Lee no worries for some time, and from the army which had beaten him Lee got reinforcements that practically made up for his heavy battle losses thus far.

There were brief lulls in the campaign but no real pauses. From Spotsylvania the Army of the Potomac again moved by its left, skirmishing every day, looking for an opening and not quite finding one. It fought minor battles along the North Anna and on Totopotomoy Creek, and it got at last to a crossroads known as Cold Harbor, near the Chickahominy River and mortally close to Richmond; and here, because there was scant room for maneuver, Grant on June 3 put on a

The first obstacle soldiers encountered on their march toward the Wilderness was the Rapidan River, over which Union engineers speedily constructed a portable pontoon bridge. The photograph below shows soldiers of the Army of the Potomac crossing from the bridge into the Wilderness on the afternoon of May 4. A Federal staff officer on the scene knew that many of the men were destined to die, and he morbidly wondered exactly which, as he watched the units passing off the bridge: "[How] strange it would be if each man who was destined to fall in the campaign had some large badge on!"

A drawing (right) by field artist Edwin Forbes shows Union gunners clearing a small field of fire in front of their position in the Wilderness. The thick underbrush of the Wilderness made it extremely difficult for troops to move in any sort of disciplined formation, and even more difficult for them to operate cannon. As a further problem, the underbrush was tinder dry; several times during the fighting, small forest fires were ignited by sparks from gunpowder. Alfred Waud's drawing (below right) shows a desperate effort to save the wounded from the flames. "The bodies of the dead were blackened and burned beyond all possibility of recognition," declared a shocked soldier on the scene.

tremendous frontal assault in the hope of breaking the Confederate line once and for all. The assault failed, with fearful losses, and the Union and Confederate armies remained in contact, each one protected by impregnable trenches, for ten days more. Then Grant made his final move—a skillful sideslip to the left, once more, and this time he went clear across the James River and advanced on the town of Petersburg. Most of the railroads that tied Richmond to the South came through Petersburg, and if the Federals could occupy the place before Lee got there, Richmond would have to be abandoned. But General William F. Smith, leading the Union advance, fumbled the attack, and when the rest of the army came up, Lee had had time to man the city's defenses. The Union attacks failed, and Grant settled down to a siege.

Two days of hand-to-hand combat in the Wilderness cost the Union army nearly 18,000 casualties, while Southern forces lost almost 11,000. Even while the injured were being carried to field hospitals, like the one near the ruins of the Chancellor House (left), Grant was planning his next move. Such heavy losses would usually compel an army to withdraw, but Grant was otherwise determined: when his troops realized that they were advancing instead of retreating, their response was to cheer the man (below) who would not be turned back.

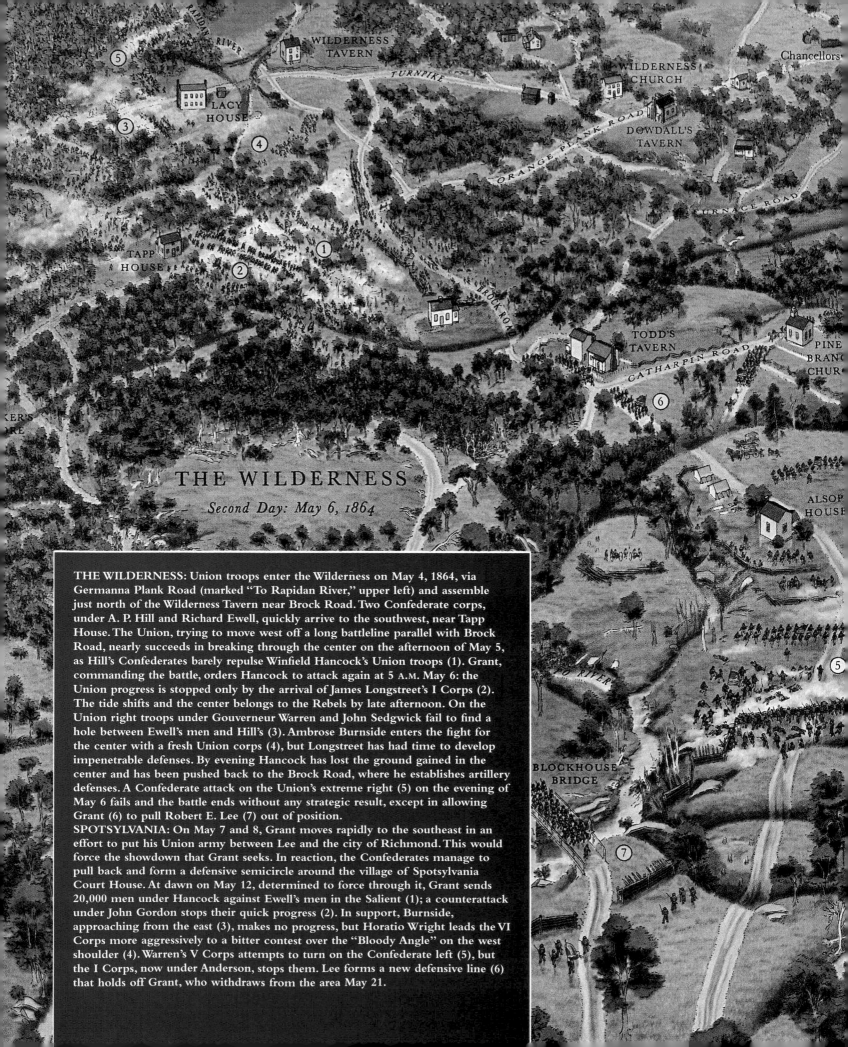

THE WILDERNESS

Second Day: May 6, 1864

THE WILDERNESS: Union troops enter the Wilderness on May 4, 1864, via Germanna Plank Road (marked "To Rapidan River," upper left) and assemble just north of the Wilderness Tavern near Brock Road. Two Confederate corps, under A. P. Hill and Richard Ewell, quickly arrive to the southwest, near Tapp House. The Union, trying to move west off a long battleline parallel with Brock Road, nearly succeeds in breaking through the center on the afternoon of May 5, as Hill's Confederates barely repulse Winfield Hancock's Union troops (1). Grant, commanding the battle, orders Hancock to attack again at 5 A.M. May 6: the Union progress is stopped only by the arrival of James Longstreet's I Corps (2). The tide shifts and the center belongs to the Rebels by late afternoon. On the Union right troops under Gouverneur Warren and John Sedgwick fail to find a hole between Ewell's men and Hill's (3). Ambrose Burnside enters the fight for the center with a fresh Union corps (4), but Longstreet has had time to develop impenetrable defenses. By evening Hancock has lost the ground gained in the center and has been pushed back to the Brock Road, where he establishes artillery defenses. A Confederate attack on the Union's extreme right (5) on the evening of May 6 fails and the battle ends without any strategic result, except in allowing Grant (6) to pull Robert E. Lee (7) out of position.

SPOTSYLVANIA: On May 7 and 8, Grant moves rapidly to the southeast in an effort to put his Union army between Lee and the city of Richmond. This would force the showdown that Grant seeks. In reaction, the Confederates manage to pull back and form a defensive semicircle around the village of Spotsylvania Court House. At dawn on May 12, determined to force through it, Grant sends 20,000 men under Hancock against Ewell's men in the Salient (1); a counterattack under John Gordon stops their quick progress (2). In support, Burnside, approaching from the east (3), makes no progress, but Horatio Wright leads the VI Corps more aggressively to a bitter contest over the "Bloody Angle" on the west shoulder (4). Warren's V Corps attempts to turn on the Confederate left (5), but the I Corps, now under Anderson, stops them. Lee forms a new defensive line (6) that holds off Grant, who withdraws from the area May 21.

Major General Winfield Scott Hancock's II Corps entered the Overland Campaign as an excellent command, probably the best in the Army of the Potomac. Hancock (seated, above) had three capable and aggressive division commanders (left to right): Brigadier General Francis C. Barlow, Major General David B. Birney, and Brigadier General John Gibbon. The fighting at Spotsylvania claimed the life of Major General John Sedgwick, commander of VI Corps and one of the Army of the Potomac's most experienced officers. Julian Scott's painting (opposite top) shows shocked Union officers bending over Sedgwick's lifeless body. Ironically, Sedgwick was shot by a sniper after stepping into the open in an effort to reassure his men. "Why, what are you dodging for?" he said to a cowering soldier. "They could not hit an elephant at that distance." Alonzo Chappel's 1865 painting *Battle of the Wilderness, Attack at Spotsylvania Courthouse* (opposite bottom), depicts an assault by the Federal II Corps led by General Winfield Scott Hancock, during the May 12 fighting. "It seemed impossible that troops could stand so severe a fire," observed one Union staff officer.

In the wake of May's fighting at the Wilderness and Spotsylvania, nearby Fredericksburg turned into one vast hospital for the Union wounded (opposite page top). Belle Plain (opposite page bottom), about ten miles east, was a holding pen for Confederate soldiers captured during the early part of the campaign and later shipped to northern prisoner-of-war camps. On May 19, Confederate efforts to flank the Union position at Spotsylvania resulted in a fight at Harris, also known as Alsop Farm. The next day the photographer Timothy O'Sullivan made a series of unforgettable images (two are presented on this page) of the bodies of Confederates killed in the fight, awaiting burial.

Major General J. E. B. Stuart (above) commanded the Confederacy's boldest cavalry corps and was the natural nemesis of Major General Philip H. Sheridan, appointed by U. S. Grant to lead the Army of the Potomac's cavalry. Determined to draw Stuart out, Sheridan persuaded Grant to let him use his riders as an independent striking force and undertake a raid toward Richmond. H. W. Chaloner's *Cavalry Charge at Yellow Tavern, Virginia, May 11, 1864* (right) depicts the resulting battle of men and horses. Amid the fighting, a dismounted Federal trooper shot and mortally wounded Stuart. "He never brought me a piece of false information," was Robert E. Lee's mournful comment when informed that Stuart had fallen. The dashing cavalryman died on May 12.

U. S. Grant was photographed (above) on May 21 conferring with his staff of the Army of the Potomac outside Massaponax Church (he is standing at the far left, leaning over a pew to examine a map). The fighting at Spotsylvania had cost Grant more than 18,000 casualties, in addition to those lost in the Battle of the Wilderness, yet he remained firm in his resolve to press forward with his campaign. In a communication Grant sent to Washington just a few days before the date of the photograph, he vowed "to fight it out on this line if it takes all summer."

. . .

THE CAMPAIGN THUS FAR had been made at a stunning cost. In the first month the Union army had lost 60,000 men. The armies were never entirely out of contact after the first shots were fired in the Wilderness; they remained in close touch, as a matter of fact, until the spring of 1865, and once they got to Petersburg they waged trench warfare strongly resembling that of World War I. Across the North people grew disheartened. Lee's army had not been broken, Richmond had not been taken, and no American had ever seen anything like the endless casualty lists that were coming out. At close range the achievement of the Army of the Potomac was hard to see. Yet it had forced Lee to fight continuously on the defensive, giving him no chance for one of those dazzling strokes by which he had disrupted every previous Federal offensive, never letting him regain the initiative. He

True to his word, Grant ordered George Meade, commander of the Army of the Potomac, to maintain the pressure on Robert E. Lee's Army of Northern Virginia, which was being forced back ever closer to Richmond. On May 23, Meade's army crossed the North Anna River at two places, one of which was near Jericho Mills (above). The fighting in that vicinity racked up at least another 2,000 Union casualties over the next three days. With Lee so well entrenched, Grant opted for a flank march, which swung the Union's army around toward the eastern side of Richmond. An effort to break through Lee's lines at Cold Harbor on June 1 (left) and June 3 proved another bloody failure, adding nearly 15,000 names to the roll of Federals killed, wounded, or missing. Grant's total casualties for the Overland Campaign came to more than 54,000.

General Grant remained confident despite the stresses on him, as is evident in the photograph (right) taken in August, 1864. Having been frustrated in his effort to draw Robert E. Lee into a decisive battle in the spring campaign of 1864, and soundly repulsed in the attack on Cold Harbor, Grant decided on an entirely new line of advance. Instead of moving on Richmond, he ordered the Army of the Potomac across the James River to strike at the strategically important railroad and manufacturing center of Petersburg, Virginia. The crossing began on June 14, as transports hauled Hancock's II Corps to the south side of the river (below) and it continued into the next day, facilitated by the construction of an immense pontoon bridge 2,100 feet long. When informed by Grant that the campaign would continue, no matter what the cost, Abraham Lincoln replied: "I begin to see it. You will succeed. God bless you all."

tried it once, sending Jubal Early and 14,000 men up on a dash through the Shenandoah Valley into Maryland. Early brushed aside a small Federal force that tried to stop him on the Monocacy River and got clear to the Washington suburb of Silver Spring, less than a dozen miles from the Capitol building; but at the last minute Grant sent an army corps north from the Army of the Potomac, and after a skirmish at Silver Spring (witnessed by a worried Abraham Lincoln, in person) Early had to go back to Virginia. No longer could a threat to Washington induce the administration to recall an army of invasion. Early's march had given the government a severe case of nerves, but it had been barren of accomplishment.

Sherman's campaign in Georgia followed a different pattern from Grant's. Sherman had both the room and the inclination to make it a war of maneuver, but

Johnston was an able strategist who could match paces with him all the way. Maneuvered out of his lines at Dalton, Johnston faded back, Sherman following. Often the Confederates would make a stand; when they did, Sherman would confront them with Thomas' Army of the Cumberland, using McPherson's and Schofield's troops for a wide flanking maneuver, and while these tactics usually made Johnston give ground, they never compelled him to fight at a disadvantage, and Sherman's progress looked better on the map than it really was. He had been ordered to go for Joe Johnston, and he could not quite crowd the man into a corner and bring his superior weight to bear. There were several pitched battles and there were innumerable skirmishes, and both armies had losses, but there was nothing like the all-consuming fighting that was going on in Virginia. Johnston made a stand once, on the slopes of Kennesaw Mountain, and Sherman tired of his flanking operations and tried to crack the center of the Confederate line. It refused to yield, and Sherman's men were repulsed with substantial losses; then, after a time, the war of movement was resumed, like a formalized military dance performed to the rhythmic music of the guns.

Andre Castaigne's 1892 painting (below) shows the 22nd U.S.C.T. (United States Colored Troops) in a successful assault against Petersburg's formidable defensive earthworks. While the Army of the Potomac was still on the way west, troops belonging to the Army of the James were already attacking Petersburg. Among them was a division of black troops, including the 22nd U.S.C.T., a unit organized at Camp William Penn near Philadelphia.

The photograph above shows Captain James H. Cooper's Battery B, 1st Pennsylvania Light Artillery in position near the Avery Farm, on June 21, in the aftermath of the Battle of Petersburg. For four days (June 15 to 18) Union forces with an overwhelming numerical advantage had battered the defenses of Petersburg, capturing some sections of the line but never achieving a breakthrough. On June 19, Grant ordered heavy guns to his lines; he was determined to lay siege to the city. After that, Union earthworks began to snake across the Virginia landscape as men such as these constructed infantry trenches and battery positions.

By the middle of July Sherman had crossed the Chattahoochee River and reached the outskirts of Atlanta, but he had by no means done what he set out to do. Johnston's army, picking up reinforcements as it retreated, was probably stronger now than when the campaign began, and Sherman for the moment was at a standstill. Grant and Meade were stalled in front of Petersburg, and Sherman was stalled in front of Atlanta. The Confederate strongholds were unconquered, and Northerners began to find the prospect discouraging.

THEY BECAME EVEN MORE discouraged late in July, when Grant's army failed in a stroke that should have taken Petersburg. Frontal attacks on properly held entrenchments were doomed to failure, and even Grant, not easily convinced, had had to admit this. But at Petersburg a new chance offered itself. A regiment of Pennsylvania coal miners dug a five-hundred-foot tunnel under the Confederate lines, several tons of powder were planted there, and at dawn on July 30 the mine was exploded. It blew an enormous gap in the defensive entrenchments, and for an hour or more the way was open for the Federal army to march almost unopposed into Petersburg.

Burnside's corps made the attempt and bungled it fearfully; the assault failed, and Grant's one great chance to end the war in one day vanished.

The people of the North were getting very war-weary as the month of July ended. Grant did not seem to be any nearer the capture of Richmond than he had

been when the campaign began; Sherman was deep in Georgia, but he had neither whipped the Confederate army which faced him nor taken Atlanta. The pressure which the Confederacy could not long endure was being applied relentlessly, but it was hard for the folks back home to see that anything was really being accomplished. They only knew that the war was costing more than it had ever cost before, and that there seemed to be nothing of any consequence to show for it; and that summer President Lincoln privately wrote down his belief that he could not be re-elected that fall. If the electorate should repudiate him, the North would almost certainly fall out of the war, and the South would have its independence.

The drawing above reflects the view looking south toward Petersburg from a signal station on Bermuda Hundred, a small peninsula formed by the confluence of the Appomattox and James rivers. Throughout the month of May, Major General Benjamin F. Butler and the Army of the James remained stalled on Bermuda Hundred, waging a fruitless campaign that was supposed to strike at Richmond's soft underbelly. After June, Bermuda Hundred represented a northern extension of the Federal siege lines at Petersburg, forcing Robert E. Lee to further spread his badly outnumbered forces in order to protect both Petersburg and Richmond.

Before Petersburg – at sunrise
July 30 1864

A.R.Waud

A Cauldron of Death

Weeks of static trench warfare prompted some industrious Pennsylvania troops to construct a five-hundred-foot tunnel at a point where the opposing lines were fairly close together, ending it under the Rebel earthworks. The man who conceived the plan, Lieutenant Colonel Henry Pleasants, had been a mining engineer before the war, and many of his men had been coal miners. They packed the end of the tunnel with 8,000 pounds of gunpowder, and at 4:44 A.M., July 30, the huge mine exploded, a moment sketched by Alfred Waud (above). "First there came a deep shock and tremor of the earth and a jar like an earthquake," said a Michigan soldier, ". . . then a monstrous tongue of flame shot fully two hundred feet into the air . . . then a great spout or fountain of red earth rose to a great height, mingled with men and guns, timbers and planks, and every kind of debris, all ascending, spreading, whirling, scattering and falling with great concussion to the earth once more."

Despite achieving a complete surprise, the attack that followed the explosion was a total failure. The infantry assault had been entrusted to Major General Ambrose E. Burnside, who had selected a division of black troops to lead the way. Twenty-four hours before the mine exploded, Major General George G. Meade told Burnside to find some white troops to take their place. Meade didn't trust the black soldiers (who had yet to see significant combat) and he worried about the political repercussions should they suffer heavy losses. This last-minute change completely confused Burnside's execution; the white troops who made the first charge were not properly briefed and their disarray in the crater left by the mine allowed the stunned Rebel defenders time to rally and counterattack. By the time the black troops were finally sent into action, it was too late. The fighting was brutal, and eventually one of the Rebel counterattacks threw back the Federal advance and trapped hundreds of men in the smoking rubble of the crater. Afterward U. S. Grant described the Battle of the Crater as the "saddest affair I have ever witnessed in the war." A weary infantryman wrote in his diary: "The old story again—a big slaughter, and nothing gained."

Among the Union soldiers taking part in the Battle of the Crater were Native Americans, such as those shown above being sworn into service. Company K of the 1st Michigan Sharpshooters was composed mostly of Ottawa and Chippewa (Ojibwa) Indians. This little unit fought in and around the crater pit throughout the day. "Some of them were mortally wounded," recalled a Federal officer, "and drawing their blouses over their faces, they chanted a death song and died. . . ."

CHAPTER 11

Two Nations at War

The inner meaning of Gettysburg had not been immediately visible. It had been a fearful and clamorous act of violence, a physical convulsion that cost the two armies close to 50,000 casualties, the most enormous battle that had ever been fought on the North American continent, and all men knew that; but the deep mystic overtones of it, the qualities that made this, more than any other battle, stand for the final significance of the war and the war's dreadful cost—these were realized slowly, fully recognized only after Abraham Lincoln made them explicit in the moving sentences of the Gettysburg Address.

In that speech Lincoln went to the core of the business. The war was not merely a test of the Union's cohesive strength, nor was it just a fight to end slavery and to extend the boundaries of human freedom. It was the final acid test

of the idea of democracy itself; in a way that went far beyond anything which either government had stated as its war aims, the conflict was somehow a definitive assaying of the values on which American society had been built. The inexplicable

The official symbols for the North and South—their flags, their currency—reflected differences at a glance (above, a portrait of Stonewall Jackson adorns a Confederate five-hundred–dollar bill). "It is sad, sad to me to face the fact that we have a family here," wrote Walt Whitman, "half the children on one side, half of them opposed, standing in antagonism. . . ." While Southerners could be expected to disparage the Lincoln administration, Northerners sometimes expressed similar contempt for their government. "By whom and when was Abraham Lincoln made dictator in this country?" asked a New York newspaper in 1864. Philadelphia artist Peter F. Rothermel seems to suggest a similar scorn in his painting (left) titled *The Republican Court in the Days of Lincoln.*

devotion which stirred the hearts of men, displayed in its last full measure on the sun-scorched fields and slopes around Gettysburg, was both the nation's principal reliance and something which must thereafter be lived up to. Gettysburg and the war itself would be forever memorable, not merely because so many men had died, but because their deaths finally did mean something that would be a light in the dark skies as long as America should exist.

. . . Thus Lincoln, considering the tragedy with the eyes of a prophet. Yet while the mystical interpretation may explain the meaning of the ultimate victory, it does not explain the victory itself. The Confederate soldier had fully as much selfless devotion as the Unionist, and he risked death with fully as much heroism; if the outcome had depended on a comparison of the moral qualities of the men who did the fighting, it would be going on yet, for the consecration that rests on the parked avenues at Gettysburg derives as much from the Southerner as from the Northerner. The war did not come out as it did because one side had better men than the other. To understand the process of victory it is necessary to examine a series of wholly material factors.

Underneath everything there was the fact that the Civil War was a modern war: an all-out war, as that generation understood the concept, in which everything that a nation has and does must be listed with its assets or its debits. Military striking power in such a war is finally supported, conditioned, and limited by the physical scope and vitality of the basic economy. Simple valor and devotion can

OPPOSITE: New York City's waterfront teemed with shipping bound for the front lines or overseas in the early 1860's. In commercial centers like New York, a new America was stirring, even as conflict raged on battlefields from Virginia to Texas. The North was becoming a more powerful, industrial, and capitalistic society. And in its harbors, strength was counted not by rows of burnished bayonets but by acres of masts and rigging.

The economic warriors of the home front fraternize with the more familiar military types in E. D. Hawthorn's *Interior of George Hayward's Porter House, 187 Sixth Avenue, N.Y.C.* (above). The artist may have exercised some license with the crowd at this elegant Manhattan saloon—grouping them neatly for the picture—but the paintings on the wall did not have to be embellished. The Hayward collection included two Hogarths and a Gilbert Stuart portrait of George Washington.

To raise funds, wartime charities offered visitors the chance to view, for example, a memorial to the Union's first military martyr, Colonel Elmer Ellsworth (right), or perhaps the latest trophies from the front lines. Such events, known as "sanitary fairs," because so many were organized by the United States Sanitary Commission, were a garish mixture of tent show, Oriental bazaar, and museum display. They showcased items for sale or merely for display: everything from homemade jams and clothing to animals and imported goods.

never be enough to win, if the war once develops past its opening stages. And for such a war the North was prepared and the South was not prepared: prepared, not in the sense that it was ready for the war—neither side was in the least ready—but in the resources which were at its disposal. The North could win a modern war and the South could not. Clinging to a society based on the completely archaic institution of slavery, the South for a whole generation had been making a valiant attempt to reject the industrial revolution, and this attempt had involved it at last in a war in which the industrial revolution would be the decisive factor.

To a Southland fighting for its existence, slavery was an asset in the farm belt. The needed crops could be produced even though the army took away so many farmers, simply because slaves could keep plantations going with very little help. But in all other respects the peculiar institution was a terrible handicap. Its existence had kept the South from developing a class of skilled workers; it had kept the South rural, and although some slaves were on occasion used as factory workers, slavery had prevented the rise of industrialism. Now, in a war whose base was industrial strength, the South was fatally limited. It could put a high percentage of its adult white manpower on the firing line, but it lacked the economic muscle on which the firing line ultimately was based. Producing ample supplies of food and fibers, it had to go hungry and inadequately clad; needing an adequate distributive mechanism, it was saddled with railroads and highways which had never been quite good enough and which now could not possibly be improved or even maintained.

The North bore a heavy load in the war. The proliferating casualty lists reached into every community, touching nearly every home. War expenditures reached what then seemed to be the incomprehensible total of more than two and

A foreign visitor to the North noted that "Everything there is movement, change, activity." When young men marched off to war, those who stayed behind found ways, as one woman put it, to have "a hand or a foot or an eye or a voice on the side of freedom." To aid the Union soldiers, volunteers (many of them women) organized fund-raising events, including one in New York City that brought in over one million dollars. The women who organized this event are pictured at left. Other women, such as those operating a volunteer refreshment saloon in Philadelphia (below), provided necessities and amenities directly to soldiers.

In John Ferguson Weir's *The Gun Foundry*
workmen are dwarfed by the great
machinery necessary to produce the
sinews of war. This factory, located in
Cold Spring across the Hudson River
from West Point, produced Parrott guns
that were used by both sides in the field.

a half million dollars a day. Inflation sent living costs rising faster than the average
man's income could rise. War profiteers were numerous and blatant, and at times
the whole struggle seemed to be waged for their benefit; to the very end of the
war there was always a chance that the South might gain its independence, not
because of victories in the field but because the people in the North simply found
the burden too heavy to carry any longer.

YET WITH ALL OF THIS the war brought to the North a period of tremendous
growth and development. A commercial and industrial boom like nothing the
country had imagined before took place. During the first year, to be sure, times
were hard: the country had not entirely recovered from the Panic of 1857, and
when the Southern states seceded the three hundred million dollars which Southerners owed to Northern businessmen went up in smoke, briefly intensifying the
depression in the North. But recovery was rapid; the Federal government was
spending so much money that no depression could endure, and by the summer of
1862 the Northern states were waist-deep in prosperity.

In the twentieth century boom times often leave the farmer out in the cold, but it was not so during the Civil War. The demand for every kind of foodstuff seemed insatiable. Middle-western farmers, who used to export corn and hogs to Southern plantation owners, quickly found that government requirements more than offset the loss of that market—which, as a matter of fact, never entirely vanished; a certain amount of intersectional trade went on throughout the war, despite efforts by both governments to check it.

Not only were grain and meat in demand, but the government was buying more leather than ever before—marching armies, after all, need shoes, and the hundreds of thousands of horses and mules used by the armies needed harness—and the market for hides was never better. A textile industry which could not get a fraction of all the cotton it wanted turned increasingly to the production of woolen fabrics (here likewise government requirements had skyrocketed), and the market for raw wool was never livelier. Taking everything into consideration, there had never before been such a prodigious rise in the demand for all kinds of Northern farm produce.

This increased demand Northern farms met with effortless ease. There might have been a crippling manpower shortage, because patriotic fervor nowhere ran stronger than in the farm belt and a high percentage of the able-bodied men had gone into the army. But the war came precisely when the industrial revolution was making itself felt on the farm. Labor-saving machinery had been perfected and was being put into use—a vastly improved plow, a corn planter, the two-horse cultivator, mowers and reapers and steam-driven threshing machines—all were available now, and under the pressure of the war the farmer had to use them. Until 1861 farm labor had been abundant and cheap, and these machines made their way slowly; now farm labor was scarce and high-priced, and the farmer who turned to machinery could actually expand his acreage and his production with fewer hands.

The expansion of acreage was almost automatic. All along the frontier, and even in the older settled areas of the East, there was much good land that had not yet been brought into agricultural use. Now it was put into service, and as this happened the government confidently looked toward the future. It passed, in 1862, the long-sought Homestead Act, which virtually gave away enormous quantities of land, in family-sized chunks, to any people who were willing to cultivate it. (The real effect of this was felt after the war rather than during it, but the act's adoption in wartime was symptomatic.) Along with this came the Morrill Land Grant Act, which offered substantial Federal support to state agricultural colleges, and which also was passed in 1862. In the middle of the war the government was declaring that all idle land was to be made available for farming, and that the American farmer was going to get the best technical education he could be given.

As acreage increased, with the aid of laborsaving machinery, the danger of a really crippling manpower shortage vanished; indeed, it probably would have vanished even without the machinery, because of the heavy stream of immigration from Europe. During 1861 and 1862 the number of immigrants fell below the level of 1860, but thereafter the European who wanted to come to America apparently stopped worrying about the war and concluded that America was still the land of promise. During the five years 1861–65 inclusive, more than 800,000 Europeans came to America; most of them from England, Ireland, and Germany. In spite of heavy casualty lists, the North's population increased during the war.

WITH ALL OF THIS, the Northern farm belt not only met wartime needs for food and fibers, but it also helped to feed Great Britain. More than 40 per cent of the wheat and flour imported into Great Britain came from the United States. The country's wheat exports tripled during the war, as if it was Northern wheat rather than Southern cotton that was king.

But if the farms enjoyed a war boom, Northern industry had a growth that was almost explosive. Like the farmer, the manufacturer had all sorts of new machinery available—new machinery, and the mass-production techniques that go with machinery—and the war took all limits off his markets. The armies needed all manner of goods: uniforms, underwear, boots and shoes, hats, blankets, tents, muskets, swords, revolvers, cannon, a bewildering variety of ammunition, wagons, canned foods, dressed lumber, shovels, steamboats, surgical instruments, and so on. During the first year industry was not geared to turn out all of these things in the quantities required, and heavy purchases were made abroad while new factories were built, old factories remodeled, and machinery acquired and installed. By 1862 the government practically stopped buying munitions abroad, because its own manufacturers could give it everything it wanted.

The heavy-goods industries needed to support all of this production were available. One of the lucky accidents that worked in favor of American industry in this war was the fact that the canal at Sault Sainte Marie, Michigan, had been built and put into service a few years before the war, and the unlimited supply of iron ore from the Lake Superior ranges could be brought down to the furnaces inexpensively. Pittsburgh was beginning to be Pittsburgh, with foundries that could turn

The major source of powder for Union guns was the Du Pont powder mills, located on Brandywine Creek, near Wilmington, Delaware (right). Industrial growth in the North was fueled by war demand as well as by the decision of the Lincoln administration to issue "greenbacks," paper currency not redeemable for gold. This influx of new money into the Northern economy supported expansion with what one writer described as a "fertilizing dew" of investment.

444

out cannon and mortars, railroad rails, iron plating for warships or for locomotives—iron, in short, for every purpose, iron enough to meet the most fantastic demands of wartime.

There was a railroad network to go with all of this. During the 1850's the Northern railroad network had been somewhat overbuilt, and many carriers had been having a hard time of it in 1860, but the war brought a heavy traffic that forced the construction of much new mileage. New locomotives and cars were needed, and the facilities to build them were at hand. The Civil War was the first of the "railroad wars," in a military sense, and the Northern railway nexus enabled the Federal government to switch troops back and forth between the Eastern and Western theaters of action with a facility the South could never match.

Altogether, it is probable that the Civil War pushed the North into the industrial age a full generation sooner than would otherwise have been the case. It was just ready to embrace the factory system in 1861, but without the war its development would have gone more slowly. The war provided a forced draft that accelerated the process enormously. By 1865 the northeastern portion of America had become an industrialized nation, with half a century of development compressed into four feverish years.

One concrete symbol of this was the speedy revision of tariff rates. Southern members had no sooner left the Congress than the low tariff rates established in 1857 came in for revision. A protective tariff was adopted, partly to raise money for war purposes but chiefly to give manufacturers what they wanted.

Machine shops such as the one in Vermont pictured above, contributed mountains of matériel to help sustain the Union's massive military effort. The poems, the songs, and the parades were for the soldier-heroes, but—as in all wars—those at home forging the tools of war had a certain part of every victory.

Northern photographer Timothy O'Sullivan captured a quartet of industrious Southern women (above) near Cedar Mountain, Virginia, in 1862. They might be mending military clothing, fashioning a unit's flag, or producing the bandages that were always in short supply. The few manufacturing centers in the South were much smaller and far less productive than those in the North. So Southern women often managed to supply those things that Southern industry could not.

The North had little trouble in financing the war. As in more modern times, it relied heavily on war loans, to float which Secretary Chase got the aid—at a price—of the Philadelphia banker Jay Cooke. Cooke sold the bonds on commission, with a flourish very much like the techniques of the 1940's, and during the war more than two billion dollars' worth were marketed. Congress also authorized the issuance of some four hundred and fifty million dollars in "greenbacks"— paper money, made legal tender by act of Congress but secured by no gold reserve. The value of these notes fluctuated, dropping at times to no more than forty cents in gold, but the issue did provide a circulating medium of exchange. More important was the passage in 1863 of a National Bank Act, which gave the country for the first time a national currency.

Wartime taxes were moderate by present-day standards, but the Federal government had never before levied many taxes, and at the time they seemed heavy. There was a long string of excise taxes on liquor, tobacco, and other goods; there were taxes on manufacturers, on professional men, on railroads and banks and insurance companies, bringing in a total of three hundred million dollars. There was also an income tax, although it never netted the Federal treasury any large sums. One point worth noting is that the supply of precious metals in the country was always adequate, thanks to the California mines and to lodes developed in other parts of the West, notably in Colorado and Nevada.

It remains to be said that the North's war-born prosperity was not evenly distributed. Prices, as usual, rose much faster than ordinary incomes: in the first two years of the war wages rose by 10 per cent and prices by 50 per cent, and people who lived on fixed incomes were squeezed by wartime inflation. In such places as the Pennsylvania coal fields there was a good deal of unrest, leading to labor troubles which, in the eyes of the government, looked like outbreaks of secessionist sympathy, but which actually were simply protests against intolerable working conditions. There were many war profiteers, some of them men apparently devoid of all conscience, who sold the government large quantities of shoddy uniforms, cardboard shoes, spavined horses, condemned weapons imperfectly reconditioned, and steamboats worth perhaps a tenth of their price, and these men did not wear their new wealth gracefully. The casualty lists produced by such battles as Murfreesboro and Gettysburg were not made any more acceptable by the ostentatious extravagance with which the war contractors spent their profits. Yet it was not all ugly. Some of the war money went to endow new colleges and universities, and such war relief organizations as the U.S. Sanitary Commission and the Christian Commission got millions to spend on their work for the soldiers.

THUS IN THE NORTH, where an economy capable of supporting a modern war was enormously expanded by war's stimulus. In the South the conditions were

Richmond's Tredegar Iron Works (above) was the most important manufacturing concern in the South. As early as 1840 it had forged anchors and munitions for the U.S. navy. For the first two years of the Civil War, it was the only foundry in the Confederacy that was capable of casting heavy artillery. In 1861 Tredegar employed some 900 men; by war's end it had expanded its work force to 2,500.

Pictured left is the Merchant's Manufacturing Company, a cotton mill in Petersburg, Virginia. As Virginia's second largest city (and the eighth biggest in the entire Confederacy), Petersburg was already a manufacturing center of considerable importance when the war began. In addition to flour mills, machine shops, and ironworks, the city had several large cotton mills.

Hardship Behind the Southern Lines

Scenes from the Confederate home front are depicted in this series of drawings by Adalbert Volck. Scarce medicines are smuggled through enemy lines (top right), women make and mend clothing for the men at the front (middle), and the dignified members of a congregation surrender their precious church bells to be melted down for bronze to make cannon (bottom). The war's adversity was felt in myriad ways. One Southern woman wrote: *Pins became scarce . . . people walked about with downcast eyes; they were looking for pins! Thorns were gathered and dried to use as pins. . . . The fashions of the day included a small round cushion worn at the back of a lady's belt, to lift the heavy hoop and many petticoats then in vogue. It was called "a bishop," and was made of silk. These were brought home from "a visit to friends at the North" filled with quinine and morphine. They were examined at the frontier by a long pin stuck through them. If the pin met no resistance, they were allowed to pass.*

tragically reversed. Instead of expanding under wartime pressures, the Southern economy all but collapsed. When the war began, the Confederacy had almost nothing but men. The men were as good as the very best, but their country simply could not support them, although the effort it made to do so was heroic and ingenious. The South was not organized for war or for independent existence in any of the essential fields—not in manufacturing, in transportation, or in finance—and it never was able during the course of the war to remedy its deficiencies.

Until 1861 the South had been almost strictly an agricultural region, and its agricultural strength rested largely on cotton. The vain hope that England and France would intervene in order to assure their own supplies of raw cotton—the hoary "cotton is king" motif—kept the Confederacy from sending enough cotton overseas during the first year of the war to establish adequate credit, and the munitions and other manufactured goods that might have been imported then appeared only in a trickle. When the government finally saw that its rosy expectations were delusions and changed its policy, the blockade had become effective enough to thwart its aims. As a result the South was compelled to remake its entire economy. It had to achieve self-sufficiency, or something very close to it, and the job was humanly impossible.

A valiant effort was made, and in retrospect the wonder is not that it failed but that it accomplished so much. To a great extent the South's farmers shifted from the production of cotton to the growth of foodstuffs. Salt works were established (in the days before artificial refrigeration salt was a military necessity of the first importance, since meat could not be preserved without it), and textile mills and processing plants were built. Powder mills, armories, and arsenals were constructed, shipyards were established, facilities to make boiler plate and cannon were expanded, and the great Tredegar Iron Works at Richmond became one of the busiest factories in America. Moonshiners' stills were collected for the copper they contained, sash weights were melted down to make bullets, all sorts of expedients were resorted to for saltpeter; and out of all these activities, together with the things that came in through the blockade and war material which not

When food became scarce in the South, government declarations like the one illustrated by a *Punch* cartoonist (above) were often met with ridicule. "Fasting in the midst of famine!" was the sardonic response. While the military took top priority for foodstuffs and clothing, the civilian market for the same necessities faced major problems: a flood of speculators diverted scarce supplies; the transportation network reeled under increased pressure, and, of course, the enemy wreaked widespread havoc. A bread riot in Richmond in early 1863 sent a strong message through the halls of government. When a War Department clerk was told by one emaciated Southerner that she and others were agitating to get something to eat, the official could not "refrain from expressing the hope that they might be successful."

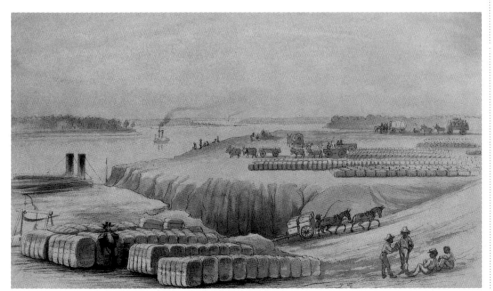

"Our cotton is . . . the tremendous lever by which we can work our destiny," declared Confederate Vice-President Alexander H. Stephens in July, 1861. Planters who voluntarily embargoed exports of that key commodity believed that by withholding cotton shipments the South could force European countries to bend to economic pressure and recognize the Confederacy. While stockpiles grew at depots such as the one at Memphis Landing, Tennessee (left), Southerners waited in vain for their strategy to work. In fact, Europe's mills were overstocked with Southern cotton when the war began, and while they suffered several harsh seasons new sources of supply were established and ultimately the embargo had no effect on European policy.

In the South the approach of the enemy created tens of thousands of refugees. When the time came to leave, the family stacked its personal belongings into a wagon and set out for safety (opposite page). A Virginia artilleryman watching one such procession wend its way out of Petersburg in the early summer of 1864 wrote, "It is hard on all; but to see the poor women with the children on one arm and their little budgets on the other seeking a safe place is enough to move the hardest heart." At the same time men, women, and children who had been slaves undertook the long-awaited journey to freedom, heading toward the Union lines by the thousands. The rare photograph at right shows one such black refugee family. Under Federal control, former slaves were often placed in contraband camps, administered by military provost marshals (below). "During all my slave life I never lost sight of freedom," wrote a North Carolina black. "It was always on my heart; it came to me like a solemn thought. . . ."

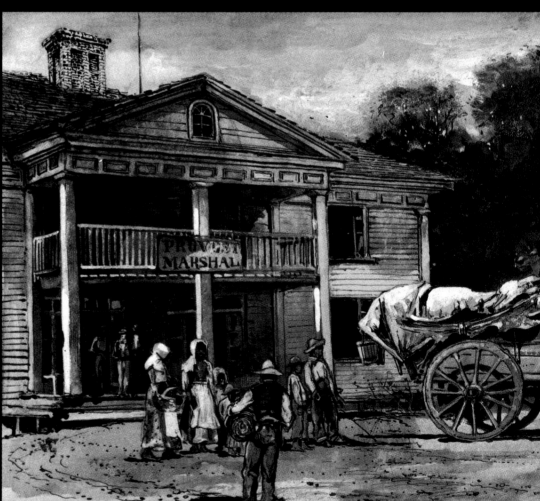

The photograph above shows slave cabins on what had been Thomas F. Drayton's plantation on Hilton Head Island. The occupants had enjoyed a sojourn of freedom under peculiar circumstances. On November 7, 1861, a combined Union army–navy force took possession of the islands adjacent to St. Helena Sound and Port Royal Inlet in order to secure a protected anchorage for U.S. warships blockading the South Carolina coast. Plantation operators fled, along with the few Rebels defending the islands, one of which was Hilton Head. The Federals who came ashore became stewards to a substantial number of black communities abandoned on the plantations.

infrequently was captured from the Yankee soldiers and supply trains, the South managed to keep its armies in the field for four years.

BUT IT WAS ATTEMPTING a job beyond its means. It was trying to build an industrial plant almost from scratch, without enough capital, without enough machinery or raw materials, and with a desperate shortage of skilled labor. From first to last it was hampered by a badly inadequate railway transportation network, and the situation here got progressively worse because the facilities to repair, to rebuild, or even properly to maintain the railroads did not exist. From the beginning of the war to the end, not one mile of railroad rail was produced in the Confederacy; when a new line had to be built, or when war-ruined track had to be rebuilt, the rails had to come from some branch line or side track. The situation in regard to rolling stock was very little better. When 20,000 troops from the Army of Northern Virginia were sent to northern Georgia by rail in the fall of 1863, a Confederate general quipped that never before had such good soldiers been moved so far on such terrible railroads. Much of the food shortage which plagued Confederate armies and civilians alike as the war grew old came not from any lack of production but from simple inability to move the products from farm to ultimate consumer.

To make matters worse, there was constant and increasing Federal interference with the resources the South did have. The Union armies' advance up the Tennessee and Cumberland rivers in the winter of 1862 meant more than a simple loss of territory for the Confederacy. It put out of action a modest industrial

452

Before the war Drayton had his slaves photographed (above); he probably did so less for sentimental reasons than to record an inventory of his property. After the Lincoln administration assumed control of the island plantations, it assigned a Boston attorney named Edward L. Pierce to assess the situation. He proposed an ambitious plan to make the plantations self-sufficient while at the same time assisting the former slaves in the difficult transition from bondage to freedom and a new life with the "full privileges of citizens." In the North the call went out for teachers of "talent and enthusiasm . . . regulated by good understanding" to go to the Port Royal area to help accomplish the task. A number of youthful activists responded and joined what a later historian termed "The Port Royal Experiment." Among their immediate accomplishments was the establishment of schools such as the one at Beaufort (left).

network; there were ironworks, foundries, and small manufacturing plants in western Tennessee which the South could not afford to lose. The early loss of such cities as New Orleans, Nashville, and Memphis further reduced manufacturing capacity. Any Union army which got into Confederate territory destroyed railway lines as a matter of course. If the soldiers simply bent the rails out of shape, and then went away, the rails could quickly be straightened and re-used; as the war progressed, however, the Federals developed a system of giving such rails a spiral

David English Henderson's painting *Departure from Fredericksburg Before the Bombardment* (above) illustrates the effect of the attack in December, 1862, on civilians. "By every road there came numbers generally on foot, with carts loaded with bedding, &c. preparing to encamp in the woods back of our lines until the battle was over," wrote a Confederate artillery officer. "The woods were full of them, mostly women & children." Another Rebel officer added that, "Many were almost destitute and had nowhere to go. . . . [T]hey . . . were forced to seek shelter in the woods and brave the icy November nights to escape the approaching assault."

twist, which meant that they were of no use unless they could be sent to a rolling mill . . . of which the Confederacy had very few.

Increasingly, the war for the Confederates became a process of doing without. Until the end the soldiers had the guns and ammunition they needed, but they did not always have much of anything else. Confederate soldiers made a practice of removing the shoes, and often the clothing, of dead or captured Federals out of sheer necessity, and it was frequently remarked that the great *élan* which the Southern soldier displayed in his attacks on Federal positions came at least partly from his knowledge that if he seized a Yankee camp he would find plenty of good things to eat.

As in the North, there were war profiteers in the South, although there were not nearly so many of them, and they put on pretty much the same sort of display. The blockade-runners brought in luxury goods as well as necessities, and the Southerner who had plenty of money could fare very well. Few people qualified in this respect, but the ones who did qualify and who chose to spend their money on themselves found all kinds of things to buy.

Perhaps the shortage that hit the Confederacy hardest of all was the shortage—

or, rather, the absolute lack—of a sound currency. This compounded and intensified all of the other shortages; to a nation which could neither produce all it needed nor get the goods which it did produce to the places where they were wanted, there came this additional, crushing disaster of leaping inflation. As a base for Confederate currency the new government possessed hardly more than one million dollars in specie. Credit resources were strictly limited, and an adequate system of taxation was never devised. From the beginning the nation put its chief reliance on printing-press money. This deteriorated rapidly, and kept on deteriorating, so that by 1864 a Confederate dollar had a gold value of just five cents. (By the end of 1864 the value had dropped very nearly to zero.) Prices went up, and wages and incomes were hopelessly outdistanced. It was in the South during the Civil War that men made the wisecrack that was re-used during Germany's inflation in the 1920's—that a citizen went to market carrying his money in a basket and came home with the goods he had bought in his wallet.

Under such conditions government finances got into a hopeless mess. One desperate expedient was a 10 per cent "tax in kind" on farm produce. This did bring needed corn and pork in to the armies, but it was one of the most unpopular

After the Federals were forced to withdraw from Fredericksburg in December, 1862, residents returned to find their beautiful town heavily scarred by cannon fire. In addition, many houses had been thoroughly ransacked by the Yankee soldiers. Henderson's painting *The Return to Fredericksburg After the Battle* (above) depicts members of a family that was lucky enough to have at least a roof left over their heads. The Union army returned to Fredericksburg briefly in 1863 and 1864. A Rebel cavalryman seeing it after the latter occupation said it "looked as if some giant pestilence had left the town nearly tenantless. . . ."

Judah P. Benjamin

James A. Seddon

Two key figures in Jefferson Davis' cabinet were Judah P. Benjamin and James A. Seddon. Benjamin, a Davis confidant since before the war, served the Confederacy, successively, as Attorney General, Secretary of War, and Secretary of State. A fellow official described Benjamin as "certainly a man of intellect, education, and extensive reading, combined with natural abilities of a tolerably high order. . . . Upon his lip there seems to bask an eternal smile; but if it be studied it is not a smile—yet it bears no unpleasing aspect." Seddon, a member of Virginia's planter-aristocracy, was the fourth man to head the War Department. One of the clerks in that department wrote of his new boss: "Secretary Seddon is gaunt and emaciated. . . . He looks like a dead man galvanized into muscular animation."

taxes ever levied, and it contributed largely to the progressive loss of public confidence in the Davis administration. To supply its armies, the government at times had to wink at violations of its own laws. It strictly prohibited the export of raw cotton to Yankee consumers, for instance, but now and then it carefully looked the other way when such deals were made: the Yankees might get the cotton, but in return the Southern armies could sometimes get munitions and medicines which were otherwise unobtainable.

By the spring of 1865, when the military effort of the Southland was at last brought to a halt, the Confederate economy had suffered an all but total collapse. The nation was able to keep an army in the field at all only because of the matchless endurance and determination of its surviving soldiers. Its ability to produce, transport, and pay for the necessities of national life was almost entirely exhausted; the nation remained on its feet only by a supreme and despairing effort of will, and it moved as in a trance. Opposing it was a nation which the war had strengthened instead of weakened—a nation which had had much the greater strength to begin with and which had now become one of the strongest powers on the globe. The war could end only as it did end. The Confederacy died because the war had finally worn it out.

ON EACH SIDE THERE WAS one man who stood at storm center, trying to lead a people who would follow no leader for long unless they felt in him some final embodiment of the deep passions and misty insights that moved them. This man was the President, given power and responsibility beyond all other men, hemmed in by insistent crowds yet always profoundly alone—Abraham Lincoln, in Washington, and Jefferson Davis, in Richmond.

They were very different, these two, alike only in their origins and in the crushing weight of the burdens they carried. On each rested an impossible imperative—to adjust himself to fate and yet at the same time somehow to control it. Miracles were expected of them by an age which had lost its belief in the miraculous.

Davis was all iron will and determination, a rigid man who might conceivably be broken but who could never be bent, proud almost to arrogance and yet humbly devoted to a cause greater than himself. Of the rightness of that cause he had never a doubt, and it was hard for him to understand that other men might not see that rightness as easily as he did. Essentially a legalist, he had been put in charge of the strangest of revolutions—an uprising of conservatives who would overturn things in order to preserve a cherished *status quo*—and he would do his unwavering best to make the revolution follow the proper forms. He had had much experience with politics, yet it had been the experience of the aristocrat-in-politics. He had never known the daily immersion in the rough-and-tumble of ward and courthouse politics, where the candidate is hammered into shape by repeated contact with the electorate.

There were other handicaps, the greatest being the fact that the kind of government Southerners wanted was not the kind that could fight and win an extended war. The administration had to have broad wartime powers, but when Davis tried to get and use them he was bitterly criticized; fighting against strong centralized government, he had to create such a government in order to win.

Salmon P. Chase

William H. Seward

Abraham Lincoln's war cabinet attracted powerful, ambitious figures such as Salmon P. Chase and William H. Seward. Chase, the radical Republican governor of Ohio, was appointed Secretary of the Treasury despite the fact that he lacked financial experience. He proved to be a quick study though, and, advised by banking wizard Jay Cooke of Philadelphia, he managed to guide the treasury through the violent turbulence of a war economy. Seward, an outspoken abolitionist, was a U.S. senator from New York when he became Lincoln's Secretary of State. In a speech delivered before the war began, Seward foretold what he described as "an irrepressible conflict between opposing and enduring forces" in American society.

States' rights made an impossible base for modern war. The doctrinaire was forever tripping up the realist.

Nor was that all. Davis' cabinet gave him little help. It contained some good men, the ablest perhaps being Judah P. Benjamin, a lawyer and former senator from Louisiana. He served, successively, as Attorney General, Secretary of War, and Secretary of State. He was a brilliant man and a hard worker, wholly devoted to the cause, and Davis trusted him and relied on him as much as a man of Davis' bristling independence could be said to rely on anyone. Other men, in the cabinet and out of it, seemed to feel that Benjamin was just a little too clever, and he was never able to bring a broad national following to the President's support. Another good man, underestimated at the time, was Stephen Mallory of Florida, the Secretary of the Navy. Mallory had very little to work with, and the Confederacy's total inability to break the strangling blockade brought him much unjust criticism, but he did a good deal better with the materials at hand than there was any reason to expect. He and John H. Reagan of Texas, the Postmaster General, were the only two who held their cabinet posts from the Confederacy's birth to its death. There were six secretaries of war, and the one who held the job longest was James A. Seddon of Virginia; like those who preceded and followed him, Seddon found his path made difficult by the fact that Davis to all intents and purposes was his own Secretary of War.

Broadly speaking, the cabinet was undistinguished, and it never contained the South's strongest men. Alexander Stephens was Vice-President, as isolated in that office as an American Vice-President invariably is; Howell Cobb was never a member, Robert Toombs was in the cabinet only briefly, and as a general thing the cabinet did not contain the men who had been most influential in bringing about secession in the first place—the men who, just before the separation took place, would have been regarded as the South's strongest leaders. More and more as the war went on the Confederate government was a one-man show.

In the sense that the President was always dominant, the Northern government too was a one-man show, but in reality it was a team of powerful men—a

A sketch by Edwin Forbes (right) shows a newsboy hawking his wares. A chaplain serving with the Union army at Petersburg wrote: "We were perhaps twelve miles or so from [the Union supply base at] City Point. . . . An enterprising boy would go to the landing on the irrepressible army mule, stay at the landing all night . . . and as soon as the steamer came with the papers he put in front of him his *quantum* of several hundreds and came galloping out to the camp, crying out at the top of his voice: 'New York *Herald!*' He charged us twenty-five cents apiece for the papers [that sold in New York for four cents], but even at that price we were delighted to get the news and he sold his papers like hot cakes."

Sometimes newspaper deliveries to soldiers were handled by individuals with a certain rakish flair (bottom right). In the rush to be first with the news, editors often reported rumors just as fast as they were sent in from the field, with the result that some published accounts bore little relation to the truth. "We have learned not to swallow anything whole that we see in the papers," declared one Union soldier. "If half the victories we read of were true the Rebellion wouldn't have a leg to stand on."

team which was unruly, stubborn, and hard to manage, but which provided a great deal of service. Lincoln put in his cabinet men of force and ability, and although some of them fought against him at times and tried to wrest leadership from him, they added strength to his administration. Lincoln had a suppleness which Davis lacked, his political experience had taught him how to win a political fight without making personal enemies out of the men he defeated, and he had as well the ability to use the talents of self-assured men who considered themselves his betters.

William H. Seward, his Secretary of State, had opposed him for the Republican Presidential nomination, entered the cabinet reluctantly, and believed that he rather than Lincoln would actually run the show. Lincoln quickly disillusioned him on this point and then made a loyal supporter of him. Edwin M. Stanton, who became Secretary of War after Simon Cameron had demonstrated his own abysmal unfitness for the post, was harsh, domineering, ruthless, forever conniving with the radical Republicans to upset Lincoln's control of high policy; yet he, like Seward, finally came to see that the President was boss, and he was an uncommonly energetic and able administrator. Salmon P. Chase, Secretary of the Treasury, was another man who had sought the Republican Presidential nomination in 1860 and who, failing to get it, believed firmly that the better man had lost. He had no conception of the loyalty which a cabinet member might be supposed to owe to the president who had appointed him, and in 1864 he tried hard, while still in Lincoln's cabinet, to take the nomination away from him. But if he was a

The sight of photographers in the field (above) was rare, since the delicate equipment necessary for their work could not easily survive the rigors of an active campaign. For eyewitness reports, newspapers turned to a cadre of correspondents who sometimes likened themselves to a "Bohemian Brigade"; the ones shown below are from the New York *Herald*. "The work needs *first class men*," wrote one of them, "men of physical courage, intelligence, tact, patience, endurance, DEVOTION." It also required a willing acceptance of physical discomfort. "I wear four shirts a week when I am at home," explained a reporter in the field to his editor in New York. "The flannel shirt I have on I have worn five weeks."

difficult man to get along with, he ran the Treasury Department ably; after removing him for unendurable political insubordination in 1864, Lincoln a few months later showed how highly he regarded Chase's services by making him Chief Justice of the United States.

Thus both Lincoln and Davis had to face intense political opposition as the war progressed. To sum up the quality of their respective cabinets, it can only be said that in the face of this opposition Lincoln's cabinet was in the long run a help to him, and that Davis' cabinet was not.

ONE QUEER ASPECT OF the political phase of the war was the fact that it was the government at Richmond which was first and boldest in its assertion of centralized control over the armies. Despite the states' rights theory, the Confederate government became a truly national government, as far as matters like conscription were concerned, much earlier and much more unequivocally than the government at Washington.

When the war began, Confederate soldiers were enlisted for a term of twelve months, which meant that in the spring of 1862 the Confederate armies were in danger of dissolving. The administration and the Congress met this problem head-on, putting through a conscription act which placed exclusive control over all male citizens between eighteen and thirty-five in the hands of the Confederate President. With certain specified exceptions and exemptions, all men within those age limits were conscripted for the duration of the war. Some of the state governors, most notably the egregious Joseph E. Brown of Georgia, complained bitterly that this was a body blow at constitutional liberties, but the President and Congress were unmoved. There might be widespread complaint about the exemptions under the

Frank Vizetelly (above) covered the Civil War for England's *Illustrated London News*. Through the first half of 1862 he filed his reports from the Union side; he then crossed the lines for the Confederate perspective and even took\part as a staff aide during the battles of Fredericksburg and Chickamauga. He witnessed the siege of Charleston and was in the Shenandoah Valley in 1864. For his help in delivering messages during the fight at Chicka-mauga, a grateful Lieutenant General James Longstreet made Vizetelly an "honorary captain."

When Timothy O'Sullivan photographed Alfred Waud (right) filling a sketch pad near Gettysburg, he caught one of the most prolific and successful artist–correspondents of the Civil War. Born in London, Waud settled in the United States when he was in his twenties, and found work drawing for illustrated dailies. He moved up to *Harper's* during the war, spending virtually all of his time in the East—from First Bull Run to Appomattox Court House. A friendly competitor described Waud: "Blue-eyed, fair-bearded, strapping and stalwart, full of loud cheery laughs and comic songs, armed to the teeth, jack-booted, gauntleted, slouch-hatted, yet clad in the shooting-jacket of a civilian. . . ."

law—the owner or overseer of twenty slaves, for instance, could not be called into military service—and in the latter part of the war there was trouble enforcing the conscription act properly, but the act itself was courageous and straightforward, and it went unmodified.

It was the Northern government that found itself unable to assert adequate central control over the lives of its citizens, and although it was driven to conscription in 1863, it never was as bold or direct about it as the government at Richmond had been, and it never adopted as good a law.

Northern armies were composed of regiments raised by the several states, and the volunteer signed up, usually, for a three-year term. When new men were

As her children parade in gentle evocation of patriotic militarism, a wife and mother anxiously scans *The New York Times* for the latest war news in Lilly Martin Spencer's painting *The War Spirit at Home—Celebrating the Victory at Vicksburg.* The young woman might well have read with gravity; in addition to providing a battle summary, with maps and drawings, the newspapers routinely published casualty lists.

A Gallery of Secret Agents

Accurate information regarding the enemy's intentions, dispositions, and strength could spell the difference between defeat and victory. The best-known "secret" agent on the Union side was Allan Pinkerton (above, standing left of Lincoln and General John McClernand), the private detective who established the Secret Service. Pinkerton enjoyed some successes and some notable failures (during the Peninsular Campaign he repeatedly provided Major General McClellan with estimates that doubled the size of the opposing forces), but he was seldom out of the public eye. For agents working undercover such publicity could mean a death sentence.

Pauline Cushman (opposite) was captured in the South after spying for the Union. Sentenced to be executed, she was spared when retreating Confederates left her behind. Operating in the heart of Washington's social whirl, Rose Greenhow (opposite) charmed information out of high-ranking Union figures and then sent it along to Richmond. Even Pinkerton, who eventually arrested her, had to acknowledge Mrs. Greenhow's "almost irresistible seductive powers." Even more flamboyant was Belle Boyd (opposite), who became a Rebel courier, conveying messages and medicines through the Union lines. Eventually deported to Canada, Miss Boyd became a tireless self-promoter after the war, telling and retelling her exploits until fact and fiction merged.

Pauline Cushman in uniform

Pauline Cushman

Belle Boyd

Rose Greenhow with her daughter

WANTED—A SUBSTITUTE for a conscript, to serve during the war. Any good man over the age of 35 years, not a resident of Virginia, or a foreigner, may hear of a good situation by calling at Mr. GEORGE BAGBY'S office, Shockoe Slip, to-day, between the hours of 9 and 11 A. M.   [jy 9—1t*]   A COUNTRYMAN.

WANTED—Two SUBSTITUTES—one for artillery, the other for infantry or cavalry service. Also, to sell, a trained, thoroughbred cavalry HORSE. Apply to   DR. BROOCKS, Corner Main and 12th streets, or to T. T. BROOCKS,
jy 9—3t*   Petersburg, Va.

WANTED—Immediately, a SUBSTITUTE. A man over 35 years old, or under 18, can get a good price by making immediate application to Room No. 50, Monument Hotel, or by addressing "J. W.," through Richmond P. O.   jy 9—1t*

WANTED—A SUBSTITUTE, to go into the 24th North Carolina State troops, for which a liberal price will be paid. Apply to me at Dispatch office this evening at 4 o'clock P. M.
jy 9—1t*   R. R. MOORE.

WANTED—A SUBSTITUTE, to go in a first-rate Georgia company of infantry, under the heroic Jackson. A gentleman whose health is impaired, will give a fair price for a substitute. Apply immediately at ROOM, No. 13, Post-Office Department, third story, between the hours of 10 and 3 o'clock.   jy 9—6t*

WANTED—Two SUBSTITUTES for the war. A good bonus will be given. None need apply except those exempt from Conscript. Apply to-day at   GEORGE I. HERRING'S,
jy 9—1t*   Grocery store, No. 56 Main st.

WANTED—Two SUBSTITUTES, over 35 years of age, for which a liberal price will be paid. Address "A," Dispatch office, stating terms.   jy 9—2t*

SUBSTITUTE WANTED—For the war. A man over the age of 35 can get employment as Substitute, by applying at 134 Main street, boarding-house, third story.   jy 9—1t*

WANTED—A SUBSTITUTE for an infantry company. A good price will be paid for one that suits. Apply at
JOHN McDONALD'S Store,
jy 9—3t*   Corner 25th and Broad sts.

A MEMBER of Company H, 15th Regiment Virginia Volunteers, who is in bad health, wishes to procure a SUBSTITUTE. Apply to GEO. F. SMITH, 5th street,
jy 9—3t*   Between Broad and Marshall.

WANTED—SUBSTITUTE—Over 35 years of age. Apply to R. J. FARLEY, Company C, H. R. Miller's 42d Mississippi regiment, at State Fair Grounds.   jy 9—3t*

WANTED—A SUBSTITUTE for Cavalry service. Call on
DEANE, HOBSON & JAMES.
jy 9—12t*

A NY person wishing to SUBSTITUTE will call

A loophole in the law allowed a draftee to hire a substitute to take his place, leading to advertisements such as those appearing in the Richmond *Dispatch* in December, 1863 (above). It also prompted cartoons mocking the Southern volunteer spirit (top right). The first conscription law in U.S. history was enacted by none other than the Confederacy (that champion of states' rights over centralized authority). "We need a large army," a Confederate senator affirmed to his reluctant colleagues. "How [else] are you going to get it?" When the North instituted its own draft it also allowed for substitutes; in Adalbert Volck's drawing (bottom right) an unscrupulous broker offers a client his pick of derelict replacements.

THE VOLUNTARY MANNER IN WHICH SOME OF THE SOUTHERN VOLUNTEERS ENLIST.

needed the Federal government set a total and assigned a quota to each state, and each state quota in turn was broken down into quotas for the separate Congressional districts. If any district or state could fill its quota with volunteers, there would be no draft, and since the draft was extremely unpopular, every state, town, and county did its best to promote volunteering. This led to the indefensible bounty system, which was enormously expensive and did the Union armies more harm than good. A state would offer a cash bounty for enlistments, cities and

MULLIGAN'S BRIGADE!

LAST CHANCE TO AVOID THE DRAFT!

$402 BOUNTY!

TO VETERANS!

$302 to all other VOLUNTEERS!

All Able-bodied Men, between the ages of 18 and 45 Years, who have heretofore served not less than nine months, who shall re-enlist for **Regiments in the field, will be deemed Veterans**, and will receive one month's pay in advance, and a bounty and premium of **$402.** To all other recruits, one month's pay in advance, and a bounty and premium of **$302** will be paid.

All who wish to join Mulligan's Irish Brigade, now in the field, and to receive the munificent bounties offered by the Government, can have the opportunity by calling at the headquarters of

CAPT. J. J. FITZGERALD

Of the Irish Brigade, 23d Regiment Illinois Volunteers, Recruiting Officer, Chicago, Illinois.

Each Recruit, Veteran or otherwise, will receive

Seventy-five Dollars Before Leaving General Rendezvous,

and the remainder of the bounty in regular instalments till all is paid. The pay, bounty and premium for three years will average **$24** per month, for Veterans; and **$21.30** per month for all others.

If the Government shall not require these troops for the full period of Three Years, and they shall be mustered honorably out of the service before the expiration of their term of enlistment, they shall receive, UPON BEING MUSTERED Of the whole amount of BOUNTY remaining unpaid, the same as if the full term had been served.

J. J. FITZGERALD.

Chicago, December, 1863.

Recruiting Officer, corner North Clark & Kenzie Street

Whenever the Federal government issued a call for new troops, each Congressional district had to deliver an assigned quota of men. Some states tried to make enlistment an attractive proposition through bonus payments and other enticements, such as those offered to prospective members of Mulligan's Brigade (left). If officials could meet the requisite numbers with such volunteers, the state would be spared a draft. Otherwise, the draft quotas had to be apportioned (below), and the conscripts hustled into uniform.

THE DRAFT.

The draft will commence in the 14th Congressional District, on

Thursday, Sept. 17th, 1863,

At 10 o'clock A. M., at the Court House in Wooster, Ohio.

The whole number required from this district is SIX HUNDRED AND NINETEEN, to which fifty per cent. will be added to cover exemptions. The following table exhibits the number to be drafted from each sub-district:

HOLMES COUNTY—To the first sub-district, 21; Second, 21; Third, 18; Fourth, 27; Fifth, 12; Sixth, 18; Seventh, 19.

ASHLAND COUNTY—Eighth sub-dist., 24; Ninth, 20; Tenth, 24; Eleventh, 27; Twelfth, 21; Thirteenth, 18; Fourteenth, 24.

WAYNE COUNTY—Fifteenth sub-district, 30; Sixteenth, 25; Seventeenth, 24; Eighteenth, 29; Nineteenth, 30; Twentieth, 23; Twenty-first, 41; Twenty-second, 24.

MEDINA COUNTY—Twenty-third sub-district, 39; twenty-fourth, 19; twenty-fifth, 27; twenty-sixth, 17; twenty-seventh, 19; twenty-eighth, 14; twenty-ninth, 12; thirtieth, 15; thirty-first, 15.

LORAIN COUNTY—32d sub-district, 16; 33d, 26; 34th, 13; 35th, 15; 36th, 29; 37th, 34; 38th, 36; 39th, 15; 40th, 23; 41st, 20; 42d, 16.

The draft will commence with the forty-second sub-district in Lorain county, and end with the first sub-district in Holmes county.

JAMES L. DRAKE,

Capt. & Provost Marshal.

Wooster, Sept. 11, 1863.

townships and counties would add their own contribution, the Federal government would make a further offer—and by 1864 there were many areas in which a man could receive more than a thousand dollars simply for joining the army.

The results were almost uniformly vicious. Men who had no intention of rendering any service at the front would enlist, collect their bounty, desert at the first opportunity, re-enlist under another name in some other locality, collect another bounty, desert again, and go on with the process indefinitely—the "bounty jumpers," who were detested by the veteran soldiers and who brought the very dregs of society into the army. Even when the high-bounty man did not desert, he did the cause little good; he was in the army because he was offered a great deal of money, not because of any patriotic impulse, and late in the war General Grant estimated that not one in eight of the high-bounty recruits ever did any useful service at the front.

On top of this, the draft act contained a couple of grotesque monstrosities.

Riots jarred the hot summer of 1863; the most serious of them took place in New York City between July 13 and 17, prompted largely by opposition to the North's first conscription law. The state's Democratic governor, Horatio Seymour, was portrayed in one contemporary cartoon (right) as a friend to the mob and an opponent of the draft.

THE MEETING OF THE FRIENDS,
CITY HALL PARK.

A Friendly Voice.—GOVERNOR, WE WANT YOU TO STAY HERE.
Horatio Seymour.—I AM GOING TO STAY HERE, "MY FRIENDS."
Second Rioter.—FAITH, AND THE GOVERNOR WILL STAY BY US.
Horatio Seymour.—I AM YOUR "FRIEND," AND THE "FRIEND" OF YOUR FAMILIES.
Third Rioter.—ARRAH, JEMMY, AND WHO SAID HE CARED ABOUT THE "DIRTY NAGURS"?
Fourth Rioter.—HOW ABOUT THE DRAFT, SAYMERE?
Governor—I HAVE ORDERED THE PRESIDENT TO STOP THE DRAFT.

A drafted man could obtain exemption by paying a commutation fee of three hundred dollars; or, if he preferred—as well he might, since the exemption thus gained would last only until a new draft was called—he could hire a substitute to go to war in his place, thus obtaining permanent release from military service. The government could hardly have devised a worse law. It put the load on the poor man and gave special favors to the well-to-do, and it brought some very poor material into the army. The substitute broker—the dealer who, for a price, would find substitutes for well-heeled draft dodgers—would take any men he could get, and some of them were mentally or physically defective. Through bribery, the broker could often get these men accepted, but they were not of much use to the army.

All in all, the conscription law was an atrocity. Comparatively few men were actually drafted; the one virtue of the law was that it stimulated recruiting, and although the volunteers it brought in were by no means the equals of the men who had enlisted in 1861 and 1862, the army could make do with them. The high-bounty laws did have one good effect. Veteran soldiers whose three-year terms were expiring often re-enlisted because the proffered bounty and the furlough that went with re-enlistment looked attractive. In the final year of the war the heaviest part of the military load was carried by the old regiments which were entitled to denominate themselves "veteran volunteers."

THAT HE ACCEPTED THINGS LIKE the bounty system and the conscription law simply indicates that Lincoln was always prepared to make political compromises to keep

466

In the early phases of the New York draft riots, the city's blacks were singled out by angry white crowds who feared losing their jobs to the undraftable black worker. The Colored Orphan Asylum on Fifth Avenue was attacked and burned (left), while the children escaped out the back. Although it was the actual implementation of conscription that sparked the riots, they were fueled by other social, ethnic, economic, and even political factors. The uprisings were only quashed when the hapless and overmatched police force was supplanted by military units that did not hesitate to fire on the mobs (below).

Newly arrived immigrants were targeted by some army recruiters; many were signed even as they stepped off their ships at entry points such as New York's Castle Garden (above). The cash incentives that some states offered to volunteers (below) bred "bounty jumpers," who would enlist and collect a bonus in one municipality, then promptly desert to repeat the process elsewhere. When squads of conscripts were finally delivered to the service, cynical veterans would hover near the first roll call to see how many would forget their own false names.

the war machine moving. He managed to keep his cabinet under moderately good control, and all things considered he got along with the Congress and with the state governors a good deal better than Davis was able to do. But the road was never smooth, and his problems multiplied as the war progressed. There were recurring cabinet crises. Lincoln had to hold the support of the radicals who followed Chase and Stanton and of the moderates who followed Seward, and there were times when it seemed all but impossible to head off an open break between the leaders of these factions. The innumerable political generals raised similar problems. Such men as Ben Butler, Nathaniel P. Banks, Franz Sigel, and John Charles Frémont were very poor generals indeed, but they held the confidence of large groups of citizens, and in the intricate game of war-plus-politics which Lincoln had to play it seemed, rightly or wrongly, that these generals must be retained in the government's service. The fearsome Congressional Joint Committee on the Conduct of the War was forever trying to interfere in the setting of administration policy and in the control of the armies; it was necessary for Lincoln to retain control without driving the energetic spellbinders who composed this committee into open opposition.

Lincoln was an adroit politician of extraordinary suppleness and agility. He had to be one, in 1864 especially, because there was about to be a Presidential election, and in the history of the world there had never been a canvass quite like this

one. Never before had a democratic nation prepared to hold free elections while it was in the midst of a bloody attempt to win a violent civil war, and the results were unpredictable. As spring gave way to summer and autumn drew near it became increasingly apparent that when it voted on the Presidency, the nation might in effect be voting whether to drop out of the war or carry on to victory at any cost.

The Republicans would of course support Lincoln, even though the party's radicals wanted someone who would wage war with more vigor and with more bitterness. Secretary Chase's bid for the nomination had failed, and although a third party tried to advance General Frémont, it got nowhere, and Frémont presently withdrew. Lincoln was renominated, by a party which called itself the Union party in deference to the support it was getting from the War Democrats, and Andrew Johnson of Tennessee was named as his running mate. Lincoln would make no election campaign. What had been done in the war would, of necessity, be the principal issue. Fighting to defeat him for re-election, the Democrats would have great difficulty to keep from fighting for a different sort of war effort; and since the people who wanted a harder war were bound to support Lincoln, the

Organized in 1861, the 4th Vermont (mustering out, above, in Brattleboro) more than proved its mettle, seeing action in the Peninsular Campaign and at Antietam, Fredericksburg, Salem Heights (part of the Chancellorsville Campaign), Gettysburg, the Wilderness, Spotsylvania Court House, North Anna, Cold Harbor, Petersburg, and in the Shenandoah Valley. Yet, when the three-year term of enlistment ended, so many of the men chose to remain under arms that the regiment retained its identity until the war's end. The 4th Vermont lost 162 men in combat action, and 280 were killed by disease.

Civil War Prisons

In the early part of the war, few prisoner-of-war camps existed, and captured soldiers were rarely incarcerated. Both sides typically paroled prisoners (allowing them to return to their homes, under the obligation not to take up arms again until properly exchanged), or else the armies arranged an even quicker swap of equal numbers of men. The exchange system collapsed in 1863, though, due to the Northern decision to enlist runaway slaves in military service and the South's refusal to acknowledge their status as Union soldiers. Captured men were sent to prisoner-of-war camps, which were often badly constructed, poorly located, and subject to all sorts of abuses and privations (some intentional, others the consequence of flawed supply systems). By war's end some 194,000 Federals and 215,000 Confederates passed through the camps; of them, nearly 30,000 Yankees and almost 26,000 Rebels died. Conditions in the prisons both North and South were shocking. Major General Lew Wallace's sketch (left), of a prisoner killed for going off limits over the so called "dead line" to get a drink of water, was based on the testimony of Federal prisoners at Andersonville; Adalbert Volck's drawing shows mistreated Confederate prisoners at Camp Douglas, near Chicago (above).

Democrats were apt to speak, or at least to appear to speak, for a softer war—which, under the circumstances, would be likely to mean no war at all.

A great many people in the North were completely disillusioned about the war. Federal troops had to be used, in Ohio and Illinois and elsewhere, to put down uprisings provoked by the draft act; and New York City went through a few bloody days just after the Battle of Gettysburg when mobs stormed draft offices, killed or beat up any Negroes they could find, battled police and soldiers, and in general acted like revolutionists. The riots were at last suppressed, after combat troops had been sent in from the Army of the Potomac, but 250 civilians and soldiers had been killed or seriously wounded and an immense amount of property had been destroyed, and the riots were a fearful symptom of deep underlying unrest and discontent. The 1864 Presidential election offered this discontent a chance to show its full strength.

In August the Democrats held their convention in Chicago, and the Copperhead wing was, if not in full control, very active and exceedingly vocal. (Copperhead: one of the anti-war Democrats, who wore in their lapels Indian heads cut from copper pennies.) They dictated a platform which declared the war a failure

This precise view of Camp Douglas (below), a prisoner-of-war camp in Illinois, was painted by a Pennsylvania private stationed there. It fails to suggest any of the suffering endured by the nearly 10,000 Confederate prisoners who were also there. As early as January and February, 1863, eighteen men died each day from disease and malnutrition; the cots in the camp infirmary didn't even have mattresses, sheets, or bedding. With a population representing the strength of two badly needed Rebel divisions, Camp Douglas became the target of several clandestine Confederate schemes intended to liberate the prisoners, but the operations were not actually carried out.

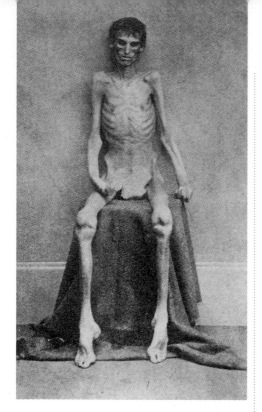

The Andersonville prison camp was established in 1864 in a remote section of southwest Georgia. It was a deadly place; nearly one in three prisoners there died from disease or malnutrition. In August, 1864, a Macon photographer named Andrew Jackson Riddle made seven images of the prison camp. This one (below) shows Andersonville's cramped conditions. During the postwar trial of the camp's commander, pictures of emaciated survivors (above) horrified the North.

and called for re-establishment of the Union on the old basis, which amounted to an open confession of lack of will to go on fighting. They accepted the nomination of General McClellan as Presidential candidate, while George H. Pendleton of Ohio, friend of the Copperhead leader, Clement Vallandigham, was named for the Vice-Presidency. Then they sat back and waited for nation-wide war weariness and disillusionment to do the job.

IT APPEARED THAT THEY MIGHT have things figured correctly. With the summer coming to a close, the campaigns that had been begun in the spring did look like failures. Neither Lee nor Johnston had been beaten, neither Richmond nor Atlanta had been taken, a Confederate army had recently menaced Washington itself, casualty lists were higher than they had ever been before, the administration had recently called for a new draft of 500,000 men, and Lincoln himself privately believed that he could not be re-elected. He believed, additionally, that if he were defeated, the man who beat him would win the election on terms which would make it humanly impossible to win the war; and although McClellan disavowed the peace plank in the Democratic platform and refused to say that the war was a failure, the Lincoln-McClellan contest was generally accepted as a test of the North's willingness to go on with the fight.

One factor in the public's war weariness was the presence of many thousands of Northern soldiers in Southern prison camps, where living conditions were atrocious and the death rate was alarmingly high. In the first years of the war the opposing governments had operated on a system of prisoner exchanges, by which prisoners were periodically repatriated on a man-for-man basis. This system had broken down by the time 1864 began, and when Grant took control of the Union armies he refused to put it in repair. The North now held more prisoners than the South held, and the manpower shortage was hurting the Confederacy

The Most Hated Man in America

As the centerpiece for the 1866 painting *Near Andersonville, or Captured Liberators*, Winslow Homer chose the mournful stare of a black woman, watching as Union prisoners are marched past her. The subject of the piece is an ill-fated Federal cavalry unit that was dispatched to liberate the camp. The unit was instead surrounded and most of its members taken prisoner. By late 1864 Confederate authorities closed Andersonville, sending the surviving occupants to repatriation centers or other camps. No longer a site of military significance, the camp was ignored by Federal authorities until May 16, when commandant, Captain Henry Wirz, wrote to the Union district commander requesting permission to return to his native Switzerland. "The duties I had to perform were arduous and unpleasant and I am satisfied that no one can or will justly blame me for things that happened here and which were beyond my power to control," he said in defense of his record. Wirz was arrested, given a much publicized trial (the verdict of which was a foregone conclusion once the bleak evidence was presented), and hanged on November 10. After standing on the scaffold and hearing the order of execution read aloud, Wirz told the officer presiding: "I know what orders are, Major. And I am being hanged for obeying them."

When the day of release actually arrived, most Civil War prisoners were simply too sick, worn out, or tired to celebrate. An 1864 photograph (above right) shows a group of Iowa soldiers waiting in New Orleans for transportation back to the North. David G. Blythe's painting (right) provides a sense of the inhumane conditions under which Union prisoners lived, crowded together at Richmond's notorious Libby Prison. A New York officer incarcerated there maintained, however, that there was a bright side to the whole experience. He wrote that, "Libby prison was a vast museum of human character, where the chances of war had brought into close communion every type and temperament; where military rank was wholly ignored and all shared a common lot. . . . It was indeed a remarkable gathering and the circumstances are not likely to arise that will reassemble its counterpart again. . . . All in all, Libby prison . . . was doubtless the best school of human nature ever seen in this country."

much more than it hurt the Union. With lucid but pitiless logic Grant argued that to resume exchanges would simply reinforce the Confederate armies. (It would also reinforce Federal armies, but these would be reinforced anyway, and the Confederate armies would not.) Unionists in Southern prison camps, therefore, would have to stay there, and if they died like flies—from dysentery, typhoid, malnutrition, and homesick despair complicated by infected quarters—that was regrettable but unavoidable.

In actual fact the Union prisoners of war were very little worse off than the Southerners who were held in Northern prisons, but most people in the North did not realize this and would not have been consoled if they had realized it. All prison camps were death traps in that war. They were overcrowded, reeking from lack of sanitation, badly policed; housing was bad, food was worse, and medical care was sometimes worst of all. This was due less to any active ill-will on either

The Knight of the Rueful Countenance

Adalbert Volck, a German immigrant who became one of the South's master satirists, drew a stinging caricature (above right) to show Lincoln playing Don Quixote to Benjamin F. Butler's Sancho Panza. Butler was one of the most hated of all Union generals, following his stormy rule of New Orleans and his often-expressed support for enlisting black soldiers in the South. A second cartoon (above) depicts Lincoln, in kingly attire, having trampled the U.S. Constitution under foot. In its issue for May 22, 1863, Richmond's *Southern Illustrated News* published a series of questions and answers titled THE LINCOLN CATECHISM:

Q. What is the Constitution?
A. A league with hell—now obsolete.
Q. What is the President?
A. A general agent for Negroes.
Q. What are the particular duties of a commander in chief?
A. To disgrace any general who does not believe that the Negro is better than a white man.
Q. What is the *habeas corpus*?
A. It is the power of the President to imprison whom he pleases.

side than to the general, unintended brutality and heartlessness of war. Army life in those days was rough, even under the best conditions, and disease killed many more men than bullets killed; in a prison camp this roughness was inevitably intensified (25,976 Southerners and 30,218 Northerners died in prison camps) even though nobody really meant it so.

No one in the North tried to analyze any of this in the summer of 1864. Heartsick parents could see only that their boys were dying in prisons because the administration, for some inscrutable reason, was refusing to bring them home. Grant was fighting the war on the theory that the North could stand heavier losses than the South could stand, and Lincoln was supporting him, but the immediate fruits of this policy did not make good election-campaign material.

Davis had no campaign problems that summer. The Confederate Constitution set the President's term at six years and ruled out a second term, and Davis did not need to ask for anybody's vote. He was devoting a good part of his attention, with a good deal of skill, to the task of making war-weary Northerners feel the burden of the war, and he was using for this purpose a device which a later generation would know as a fifth column.

THIS FIFTH COLUMN WAS DIRECTED from bases in neutral Canada, where certain Confederate emissaries, their operations amply financed by the sale of cotton, kept in touch with agents in the Northern states. They were in touch also with a good many of the Copperhead leaders, and they worked closely with a strange, amorphous, and slightly unreal secret society known variously as the Order of American Knights or the Sons of Liberty; a pro-Confederate peace organization which had

In Adalbert Volck's *Worship of the North* (below) a white man is sacrificed on an altar bearing the figure of a black man and a bust of Lincoln. Presiding over this ceremony is the Northern abolitionist preacher Henry Ward Beecher; among the supplicants are Benjamin F. Butler (kneeling in front of the altar) and the newspaper editor Horace Greeley (lower left in the picture). On August 20, 1862, Greeley (left) published an open letter to the President in his New York *Tribune*, asking Lincoln to state his position on slave emancipation. In his reply Lincoln wrote: "My paramount object in this struggle is to save the Union, and is not either to save or to destroy slavery. If I could save the Union without freeing any slave I would do it, and if I could save it by freeing all the slaves I would do it; and if I could save it by freeing some and leaving others alone, I would also do that."

The Fifth Column of the Civil War

Within the Union, challenges to Lincoln came in many forms. The outspoken anti-war faction of the Democratic party was likened by opponents to the venomous "Copperhead" snake (bottom right). Such Democrats didn't mind the nickname; they embraced it by wearing something reminiscent of copper: a likeness of Liberty, as found on copper penny coins. It symbolized their opposition to Republican tyranny. The acknowledged leader of these "Copperheads" was Clement L. Vallandigham (sitting in the center of the photograph at right), an Ohio congressman who traveled around the country expounding advice on how Lincoln could end the war. "Stop fighting," he said. "Make an armistice. . . . Withdraw your army from the seceded states. . . . In considering terms of settlement we [should] look only to the welfare, peace, and safety of the white race, without reference to the effect that settlement may have on the African." Even more ominous, though, were the fringe groups that splintered from the peace movement. Three of them—the Knights of the Golden Circle, the Order of American Knights, and the Sons of Liberty—were rumored to be endowed with large memberships and sinister purpose. In fact, these organizations were empty facades, with few followers, vague goals, and little ability to carry out any serious plan of action.

proliferated all across the Middle West, claiming hundreds of thousands of members and supposedly preparing to take up arms against the Federal government. The plots that were laid for armed uprisings never came to anything—there was one scheme for a wholesale prison delivery in the Northern states, but it died a-borning—but their existence was an open secret, and the whole business tended to spread defeatist talk and defeatist feelings across the North as nothing else could have done. The fifth column attempted other things—to burn New York City, to capture a warship on the Great Lakes, to destroy railroad bridges, and to enrich the Confederacy with money taken from Yankee banks—and although the actual results were small, the program itself was as desperate as anything a modern fifth columnist would be likely to attempt.

Although Jefferson Davis lacked Lincoln's political address, he was adapting himself to the war situation with real skill. He was, to repeat, a legalist, insisting that the revolution which he led was in fact no revolution at all but something fully sanctioned by constitution and law; but he was laying his hands on a revolutionary weapon with genuine earnestness and ruthless energy, and it was no fault of his that the great fifth-column movement of 1864 came to so little. If the Northern Copperhead leaders had been able to deliver on a fifth of their promises, the Confederacy might that summer have given the Northern home front a good deal more than it could conveniently handle.

The Presidential campaign of 1864 was, all in all, about the most crucial political contest in American history, but it was a campaign in which what men said made very little difference. Speeches were of small account. It was what the

In David G. Blythe's 1862 painting (below left) Lincoln is shackled to strict adherence to the Constitution by New York's Tammany Hall Democrats, while, at the same time, he battles the dragon of rebellion. At a mass meeting held in early 1863 New York Democrats issued a resolution that the war "against the South is illegal . . . and should not be sustained." Even as Lincoln faced overt political threats, there were subversive ones as well. The eerie image in the drawing that appeared in *Harper's Weekly* (above) depicts a real incident. On November 25, 1864, Confederate agents in New York set fires in twenty-two hotel rooms and P. T. Barnum's grand museum. However, to slow the fires until they had time to escape, most of the arsonists locked up the rooms behind them; the lack of oxygen either snuffed out the flames or produced more smoke than flame. The operation may have been bungled, but the fear it inspired was real.

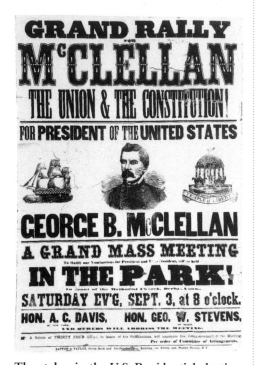

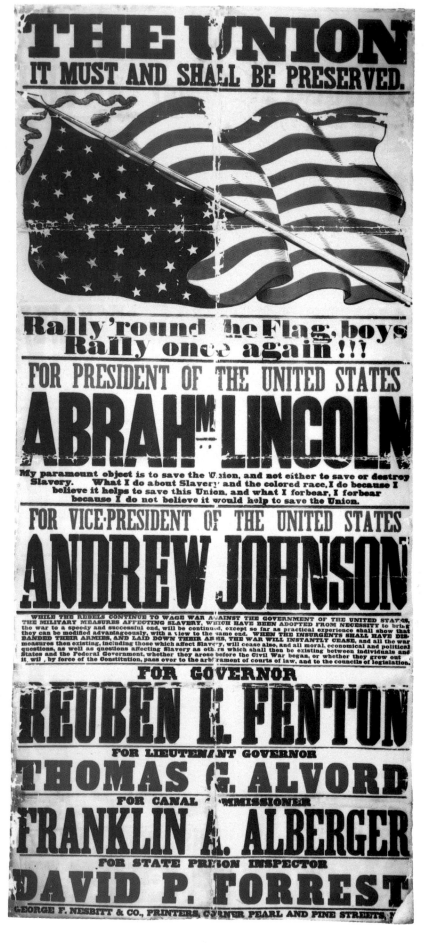

The stakes in the U.S. Presidential election were high in the summer of 1864. The Democratic candidate was George B. McClellan, who had commanded the Union army at Antietam. While McClellan pointedly refrained from endorsing his party's anti-war plank, he nevertheless promised a cessation of hostilities, using "every means to secure peace without further bloodshed." "Grand rallies" took place around the country (a poster for one such event is reproduced above) as Democrats touted their man. According to the Democrats, a vote for Lincoln (one of his campaign posters is shown at right) was a vote to continue a war which seemed to produce no victories, only long casualty lists. Convinced that his policies would be repudiated at the polls, Lincoln had his cabinet members sign their names to a blind memorandum. Only after the election did he reveal that they had signed a pledge to fully assist in the transition of power in the event of a Democratic victory.

In the custom of the day, the Presidential candidates themselves did very little politicking in 1864. Instead, party officials organized colorful events, such as the one depicted in G. Anton Uhle's painting (above) showing Philadelphians bearing torches on behalf of their choice, though the artist (either through design or forgetfulness) did not specify which Presidential nominee was being feted. Much of the rhetorical burden of the campaign was carried by partisan newspapers, which were seldom restrained in what they said. "The doom of Lincoln and black republicanism is sealed," proclaimed the Illinois *State Register*. "Corruption and the bayonet are impotent to save them. The sovereign people have willed it, and the would-be despots at Washington must succumb to their fate."

RUNNING THE "MACHINE".

The political cartoons of 1864 provided lively glimpses into the issues and personalities of the Presidential election. Currier & Ives' *Running the "Machine"* (above) shows the foibles of Lincoln's cabinet: while the President laughs at their foolishness, greenbacks pour out of a contraption operated by Treasury Secretary William P. Fessenden, Secretary of State Seward proclaims meaningless victories, and Navy Secretary Welles appears simple-minded.

The elephant was not yet a Republican symbol when the New York humor magazine *Phun* ran this cartoon (right). After toppling Abraham Lincoln and Ulysses S. Grant, publisher James Gordon Bennett of the New York *Herald* helps George B. McClellan climb aboard the elephant. Bennett would soon change his opinion of Lincoln; by early 1865 his paper would proclaim the President "the unquestioned master of the situation in reference to American affairs, at home and abroad."

THE CHICAGO PLATFORM AND CANDIDATE.

men in uniform did that mattered. The war effort was alleged to be a failure; if most people felt, by election day, that it really was a failure, then it would in fact become one through the defeat of the candidate and the party which had had direction of the war effort. On the other hand, if by election day the war was clearly being won, the Democratic campaign would inevitably come to nothing. Everything depended on the fighting men. If they should start to win, Lincoln would win. He would not win otherwise.

Currier & Ives' *The Chicago Platform and Candidate* (above) depicts the dilemma faced by Democratic nominee George B. McClellan. Although anxious for a negotiated end of the war, McClellan refused to repudiate the efforts of his beloved soldiers. "I could not look in the faces of gallant comrades of the army and navy . . . and tell them that their labor and the sacrifice of our slain and wounded brethren had been in vain," he said. McClellan, who had moved his army at such a plodding pace up Virginia's Peninsula in 1862, took a full ten days to actually accept the nomination, leading one Republican wag to quip that he was "about as slow in getting up on the platform as he was in taking Richmond."

CHAPTER 12

Total Warfare

I n the early summer of 1864 General Joseph E. Johnston understood the military situation very clearly. Sherman had driven him from the Tennessee border to the edge of Atlanta, and in Richmond this looked like the equivalent of a Confederate disaster; but to Johnston it looked very different. Sherman had done a great deal, but he had neither routed Johnston's army nor taken Atlanta, and until he did at least one of these things the Northern public would consider his campaign a failure. Feeling so, it might very well beat Lincoln at the polls—and this, as things stood in the fourth year of the war, represented the Confederacy's last and best hope for victory. As Johnston appraised things, his cue was to play a waiting game; stall for time, avert a showdown at all costs, let Sherman dangle ineffectually at the end of that long, tenuous supply line, and count on Northern depression and weariness to turn the tide.

But Davis saw it otherwise, and Davis had the final responsibility. He was a man beset by rising

Ammunition, as the soldiers received it and used it, is shown above.

A string of decisive Union military victories toward the end of 1864 marked the beginning of the end for the Confederacy. On the morning of August 5 U.S. naval forces, commanded by Rear Admiral David G. Farragut, seized the mouth of Mobile Bay, Alabama, closing one of the few remaining havens for blockade-runners. This lithograph, created after Julian O. Davidson's painting *Battle of Mobile Bay* (right), telescopes the action to show the Union warships blasting their way past Confederate Fort Morgan while the small Rebel defensive squadron, led by the ironclad ram *Tennessee*, steams out to challenge them. On the right side of the picture the Federal monitor *Tecumseh* heels over from the blast of a mine on its port side.

In the western theater Sherman's campaign to capture Atlanta stretched from May to July and then well into August without victory. An important change on the Confederate side took place on July 18 when conservative, defensive-minded Joseph E. Johnston was replaced as army commander by one of his subordinates, Lieutenant General John B. Hood (right). A fiercely aggressive and ambitious officer, Hood had suffered two terrible wounds: his left arm had been paralyzed at Gettysburg and his right leg amputated after Chickamauga. "General John B. Hood," said one of his soldiers, "had the reputation of being a fighting man. . . ." Promising a new strategy of attack, he was to face, among others, Major General James B. McPherson (below), one of Sherman's best combat leaders.

shadows, and as he struggled gallantly to keep life in a dying cause, refusing to recognize the omens of doom, he looked about him with the eyes of a soldier rather than with the eyes of a politician. What might happen in the November elections was a politician's concern; to Davis the victories that would save the Confederacy must be won in the field, and they would never be won unless the Confederate armies turned and fought the invader until the invader had had enough. So Davis relieved Johnston of his command and put General John Bell Hood in his place. Doing so, he made one of the fateful decisions of the war.

Hood was a combat soldier of proved effectiveness. He had commanded a brigade and then a division in Lee's army, fighting with great dash and valor; had been badly wounded in the arm at Gettysburg, had recovered in time to fight at Chickamauga, and there had lost a leg. Patched up, and riding strapped to his saddle, he had been given corps command under Johnston, and he had been bitterly critical of Johnston's series of feints and retreats. He understood stand-up fighting, and now Davis wanted a stand-up fighter and gave Hood Johnston's

job. Unfortunately, Hood was suited for subordinate command but not for the top job. The transfer worked to Sherman's immense advantage.

Hood was aware that he had been put in charge of the army to fight, and he lost no time in getting at it. Sherman had crossed the Chattahoochee River and was moving so as to come down on Atlanta from the north and east. Atlanta was ringed with earthworks, and Sherman had no intention of attacking these. He hoped to cut the four railroad lines that converged on the city and thus compel the Confederates either to retreat or to come out and make a stand-up fight in the open. Moving out to attack, Hood was doing just what Sherman wanted.

Hood was not being stupid, for Sherman had in fact incautiously left an opening. McPherson, with Schofield and rather less than half of the Federal troops, had moved to a point on the Georgia Railroad, east of the city, and was marching in, tearing up the railroad as he advanced. Thomas, with the rest of the army, was crossing Peachtree Creek, and there was a gap of several miles between his forces and the men of McPherson and Schofield; and on July 20 Hood attacked Thomas savagely, hoping to destroy him before Sherman could reunite his forces.

Hood's troops attacked with spirit, but there never was a better defensive fighter than George Thomas, and his troops were as good as their general. Hood's attack was beaten off, the Confederates had substantial losses, and Thomas' army was able to re-establish contact with McPherson and Schofield.

Two days later Hood struck again. This time he swung east, seeking to hit

As Sherman pressed closer to Atlanta, his lines of supply and communication with Chattanooga grew ever more vulnerable. His greatest concern came from raids mounted by Confederate cavalry forces under Major General Joseph Wheeler (above left) and Major General Nathan B. Forrest (above right). Wheeler commanded the troopers with the Army of Tennessee, serving under Johnston and then Hood. A small man (he stood five feet five inches tall), Wheeler was, in the words of one observer, as "restless as a disembodied spirit and as active as a cat." Forrest was in charge of Confederate troops in northern Mississippi and western Tennessee. He was any opponent's nightmare: a ferociously combative and courageous officer capable of brilliant tactical improvisations. "Forrest is the very devil," Sherman declared during the Atlanta Campaign.

For Major General William T. Sherman (watching his troops pass by along a winding Georgia road in Thure de Thulstrup's painting, opposite page), the stakes of the Atlanta Campaign were the highest possible. The objectives that rested on his shoulders, as he explained to his brother (a U.S. senator), "would probably decide the fate of the Union." As his army drew near to well-fortified Atlanta (above), Sherman was faced with both logistical and combat challenges. Valuable troops (such as those depicted in Theodore R. Davis' drawing, below) had to be relegated to protecting supply trains, making them unavailable when Confederates swarmed from the city to attack on July 20. Hood's strategy was to strike at a gap in Sherman's shifting deployment north of Atlanta, along Peachtree Creek (above right). According to one of Sherman's commanders, "the fury of the battle . . . could not be surpassed." Hood's attacks failed, at a cost to him of approximately 2,500 men, irreplaceable by that point in the war.

McPherson in the flank the way Jackson had hit Hooker at Chancellorsville. The fight that resulted, known as the Battle of Atlanta, was desperate, and it came fairly close to success. McPherson himself was killed, and for a time part of his army was being assailed from front and rear simultaneously. But the Unionists rallied at last, the Confederate assaults failed, and Hood pulled his men back inside the fortified lines. The two battles together had cost him upward of 13,000 men, and Sherman now was pinning him in his earthworks. The railroads that came to Atlanta from the north and east had been cut, and Sherman began to swing ponderously around by his right, hoping to reach the Macon and Western that ran southwest from Atlanta. Once more Hood came out to attack him, and there was a hard fight

Just two days after defeat at Peachtree Creek, General Hood, true to his fighting spirit, mounted a surprise attack against the Union lines southeast of the city. The July 22 fight, known as the Battle of Atlanta, was the subject of a mammoth cyclorama-painting created by the American Panorama Company of Milwaukee, and first displayed in 1887. From their study of the engagement, the painters selected the moment Major General Benjamin Cheatham's Confederate corps pierced the Federal line, only to be hurled back by a counterattack led by Major General John A. Logan. The unfinished brick dwelling in the portion of the cyclorama below belonged to George M. Troup Hurt. Held by five Ohio regiments in Brigadier General Joseph Lightburn's division, it changed hands in a fierce assault led by Confederate Brigadier General Arthur M. Manigault's brigade. The Southerners are shown defending their gains against a spirited counterattack spearheaded by Colonel August Mersy's brigade.

at Ezra Church west of the city; once again the Confederates were repulsed, with losses heavier than they could afford, and Sherman was a long step nearer the capture of Atlanta.

IT WAS ATLANTA THAT he wanted, now. He had started out to destroy the Confederate army in his front, and this he had never been able to do; since Hood replaced Johnston that army had been badly mangled, but it still existed as an effective fighting force, and Sherman had been changing his objective. If he could get the city, the campaign would be a success, even though it would not be the final, conclusive success he had hoped to win. Hood alone could not keep him out of Atlanta indefinitely; Sherman had more than a two-to-one advantage in numbers now, and he could reach farther and farther around the city, snipping the railroad connections and compelling the defenders at last to evacuate. Sherman's chief worry now was his own rear—the railroad that went back to Chattanooga, down the Tennessee Valley to Bridgeport, and up through Nashville to Kentucky. There was in the Confederacy one man who might operate on that line so effectively that Sherman would have to retreat—Bedford Forrest—and as the siege of Atlanta began, Sherman's great concern was to put Forrest out of action.

Unfortunately for Sherman, all attempts to do this ended in ignominious

defeat; the Federal army, apparently, contained no subordinate general capable of handling this self-taught soldier. Early in June, Sherman sent a strong cavalry column under Major General Samuel D. Sturgis down into Mississippi from Memphis, in the hope that Forrest could be forced into a losing battle. It did not work out as he hoped. Forrest met Sturgis, who had twice his strength, at Brice's Crossroads, Mississippi, on June 10, and gave him one of the classic beatings of the Civil War. Sturgis drew off in disgrace, and Sherman had to make another effort.

He made it in July. With his own army nearing Atlanta, Sherman ordered a powerful expedition under Major General A. J. Smith to move down from Memphis into Mississippi to keep Forrest busy. Top Confederate commander in that area was General Stephen D. Lee, and he and Forrest with a mixed force ran into Smith's expedition near the town of Tupelo. There was a brisk fight in which Forrest was wounded and the Confederates were driven off, a clear tactical victory for the Unionists; but Smith did not like the looks of things, and he beat a hasty retreat to Memphis, his withdrawal badly harassed by Forrest's cavalry. In August he was sent out to try again; and this time Forrest slipped past him and rode into Memphis itself—he was traveling in a buggy just now, his wounded foot propped up on a special rack, but he could still move faster and more elusively than any other cavalry commander. He could not stay in Memphis more than a

In the center and right center of the panel shown below, the horses of Captain Francis DeGress' Illinois battery writhe in agony, having been shot by Federal gunners to keep Confederates from removing the four cannon they have captured.

moment, and he did no especial harm there, but he did force the authorities to recall Smith's expedition. The moral apparently was that no one could invade the interior of Mississippi as long as Forrest was around.

Brilliant as Forrest's tactics had been, however, the Federal moves had done what Sherman wanted done; that is, they had kept Forrest so busy in the deep South that he had not been able to get into Tennessee and strike the sort of blow against Sherman's long supply line that would have pulled Sherman back from Atlanta. With Forrest otherwise engaged, Hood could not hold the place forever. On August 25 Sherman broke off his intermittent bombardment of the Confederate lines and began another circling movement to the southwest and south of the city. Hood's efforts to drive the advancing columns back failed, and it was clear now that Atlanta was going to fall. Hood got his army out smartly, and on September 2 the Federals occupied the city.

Here was a victory which the administration could toss into the teeth of the Democrats who were basing their Presidential campaign on the assertion that the war was a failure. (The fact that this was not the kind of victory Sherman and Grant had hoped for in the spring was irrelevant; the fragmentation of the Confederacy was visibly progressing, and the capture of Atlanta was something to crow about.) The victory came on the heels of another one, at Mobile Bay, where tough

On the left, Major General Logan rides forward to rally his men; mounted immediately behind him is Captain DeGress, hatless and holding a revolver.

old Admiral Farragut on August 5 had hammered his way past the defending forts and, after a hard fight, had taken the ironclad ram *Tennessee*. This victory effectively closed the port of Mobile, and although that city itself would hold out for months to come, it would receive and dispatch no more blockade-runners. One more Confederate gate to the outer world had been nailed shut, and there had been a spectacular quality to Farragut's victory that took men's imaginations. He had steamed in through a Confederate mine field (they called mines "torpedoes" in those days) and one of his monitors had run on one of the mines and had been lost, whereat the rest of the battleline hesitated and fell into confusion; but Farragut bulled his way in, and his "Damn the torpedoes—full speed ahead!" was a battle cry that stuck in the public's mind as if robust confidence in ultimate victory had been reborn.

NOT LONG AFTER THIS a third Federal triumph was recorded, and Northern spirits rose still higher.

Jubal Early had led his diminutive Confederate army to the very suburbs of Washington, but he had not been able to force his way in or to stay where he was, and he had retreated to the upper end of the Shenandoah Valley. The War Department had assembled troops to drive him away, but although Early was very

Having lost the section of the line near Troup Hurt House, Ohio soldiers belonging to Brigadier General Joseph Lightburn's division are shown below as they advance to retake the position. Stretching to the horizon behind the Federal battlelines are the damaged tracks of the Georgia Railroad. Afterward General Lightburn made his report: "I take pleasure in saying that the officers behaved gallantly in reforming the command and retaking our former position."

Hood's weary, dispirited army was ordered to abandon Atlanta as September 1 drew to a close, marching off so quietly that it was not until the next day that General Sherman, riding with his forces south of the city, learned the news. At almost the same instant, thanks to the army "grapevine," his soldiers got the word; Sherman later wrote of the "shouts that arouse from our men, the wild hallooing and glorious laughter." Even as Union guards appeared throughout the city and its fortifications (above), Sherman was reporting his success to Washington. "Atlanta is ours," he wired Chief of Staff Halleck on September 2, "and fairly won."

badly outnumbered—he had about 23,000 men with him, and the Federals mustered three army corps and a good body of cavalry, 48,000 men or more—everybody was being very cautious, and Grant in front of Petersburg found it impossible to get aggressive action by remote control. He finally put Phil Sheridan in charge of the operation, went to the scene himself long enough to make sure that Sheridan understood what he was supposed to do, and returned to Petersburg to await results.

Sheridan was supposed to do two things—beat Early and take the Shenandoah Valley out of the war. This Valley, running southwest from the Potomac behind the shield of the Blue Ridge, had been of great strategic value to the Confederacy ever since Stonewall Jackson had demonstrated its possibilities. A Confederate army moving down the Valley was heading straight for the Northern heartland, threatening both the capital and such cities as Philadelphia and Baltimore, to say nothing of the North's east–west railway connections; but a Northern army moving up the Valley was heading nowhere in particular, since the Valley went off into

mountain country and led the invader far away from Richmond. The Valley was immensely fertile, producing meat and grain that were of great importance to Lee's army defending Richmond, and a Confederate army operating in the lower Valley could supply itself with food and forage from the Valley itself. All in all, a Federal army trying to take Richmond could never be entirely secure until the Confederates were deprived of all use of the Shenandoah Valley, and it was up to Sheridan to deprive them of it.

Grant's instructions were grimly specific. He wanted the rich farmlands of the Valley despoiled so thoroughly that the place could no longer support a Confederate army; he told Sheridan to devastate the whole area so thoroughly that a crow flying across over the Valley would have to carry its own rations. This work Sheridan set out to do.

And now, in September of 1864, total war began to be waged in full earnest. Grant and Sheridan were striking directly at the Southern economy, and what happened to Early's army was more or less incidental; barns and corncribs and

The destruction visited upon the Potter family property when it became enveloped in Hood's defensive scheme (above) was recorded in one of the many pictures taken by George N. Barnard. Confederate soldiers stripped the wood-frame houses bare, and used the lumber to build bunkers and trench shelters. Immediately after the fall of Atlanta, Captain Orlando M. Poe, Sherman's chief of engineers, summoned Barnard from Nashville. Barnard and his crew arrived in mid-September; they immediately went to work to assist Poe's engineers by taking pictures of the city's principal buildings and fortifications.

When the powerful ironclad *Tennessee* challenged Farragut's fleet on Mobile Bay, August 5, 1864, it was under the firm direction of Admiral Franklin Buchanan, who had skippered the *Merrimac* in its historic battle against the *Monitor*. Though vastly outnumbered, Buchanan promptly engaged the Federal warships, including the U.S.S. *Richmond* (above). The *Tennessee*, nearly alone in its defense of the bay, was forced to surrender after two hours of what Union Rear Admiral Farragut called "one of the fiercest naval contests on record." Fort Morgan was to have helped defend Mobile Bay, but let Farragut's fleet run through the entrance.

gristmills and herds of cattle were military objectives now, and if thousands of civilians whose property this was had to suffer heartbreaking loss as a result, that also was incidental. A garden spot was to be turned into a desert in order that the Southern nation might be destroyed.

Sheridan began cautiously. Early was a hard hitter, and although his army was small, it was lean and sinewy, composed of veterans—altogether, an outfit to be treated with much respect. Sheridan did not really make his move until September, and on the nineteenth of that month he fought Early near the town of Winchester, Virginia. The battle began before half of Sheridan's army had reached the scene, and the morning hours saw a Union repulse, but by midafternoon Sheridan had all of his men in hand, and Early was badly beaten and compelled to retreat. Sheridan pursued, winning another battle at Fisher's Hill three days later, and Early continued on up the Valley while Sheridan's men got on with the job of devastation Grant had ordered.

Few campaigns in the war aroused more bitterness than this one. The Union troopers carried out their orders with a heavy hand, and as they did so they were plagued by the attacks of bands of Confederate guerrillas—irregular fighters who were of small account in a pitched battle, but who raided outposts, burned Yankee wagon trains, shot sentries and couriers, and compelled Sheridan to use a sizable percentage of his force for simple guard duty. The Federal soldiers considered the

As the Union warships steamed into Mobile Bay, Rear Admiral Farragut positioned himself high in the rigging of his flagship, *Hartford,* so that he could watch the action from a point above the low-lying gunsmoke. William Heysham Overend's 1883 painting *An August Morning with Farragut: The Battle of Mobile Bay, August 5, 1864* (below), shows the *Hartford* in close combat with the Rebel ram *Tennessee.* After the Union fleet had anchored in Mobile Bay, Farragut's sailors joined with U.S. army forces to capture the three Rebel forts defending the bay: Fort Powell, Fort Gaines and Fort Morgan. Powell fell August 5; Gaines, August 6. Morgan held out until August 23, enduring several days of a destructive Federal bombardment—some of the results of which can be seen in a picture taken soon after its surrender (left).

Albert Bierstadt's 1862 painting, showing a Yankee patrol that has ambushed a band of Southern irregulars, is titled *Guerrilla Warfare, Civil War*. While the Civil War's great battles and large-scale campaigns received the most attention, the fighting took place on every level. In many corners, the conflict was left to small bands of part-time soldiers, so-called irregulars, who would carry out hit-and-run raids and then melt back into the local civilian population. Some of these guerrillas faithfully served their cause, while others used the opportunity to rob and pillage both sides. For the uniformed troops in the field, dealing with these partisan fighters was a constant problem.

guerrillas no better than highwaymen, and when they captured any of them they usually hanged them. The guerrillas hanged Yankees in return, naturally enough; and from all of this there was a deep scar, burned into the American memory, as the romanticized "war between brothers" took on an ugly phase.

GUERRILLA WARFARE TENDED to get out of hand. Most bands were semi-independent, and in some areas they did the Confederacy harm by draining able-bodied men away from the regular fighting forces and by stimulating the Federals to vicious reprisals. Best of the guerrilla leaders was Colonel John S. Mosby, who harassed Sheridan's supply lines so effectively that substantial numbers of Sheridan's troops had to be kept on duty patrolling roads back of the front, but most partisan leaders were far below Mosby's stature. In Missouri guerrilla warfare was especially rough; neighborhood feuds got all mixed in with the business of fighting the Yankees, and the notorious W. C. Quantrill, whose desperadoes sacked Lawrence, Kansas, in 1863, killing about 150 citizens, often looked more like an outlaw than a soldier.

The middle of October found Sheridan's army encamped near Cedar Creek, twenty miles south of Winchester. Early was not far away, but he had been beaten twice and it seemed unlikely that he retained any aggressive intentions, and Sheridan left the army briefly to visit Washington. At dawn on the morning of October 19, just as Sheridan was preparing to leave Winchester and return to camp, Early launched a sudden attack that took the Union army completely by surprise, broke it, and drove various fragments down the road in a highly disordered retreat. Sheridan met these fragments as he was riding back to camp, hauled them back into formation, got them to the battle front, put them in line with the soldiers who had not run away, and late in the afternoon made a furious counterattack which was overwhelmingly successful. Early was driven off, his army too badly manhandled to be a substantial menace any longer, and it was plain to all men that the Confederacy would never again threaten the North by way of the Shenandoah Valley.

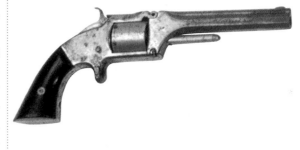

This victory aroused much enthusiasm. Like Farragut's fight, it was intensely dramatic; men made a legend out of Sheridan's ride from Winchester and about the way his rallied troops broke the Confederate line, and a catchy little ballad describing the business went all across the North. Coming on the heels of Mobile Bay and Atlanta, Sheridan's conquest was a tonic that checked war weariness and created a new spirit of optimism. No longer could the Democrats make an effective campaign on the argument that the war was a failure. The war was visibly being won, and although the price remained high it was obvious that the last crisis had been passed. Sherman, Farragut, and Sheridan were winning Lincoln's election for him.

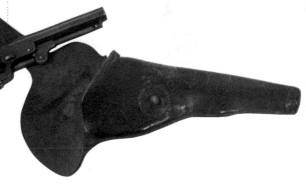

Which is to say that they were winning it in part. The victory which Lincoln was to gain when the nation cast its ballots in November was fundamentally of his own making. In his conduct of the war he had made many mistakes, especially in his handling of military matters in the first two years. He had seemed, at times, to be more politician than statesman, he had been bitterly criticized both for moving

Large factories and small, at home and abroad, poured forth service revolvers for use in the Civil War. Top: Adams revolver, imported from England; middle: Smith & Wesson Army No. 2 revolver; bottom: Colt 1844 Model pocket revolver with holster. Colt was the leading supplier of pistols to the Union army.

An Infamous Order

Outrage matched outrage on the Western border in 1863. Union general Thomas Ewing, commanding the District of the Border, was battling a band of raiders serving under the notorious partisan leader William Quantrill. Convinced that some raiders were receiving direct aid from their wives and sisters, Ewing had the women arrested and held in a building in Kansas City, but five of them died on August 13 when the dilapidated building collapsed. Even before that tragedy, Quantrill had conceived of a plan to bring 450 raiders into the Kansas town of Lawrence one week later. When the plan was carried out, the raiders murdered 182 men and boys; there is little doubt that the deaths of the women fueled their vengeance. Four days later Ewing issued General Order Number 11, which directed all civilians in Missouri's Jackson, Cass, and Bates counties, and the upper half of Vernon County to clear out within fifteen days. Anyone found remaining after the grace period would be considered an outlaw and executed. Ewing inflicted profound hardship on thousands of Missouri residents, until he was transferred to a new command at St. Louis, but the horrors of his policy remained vivid in the minds of those who were there. In 1870 George Caleb Bingham, a Virginian who grew up in Missouri, portrayed Ewing's infamous decree in the painting titled *Order No. 11*.

Quantrill's raid on Lawrence (pictured in Union cavalryman Sherman Enderton's drawing, above right) was but the prelude to a terrible period in the central Midwest. Neither the Union nor the Confederacy was able to dominate Missouri and lower Kansas, so lawlessness reigned. Among the infamous men who rose to partisan leadership at this time was William Anderson, known as "Bloody Bill," a murderer, cattle rustler, and highwayman. On September 27, 1864, Anderson led his raiders into Centralia, Missouri, where they slaughtered 148 Union soldiers and looted the town's banks. In response to atrocities such as the one in Centralia, citizens organized into militia units that marched through the troubled land seeking vengeance. One of them, the 2nd Kansas State Militia, is pictured (right) crossing into Missouri in late 1864. Within a month of the Centralia massacre, justice caught up with "Bloody Bill" Anderson: his dead body was carefully photographed (above) as proof to disbelievers.

Regaining control of Missouri was a dream that grew to an obsession with western Confederate leaders. In the latter part of 1864, Major General Sterling Price gathered troops from as far away as Texas to form a 12,000-man invasion army to drive into the state. As this rag-tag force pushed forward, Price's men made a sweep of Union sympathizers, some of whom were dragooned into Confederate service, while others were marched to prison camps. Samuel J. Reader's 1865 watercolor, *Captured by Price's Confederate Raiders,* shows a few of these helpless Federals under guard.

too fast on the slavery question and for not moving fast enough, and there had always been sincere patriots to complain that he had lacked drive and firmness in his leadership. But he had gained and kept, somehow, the confidence of the average citizen of the North. If his leadership had at times been tentative, almost fumbling, it had firmly taken the mass of the people in the direction they themselves deeply wanted. The determination and the flexible but unbreakable will that kept on waging war in the face of all manner of reverses had been his. The military victories won in the late summer and early fall of 1864 did reverse an unfavorable political current, but in the last analysis it was a majority belief in Lincoln himself that carried the day.

WHILE THESE TRIUMPHS were being won, Grant's army was still dug in at Petersburg. It had had a fearful campaign. Coming to grips with Lee's army in the first week of May, it had remained in daily contact with its foes (except for the two-day interlude provided by the shift from Cold Harbor to Petersburg) for more than five months. It had fought the hardest, longest, costliest battles ever seen on the

The 43rd Battalion of Virginia Cavalry, with its brilliant, dedicated leader, Colonel John Singleton Mosby (right), was perhaps the most successful Confederate guerrilla unit throughout the war. Operating with impunity from a four-county region in northern Virginia that became known as "Mosby's Confederacy," the unit excelled in hit-and-run tactics against Federal outposts and supply lines. Whether toppling railroad engines (below) or descending on a hapless Union wagon train (Henri Emmanuel Félix Philippoteaux' painting, opposite page top), Mosby's men generally rode roughshod over Yankee efforts to stop them. While their service was not without its hardships, tragedies, and brushes with death, a certain daredevil spirit inspired the actions of Mosby's men. Painter Charles Edouard Armand-Dumaresq was clearly captivated by the romantic aura of the 43rd Battalion of Virginia Cavalry when he painted *Mosby Returning from a Raid with Prisoners* (opposite page bottom).

Decision in the Valley

For residents of Virginia's lovely Shenandoah Valley, who had already suffered through military campaigns in 1862 and 1863, the worst was yet to come. As part of U. S. Grant's grand design for 1864, a 9,000-man Union army under Major General Franz Sigel was to move south through the Valley from Martinsburg. Stopped at New Market by a mixed force of veterans, militia, and cadets from the Virginia Military Institute, Sigel was replaced by Major General David Hunter (above left), who directed a campaign of widespread destruction, leaving such a trail of burnt property behind him, that his men took to calling him "Black Dave." At Piedmont, on June 5, Hunter crushed the small Confederate force sent to oppose him; six later days his troops entered Lexington, home of the military institute. The vengeful Union general ordered the school put to the torch (save the building he used for his headquarters), and let his soldiers live off the surrounding countryside for the next three days. General Robert E. Lee, fighting Grant near Richmond, not only was appalled by Hunter's ravages, but also was conscious that maintaining an effective Confederate presence in the Valley directly threatened the city of Washington. He sent a reduced army corps under Lieutenant General Jubal A. Early (above right) to re-establish Southern control of the Shenandoah. When Hunter learned of Early's approach, he retreated into the Kanawha Valley of West Virginia, effectively returning the Shenandoah Valley to Confederate control. Having accomplished his mission of chasing Hunter out, Jubal Early then decided to strike out for the U.S. capital itself.

American continent, and its casualties had been so heavy that it was not really the same army it had been in the spring; most of the veterans were gone now, and some of the most famous fighting units had ceased to exist, and in all of this wearing fighting there had been nothing that could be pointed to as a clear-cut victory. The Army of the Potomac had won no glory, and it had been chewed up almost beyond recognition. It had done just one thing, but that one thing was essential to the final Union triumph: it had compelled Lee to stay in the immediate vicinity of Richmond and fight a consuming defensive fight which he could not win.

For the Army of Northern Virginia, doggedly barring the way to Richmond, had paid a price in this campaign too. It had been worn down hard, and if its losses were not nearly as heavy as the losses which it had inflicted, its numbers had never been as great, and the capacity to recuperate quickly from a hard bloodletting was gone. In all previous campaigns in Virginia this army, under Lee's direction, had been able to make a hard counterblow that robbed the Federals of the initiative and restored the offensive to the Confederacy. That had not happened in

On July 5 Jubal Early's columns crossed the Potomac River from Shepherdstown into Maryland; three days later his men occupied Frederick, where Early (as depicted in Charles W. Reed's sketch, above) demanded $200,000 from the city's leaders or he would burn the town. On July 9 his little army defeated a smaller Union force that tried to dispute his crossing of the Monocacy River south of Frederick. By July 12 Early's men were actually probing the outer defenses of Washington, though it is unclear whether or not he contemplated an actual attack. In the face of heavy Federal reinforcements which had been rushed to Washington from Petersburg, Early pulled back into the Shenandoah Valley, where he sparred with Union columns in the following weeks. As part of this series of actions, Early's cavalry, under Brigadier General John McCausland, swept into Chambersburg, Pennsylvania, on July 30. When the civilian leaders failed to raise the $100,000 in gold that McCausland demanded, much of the town was put to the torch, including the Bank of Chambersburg and the Franklin County Courthouse (left).

B-67

To establish Union control over the Shenandoah Valley once and for all, U. S. Grant needed a strong, aggressive, and trustworthy officer. He selected Major General Philip H. Sheridan (above).

Sheridan was a fighter and an inspiring leader. "He had that magnetic quality of swaying men which I wish I had," declared Grant, "a rare quality in a general." Grant's directive, as laid out for Chief of Staff Henry Halleck, made it clear that he expected a fight to the finish in the

Shenandoah Valley. "I want Sheridan put in command of all the troops in the field," said Grant, "with instructions to put himself south of the enemy and follow him to the death."

the 1864 campaign, partly because Grant had crowded Lee too hard, but even more because the Army of Northern Virginia was not quite the instrument it had been. The razor-sharp edge was gone. The army was still unconquerable on the defensive, and it was still knocking back offensive thrusts made by its rival, but it was no longer up to the kind of thing that had made Second Bull Run and Chancellorsville such triumphs.

In plain words, these two armies had worn each other out. The significance of this was the fact that the really decisive campaigns—the campaigns which

Alfred Waud's sketch (above) shows Brigadier General Cuvier Grover's division in action during the battle known as both Third Winchester and Opequon Creek. At first, as Sheridan later wrote, he "deemed it necessary to be very cautious" in the Shenandoah Campaign. Worried that any defeat could affect the upcoming Presidential election, Sheridan held back until Grant himself traveled from Petersburg to see what was happening. Although Grant brought along his own plan, he kept it in his pocket while Sheridan outlined his campaign. Afterward, Grant issued perhaps the briefest affirmation on record. "Go in," he told Sheridan. On September 19 Sheridan did just that, advancing into the Valley from the east to confront Jubal Early's army outside Winchester. In the battle, Grover's Union division, one of those advancing against the smaller Southern forces, was initially successful, but was badly confused by a ferocious counterattack. Ultimately, the Union prevailed on the strength of its superior numbers. Sheridan pursued Early's beaten army, forcing it out of the Valley after a clash at Fisher's Hill on September 22. Determined to destroy the Shenandoah Valley as a source of supply to the Confederacy, Sheridan directed a campaign intended to leave behind "a barren waste." Theodore R. Davis' drawing (left) shows some of Sheridan's cavalrymen at work. Said a Michigan trooper, "Clouds of smoke marked the passage of the Federal army."

These drawings by the former Union soldier James E. Taylor, who worked as a special artist for *Leslie's Illustrated* newspaper, show scenes from the Battle of Cedar Creek. In October Jubal Early learned that an overconfident Sheridan had not only ordered some of his troops back to Petersburg, but was himself absent from the field, on business in Washington. On the nineteenth Early launched a surprise attack on the reduced Union force camped near Cedar Creek, Virginia. The opening stages of the engagement belonged to Early; his men had the Federals reeling and in a near rout after just a few hours fighting. Sheridan, on his way back from Washington, was fifteen miles away in Winchester when the fighting began. Riding back to join his army, his attitude was casual and unhurried, until he met the first panic-stricken soldiers tumbling back from Cedar Creek. Sheridan picked up his pace (opposite page top), stopping only long enough to rally men who moments before had been in abject retreat. In a fury of activity, Sheridan re-formed his scattered army and personally waved it forward (opposite page bottom). Fierce combat followed, costing the South one of its brightest stars, young Major General Stephen D. Ramseur, mortally wounded at about 5:00 P.M. while rallying his men (above). By nightfall Sheridan had turned the defeat to a great victory for the Union, an event celebrated by cavalry general George A. Custer who hoisted his superior officer in a joyful bear hug (left).

Voice of the People

In 1864 soldiers participated in a U.S. Presidential election for the first time. Some were sent home to vote, while others (such as the Pennsylvanians in William Waud's pencil sketch, above) cast absentee ballots in camp. War-weary Confederates rooted for the Democratic candidate, George B. McClellan, whose party platform included a peace plank. "I hope this war will soon end now and I think will if McClellan is elected, and I hope he will be," declared a North Carolina cavalryman. "It seems to be the general impression if he is elected we will soon have peace." On the Petersburg front, a few Rebels even tried to influence the balloting. "Two of our pickets were captured. . . ," related a New York soldier, "and on being asked who they would vote for, replying that they were McClellan men, they were promptly released by the rebel scoundrels, and allowed to poll their votes at liberty." The Democratic Party's choice of McClellan put many of the Federal soldiers in a difficult position, because "Little Mac" was much loved by his men. "As for McClellan," declared an infantryman in the Army of the Potomac, "I don't think I shall let my love for the soldier do injury to my principles as a man." In the end, the election was a referendum on the war itself: whether to carry it to the finish or to seek an accommodation with the South. Lincoln received 78 per cent of the soldier vote, which helped him win a half-million vote plurality and an electoral advantage of 212 to 21. *Harper's Monthly* captioned its cartoon of the victorious incumbent (opposite), "Long Abraham Lincoln a Little Longer."

would determine the outcome of the war—would therefore be made far to the south and west, where the Confederacy operated at a ruinous disadvantage. A stalemate in Virginia meant victory for the North. Only when the Army of Northern Virginia had the room and the strength to maneuver as of old could the nation which it carried on its shoulders hope to survive. Crippled and driven into a corner, it could do no more than protect the capital while the overwhelming weight of other Federal armies crushed the life out of the Confederacy.

Lincoln's re-election was the clincher. It meant that the pressure would never be relaxed; that Grant would be sustained in his application of a strategy that was as expensive as it was remorseless, and that no loss of spirit back home would cancel out what the armies in the field were winning. It should be pointed out that the Federal government used every political trick at its command to win the election; many soldiers were permitted to cast their ballots in camp, and where this was not possible, whole regiments were furloughed so that the men could go home and vote. However, Lincoln would have won even without the soldier vote. He got 2,203,831 votes to McClellan's 1,797,019, winning 212 electoral votes to 21 for his rival. In some states, notably New York, the winning margin was painfully narrow, and the fact that McClellan could get as much as 45 per cent of the total vote indicates that a surprisingly large number in the North were not happy about the course of events since March 4, 1861. However, 45 per cent remains a losing minority. By a substantial majority the people of the North had told Lincoln to carry the war on to a victorious conclusion. After November, triumph for the Union could only be a question of time.

Long ABRAHAM LINCOLN a Little Longer.

CHAPTER 13

The Forlorn Hope

The Federal occupation of Atlanta led to a brief lull—a final intermission, so to speak, before the curtain should rise for the last act in the war. Sherman undertook to make a fortress out of Atlanta, and he ordered all noncombatants to leave—one of the harsh acts for which Georgians never forgave him. There was a brief truce, and Union army teamsters helped the exiles get their pathetic bundles of personal property south of the city and inside the Confederate lines. Not all civilians left Atlanta, but a great many did. The town was more than half depopulated, and many abandoned homes were looted or destroyed outright. Meanwhile, the rival commanders tried to devise new strategic plans.

Sherman welcomed the breathing spell. His army needed rest and a refit, and he himself needed time to decide on his next step. Under the program Grant had laid down in the spring, Sherman had not yet attained his true objective, the destruction of Hood's army; but as he studied the situation now he began to realize that the whole nature of the war had changed, and that a radical reconsideration of possible objectives might be necessary. He was in the very heart of the South, and he had subject to his orders many more soldiers than his foe could bring against him. He could go anywhere he chose to go, and when he selected his goal he might not be bound by the tenets of military orthodoxy. He had broken the shell of the Confederacy, and—as he was to remark—he was finding hollowness within. His problem was to find the best way to exploit that hollowness.

When it was first displayed in 1866, Winslow Homer's painting *Prisoners from the Front* (left) was widely hailed for its symbolic depiction of the Civil War. The central figures, wrote one critic, showed "the South, ardent and audacious at the first, like the young Virginian rebel; bound to the past, and bewildered by the threatened severance of that connection with the past, like the poor old man nervously holding his hat; resting on ignorance and servile habits, as expressed by the 'poor white,' the third prisoner of the group. These are confronted by the dry, unsympathetic, firm face of the Federal officer, who represents the reserved but persistent North."

The Union siege lines at Petersburg, Virginia, snaked for miles along the eastern and southern outskirts of the city. While Southern soldiers endured shortages of food, ammunition, and clothing, Federal troops were well supplied by the U.S. Military Railroad. Built parallel to the Union trench lines by work crews, like those taking a break near City Point in A. J. Russell's photograph (above), the U.S.M.R.R. was a monument, of sorts, to rapid construction. "There was no pretense of grading," said one infantryman. "They just placed ties on top of the ground and laid the rails across them." Said a staff officer: "It ran up a hill and down dale, and its undulations were so marked that a train moving along it looked in the distance like a fly crawling over a corrugated washboard."

Hood's problem was to get Sherman out of the South. The Confederate could hardly hope to do this by a direct attack. The inequality of the opposing forces ruled this out, and the battles around Atlanta had hurt Hood far more than they had hurt Sherman. If Sherman was to be dislodged, it must be by maneuver, and Hood concluded that his best hope was to go west of Atlanta, swing north, and attack Sherman's communications. This would force Sherman to follow him, and in the tangled country of northern Georgia an opportunity for a winning battle might somehow be developed.

So Hood put his army on the march, and as he did so Forrest went up into Tennessee and broke an important section of the railroad between Nashville and the Tennessee River. If this move had been made before the capture of Atlanta, it would have given Sherman serious trouble; even as it was, the Federals assembled 30,000 men to get Forrest out of Tennessee, and Sherman sent his ablest subordinate, Thomas, back to Nashville to make Tennessee secure. Forrest escaped the Federal net and withdrew to northern Mississippi. He got there early in October, just as Hood began his operations against Sherman's railroad line in Georgia.

Sherman left an army corps to hold Atlanta and set out after Hood, and for a fortnight or more the two armies sparred at long range and maneuvered for position. At Allatoona Pass on October 5 Hood saw an opportunity to capture large

William Tecumseh Sherman posed in the center of the picture at left, surrounded by officers who were with him during his Atlanta Campaign. Earlier in the war Sherman was so tormented by his own intensity that he suffered a breakdown, and had to return home to Ohio for respite. Returning to war, and leadership in some of the Union's most important successes, he regained his emotional balance, without losing his relentless need for victory. North of Sherman's operations in Georgia, approximately 60,000 Confederates, commanded by General Robert E. Lee, opposed more than 112,500 Union troops directed by Lieutenant General U. S. Grant, in Petersburg, Virginia. To supply such a large U.S. army, Grant's principal depot turned City Point from a sleepy village of half a dozen houses into what was, for a short while, one of the busiest river ports in the world (below).

In the picture (right) of U. S. Grant with his command staff at Petersburg, the officer sitting second from the right is Lieutenant Colonel Ely S. Parker. A Seneca Indian and the principle leader of the Iroquois Confederacy, he was Grant's assistant adjutant general. The logistics of maintaining Grant's army at Petersburg were staggering. More than six hundred tons of grain and hay were needed each day just to feed thousands of army animals, most of which were horses. Edward Lamson Henry's drawing *The Great Horse Depot at Giesboro on the Potomac* (below) shows the area near Washington where cavalry and artillery horses were inspected and treated before being sent to the Virginia front.

Federal stores of supplies, which were lightly guarded by a detachment under Brigadier General John M. Corse. The Confederates sent Corse a demand for immediate surrender "to avoid a needless effusion of blood," but the Unionist stoutly replied that he was ready for just such an effusion "whenever it is agreeable to you." From nearby Kennesaw Mountain, Sherman signaled Corse—an interchange of messages which inspired a popular patriotic ballad entitled "Hold the Fort"—and in the fight that followed Corse stubbornly held on, and the Rebels were eventually forced to retire.

Hood could never quite make a real break in Sherman's railroad, and Sherman could never pin the elusive Confederate down for a finish fight; and late in October the two armies turned their backs on one another and set off in opposite directions, each general having at last evolved a new program. Taken together, the decisions of Hood and Sherman put the war into its concluding phase.

Hood had settled on a bold and desperate gamble. He would go over into northern Alabama, and from that area he would march his entire army into Tennessee, in the belief that this would force Sherman to evacuate Atlanta and come after him. Joe Wheeler, with Hood's cavalry, would remain in Georgia to keep an eye on Sherman and hurt him as much as possible. When Hood crossed the Tennessee River and started north, Forrest would go with him in Wheeler's stead. Even if this move did not persuade the Federal authorities to call off Sherman's gigantic raid, Hood might possibly overwhelm Thomas and regain Tennessee for the Confederacy, and after refitting at Nashville, he could drive north into Kentucky. From that state, Hood reasoned, he could threaten Cincinnati, and he

Edward Lamson Henry's painting *The Old Westover Mansion* (below) portrays the unsettling situation faced by many plantation owners caught behind the Union lines in eastern Virginia in 1864 and 1865. If a family was lucky, it was allowed to occupy one or two rooms in the back, while Federal officers and their staffs took over the rest of the house and the outlying buildings. With the addition of guards camped nearby, and a signal unit perched on the roof, a pastoral setting could be transformed into a little military base.

Nearly ten months of manning the siege at Petersburg taught Union soldiers to depend on tried-and-true protection. The men became adept at constructing log and dirt enclosures called "bombproofs" (one is shown above) that remained secure even after a direct hit. The enemy weapon the Yankees hated most was the mortar, a stubby artillery piece with a high trajectory that allowed it to drop sputtering explosives into the trenches among the men. "Mortar shells fly into the works occasionally," wrote a Maine soldier, "at which times we get out in double-quick time." To offset the numerical advantage of the enemy, Confederate soldiers built row upon row of earthworks (the picture at right shows a representative section at Petersburg), which allowed a relatively small number of men to defend against many more attackers. Service in the trenches was far from easy. "It was endurance without relief," declared a Confederate at Petersburg; "sleeplessness without exhilaration; inactivity without rest; constant apprehension requiring ceaseless watching...."

might even cross the Cumberland Mountains to fall upon Grant's rear and thus come to the aid of Lee before Richmond. It was a plan born of desperation, and, as it turned out, it was a strategic error of the first magnitude, but the plain fact of the matter was that Hood had no good choice to make.

SHERMAN, MEANWHILE, WAS looking southeast to the sea, meditating a bold gamble of his own—a gamble all the more remarkable in that it involved a complete reversal of the strategic plan laid down by Grant six months earlier. Grant had insisted that Confederate armies were the chief objectives for Union strategy. What Sherman was saying now was that he would completely ignore the Confederate army which was supposed to be his target, and that he would go instead for a military intangible—the spirit that sustained the Confederate nation itself. He would march for Savannah and the seacoast, abandoning his own line of supply, living off the lush Georgia country—the harvest was in, there was corn in the bins and forage in the barns, plantation smokehouses were crammed with bacon and ham, and there were hogs and cattle in the fields. If 60,000 Union soldiers (Sherman argued) could go anywhere in the South they wanted to go, making the South support them as they moved and paying no attention to anything the

In Winslow Homer's oil painting *Inviting a Shot Before Petersburg, Virginia* **(below), a bored Rebel soldier taunts enemy snipers, while a black servant provides a little musical accompaniment. Two Federal riflemen, whose muzzle flashes can be seen on the left side of the picture, have taken up the challenge.**

Union operations against Petersburg and Richmond in 1864 and 1865 included several ambitious and unusual schemes, most notably the construction of the Dutch Gap Canal, shown above in a sketch by William Waud. It was conceived by Major General Benjamin F. Butler, whose Army of the James was being held at bay on the twisting James River below Richmond. Butler believed that by digging a canal across Dutch Gap, the narrow neck of a particular loop in the river, he could bypass powerful Rebel batteries and allow Union gunboats to approach the city. Construction of the 500-foot canal began in August, 1864; the effort was frustrated by enemy action and natural conditions. Finally, the last earthen bulkhead holding back the river was exploded on December 31, but the fallout refilled much of the canal. An observer called it a "perfect fizzle," but he could have been describing the whole effort. The Dutch Gap Canal would not be open to river traffic until after the end of the war.

South's army might try to do, they would prove once and for all that the Confederate nation was too weak to live. Lee and Hood might make war along the Southland's frontier; Sherman would make the Southern heartland his own, proving that the Confederacy could not protect the homes, the property, or the families of its own defenders. Grant was skeptical at first, but he finally approved Sherman's plan, and Sherman set off to implement it.

By November 16 the strangest movements of the war were under way: Hood was going north, striking for Nashville, and Sherman was marching southeast for Savannah. Atlanta Sherman left in flames: he had ordered that only buildings of some military potentiality should be destroyed, but his soldiers were careless with matches, and the place was full of empty dwellings, and as the Union army left most of Atlanta went up in smoke. With some 60,000 men Sherman set out for the sea.

Nowhere in Georgia was there any force that could give him serious opposition, and the march seemed to the soldiers more like a prolonged picnic than like regular war. The march was leisurely, and as it moved the army fanned out widely, covering a front sixty miles from wing to wing; and, by orders and by the inclination of its imperfectly disciplined soldiers, the army laid waste the land as it moved, doing much the same thing Sheridan had done in the Shenandoah Valley but doing it jocosely, like Halloween rowdies on a spree, rather than with the cold grimness of Sheridan's troopers. Regular foraging parties were sent out by each brigade, every morning, to bring in supplies, and these brought in far more than the army needed. Soldiers used to a diet of salt pork and hardtack ate chicken and sweet potatoes, fresh beef and southern ham, anything and everything that a rich agricultural region could provide. The supply wagons were always full, and when the army moved on, it destroyed or gave away to the runaway slaves who clustered about it more food than it had eaten.

In addition, the army was preceded, surrounded, and followed by a destructive horde of lawless stragglers. These included outright deserters, who had abandoned their regiments and had no intention of returning to them, and who were going along now on the fringe of the army just for the fun of it; they included, also, men temporarily absent without leave, who would return to duty later but who were freewheeling it for the time being; and they included, oddly enough, certain numbers of deserters from the Confederate army, who found kindred spirits among these lawless marauders and went with them for the sake of the loot. All of these characters, out from under anyone's control, went under the generic name of "bummers," and they made Georgia's lot far more grievous than Sherman's orders intended. They robbed and pillaged and burned all the way from Atlanta to the sea, not because they had anything against the people they were afflicting, but simply because they had gone outside of all normal controls—including their own.

SHERMAN PROBABLY COULD have suppressed them if he had tried hard. He did not try. He argued, with some justification, that his responsibility was to get his army safely to the sea, and that he could spare neither the manpower nor the energy to protect the people of Georgia while he got it there. But in point of plain fact the bummers were doing pretty largely what Sherman wanted done. They were undoubtedly being a great deal more brutal and wanton than he

On the orders of U. S. Grant, Butler's Army of the James attacked Richmond's outer line of defenses in late September, 1864, capturing a key sector centering on Fort Harrison and posing a serious threat to the Confederate capital. In an all-out effort to regain the lost ground, General Robert E. Lee mounted an offensive on October 7 that successfully flanked Butler's line and appeared poised to shove the Federals back to the James River. A stubborn stand made by Union troops positioned along the New Market Road (sketched by William Waud, below) repulsed the attack Lee launched from the Darbytown Road, preserving the Federal presence on Richmond's doorstep.

would have wanted them to be, but they were effectively laying waste the Confederate homeland, and that was all that mattered—to Sherman. He had said that he would make Georgia howl; Georgia was howling to the high heavens, and much of the impetus was coming from the work of the bummers. It is hard to imagine Sherman making a really serious effort to put all of these characters under proper restraint.

For this, again, was total war. Sherman's march to the sea was the demonstration that the Confederacy could not protect its own; it was also the nineteenth-century equivalent of the modern bombing raid, a blow at the civilian underpinning of the military machine. Bridges, railroads, machine shops, warehouses—anything of this nature that lay in Sherman's path was burned or dismantled. Barns were burned, with their contents; food to feed the army and its animals was taken, and three or four times as much as the army needed was simply spoiled . . . and partly because of all of this, Lee's soldiers would be on starvation rations, and the whole Confederate war effort would become progressively weaker. Wholesale destruction was one of the points of this movement. The process through which that destruction was brought about was not pretty to watch, nor is it pleasant to read about today.

Sherman went on toward the sea, taking his time about it, and the Confederacy could do nothing to stop him. Hood, who might have engaged his attention,

Doomed Atlanta

George N. Barnard's photograph of an Atlanta street after General Sherman's departure shows a burned-out bank, right next to a saloon that was spared by the Federals. Sherman intended that his treatment of Atlanta would teach the Confederacy a lesson: further resistance was hopeless. "Let us destroy Atlanta," he told a subordinate, "and make it a desolation." After evacuating the civilians, the Union troops set Atlanta's public buildings on fire. "If the people raise a howl against my barbarity and cruelty," declared Sherman, "I will answer that war is war and not popularity-seeking." Sherman later recalled his last image of Atlanta, as his armies left for their march to the sea in mid-November: "smouldering and in ruins, the black smoke rising high in the air, and hanging like a pall over the ruined city."

George N. Barnard's photograph shows one of the last trains leaving Atlanta after Sherman ordered the city evacuated, loaded with luggage and personal property belonging to residents. Although expulsion orders had displaced other civilian populations during the war, Sherman's was perhaps the harshest of them all. Writing from behind a desk in far away Washington, the army chief of staff, Major General Henry W. Halleck, fully supported Sherman's decision. "Your mode of conducting war is just the thing we want now," stated Halleck. "We tried the kid-glove policy long enough."

was going on into central Tennessee, his gamble a failure before it was made. Thomas was assembling an army of more than 50,000 men at Nashville, and Hood was a great deal weaker. The odds were great, and the fact that they were so great was a conclusive demonstration of the North's overwhelming power; the Federal government could take Sherman's army clear off the board and still outnumber the best force Hood could bring to the field.

IT TOOK THOMAS A CERTAIN amount of time, however, to get all of his forces together, and Hood was an aggressive fighter who would use his hitting power to the utmost. He was moving up from the Muscle Shoals crossing of the Tennessee, heading for Nashville by way of Franklin, and Federal General Schofield, commanding two army corps, was falling back from in front of him. Hood outmaneuvered Schofield and at Spring Hill had a chance to cut in behind him and put his whole force out of action—a blow which would have compelled the Federal high command to take Hood's movement very seriously indeed. Hood had particular

Sherman's men paid special attention to wrecking rail lines, the iron arteries that made Atlanta the heart of the deep South (the picture at left shows the Atlanta depot after it was destroyed). Railroads radiated to every point on the compass: the Georgia Railroad ran eastward to Augusta, with connections to Richmond; the Macon and Western, running southward, eventually connected to the city of Savannah; the Atlanta and West Point line stretched toward the west, linking it to Montgomery and Mobile, and the Western and Atlantic threaded toward the northwest, all the way (in better times) to Chattanooga.

admiration for the fighting qualities and generalship of the late Stonewall Jackson, and his move was now patterned after Jackson's spectacularly successful flanking march and attack at Chancellorsville. At Spring Hill he came very close to duplicating it, but at the last minute his command arrangements got completely snarled, in one way or another he failed to take advantage of his opportunity, and Schofield's army marched unmolested across the Confederate front, wagon trains and all, to escape the trap. On November 30 Hood overtook him at Franklin; furious because of the chance he had missed, Hood ordered a frontal assault on the Federal line, sending 18,000 men forward through the haze of an Indian-summer afternoon in an attack as spectacular, and as hopeless, as Pickett's famous charge at Gettysburg.

Never was a charge driven home more heroically, or at greater cost—to a more dismal defeat. In a few hours' time Hood's army lost 6,252 men, including five generals killed. The Union lines held firmly, and Hood gained nothing whatever by the assault. After dark Schofield drew away and continued his retreat to

Iron Neckties

By the time Sherman's men began wrecking Atlanta's railroad lines (above), they had become coldly efficient at the job. "The way this is done is to string the troops out along the track, two men to a tie...," wrote a Federal soldier. "[E]very man grabs a tie and lifts. Up comes the whole track and slowly tips over. Then with sledge hammers ... the ties are knocked loose from the rails, ... the pine ties made into piles, set on fire, and the rails laid on top.

When they get red hot in the center about 20 men get hold of the ends and wind them edgewise around a telegraph pole or small tree." Sections of rail were twisted into a certain shape, which the Yankee boys called "Sherman's neckties." The work was inadvertantly augmented by confusion in the Confederate high command. A few days prior to abandoning Atlanta, Lieutenant General Hood ordered that his reserve ordnance be taken away on trains. Twenty-eight cars were duly loaded, but through a mix-up in orders,

the trains were never dispatched. In one of the final acts of the Confederate withdrawal, the cars were set on fire to prevent their falling into the enemy's hands. The resulting explosions drew hundreds of spectators who were mesmerized by the "volcanic scene on the Georgia Railroad." George N. Barnard's photograph (opposite), taken long after the fires had cooled, nonetheless conveys the unforgettable scene of absolute desolation.

Thomas Nast's painting (above) reflects Sherman's bold decision during his march to the sea to move through the deep South from Atlanta to the Atlantic coast without a supply line. In Nast's piece, Sherman's men call at a Southern plantation, attracting the intense curiosity of the slaves living there. "We went to sleep one night with a plantation full of negroes," wrote the mistress of one plantation visited by the Federals, "and woke to find not one on the place." As another Southern belle recorded, "[t]hose [slaves] that we depended most upon and trusted and believed they would stay with us through it all were the first to go."

Nashville, and Hood was left in possession of the field, which he would have gained without fighting at all because Schofield had no intention of remaining there. Weaker than Thomas to begin with, Hood had further weakened his army; worse yet, his men had lost confidence in him, realizing that the whole battle had been useless.

No army in the war was unluckier than Hood's army, the gallant Army of Tennessee. It had fought as well as any army ever fought, but mistakes in leadership always intervened to cancel out gains that were won on battlefields. Bragg had taken it far up into Kentucky and then had been able to do nothing better than lead it back south again, its mission unaccomplished. The army had nearly destroyed Rosecrans at Murfreesboro only to see its near-victory turned into defeat. It had completely routed Rosecrans at Chickamauga, but Bragg's inept handling of it thereafter had made the victory barren. It had lost more men than it could afford to lose in the heroic assaults on Sherman's troops around Atlanta, and now, at Franklin, it had almost wrecked itself in an attack that should never have been ordered. It was at a dead end. It could continue to advance, but it was on the road to nowhere.

Hood followed hard, once the Battle of Franklin was over. The Federals in Nashville were solidly entrenched; they had been occupying the city for three years, and by now it was one of the best-fortified places in the country, and

Thomas had put together a force at least twice the size of Hood's. Hood put his men in camp on high ground a few miles south of Nashville and waited—for what, it is hard to determine, since he had nothing to gain by hanging on in front of Nashville. He could not conceivably take the place by storm, his force was altogether too small for him to lay siege to it, he could not side-step and march north without inviting Thomas to attack his flank and rear, and he believed that if he tamely retreated his army would disintegrate. In simple fact he had run out of strategic ideas, even of strategic possibilities, and as he waited he was no better than a sitting duck for the ablest Federal commander in the West.

Thomas was still holding back, preferring not to strike until everything was ready. Just when he completed his preparations a hard sleet storm came down, sheathing the roads and hills with glare ice and making movement impossible, so Thomas waited a few days longer for a thaw. Far off in Virginia, Grant, ordinarily a man without nerves, grew worried. He could not, at that distance, see how completely Thomas was in control of the situation; he feared that Hood would get away from him and march all the way north to the Ohio; and after fruitlessly bombarding Thomas with orders to attack at once, Grant prepared orders relieving the general from command and set out himself to go west and take control.

For the only time in his career Grant was suffering from a case of the jitters. The war was on the edge of being won, but if Hood eluded Thomas and kept on to the north the balance might be upset disastrously, and Grant was fretting about it, not realizing that Hood could do nothing whatever but await Thomas' assault. It appears that under everything there was some coolness between Grant and Thomas. Ordinarily a first-rate judge of soldiers, Grant apparently never quite rated Thomas at his true worth, and now he was unable to contain himself. It quickly became evident that Grant was indulging in a lot of quite needless worry.

BEFORE THE ORDER RELIEVING Thomas could be transmitted, and before Grant had got any farther on his way than Washington, Thomas struck, the ice at last having melted. On December 15 and 16 the Unionists attacked Hood's army, crushed it, and drove it south in headlong retreat. A rear guard of 5,000 men under Forrest fought a series of delaying actions, and the remnants of Hood's command at last got to safety south of the Tennessee River, but the Confederacy's great Army of Tennessee was no longer an effective fighting force. Hood was relieved from a command which had ceased to mean much, and the bits and pieces of the broken army were assigned to other areas of combat. For the one and only time in all the war, a Confederate army had been totally routed on the field of battle. It goes without saying that Grant never finished his trip west, and his order relieving Thomas was immediately canceled.

Meanwhile, Sherman had kept on moving. As far as the people of the

To keep his army supplied on the march, Sherman authorized a policy of foraging, allowing the soldiers to take what they needed from the surrounding countryside. Small units were specifically organized for the purpose, but certain individual soldiers excelled in searching out well-hidden Rebel supplies. These independent foragers became known as "bummers," a name probably derived from a pre-war appellation for a tramp or wastrel. A typical bummer (above, as drawn by an unidentified Yankee soldier) described his kind as, "dressed in a nondescript suit, . . . with a white hat and tremendous rents in his Breeches, . . . with his Belt & cartridge box on (for we always go well armed), his trusty carbine by his side, and a revolver stuck in his belt."

Sherman carefully kept his opponents guessing at his real destination as he passed through Georgia. His men were drawing near to the Atlantic coast when he finally named the objective he had had in mind all the time: the port city of Savannah, Georgia. It was occupied by Federal troops on December 21. A tidy town, Savannah's bustling wharves had been quieted earlier in the war (below), when the Federals seized Fort Pulaski at the mouth of the Savannah River. A jubilant Sherman (sketched by William Waud, right) reviewed his troops shortly after taking possession of the town and sent a message to President Lincoln: "I beg to present to you as a Christmas gift the city of Savannah, with one hundred fifty heavy guns and plenty of ammunition. . . ."

By Sherman's own estimate, the capture of Savannah provided the North with 25,000 bales of cotton, some of which can be seen in the sketch below, drawn as U.S. merchant ships queued up at the city's docks for their share of the spoils. On reaching the Atlantic coast, Sherman's force was able to make contact with the U.S. navy, and communicate with the North for the first time since leaving Atlanta. William T. Crane's drawing (left) shows Sherman being greeted by Major General John G. Foster, who commanded Union troops along the coast from South Carolina to Florida. A personal emissary of President Lincoln also caught up with Sherman at this time. "He asked me to take you by the hand wherever I met you and say 'God bless you and the army,'" Sherman was told.

Shipping cotton captured by Genl Sherman at Savannah for New York

John M. Schofield

Benjamin F. Cheatham

Patrick Cleburne

When Sherman departed Atlanta he left the Confederate Army of Tennessee, under Hood. Although badly battered, it was still a potent military force. While Sherman headed east, Hood turned north, and his first target was a Union corps, detached from Sherman's army under the command of Major General John M. Schofield. Hood pursued Schofield with three infantry corps; included in the one commanded by Major General Benjamin F. Cheatham was the hard-fighting division of Major General Patrick Cleburne. If Schofield could be defeated, Hood's plan was to strike either northeast toward Nashville or west toward Memphis, where the 1st Tennessee Regiment of Heavy Artillery (African Descent), shown in the photo at right, was posted.

North were concerned, he had disappeared from sight when he left Atlanta. He sent back no progress reports—could not, since all lines of communication with the North were cut—and if he and his whole army had gone underground they could not have been more completely out of touch with the home folks. Lincoln was somewhat worried, at times, but he comforted himself with the grim thought

FRANKLIN: Through a series of rapid marches, Hood traps Schofield's corps at Spring Hill, Tennessee, but lackluster execution of orders by his subordinate commanders allows the Federals to escape. A frustrated Hood renews the pursuit with his 38,000 men, catching up with Schofield at the town of Franklin, where the slightly smaller Federal force has entrenched, while its supply wagons get across the Harpeth River (1). Arriving in sight of Franklin (2), Hood finds two Union brigades, under George Wagner, lying in a vulnerable position in advance of their own lines. A fierce assault, personally led by the dashing Patrick Cleburne, briefly breaks the Union line near the Gin House (3), as Wagner's men confuse Union defenses in their panicked retreat. Reserve troops under Emerson Opdycke stem the Confederate charge (4). General Cleburne is killed in this fighting. Subsequent attacks against the Federal left flank (near the Harpeth River) and right (5) prove fruitless. Schofield's corps, having suffered about 2,500 casualties, withdraws in good order across the river, leaving Hood in uncontested possession of the field, at the dire cost to his army of more than 6,000 men.

N

FRANKLIN
November 30, 1864

TO NASHVILLE

FORT GRANGER

HARPETH RIVER

Franklin

CARTER HOUSE

GIN HOUSE

COLUMBIA PIKE

LEWISBURG PIKE

NASHVILLE

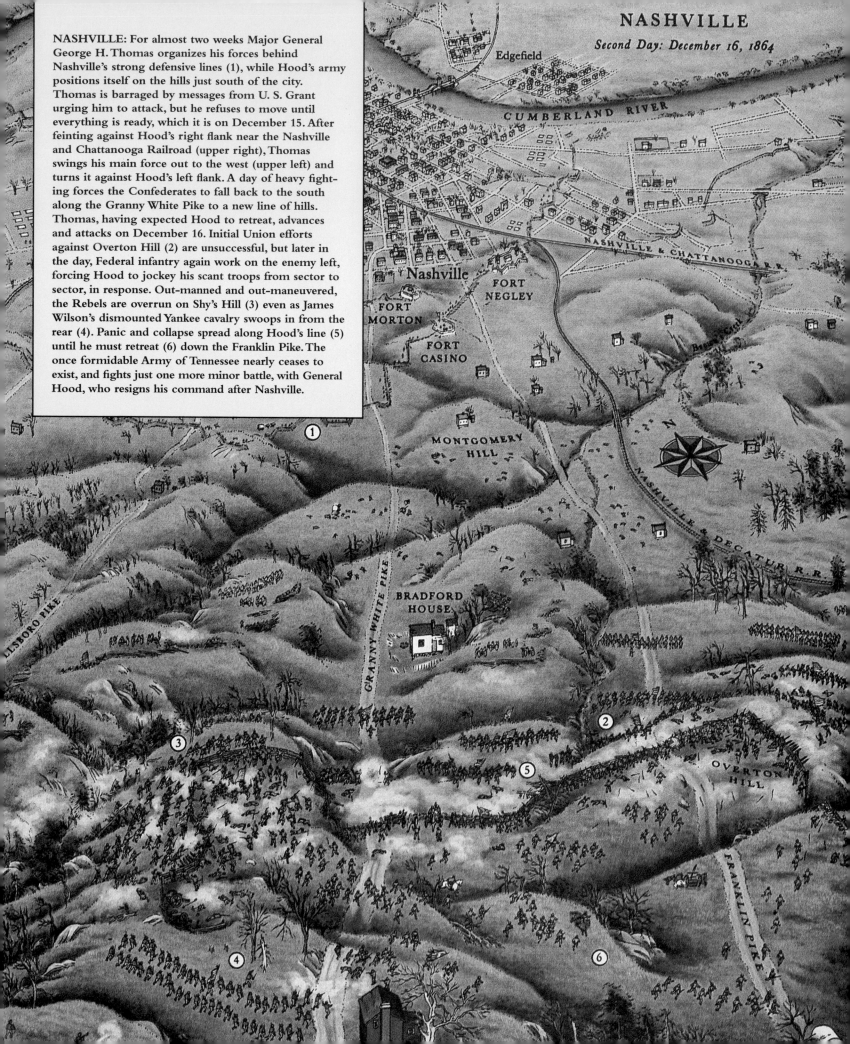

NASHVILLE

Second Day: December 16, 1864

NASHVILLE: For almost two weeks Major General George H. Thomas organizes his forces behind Nashville's strong defensive lines (1), while Hood's army positions itself on the hills just south of the city. Thomas is barraged by messages from U. S. Grant urging him to attack, but he refuses to move until everything is ready, which it is on December 15. After feinting against Hood's right flank near the Nashville and Chattanooga Railroad (upper right), Thomas swings his main force out to the west (upper left) and turns it against Hood's left flank. A day of heavy fighting forces the Confederates to fall back to the south along the Granny White Pike to a new line of hills. Thomas, having expected Hood to retreat, advances and attacks on December 16. Initial Union efforts against Overton Hill (2) are unsuccessful, but later in the day, Federal infantry again work on the enemy left, forcing Hood to jockey his scant troops from sector to sector, in response. Out-manned and out-maneuvered, the Rebels are overrun on Shy's Hill (3) even as James Wilson's dismounted Yankee cavalry swoops in from the rear (4). Panic and collapse spread along Hood's line (5) until he must retreat (6) down the Franklin Pike. The once formidable Army of Tennessee nearly ceases to exist, and fights just one more minor battle, with General Hood, who resigns his command after Nashville.

The Federal victory at Nashville had been dependent on the ability of Union troops to maintain vital supply lines from the north. George N. Barnard's 1864 photograph (left), of the Louisville and Nashville Railroad's fortified bridge over the Cumberland River, shows one way that the Federals protected critical railroad routes. By closing the doors at either end of the structure, and manning the enclosed turrets, Union troops could defend the bridge against Rebel raiders.

that even if Sherman's army were entirely lost, the North would still have enough soldiers to handle the Confederacy's declining armies; besides which, the President by this time had full confidence in Grant and Sherman, and he was willing to assume that they knew what they were about.

On December 10 Sherman reached the coast just below Savannah, capturing Confederate Fort McAllister, at the mouth of the Ogeechee River, and getting in touch with the U.S. fleet. News of his safe arrival went north promptly, and Sherman drew his lines to capture Savannah and the force of 10,000 which had been scraped together to defend it.

He succeeded in taking the city—it was bound to fall, once Sherman's army had attained full contact with the navy—but Confederate General William J. Hardee managed to get the garrison out safely. The Confederate troops moved up into South Carolina, and Sherman's men marched proudly into Savannah. On December 24 Sherman sent Lincoln a whimsical telegram, offering him the city of Savannah as a Christmas present.

So 1864 came to an end, and as it did the approaching end of the war was visible for all to see. The Confederacy still had an army west of the Mississippi, where it could have no effect on the outcome of the struggle, and it had isolated forces at Mobile and elsewhere in the deep South, but it had nothing to oppose Thomas' victorious troops in Tennessee, it had no chance to bring together enough men to keep Sherman from coming north from Savannah whenever he

Union rear echelon troops (above) passed a quiet day behind the lines in Nashville on December 16, even as fierce fighting was taking place a few miles to the south. That morning the city laid under what one observer termed a "Scotch mist," which burned off by midday, when the temperature reached the mid-60's. The soldiers pictured were part of a garrison that had occupied Nashville since mid-1863, a period of eighteen months during which the once picturesque town became, according to one diarist, a "dreary waste."

elected to try it, and Lee was still pinned in the lines at Petersburg, unable to do more than hold on. To all intents and purposes, the Confederacy at the beginning of 1865 consisted of the Carolinas and of the southern strip of Virginia.

ONE SUCCESS THE SOUTH HAD had, in December. An amphibious expedition under Benjamin Butler had tried to capture Wilmington, North Carolina, the one remaining seaport through which the South could communicate with the outer world. A Union fleet had bombarded Fort Fisher, which commanded the entrance to the Cape Fear River on which Wilmington was situated, Butler had put troops ashore—and then, growing panicky, had concluded that the place was too strong to be taken, had re-embarked his men, and had sailed north in disgraceful panic. But even the savor of this defensive victory did not last long. Butler was removed, and early in January Grant sent down a new expedition, with Admiral Porter commanding for the navy and General A. H. Terry commanding for the army. This time there was no hesitation. The navy pounded the fort hard, then Terry got his troops on the beach and sent them swarming over the defenses. Fort Fisher surrendered, and the Confederacy's last door to the outer world was closed.

Sherman was preparing to march north. In Tennessee a powerful Federal mounted force of 12,000 men armed with repeating carbines was getting ready to cut down into Alabama. Another Federal army was besieging Mobile. Grant was ordering 21,000 Western troops brought east, to move inland from captured Wilmington and join Sherman as he came north. The war was all but finished.

The Tennessee State House in Nashville becomes just another Union stronghold in late 1864, as artillery units stand ready on the north (left), and south sides (below). The city was ill-prepared for the influx of fortune hunters, speculators, and others who descended upon it during the Federal occupation. Nashville, complained a local newspaper just one month before the great battle, "swarms with a host of burglars, brass-knuck and slingshot ruffians, pickpockets and highwaymen, who have flocked hither from all parts of the country."

OVERLEAF: In Xanthus Russell Smith's oil painting *Attack on Fort Fisher, North Carolina,* the Union fleet pounds Confederate defenses at the mouth of the Cape Fear River on January 15, 1865. The combined army-navy operation captured the fort and closed the river, ending the reign of Wilmington, North Carolina (located twenty miles upriver), as the South's last usable seaport.

CHAPTER 14

Victory

On the first of February, 1865, Sherman and his army started north from Savannah, and the war shuddered toward its conclusion. Sherman had some 60,000 veterans, and when he reached North Carolina he would be reinforced by 21,000 more under Schofield. To oppose him, the Confederacy had the troops that had been pulled out of Savannah, some threadbare levies from the broken Army of Tennessee, and sundry home-guard and cavalry units—upwards of 30,000 men in all, many of them not first-line troops. There was not the slightest possibility that it could increase this number substantially; Joe Johnston, brought back from retirement and put in charge in the hope that he might somehow find a way to halt Sherman, confessed sadly: "I can do no more than annoy him."

Johnston's return was a sign of belated and unavailing effort to put new vigor into the defense of the dwindling Southern nation. Late in January the Congress at Richmond had passed an act providing for a general in

George P. A. Healy's painting *The Peacemakers* (right) depicts a telling incident that took place at City Point, Virginia. On March 28, 1865, Abraham Lincoln held a war strategy session with generals William Tecumseh Sherman and U. S. Grant (at left in picture) and Admiral David Dixon Porter (at right). Following an over-all review of recent events, the discussion turned, not to the further destruction of the Confederacy, but to plans for rebuilding the battered nation. "I know when I left him," wrote Sherman later, "that I was more than ever impressed by his kindly nature, his deep and earnest sympathy with the afflictions of the whole people . . . and that his earnest desire seemed to be to end the war speedily. . . ." Lincoln's conciliatory impulse was not shared by Southern leaders; in nearby Richmond, the coming of spring brought forth renewed calls to arms (above).

TO THE Citizens of the State, AND THE PEOPLE of RICHMOND

THE ENEMY UNDOUBTEDLY **ARE APPROACHING THE CITY!** And may be expected at any hour, with a view to its capture, its pillage, and its destruction. The strongest considerations of self and of duty to the country, **CALL EVERY MAN TO ARMS!** A duty which none can refuse without dishonor. All persons, therefore, able to wield a musket, will immediately **Assemble upon the Public Square** Where a regiment will be found in arms, and around which all can rally, and where the requisite directions will be given for arming and equipping those who respond to this call.

☞The Governor confidently relies that this appeal will not be made in vain.

WM. SMITH, GOVERNOR OF VIRGINIA.

chief for the armies of the Confederacy, and Robert E. Lee, inevitably, had been given this position. Lee restored Johnston to command in the Carolinas, but he could do very little to help him, and there was not much Johnston himself could do. His chief immediate reliance would have to be on the weather and geography. Sherman's line of march would carry him through swampy lowland regions, cut by many rivers, and in rainy winter weather roads would be almost impassable and the streams would be swollen; all in all, it seemed improbable that he could make much progress during the winter months.

But Sherman's army had special qualities. Like the Confederate armies, it contained men who had lived close to the frontier, backwoods people who could use the axe and who could improvise their way through almost any obstacle, and these men came up through South Carolina as rapidly as they had gone across Georgia, corduroying roads, building bridges, and fording icy rivers as they came. Johnston, watching from afar, remarked afterward that there had been no such army since the days of Julius Caesar.

Sherman's men laid hard hands on South Carolina. They had been very much on their good behavior in Savannah, but they relapsed into their old habits once they left Georgia, burning and looting and destroying as they marched. There

OPPOSITE: After reaching Savannah from Atlanta, General Sherman decided to continue his march, through South and North Carolina. The route was a difficult one, cluttered with swamps, forcing the men to wade for miles through waist-deep muck (bottom). As to enemy opposition, William Waud's sketch (top) depicts an incident that occurred in early March, near Cheraw, South Carolina, when Sherman's men had to race through woods and then over a foot bridge that retreating Rebels had set afire.

Soon after Sherman's men entered South Carolina, they met Confederate forces that were making a stand along the Salkehatchie River. After three days of preparation, Federals attacked boldly, crossing the boggy woodlands (left) and routing the Rebels. As Sherman's Yankees marched with vengeance in their hearts, towns in their path were doomed. Most of the residents of McPhersonville fled before Sherman's approach, but that did not dissuade his men from setting it ablaze (below).

Columbia the morning after the fire

William Waud's panoramic sketch (above) shows the devastation visited upon South Carolina's capital, Columbia, as Sherman's men took possession February 17. An Ohio boy wrote home that "Our men had such a spite against the place they swore they would burn the city, if they should enter it, and they did." The fire bells began to ring at dusk, February 17. "The winds blew terribly," recalled a more sympathetic Union soldier. "It would pick up flakes of the burning cotton and carry it a long ways. If it fell on a roof it set fire to that building. Burning shingles and pieces of boards flew before the wind. We soon began to help the women and children. Poor souls! They did not know what to do. All we could do was to hustle them out and if they had any little valuables help them get them to a safe place." After the war, Sherman maintained that retreating Confederate soldiers had started the fire, and his men had worked to contain it. In the aftermath he did post guards to prevent looting and to protect Columbia's surviving landmarks, like the Palmetto monument (opposite).

was a personal fury in their behavior now that had been missing in Georgia; to a man, they felt that South Carolina had started the war and that her people deserved rough treatment, and such treatment the unhappy South Carolinians assuredly got. The capital, Columbia, was burned after Sherman's men moved in, and although the Federals insisted that the burning had been accidental—a point which is in dispute to this day—most of the soldiers agreed that if the accident had not taken place they themselves would have burned the place anyway. As they came north their path was marked, Old Testament style, by a pillar of smoke by day and pillars of fire by night. South Carolina paid a fearful price for having led the way in secession.

In Richmond approaching doom was clearly visible, and the sight stirred men to consider doing what had previously been unthinkable—to lay hands on the institution of slavery itself. After much debate the Confederate Congress voted a bill to make soldiers out of Negro slaves. That this implied an end to slavery itself was obvious; to turn a slave into a soldier automatically brought freedom, and if part of the race lost its chains, all of the race must eventually be freed; and there was bitter opposition when the measure was first suggested. As recently as one year earlier the idea had been quite unthinkable. One of the best combat soldiers in the Army of Tennessee, Irish-born General Pat Cleburne, had proposed such a step at a conclave of generals, and the proposal had been hushed up immediately. But Cleburne was

The Night Columbia Burned

Each side blamed the other for the burning of Columbia on the night of February 17, 1865. Those who considered it a war crime dogged Sherman throughout the rest of his life, and in 1880, a committee in Columbia published a record of testimony regarding the conflagration. It included this entry: *One of my maids brought me a paper, left, she told me, by a Yankee soldier; it was an ill-spelled but kindly warning of the horrors to come, written upon a torn sheet of my dead son's note-book, which, with private papers of every kind, now strewed my yard; it was signed by a lieutenant, but of what company and regiment I did not take note. The writer said he had relatives and friends at the South, and that he felt for us; that his heart bled to think of what was threatening. "Ladies," he wrote, "I pity you; leave this town, go anywhere to be safer than here." This was written in the morning; the fires were in the evening and night.*

Whoever started the fires that ravaged Columbia, the city was completely out of control on the night that Sherman's men marched in and took charge. Yet, though the general would be personally blamed for the destruction (as photographed by George N. Barnard from the State House grounds, above), the occupation was a proud triumph for him. He took special pleasure in greeting some Federal soldiers who had been liberated from the city's prison camp. "Not when meeting his dearest friends, not in the . . . moment of victory . . . have I seen his face beam with such exultation and kindly greeting," said an observer. His troops were exultant, too, and soon the whiskey that had filled Columbia's warehouses filled many of them. "The soldiers had a terrible drunk and run riot all night," declared a surgeon with an Illinois regiment.

dead now, one of the generals killed at Franklin, and Lee himself was supporting the plan; and as spring came the Confederacy was taking halting steps to arm and train black troops.

AT THE SAME TIME Secretary of State Benjamin played a card which might have been very effective if it had been played two or three years earlier. To France and Great Britain he had the Confederacy's emissaries abroad offer the abolition of slavery in return for recognition. Neither London nor Paris was interested: the Confederacy was beyond recognition now, and nobody could mistake the fact, so the offer fell flat. If it had been made in 1862 or in the spring of 1863, it might possibly have bought what Richmond wanted, but like Confederate currency it had depreciated so badly by this time that it would buy nothing of any consequence.

If there was to be a negotiated peace, then, it would have to come from Washington, and in February the government at Richmond tried to find out if Washington cared to talk terms. It was encouraged to take this step by a recent visit paid to the Confederate capital by old Francis P. Blair, Sr., one of whose sons had been Postmaster General in Lincoln's cabinet, while the other was a corps commander in Sherman's army. Old man Blair was believed to be in Lincoln's confidence, and in January he came through the lines and went to the Confederate White House for a talk with Jefferson Davis; to Davis he suggested a reunion of the states and a concerted effort by the restored nation to drive the French out of Mexico. Davis refused to commit himself on this eccentric proposal, and it developed presently that Blair had made the trip on his own hook and definitely had not been speaking for Lincoln; but the mere fact that the feeler had been put out seemed to indicate that the Lincoln government might be willing to talk terms, and a semiformal conference was arranged for February 3 on a Federal steamer in Hampton Roads, Virginia. Representing the Confederacy were Vice-President Alexander Stephens, R. M. T. Hunter of Virginia, president pro tem of the Senate, and Judge John A. Campbell of Alabama, formerly of the United States Supreme Court. Speaking for the Union at this conference were President Lincoln and Secretary Seward.

The conferees seem to have had a pleasant chat, but they got nowhere. Lincoln was leading from strength, and he had no concessions to offer. It was told, later, as a pleasant myth, that he had taken a sheet of paper, had written "Reunion" at the top of it, and then had handed it to little Stephens with the remark that Stephens might fill in the rest of the terms to suit himself, but there was no truth in this tale. Lincoln's position was inflexible: there would be peace when the Confederate armies were disbanded and the national authority was recognized throughout the South, and there would be no peace until then. With acceptance of national authority, of course, would go acceptance of the abolition of slavery; the thirteenth amendment to the Constitution, ending slavery forever, had already been submitted to the states for ratification.

The stark debris of a devastated city (below) became an object of great fascination for photographers, but mere pictures could not fully convey the horror of the night Columbia burned. A novelist later wrote of that infamous event: "You might see the ruined owner, standing woebegone, aghast, gazing at his tumbling dwelling, his scattered property, with a dumb agony on his face. . . . Others you might hear . . . with wild blasphemies assailing the justice of Heaven, or invoking, with lifted and clenched hands, the fiery wrath of the avenger. But the soldiers plundered and drank, the fiery work raged, and the moon sailed over all. . . ."

After holding out for years, Charleston's defenders quietly abandoned the port city on the night of February 17, 1865, fearing that they would be trapped by Sherman as he marched through the state's interior. The first unit to occupy Charleston was the 55th Massachusetts, a black regiment that had spent much of its service on nearby Morris and Folly islands. The moment captured by Thomas Nast in his *Entrance of the 55th Massachusetts (Colored) Regiment into Charleston, S.C., February 21, 1865,* illustrates the testimony of one of the unit's white officers: "Words fail to describe the scene which those who witnessed it will never forget,—the welcome given to a regiment of colored troops by their people redeemed from slavery."

What this meant was that the Confederates must simply surrender unconditionally and rely on the liberality of the Federal administration for a reconstruction program that would make the lot of the Southland endurable. Of Lincoln's own liberality there was no question; he was even willing to try to get a Federal appropriation to pay slaveowners for the loss of their human property, and it was clear that he planned no proscription list or other punitive measures. But no Southerner could forget that what would finally happen would depend in large part on the Northern Congress, and such leaders as Thaddeus Stevens, Ben Wade, Zachariah Chandler, and Charles Sumner had ideas very different from Lincoln's. In the end the conference adjourned with nothing accomplished, the Southern delegates went back to Richmond, and Davis told his people that their only hope lay in war to the last ditch.

Sherman kept moving north, inexorably. As he came up through South Carolina his army sliced across the railroad lines that led to Charleston, and that famous city fell at last into Union hands. It had withstood the most violent attacks the Federal army and navy could make, but it had to be abandoned at last because the whole interior of the state was lost. The national flag went up on the rubble-heap that had been Fort Sumter, the Palmetto State was out of the war forever, and Sherman's hard-boiled soldiers tramped on into North Carolina. In this state they

For much of 1863 and all of 1864, Charleston was the target of steady bombardment from Union Parrott rifles on Morris Island near the harbor mouth. This shelling, and a series of fires, resulted in the destruction which was vividly recorded by photographers who rushed into the city after its capture (left and above). Yet, more than a year later, a visitor still found much of the devastation remained. "Above the monotonous gloom of the ordinary ruins rise the churches—the stone tower and roofless walls of the Catholic cathedral, deserted and solitary, a roost for buzzards; the burned-out shell of the Circular Church, with its dismantled columns still standing, like those of an antique temple."

INAUGURATION PROGRAMME.

AIDS.   THE MARSHAL-IN-CHIEF.   AIDS.

THE MILITARY ESCORT.

The President of the United States

And his Private Secretary, with the Marshal of the
District of Columbia and his Deputies
on right and Left.

EX-PRESIDENTS.

The Vice President and Vice President Elect,

THE CABINET.

The CORPS DIPLOMATIQUE.

THE JUDICIARY.

Senators and Representatives.
Ex-Senators and Representatives.

HEADS OF BUREAUS AND ASSISTANTS.

Officers and Soldiers of the Revolution, and of the War of
1812.

THE NATIONAL UNION COLLEGE BAND,

The National Union Executive Committee.
The National Executive Committee of Loyal Leagues.

STATE AND CITY AUTHORITIES.

The Lincoln and Johnson Clubs, with Car, &c.

STATE ORGANIZATIONS.

EAST WASHINGTON LINCOLN and JOHNSON
CLUB, WITH MONITOR, &c.

FIRE ORGANIZATIONS.

The Washington Press.

OFFICERS OF THE ARMY, NAVY, MARINE
CORPS, AND MILITIA.

Detachment of the United States Marine Corps.
Detachment of the 1st Brigade of Quartermaster Volunteers.

Other Military Organizations.

GIESBORO' CAVALCADE.

Turner Associations of Washington and Georgetown.
Odd Fellows and other Benevolent Associations.

The following names have been sent in to
represent the States and Territories :

Maine—General John O. Caldwell.
New Hampshire—Major Evarts W. Farr.
Vermont—Edward S Dana.
Massachusetts—Major Charles N. O. Rogers.
Rhode Island—Walter O. Simmons.
Connecticut—Hon. Benj Noyes.
New York—Colonel E M. Whitaker.
New Jersey—r. A. P. Fardon.
Pennsylvania—A. S. Fuller.
Maryland—B. F M. Hurley.
Ohio—H. M. Slade.
Virginia—James H. Clements.
North Carolina—Professor H. S. Hedrick.
South Carolina—J. P. M. Epping.
Florida—Harrison Reid.
Alabama—Captain Daniel H. Bingham.
Mississippi—General A. Alderson.
Louisiana—E. Murphy.
Tennessee—Governor William Bebb.
Kentucky—Colonel James W. Irwin.
Indiana—I. J. Cummings.
Illinois—Dr. J. S. Bangs.
Michigan—H. J. Gray.
Missouri—G. W. Moran.
California—Major Robert J. Stevens.
Iowa—B. N. Hawes.
Wisconsin—Major George W. Barter.
Minnesota—H. H. Brackett.
Kansas—Edward E. Fuller.
Nebraska—Colonel R W. Furnas.
Nevada—Stephen Gage.
Montana—Hon G. E Upson.
Dakota—William H. Burleigh.

The following Aids, Marshals, and Marshals
representing States, have been selected to act
on the occasion :

AIDS.

Capt. J. S. Poland.
Lewis Clephane.
George H. Plant.
Dr. D. W. Bliss.
Z. C Robbins.
Wm. S. Mitchell.
J. L. Henshaw.

Maj. G. W. DeCosta.
Col. A.G M. Provest
Dr. Z. D. Gilman.
I. T. Clements Jr.
Z. Richards.
B. B. French, Jr.

MARSHALS.

Major Charles Hamlin.
De Vere Burr.
Alexander Shepherd.
James W. Deeole,
Job Angus.
Lt. Col. Gardner Tufts,
J. S. Brown,
Jno. G. Adams,
H. C Addison.
Lt. Samuel Fessenden,
Ino. P. Hilton,
W. H. Craig,
Seward A. Foot,
A. G Hall,
George Hill, Jr.,
H. C. Field,
Dr. G. K. Smith,
John W. Jones,
Dr. H. A. Robbins,
Franklin Rives,
Major E. E. Paulding,
Robert S. Stevens,
Willard Seares,
Clement L. West,
Major E. M. Stebbins,
Lt. Col. Jas. A. Hall,
A. L. Hayes,
John R. Thompson.
George H. Plant, Jr.,
C H Snow,
R. B. Clark
Dr. Daniel B Clark,
E. J. Brooks,
O. M. Keyes,
Serg. Maj A. S. Perham.
I. E. Bartholow,
Obrey White,
H. Grossmayer,
James Galway,
John W. Fitzhugh,
W. J. Stephenson,
A. H. Sawyer,
A. Cluss,
Lewis F. Perry,
L. C. Campbell,
George W. Brown ;
J W. Thompson,
Thos E Baden,
Warren J. Gollamer,
Franklin Philp,
O. A. Stevens,
Edward Griggs,
T. B. Brown,
L. B. Jackson,
Gratiot Washburne,
Jas. Topham.

Lieut. G. A. Whitman,
M. G. Emery,
Thos. Lewis,
Asbury Lloyd
Wm. Orme,
Fielder Dorsett,
John Alexander,
Major T. H. Gardner,
Chas. J. Frazier,
R. J. Meigs, Jr.,
F A. Boswell.
Lieut. Albion Howe,
Geo. A. Bassett,
Geo N. Beall,
Capt. N. Darling,
L. P. Parker,
George A. Bates,
Jas. Kelly.
Ch. S. English,
J. A. Magruder,
R. A. Shinn,
Jas. A. McKean,
Jos Gerhardt,
Fred. Myers,
D. C Fortey,
Edward Baldwin,
S. P. Bell,
F. N. Blake,
Jonas B. Ellis,
Wm H. Rohrer,
Wm. J. Murtagh,
John Paxton,
H. O Reever,
M. Willian,
Richmond J. Southworth
Dr. Julius Nichols,
W. O Tuck
B F. Guy,
J. R. Dodge,
R. T. McLain,
Prof. W E. Jilson,
Gilbert B. Towles,
U R Vaugan,
Samuel T. Ellis,
Charles E Lathrop,
Daniel Baker,
Thomas Adams
J. H. Thomas,
Wm. A Cook,
Samuel Weis
W. D. Moore,
Capt. Jas. Lawrence,
Dr. S. A. H. McKim,
D. H. Walker,
Capt. R. T Shillinglaw.

REGALIA.

The following regalia is prescribed for the
occasion: The marshal-in-chief will be designated by an orange-colored scarf with white
rosettes, and blue saddle-cloth with gilt trim-
mings. His aids, thirteen in number, will wear
cherry-colored scarfs with white rosettes; their
saddle-cloths will be white, trimmed with blue.
The marshal-in-chief and his aids will wear
yellow gauntlets, and use blue batons two feet
in length, with gilt ends two inches deep.

The marshals will be designated by blue
scarfs with white rosettes, white saddle-cloths
trimmed with red, white gloves, and pink
colored batons, with white ends two inches
deep.

The marshals representing States and Territories will be designated by white scarfs with
blue rosettes, white saddle-cloths trimmed with
red, white gloves, and white batons two feet

long, with pink ends two inches deep.

The marshal-in-chief, the aids, and the marshals will wear common black hats, black
frock-coats, and black pantaloons.

THE RENDEZVOUS.

Owing to the almost impassable condition of
the unpaved streets through which it was originally intended to lead the procession, it has
been thought expedient to change the programme in that particular ; and the following
places are designated as the rendezvous for the
several organizations which will join in the Inaugural procession :

The Marshal-in-chief, his Aids, Marshals,
and Marshals representing States, will meet at
the corner of Sixteen-and-a-half street and
Pennsylvania avenue, near the War Department.

The military escort, with band, on Seventeenth street, south of Pennsylvania avenue.

The officers and soldiers of the Revolution,
and the war of 1812, on Pennsylvania avenue,
corner of Fifteen-and-a-half street.

The National Union College Band, the National Union Executive Committee of the Loyal
Leagues, the Lincoln and Johnson Clubs, the
State and city authorities, and State organizations on spaces at intersection of Pennsylvania
avenue and adjacent streets.

The Fire organizations on Nineteenth street,
south of Pennsylvania avenue.

Washington City Press, Nineteenth street,
north of the avenue.

Officers of the army and navy, Marine corps,
and Militia, Seventeenth street, north of Pennsylvania avenue.

Detachment of United States Marines, 1st
brigade of Quartermaster's volunteers, other
military organizations, and the Giesboro cavalcade, on Pennsylvania avenue from Twentieth
street west.

Turner Associations of Washington and
Georgetown, on spaces at intersection of Twenty-first street and Pennsylvania avenue.

Odd Fellows and other benevolent organizations, on Twentieth street, south of Pennsylvania avenue.

The various organizations are expected to
present themselves punctually by 10 30 o'clock,
and will be shown to their respective rendezvous by the aids and marshals.

DANIEL R. GOODLOE,
Marshal in Chief.

The Senate Committee have made the follow-
ing arrangements for the inauguration of the
President of the United States, on the 4th of
March, 1865 :

PROGRAMME.

The doors of the Senate Chamber will be
opened at 11 o'clock, a. m., for the admission
of Senators, and others who, by the arrangement of the committee, are entitled to admission, as follows :

Ex-Presidents and Vice Presidents.

The Chief Justice and Associate Justices of
the Supreme Court.

The Diplomatic Corps, Heads of Departments,
Ex-Members of either branch of Congress, and
Members of Congress elect.

Officers of the Army and Navy, who, by name,
have received the thanks of Congress.

41052

On March 4, 1865, Abraham Lincoln was
inaugurated to his second term as U.S.
President. Thousands gathered at the
Capitol for a program of events (above)
that included a much-anticipated speech
by the Chief Executive. Using phrases
that sounded as if they had come from
the Old Testament, Lincoln said that God
had his own purpose in the war, and that
purpose may have been to continue the
war, even if it meant that "all wealth
piled by the bond-men's two hundred
and fifty years of unrequited toil shall be
sunk, and until every drop of blood
drawn with the lash shall be paid by
another drawn with the sword. . . ."
While the Southern press rejected his
words as "being a compound of philan-
thropy, fanaticism and scriptural morality,"
some Northern writers said that Lincoln's
text should be "printed in gold." A young
Union officer, Charles Francis Adams,
Jr., writing to his father (the American
Minister to England), asked: "What will
Europe think of this utterance of the rude
ruler, of whom they have nourished so
lofty a contempt? Not a prince or minister
in all Europe could have risen to such an
equality with the occasion."

Alfred Waud's sketch (right) shows the Union V Corps attacking at Five Forks, Virginia, an encounter that was key to breaking the ten-month stalemate at Petersburg. At Five Forks, an important intersection, Union infantry and cavalry, under Major General Philip H. Sheridan, crushed a smaller Rebel force and took control of Robert E. Lee's last supply route. Sheridan captured approximately 2,400 Confederate soldiers, some of whom were photographed (below), near City Point, on their way to Northern prison camps. As they passed by miles of loaded wagons and mounds of plentiful supplies, one emaciated prisoner wondered "how our little army had so long held at bay so mighty a force."

went on their good behavior, and the burning and devastation that had marked their path ever since they left Atlanta were held to a minimum. They did not feel the hatred for North Carolina that they had felt for her sister state; and, in point of fact, there was no military need for a policy of destruction now, because the war could not possibly last very much longer.

TO THE CONFEDERACY there remained just one chance—a very slim chance, with heavy odds against it. In the lines at Petersburg, Lee faced double his own numbers; in North Carolina, Johnston was up against odds that were even longer. The one hope was that Lee might somehow give Grant the slip, get his army into North Carolina, join forces with Johnston, and defeat Sherman in pitched battle. This done, Lee and Johnston might turn back toward Virginia and meet Grant on something like even terms. It was most unlikely that all of this could be done, but it had to be tried because it was the only card that could be played. Lee would try it as soon as the arriving spring made the roads dry enough to permit his army to move.

This photograph (below), often described as showing the first Union wagons entering Petersburg, was actually taken nearly a week after Federal troops entered the town on April 3. It is likely that this supply train, which is shown heading west out of town on Washington Street, was bringing food to the hard-pressing Union columns spread along a line from Petersburg to Appomattox Court House.

Even as Richmond was in the process of evacuation, on April 2, Union and Confederate troops continued to battle for control of Petersburg's defensive lines. To the west of the town the Federals finally scored a major breakthrough, forcing Robert E. Lee to evacuate his troops; southeast of Petersburg there were bitter clashes over several Confederate strongpoints, one of which was known as Fort Mahone. Soon after Union troops occupied it, they posed along Mahone's ramparts (above). Of especial interest to the cameramen who entered with them were the remains of the fort's Rebel defenders (right), left unburied by comrades in hasty retreat.

The Federal army in Lee's front occupied a huge semicircle more than forty miles long, the northern tip of it opposite Richmond itself, the southern tip curling around southwest of Petersburg in an attempt to cut the railroads that led south. Lee proposed to form a striking force with troops pulled out of his attenuated lines and to make a sudden attack on the Federal center. If the striking force could punch a substantial hole and break the military railroad that supplied Grant's army, the Union left would have to be pulled back to avoid being cut off. That would make possible a Confederate march south and would pave the way for the combined attack on Sherman.

On March 25 the Army of Northern Virginia launched its last great counterpunch. Lee's striking force, led by the fiery young Georgian, General John B. Gordon, made a dawn attack on the Federal Fort Stedman; carried the fort, sent patrols

Having taken the picture at left, photographer T. C. Roche also wrote the caption: "Rebel soldiers killed in the trenches of fort Mahone, called by the soldiers 'fort Damnation.' This view shows the construction of their bomb proofs and covered passages, which branch off in every direction. This view was taken the morning after the storming of Petersburg, Va. 1865."

back toward the railroad, seized a portion of the Federal trenches—and then ran out of steam, crumpled under a heavy Union fire, and at last had to confess failure. By noon the survivors of the attack were back in the Confederate lines. Lee's last expedient had misfired; now Grant would take and keep the initiative.

For many months Grant had refused to make frontal attacks on the Confederate fortifications. They were simply too strong to be taken by direct assault, so long as even a skeleton force remained to hold them, and the fearful losses of the first months of 1864 had taught the Federals the folly of trying to drive Lee's men out of prepared positions. Grant's tactics ever since had been to extend his lines to the west, using his superior manpower to compel Lee to stretch his own army past the breaking point. Sooner or later, Grant would be able to put a force out beyond Lee's flank and compel the Confederates to quit their position or fight a battle they could not win. The impassable roads of midwinter had caused a suspension of this movement, but after Fort Stedman it was resumed.

DURING THE FINAL DAYS of March, Federal infantry tried to drive in past Lee's extreme right. The Confederate defenders were alert, and this infantry move was roughly handled; but Phil Sheridan, meanwhile, had brought his cavalry down from the Shenandoah Valley, after cleaning out the last pockets of Confederate resistance there, and with 12,000 mounted men he moved out to Dinwiddie Court House, south and west of the place where Union and Confederate infantry had been fighting for control of the flank. On the last day of the month Sheridan moved north from Dinwiddie Court House, aiming for a road junction known as Five Forks. This was well beyond Lee's lines; if the Federals could seize and hold it

The Virginia State House, overlooking Richmond as seen in the view (above) of the city across the James River, survived the conflagrations with little damage, except for a few broken windows. A Northern reporter on the scene believed that most of Richmond's destruction was well-deserved. "The offices of the newspapers, whose columns have been charged with the foulest vituperation against our Government, were on fire;" he wrote, "two of them have been reduced to ashes. . . . Every bank which had emitted the spurious notes of the rebels was consumed to ruins. Churches no longer gave audience to empty prayers, but burst forth in furious flames. . . . In short, Secession was burnt out, and the city purified as far as fire could accomplish it."

they could break Lee's railroad connections with the South, compel the evacuation of Petersburg and Richmond, and interpose themselves between Lee and Johnston. Lee sent a mixed force of cavalry and infantry out to hold Five Forks, and Sheridan called to his aid a veteran infantry corps from Grant's left flank.

On April 1 Sheridan and his powerful column routed the Confederate defenders at Five Forks. The Rebel force there was commanded by George Pickett, who would forever wear the glamour of that magnificent charge at Gettysburg, and Pickett was badly overmatched now. Sheridan had too many men and too much impetus, Pickett appears to have handled his own part of the assignment inexpertly, and as dusk came down on April 1 Pickett's column had been almost wiped out, with about 4,500 men taken prisoner, and most of the survivors fleeing without military formation or control.

Oddly enough, at the very moment that this sweeping victory was being won Sheridan removed Major General G. K. Warren from command of the Federal infantry involved, on the ground that Warren had been slow and inexpert in getting his men into action. Warren had brought the V Corps over from the left end of

When Madness Ruled the Streets

The night of April 2 was terrifying for residents of Richmond. As buildings burned, mobs roamed the streets in a frenzy of looting and destruction, the results of which are shown here. A Confederate officer, leaving the city in retreat, remembered:

As I rode by the principal jewelry store I saw an old woman crawling backwards out of a window. One of the mounted men [with me] rode up and whacked her with the flat of his sword when she tumbled out with a yell, and her lap full of plunder from [jewelry] . . . show cases poured over the sidewalk. At another store, a party was

beating in the door which burst in only to show the owner standing armed and firing on his assailants. One of them fell, but instantly the poor fellow [the owner] fell, shot to death.

the Federal entrenched position; he had had a hard march in the darkness over bad roads, the orders he had been given were somewhat confusing, and the delay was not really his fault—and in any case the Union had won the battle and no real harm had been done. But Sheridan was a driver. At the very end of the war the Army of the Potomac was being given a sample of the pitiless insistence on flawless performance which it had never known before. Warren was treated unjustly, but the army might have been better off if similar treatment had been meted out to some of its generals two years earlier.

The way was clear now for Grant to get in behind the Army of Northern Virginia; to emphasize the extent of the Union victory, Grant ordered a blow at the center of the Petersburg lines for the early morning of April 2. The lines had been stretched so taut that this blow broke them once and for all. That evening the Confederates evacuated Richmond and Petersburg, the government headed for some Carolina haven where it might continue to function, and Lee put his tired army on the road and began a forced march to join forces with Johnston.

He was never able to make it. The Union advance, led by Sheridan, outpaced him, and instead of going south the Army of Northern Virginia was compelled to drift west, with Federals on its flank and following close in its rear. In the confusion that surrounded the evacuation of Richmond the Confederate government got its victualling arrangements into a tangle, and the rations which were supposed to meet Lee's almost exhausted army along the line of march did not appear. The army stumbled on, its march harassed by constant stabs from Yankee cavalry, its men hungry and worn out, staying with the colors only because of their unshakable confidence in Lee himself. At Sayler's Creek, Federal cavalry and infantry

Alfred Waud's sketch (above) shows Confederate soldiers incarcerated on the grounds of Libby Prison where Union officers had been held earlier in the war. As Union troops began to enter Richmond on the morning of April 3, the 81st New York claimed the honor of raising the U.S. flag over one of the South's most notorious prisoner compounds. A member of that regiment noted that "Details were made to pick up all men that wore the gray uniform and bring them into the prison, which was soon pretty well filled." The heavy guns that had kept U.S. warships at bay from approaching on the James were also collected under Union control (below right).

PREVIOUS SPREAD: Richmond's business district, as photographed soon after the fires had been extinguished.

The President in a Captured Capital

Abraham Lincoln was ending an extended visit to the Petersburg front when word arrived that Richmond had been captured. On April 4, unannounced and accompanied only by a small escort, Lincoln visited the conquered capital. Denis Malone Carter's painting (below) exaggerates the response of the city's white population, but when black residents learned that the author of the Emancipation Proclamation was in their midst, they crowded around him. An officer with the escort thought the President "stood a chance of being crushed to death." Finally, Lincoln spoke to the admiring crowd: *My poor friends, you are free—free as air. . . . Liberty is your birthright. God gave it to you as he gave it to others, and it is a sin that you have been deprived of it for so many years. But you must try to deserve this priceless boon. . . . Don't let your joy carry you into excesses. Learn the laws and obey them; obey God's commandments and thank him for giving you liberty, for to him you owe all things.*

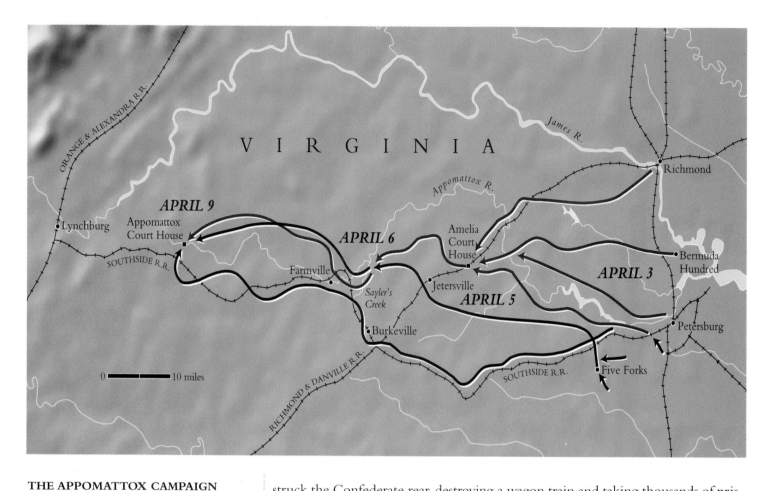

VIRGINIA

James R.

Richmond

Appomattox R.

APRIL 9

Lynchburg

Appomattox
Court House

APRIL 6

Amelia
Court
House

APRIL 3

ORANGE & ALEXANDRA R.R.

SOUTHSIDE R.R.

Farmville

Sayler's
Creek

Jetersville

Bermuda
Hundred

APRIL 5

Burkeville

Petersburg

0   10 miles

RICHMOND & DANVILLE R.R.

SOUTHSIDE R.R.

Five Forks

THE APPOMATTOX CAMPAIGN (above): After Lee orders his forces to abandon the Richmond–Petersburg front on the night of April 2, his plan is to concentrate his scattered commands at Amelia Court House, provision them, and then march along the Richmond and Danville Railroad to link up with General Joseph E. Johnston's army in North Carolina (Lee's flight is marked by the red arrows). Realizing this, U. S. Grant does not pursue Lee directly, but moves along a parallel line to the south, in order to foil any attempt at a rendezvous (Grant's pursuit of Lee is marked by the black arrows). Lee loses a day at Amelia Court House when the desperately needed rations fail to arrive and his men must forage from the surrounding countryside. When he does start south, he finds the way blocked at Jetersville and he turns to the west, hoping to both meet supplies sent from Lynchburg and overreach the Union columns. The Federal pursuit is relentless, though: most of the supplies are intercepted, the rear of Lee's column is trapped at Sayler's Creek, and Lee himself is finally cornered at Appomattox Court House, where he surrenders to Grant on April 9.

struck the Confederate rear, destroying a wagon train and taking thousands of prisoners. Witnessing the rout from high ground in the rear, Lee remarked grimly: "General, that half of our army is destroyed."

THE END CAME ON April 9, at a little town named Appomattox Court House. Federal cavalry and infantry had got across Lee's line of march, other powerful forces were on his flank, and a huge mass of infantry was pressing on his rear. He had no chance to get in touch with Johnston, no chance to continue his flight toward the west, no chance to put up a fight that would drive his foes out of the way; Lee had fewer than 30,000 soldiers with him by now, and not half of these were armed and in usable military formation. The rest were worn-out men who were pathetically doing their best to stay with the army, but who could not this day be used in battle.

The break came just as Federal infantry and cavalry were ready to make a final, crushing assault on the thin lines in Lee's front. Out between the lines came a Confederate horseman, a white flag fluttering at the end of a staff, and a sudden quiet descended on the broad field. While the soldiers in both armies stared at one another, unable to believe that the fighting at last was over, the commanding generals made their separate ways into the little town to settle things for good.

So Lee met Grant in the bare parlor of a private home at Appomattox Court House and surrendered his army. For four long years that army had been unconquerable. Twice it had carried the war north of the Potomac. Time and again it had beaten back the strongest forces the North could send against it. It had given to the Confederate nation the only hope of growth and survival which that

After Amelia Court House, Lee's army was forced by lack of sufficient roads to move in a long single column that was impossible to protect from Union cavalrymen sweeping into the flanks and rear. Alfred Waud's sketch (left) records the scene when Sheridan's cavalry trapped some of Lee's men in this way. After failing to break through a Federal cordon thrown across his line of march at Appomattox Court House on April 9, Lee arranged to discuss terms with U. S. Grant. While the talks were being set up, a series of truces were established between the two sides. The drawing by Alfred Waud (below) shows an officer bearing a truce flag approaching Brigadier General George A. Custer.

Custer receiving the flag of Truce appomatox 1865

At Appomattox Station (above), Robert E. Lee hoped to find supplies sent from Lynchburg. They had arrived, all right; however, so had three brigades of Yankee cavalry under dashing George Custer, who corralled the cars in a wild charge. "Go in, old fellow, don't let anything stop you, now is the chance for your stars," Custer told the officer commanding his lead regiment. "Whoop 'em up. I'll be after you." While Custer's riders grabbed the supplies, other troops, under Philip Sheridan's command, put up roadblocks the following day, to stop Lee's advance altogether. Once the Confederates realized that hard-marching Federal infantry was on the scene to back up the cavalry, they knew that the end had come. When both sides agreed to meet to discuss terms of surrender, one of Lee's staff officers selected a suitable location, the Wilmer McLean House (right), in the nearby village of Appomattox Court House.

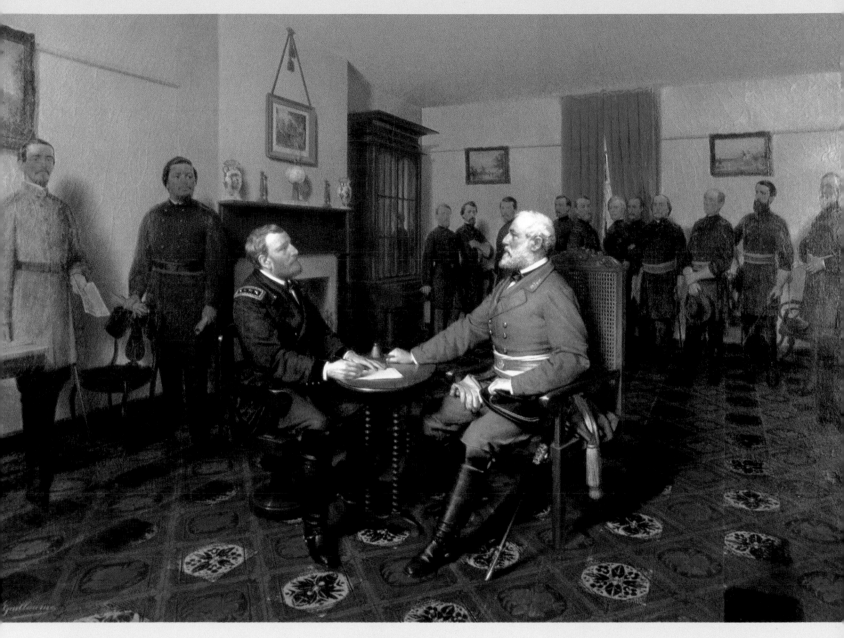

The End of the Army of Northern Virginia

Louis Guillaume's painting of the surrender ceremony in the parlor of the McLean House (above) takes artistic license with some of the details: it makes the room seem much larger than it actually is, and erroneously places Grant and Lee at the same table (they sat at separate tables about five feet apart). The meeting, so long awaited, began with idle chatter and only turned to the matter at hand when Lee pointedly reminded Grant why they were meeting. Grant immediately called for writing implements. "When I put my pen to the paper I did not know the first word that I should make use of in writing the terms," he recalled. "I only knew what was in my mind, and I wished to express it clearly, so that there could be no mistaking it." His terms were generous: soldiers of the Confederate army would be paroled, not sent to prison camps; officers could keep their side arms, and personal property would be respected. Although it was not included in the written terms, he also agreed to Lee's request that enlisted men who claimed horses or mules as their own would be allowed to keep them. As a final gesture of reconciliation, he also provided rations for Lee's men. Grant ordered there be no celebrations in the Union armies to mark Lee's surrender. "The Confederates were now our prisoners," he later explained, "and we did not want to exult over their downfall." It was a dignified gesture, but as an order, it was widely ignored.

Lee

A Ride Among the Troops

General Robert E. Lee was sketched by Alfred Waud as he left the McLean House (above) on his final return to his headquarters. The ride took Lee past his surrendered soldiers, whose personal affection for him had often superseded any formal military obedience. According to one of Lee's artillery officers:

The universal desire to express to him the unabated love and confidence of the army had led to the formation of the gunners of a few battalions of artillery along the roadside, with orders to take off their hats in silence as he rode by. When he approached, however, the men could not be restrained, but burst into the wildest cheering. . . . Gen. Lee

stopped his horse, and after gaining silence, made the only speech to his men that he ever made. He was very brief, and gave no excuses or apologies for his surrender, but said he had done all in his power for his men, and urged them to go as quickly and quietly to their homes as possible, . . . and to be good citizens as they had been soldiers. . . .

nation had ever had, and to the American nation of reunited North and South it gave a tradition of undying valor and constancy which would be a vibrant heritage for all generations. Not many armies in the world's history have done more. Now the Army of Northern Virginia had come to the end of the road, and it was time to quit.

One option Lee did have, that day, which—to the lasting good fortune of his countrymen—he did not exercise. Instead of surrendering he might simply have told his troops to disband, to take to the hills, and to carry on guerrilla warfare as long as there was a Yankee south of the Mason and Dixon Line. There were generals in his army who hoped he would do this, and Washington unquestionably would have had immense difficulty stamping out a rebellion of that nature. But the results of such a course would have been tragic beyond comprehension—tragic for Northerners and Southerners of that day and for their descendants forever after. There would have been a sharing in repeated atrocities, a mutual descent into brutality and bitterness and enduring hatred, which would have created a wound beyond healing. Neither as one nation nor as two could the people of America have gone on to any lofty destiny after that. All of this Lee realized, and he set his face against it. He and the men who followed him had been fighting for an accepted place in the family of nations. When the fight was finally lost, they would try to make the best of what remained to them.

When the South surrendered, U. S. Grant decided that there should be a formal laying down of arms. After three days of preparation, the ceremony took place at Appomattox Court House on April 12. John R. Chapin's pencil sketch (above) shows a Confederate unit that stacked its weapons and unslung its cartridge boxes before a line of Union troops. One Federal soldier recounted a few of the "very witty things" that Lee's men said as they gave up their guns. "If you kill as many Rebels as you have killed Yanks, you will do very well," remarked one to his weapon. Said another: "Good-bye gun; I am darned glad to get rid of you. I have been trying to for two years."

Richard Norris Brooke's postwar painting *Furling the Flag* shows the most difficult part of the entire surrender ceremony for many of the veteran soldiers—of both sides—at Appomattox on April 13. A soldier present in the Union ranks recalled that it was "quite an affecting scene to see some of the various color guards, as they were about to leave the old flags they had carried so long and defended so bravely, turn and tear small pieces from the old banner, and hastily put them in their pockets as if fearing our officers would forbid their doing it." In some regiments the soldiers burned or buried their standards rather than give them up.

SURRENDER OF GEN. LEE!

"The Year of Jubilee has come! Let all the People Rejoice!"

200 GUNS WILL BE FIRED

On the Campus Martius,
AT 3 O'CLOCK TO-DAY, APRIL 10,
To Celebrate the Victories of our Armies. *1865*

Every Man, Woman and Child is hereby ordered to be on hand prepared to Sing and Rejoice. The crowd are expected to join in singing Patriotic Songs.

ALL PLACES OF BUSINESS MUST BE CLOSED AT 2 O'CLOCK.

Hurrah for Grant and his noble Army.

By Order of the People.

The joyous news of Lee's surrender spread like wildfire throughout the North. Banner newspaper headlines shouted it, and city walls were plastered with broadsides (such as the one, above, that appeared in Detroit), announcing the glad tidings. In New England the philosopher Ralph Waldo Emerson wrote that the surrender made it "a joyful day . . . & proud to Allegheny ranges, Northern Lakes, Mississippi rivers & all kinds & men between the two Oceans, between morning & evening stars."

In Grant, Lee met a man who was as anxious as himself to see this hardest of wars followed by a good peace. Grant believed that the whole point of the war had been the effort to prove that Northerners and Southerners were and always would be fellow citizens, and the moment the fighting stopped he believed that they ought to begin behaving that way. In effect, he told Lee to have his men lay down their arms and go home; and into the terms of surrender he wrote the binding pledge that if they did this, signing and then living up to the formal articles of parole, they would not at any time be disturbed by Federal authority. This pledge had far-reaching importance, because there were in the North many men who wanted to see leading Confederates hanged; but what Grant had written and signed made it impossible to hang Lee, and if Lee could not be hanged no lesser Confederates could be. If Lee's decision spared the country the horror of continued guerrilla warfare, Grant's decision ruled out the infamy that would have come with proscription lists and hangings. Between them, these rival soldiers served their country fairly well on April 9, 1865.

TO ALL INTENTS AND PURPOSES, Lee's surrender ended things. Johnston had fought his last fight—a valiant but unavailing blow at Sherman's army at Bentonville,

North Carolina, late in March—and when the news of Lee's surrender reached him he knew better than to try to continue the fight. He would surrender, too, and nowhere in the Southland was there any other army that could hope to carry on. A ponderous Federal cavalry force was sweeping through Alabama, taking the last war-production center at Selma, and going on to occupy the onetime Confederate capital, Montgomery; and this force was so strong that even Bedford Forrest was unable to stop its progress. On the Gulf coast the city of Mobile was forced to surrender; and although there was still an army west of the Mississippi it no longer had any useful function, and it would eventually lay down its arms like all the rest. Lee and his army had been the keystone of the arch, and when the keystone was removed the arch was bound to collapse.

Amid the downfall President Davis and his cabinet moved across the Carolinas and into Georgia, hoping to reach the trans-Mississippi and find some way to continue the struggle. It could not be done, and the cabinet at last dispersed.

The frenzied relief at the word of Lee's surrender, depicted in this painting by an unknown artist (below), was repeated with countless variations throughout the country. "Everybody here is half crazy," a Delaware woman wrote. In distant Iowa, the sister of a soldier serving with Sherman noted that every bell in her town "jangled together. The fire companies displayed their skill by throwing a stream of water over the [hospital]. . . . I never saw Main Street look as gay as it did with the flags today."

Even after Lee's surrender at Appomattox Court House, three other significant Confederate military forces remained officially at war. At the James Bennett farmhouse (above), just outside Durham, North Carolina, Confederate General Joseph E. Johnston and Union Major General William T. Sherman settled on terms that surrendered the Army of Tennessee, the last major fighting force in the East. It was a bitter blow for some of the Southern soldiers. "Everything we had fought for and believed in had come down to nothing," declared a Louisiana cavalryman. Confederate forces in Alabama, Mississippi, and east Louisiana capitulated on May 4 while those west of the Mississippi River were surrendered in yet another military convention that was signed on June 2.

Davis himself was captured by Federal cavalry, and the government of the Confederate States of America at last went out of existence. The war was over.

Davis went to a prison cell in Fort Monroe, and for two years furious bitter-enders in the North demanded that he be tried and hanged for treason. The demand was never granted; despite the furies that had been turned loose by four years of war, enough sanity and common decency remained to rule out anything like that. Davis' imprisonment, and the harsh treatment visited on him by his jailers, won him new sympathy in the South, where there had been many men who held him chiefly responsible for loss of the war, and he emerged from prison at last to become the embodiment of the Lost Cause, standing in the haunted sunset where the Confederate horizon ended.

He had done the best he could do in an impossible job, and if it is easy to show where he made grievous mistakes, it is difficult to show that any other man, given the materials available, could have done much better. He had great courage, integrity, tenacity, devotion to his cause, and like Old Testament Sisera the stars in their courses marched against him.

The Rebel Raider That Wouldn't Surrender

The Rebel commerce-raider *Shenandoah* (above) was purchased from an English shipbuilder and outfitted in mid-October, 1864. The vessel then began a cruise of destruction through the South Atlantic, across the Indian Ocean, and into the Pacific. In June, 1865, the *Shenandoah,* oblivious of the events at Appomattox, entered the Bering Sea, and found and burned a veritable fleet of U.S. whaling ships. Snippets of news about the fading fortunes of the Confederacy induced the captain of the *Shenandoah,* James Waddell, to embark on a desperate plan: using the ship's guns, he would hold the city of San Francisco hostage for ransom. While sailing toward the target, though, the *Shenandoah* intercepted a British ship carrying newspapers that confirmed that the Civil War was indeed over. Determined never to surrender the *Shenandoah* to the Union navy, Waddell sailed for England, where the Royal Navy took charge of the ship on November 6, 1865. The captain declared in his final report, that the *Shenandoah* "was the only vessel that carried the [Confederate] flag around the world, and she flew it six months after the overthrow of the South. . . ."

A PROPER FAMILY RE-UNION.

OPPOSITE: Paroled Confederate soldiers started for home and spread across the landscape of the South (the ones pictured pose in front of Richmond's equestrian statue of Washington, top), even as the national dialogue turned to the fate of Confederate leaders. *A Proper Family Reunion* (bottom left) extended no mercy toward Confederate President Jefferson Davis, who was not captured by Federal authorities until May 10. Once in custody, Davis was incarcerated in a cell at Fortress Monroe, where he was watched constantly by guards (bottom right).

One of the Confederate officers paroled at Appomattox Court House was Robert E. Lee, photographed by Mathew Brady soon after his return home to Richmond (left). Lee harbored no thoughts about continuing the struggle on any level; a few months after he surrendered, he declared: "I think it the duty of every citizen, in the present condition of the Country, to do all in his power to aid in the restoration of peace and harmony, and in no way to oppose the policy of the State or General Government directed to that object."

CHAPTER 15

End and Beginning

The war had lasted for four years and it had consumed hundreds of thousands of lives and billions of dollars in treasure. It had destroyed one of the two American ways of life forever, and it had changed the other almost beyond recognition; and it ended as it had begun, in a mystery of darkness and passion. If no one could say exactly why it had come about in the first place, no one could quite say what it meant now that it was finished. (Many decades of reflection have not wholly answered either riddle.) Things done by men born generations after Appomattox would continue to shed light on the significance of this greatest of all convulsions of the American spirit.

Of all men, Abraham Lincoln came the closest to understanding what had happened; yet even he, in his final backward glance, had to confess that something that went beyond words had been at work in the land. When he tried to sum it up, delivering his second inaugural address on March 4, 1865, he could do no more than remind his countrymen that they had somehow done more than they intended to do, as if without knowing it they had served a purpose that lay far beyond their comprehension.

"Neither party," he said, "expected for the war the magnitude or the duration which it has already attained. Neither anticipated that the cause of the conflict might cease with, or even before, the conflict itself should cease." (As he spoke, the Federal Congress had passed the thirteenth amendment and seventeen states had already ratified it; and in Richmond the Congress of the Confederacy was preparing to vote regiments of slaves into the Confederate service. Slavery was

Union veteran James E. Taylor's 1881 watercolor *The Grand Parade of General Sherman's Army in Washington* (left) evokes the martial splendor of the Grand Review, a victory parade organized by U.S. leaders to symbolize, for the sake of the nation, that the terrible Civil War was over. Soldiers taking part represented the "eastern" Army of the Potomac that had defeated Lee and the "western" armies, under Sherman, that had wrought destruction throughout the South. Because of intense rivalries between the two, the Grand Review was spread over two days, with the former marching on May 23 and the latter, as depicted in Taylor's painting, on May 24.

A Weary Leader's Prophetic Dream

The personal price paid by Abraham Lincoln in guiding the nation through the Civil War was etched on his face; compare the image made in Springfield, Illinois, on June 3, 1860 (above) with the one taken in Washington on April 10, 1865 (opposite). During the last days of the conflict, Lincoln was asleep in the White House when he had a disturbing dream. As he described it to a friend: *There seemed to be a death-like stillness about me. Then I heard subdued sobs, as if a number of people were weeping. I thought I left my bed and wandered downstairs. There the silence was broken by the same pitiful sobbing, but the mourners were invisible. I went from room to room; no living person was in sight, but the same mournful sounds of distress met me as I passed along. It was light in all the rooms; every object was familiar to me; but where were all the people who were*

grieving as if their hearts would break? Determined to find the cause of a state of things so mysterious and so shocking, I kept on until I arrived at the East Room, which I entered. There I met with a sickening surprise. Before me was a catafalque, on which rested a corpse wrapped in funeral vestments. Around it were stationed soldiers who were acting as guards; and there was a throng of people, some gazing mournfully upon the corpse, whose face was covered, others weeping pitifully. "Who is dead in the White House?" I demanded of one of the soldiers.

"The President," was his answer; "he was killed by an assassin!" Then came a loud burst of grief from the crowd, which awoke me from my dream. I slept no more that night; and although it was only a dream, I have been strangely annoyed by it ever since.

As the war began to wind down in early 1865, both sides renewed the effort to exchange prisoners. William Waud's 1865 sketch (right) shows repatriated Federal prisoners of war as they strip off their filthy prison clothes and fling them from the transport carrying them North. A reporter described a similar group from Andersonville: "Their clothing was in tatters; their faces were begrimed with dirt and black smoke from pine wood; they nearly were all without shoes; many were without hats. Large numbers were affected with scurvy." Declared one Yankee as he reached friendly lines: "We are again under the old flag. God be praised."

dead no matter how the war came out.) "Both read the same Bible and pray to the same God, and each invokes His aid against the other. . . . The prayers of both could not be answered; that of neither has been answered fully. The Almighty has His own purposes."

It was a thing to brood over, this war with its terrible cost and its veiled meanings, and the wisest man could perhaps do little more than ask searching questions about it. As he went on with his speech Lincoln was doing nothing less than remind the people of America that they could not hope to understand what they had done and what had been done to them without examining the central riddle of human existence. As the war storm slowly ebbed he left one of the great questions for all men to ponder: "If we shall suppose that American slavery is one of those offenses which, in the providence of God, must needs come, but which, having continued through His appointed time, He now wills to remove, and that He gives to both North and South, this terrible war, as the woe due to those by whom the offense came, shall we discern therein any departure from those divine attributes which the believers in a living God always ascribe to Him?"

This question was propounded by a man who believed that both sides shared in the blame for the war, just as they had shared in the cost of it. Out of such a belief had to come a determination that both sections must also share in the victory. The peace that would come out of the war must, in Lincoln's view, be broad enough and humane enough to mean some sort of gain for everyone in the land—for the Northerner who had fought to reunite the country and to end slavery, for the Southerner who had fought against that goal, for the Negro who had humbly endured the struggle. In such a peace there could be no question of any punitive measures, any more than there could be any question of seeking to restore what the war had destroyed. If there was a triumph to celebrate, it was not the triumph of one set of men over another set, but of all men together over a common affliction.

Even the title of William Waud's sketch (left) is exuberant: *Released Union Prisoners Dancing on Board the* Star of the North *at Charleston, South Carolina*. An observer wrote of the same scene: ". . . [T]hey shouted, danced, wept, even kissed the mute folds of those loved colors!" Southern prisoners of war also celebrated their liberation at the end of the war, and were understandably less concerned than others that their cause had been defeated. An artilleryman freed from Fort Delaware recalled that "men were so wild with joy that old veterans playfully tumbled and rolled on the grass like young schoolboys."

. . .

TO HIS GREAT LIEUTENANTS, Grant and Sherman, Lincoln gave a glimpse of his policy in a meeting on board Lincoln's steamer *River Queen* at City Point, just before the beginning of the last campaign of the war. It was a policy rather than a detailed program, summarized in Lincoln's homely injunction: "Let 'em up easy." He wanted to see the Confederate armies disbanded and the men back at work on their farms and in the shops, and he wanted civil governments re-established in the secessionist states at the earliest possible moment. Sherman got the impression that Lincoln was perfectly willing to deal with the existing state governments in the South in order to maintain order, until Congress could provide for a more permanent arrangement. When Sherman returned to North Carolina to finish the job against Johnston, he took with him the conviction that Lincoln wanted a peace of reconciliation with no particular concern about formalities.

So when Johnston surrendered, Sherman was guided by what he thought Lincoln wanted. Two things, however, were wrong: Sherman appears to have gone beyond anything Lincoln was prepared to offer—and when he and Johnston met to discuss surrender terms Lincoln was dead, and the atmosphere in which Northern politicians could be magnanimous and farsighted had been fatally poisoned.

Johnston was brought to bay a few days after Lee surrendered. The Union army, more than 80,000 strong, was in camp around Raleigh, North Carolina. Johnston had fewer than half that many men, and not all of them were fully armed and organized. He and Sherman met near a place called Durham's Station, aware that Lee had given up and that the only task remaining was to get the Confederacy out of existence as smoothly as possible, and on April 18 they agreed on a document. Considering the fact that Sherman was looked upon as the South's most pitiless enemy, the hard man of war who struck without compassion and laid waste whole states without remorse, it was an amazing agreement.

To begin with, it covered not simply Johnston's army, but all of the remaining armed forces of the Confederacy. (Johnston had no authority over these, but he had with him the Confederate Secretary of War, General John C. Breckinridge,

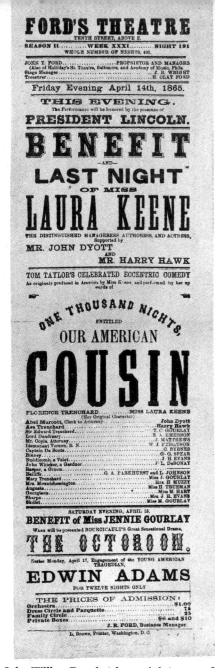

John Wilkes Booth (above right), one of the youngest members of a distinguished American stage family, was a man consumed by a sense of personal destiny. Several of his acquaintances remembered what one described as his "desire to do some deed or accomplish some act that had never been done by any other man, so that his name might live in history." This Booth did, on the evening of April 14, 1865, when Abraham Lincoln was at Ford's Theatre in Washington to see a production of the popular period comedy *Our American Cousin* (the playbill for which is shown above). After making his way unnoticed to the rear of the Presidential box, Booth waited for one of the play's funniest lines; then, during the laughter, he stepped forward and shot Lincoln in the head. "I struck boldly," Booth wrote in the diary he kept during the following, remaining week of his life.

and Breckinridge's word would be binding.) It went far beyond the terms Grant had given Lee. Confederate regiments were to march to their respective state capitals, deposit their weapons there, and then disband, each man signing a pledge not to take up arms again. Each state government would be recognized as lawful once its officers had taken oath to support the Constitution of the United States. No one was to be punished for the part he had taken in bringing on or supporting secession, all political rights were to be guaranteed, and the rights of person and property as defined in the Federal Constitution were to be fully respected—which might, conceivably, give slavery a new lease on life. All in all, this treaty—for it was a treaty of peace, rather than a simple surrender document—gave all that any Southerner in this spring of 1865 could hope to ask; and by this time there was not a chance in the world that the government in Washington would ratify it.

Lincoln himself would almost certainly have modified it. From the moment when Confederate surrender became an imminent probability, he had insisted that generals in the field were not to concern themselves with political questions; they should give liberal terms to the surrendering armies, but all issues involving the readmission of the states to the Union, the restoration of civil and political rights, and the abolition of slavery, they were to leave in the President's hands. (Sherman apparently had missed this particular point.) To bring the seceded states back into full relationship with the rest of the Union would take the most delicate kind of

Lewis Paine

George Atzerodt

Mary Surratt

David Herold

Samuel Arnold

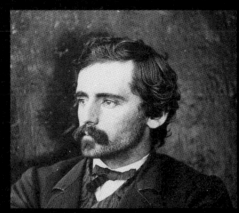

Michael O'Laughlin

John Surratt

Edward Spangler

Questions Remain

Deep clouds of mystery still obscure the motives of John Wilkes Booth and his associates (left) in the assassination of President Lincoln and the attempted murders of Vice-President Andrew Johnson, Secretary of State William Seward, and Lieutenant General Ulysses S. Grant. Many years after the event, a Confederate officer associated with Booth was quoted as saying:

We knew that we were beaten, and there was a general fear among Southern men that the North would impose terms so severe that the . . . South could not meet them. Many plans were discussed . . . looking to the reaching of a settlement on terms the South could endure. One plan which found favor was to capture Lincoln, take him into the Confederacy, and with him as a hostage, treat for peace. I was party to this plot. . . . The venture needed desperate men and the exercise of great caution and skill as well. Somehow the men in the plot became impatient and finally a new conspiracy was hatched which contemplated the killing of Lincoln.

Alfred Waud's sketch of Ford's Theatre (right) shows the box where Lincoln and his wife were seated with another couple, as well as the stage to which John Wilkes Booth jumped, after firing the fatal shot. (The figure stands where Booth landed.) A businessman present in the audience that night recalled that a "man of about 5 ft. 9 inches dressed in a black suit of clothes leaped onto the stage apparently from the President's box. . . . He did not strike the stage *fairly* on his feet, but appeared to stumble slightly. Quickly recovering himself he ran with lightning speed across the stage & disappeared. . . . The whole occurrence, the shot, the leap, the escape—was done while you could count eight."

political finesse, and Lincoln proposed to handle all of this himself. Congress would not be in session until late in the fall, and it was just possible that Lincoln could have his moderate reconstruction program well enough established by that time so that the bitter-enders in House and Senate could not upset it, but he never would have let any general set the pattern for him.

BUT AN ACTOR NAMED John Wilkes Booth had chosen this moment to upset everything. On Good Friday evening, April 14—driven by an insane compulsion of hatred and perverted loyalty to a cause which he had never felt obliged to fight for as a soldier—Booth strode into the President's box at Ford's Theatre in Washington, fired a bullet into Lincoln's brain, vaulted from the box to the stage, and rode off desperately through the night, fancying that if he could just reach Confederate territory he would be hailed as a hero and a savior. His twisted, inadequate mind was never able to see that his trigger finger had done the South more harm than all the lawless bummers in Sherman's army.

In all American history there is no stranger story than the story of the plot that took Lincoln's life. Booth had been conspiring for months, doing it flamboyantly, dramatically, in a way that fairly invited detection. He had first nourished a crackbrained plan to kidnap Lincoln alive and take him down to Richmond, shifting to a scheme for wholesale murder after Lee surrendered and Richmond was captured. He planned to kill Lincoln, Grant, Vice-President Johnson, and Secretary of State Seward, and he conspired with a weird set of dimwitted incompetents who could hardly have carried out a plan to rob a corner newsstand. The odds that the whole scheme would fall of its own weight were fantastically long. And yet, somehow—the luck of the American people just then being out—the thing worked. Lincoln was assassinated; Seward barely escaped death when one of Booth's minions forced a way into his sickroom and slashed him with a knife. The plot to kill Grant and Johnson missed fire, but the central, disastrous feature of the plan worked. Lincoln died.

Lincoln died early on the morning of April 15, and his death left the Republican radicals—the men who hated the South and hoped to see stern punishment inflicted on it—in full control of the Federal government. Vice-President Andrew Johnson had demanded that treason be made odious: now he was President, with full power to make the peace as stern as anyone could wish, and although he would finally come to see that Lincoln's policy was the better one, and would wreck his career trying to put it into effect, he was surrounded by men of great force and determination who would put Lincoln's ideas into the grave along with Lincoln's lifeless body.

For the immediate present the Federal government would be effectively operated by Secretary of War Stanton, who made himself something very like a dictator during the first week or two of Johnson's regime.

Stanton was a man of immense drive; ruthless, often arrogant, of an incurably suspicious nature. The task of unraveling Booth's mad plot was in his hands, and as the details of the scheme came to light Stanton was convinced that Booth was no lone-wolf operator, but was in fact an agent for the Confederate government itself. In part this deduction came simply because Stanton was always ready to believe the worst, especially where his enemies were concerned; and in part it rested on the fact that the Confederate government had been operating that

The first doctor to reach Lincoln was Charles Leale, a twenty-three-year-old army surgeon. After examining Lincoln's wound and performing first aid, Leale was asked if the President could be transported back to the White House. "If it is attempted," he said, "he will be dead before we reach there." Four soldiers carried Lincoln down to the street; once there, they looked for a suitable place to shelter the President and settled on William Petersen's house at 453 Tenth Street. Carl Bersch's painting *Lincoln Borne by Loving Hands* shows the soldiers, as they exit Ford's Theatre, surrounded by anxious spectators.

During the eight hours that Lincoln lay mortally wounded on a bed in the Petersen House, approximately sixty-five people went in and out of his room. Hermann Faber based his sketch (right) on the testimony of some of those present. In the drawing, Secretary of the Navy Gideon Welles is sitting on the bed next to the President, while Secretary of War Edwin Stanton stands to the right. When Lincoln died, at 7:22 A.M., April 15, Stanton reportedly remarked, "Now he belongs to the ages."

fifth-column business in the North, with agents trying to burn Northern cities, wreck railroads, seize military prison camps, and raid Yankee banks. The War Department had collected a great deal of information about this operation, some of it false, some of it true. It knew, among other things, that these operations had been directed by Confederate agents established in Canada, and it also knew that Booth himself had recently been in Canada. Under the circumstances it is hardly surprising that a man like Stanton should suspect that Booth might be a part of the Southern conspiracy which had been keeping Federal counterespionage operatives so busy.

Stanton did more than suspect: he informed the nation, without any qualifications, that Lincoln had been murdered by Jefferson Davis' agents, and that the whole tragedy was a direct part of the dying Confederate war effort. (It seems that in fact Booth had had an earlier connection with the authorities in Richmond, but that trail fades out before it connects to the murder plot. No solid evidence has surfaced to show that Booth was anything but an irresponsible fanatic, just as John Brown had been when he descended on Harpers Ferry.) Stanton was never able to prove a word of these charges, but that made no difference whatever. The damage was done; in the terrible revulsion of feeling that swept across the North few people would bother to speak out for the sort of peace Lincoln himself had wanted.

Stanton and the other bitter-enders saw to it that no one in the North was allowed to get over his grief quickly. Lincoln's body lay in state beneath the Capitol dome, and there was a state funeral in the White House. Then, in a special train, the body was taken back to Springfield, Illinois, for burial—taken there in the most roundabout way imaginable, put on display in New York and Chicago and in many other cities, made the occasion for the most elaborately contrived funeral procession in American history. Millions of Americans saw it. Those who could not file past the open casket, in places where it was on display, at least could gather by the railroad tracks and watch the train as it moved slowly past. Millions of people took part in this parade of sorrow. It lasted for two weeks, and although the

SURRAT.   BOOTH.   HAROLD.

War Department, Washington, April 20, 1865,

$100,000 REWARD!

THE MURDERER

Of our late beloved President, Abraham Lincoln,

IS STILL AT LARGE.

$50,000 REWARD

Will be paid by this Department for his apprehension, in addition to any reward offered by Municipal Authorities or State Executives.

$25,000 REWARD

Will be paid for the apprehension of JOHN H. SURRATT, one of Booth's Accomplices.

$25,000 REWARD

Will be paid for the apprehension of David C. Harold, another of Booth's accomplices.

LIBERAL REWARDS will be paid for any information that shall conduce to the arrest of either of the above-named criminals, or their accomplices.

All persons harboring or secreting the said persons, or either of them, or aiding or assisting their concealment or escape, will be treated as accomplices in the murder of the President and the attempted assassination of the Secretary of State, and shall be subject to trial before a Military Commission and the punishment of DEATH.

Let the stain of innocent blood be removed from the land by the arrest and punishment of the murderers.

All good citizens are exhorted to aid public justice on this occasion. Every man should consider his own conscience charged with this solemn duty, and rest neither night nor day until it be accomplished.

EDWIN M. STANTON, Secretary of War.

DESCRIPTIONS.—BOOTH is Five Feet 7 or 8 inches high, slender build, high forehead, black hair, black eyes, and wears a heavy black moustache.

JOHN H. SURRAT is about 5 feet, 9 inches. Hair rather thin and dark; eyes rather light; no beard. Would weigh 145 or 150 pounds. Complexion rather pale and clear, with color in his cheeks. Wore light clothes of fine quality. Shoulders square; cheek bones rather prominent; chin narrow; ears projecting at the top; forehead rather low and square, but broad. Parts his hair on the right side; neck rather long. His lips are firmly set. A slim man.

DAVID C. HAROLD is five feet six inches high, hair dark, eyes dark, eyebrows rather heavy, full face, nose short, hand short and fleshy, feet small, instep high, round bodied, naturally quick and active, slightly closes his eyes when looking at a person.

NOTICE.—In addition to the above, State and other authorities have offered rewards amounting to almost one hundred thousand dollars, making an aggregate of about TWO HUNDRED THOUSAND DOLLARS.

Five days after the assassination, the largest manhunt in U.S. history to that point had still failed to capture Booth and all of his fellow conspirators, leading the government to offer substantial rewards for their apprehension (left). At the time, Booth was moving slowly through southern Maryland, hiding for days at a time in the open country or sheltered by residents sympathetic to his crime. While in hiding, he scribbled occasionally in his diary. On the day after the reward poster appeared, Booth wrote: ". . . I am here in despair. And why; For doing what Brutus was honored for, what made [William] Tell a Hero. And yet I for striking down a greater tyrant than they ever knew am looked upon as a common cutthroat. My action was purer than either of theirs. . . . I hoped for no gain. I knew no private wrong. I struck for my country and that alone." Early on the morning of April 26 Booth was cornered in a barn in northern Virginia. Shot and mortally wounded, he died within a few hours.

On June 30, 1865, a specially assembled military commission returned a guilty verdict against the eight individuals arrested for their part in the Lincoln assassination. Most objective observers agreed that the trial was blatantly biased against the defendants. Four of the eight including one woman, Mary Surratt, were sentenced to hang. On July 7 they were brought to Washington's Old Arsenal Prison, where a gallows had been constructed to carry out the verdict. Only one photographer, Alexander Gardner, was allowed to record the executions. Assisted by Timothy O'Sullivan, he set up his cameras on the second floor of a building facing the scaffold. The two men recorded each step in the conduct of the hangings, including the moment, at 1:26 P.M. (below), right after the trap was sprung beneath the feet of the convicts.

grief which was expressed was undoubtedly sincere, the whole affair amounted to turning a knife in a wound—turning it again and again, so that the shock of sorrow and outraged indignation which had gone all across the North might continue to be felt.

IN TRYING TO CAPITALIZE on the nation's tragedy the radicals had something real and deep to work with. The millions who stood in silence to watch the funeral car, with its black bunting, drift past on its way to Illinois were the people who had supported Lincoln through thick and thin. They had provided the armies that he had called into being. They had sustained him at the polls when the issue was in doubt. He had spoken to their hearts, in a way no one else had ever done, when he explained the ultimate meaning of the war in his address at Gettysburg and groped for the unattainable truth in his second inaugural. He had expressed the best that was in them, speaking not so much to them as for them, and he had gone with them through four years of trial by doubt and fire. As the war ended they had come to understand his greatness: and now, when he was struck down at the very moment of his triumph, they felt an anger so black that Lincoln's own vision was blotted out.

The first step was to undo what Sherman had tried to do. His treaty with Johnston went first to Grant, who could see that Sherman had done much more than any general was authorized to do. Grant sent the papers on to Stanton and suggested that the whole cabinet might want to consider them. The cabinet did want to consider them, and it disapproved them in short order; Grant was ordered to go to Sherman at once, to cancel the armistice which was a part of the Sherman-Johnston agreement, and to resume hostilities. Grant obeyed and Johnston was notified that the deal was off. There was no more fighting, as he promptly surrendered on terms identical with those Grant had given Lee.

None of this disturbed Sherman greatly. He could see that he had tried to exercise powers which belonged to the civil government, and when he was overruled he was ready to accept the fact quietly. What infuriated him was the way Stanton used the whole episode to inflame public opinion.

For Stanton made a public announcement concerning the Sherman-Johnston agreement in a way which strongly suggested that Sherman was disloyal or crazy. This agreement, Stanton declared, practically recognized the Confederacy, re-established the secessionist state governments, put arms and ammunition in the hands of Rebels, permitted the re-establishment of slavery, possibly made the Northern taxpayer responsible for debts run up by the Confederate government, and left the defeated Rebels in position to renew the rebellion whenever they saw fit.

An announcement of this kind, coming at the moment when the electorate was still in a state of shock because of Lincoln's assassination, and coming also at a time when the complicity of the Confederate government in Booth's murder plot was being proclaimed as an established fact, was a stunner. It raised Sherman to a high pitch of rage, and made him one of Stanton's most devout and enduring enemies; but this did no particular damage, since Sherman was a good hater and Stanton already had many enemies, and the public outcry that was raised against the general eventually subsided. In a few years no one in the North or the South would remember that Sherman had nearly wrecked his career in his attempt to befriend the South, and he would be enshrined as an unstained hero in the North and as an unmitigated villain in Southern memories. The real harm that was done was the mortal injury that was inflicted on the Lincolnian policy which Sherman, however clumsily, had tried to put into effect.

FOR THE BASIS OF Lincoln's whole approach to reconstruction was the belief that the broken halves of the Union could be fitted together without bitterness and in a spirit of mutual understanding and good will. The war was over, and there was no undoing of anything that had happened. No one had really intended that things should go as they had gone; the responsibility for it all was strangely divided, just as the almost unendurable suffering and heartache had been divided ... the Almighty did indeed have His own purposes, and now it was up to the people of both sections to try to adjust themselves to those purposes and to work together in the adjustment. But by the time Lincoln's body had finished its long journey and lay in the tomb at Springfield, an atmosphere had been created in the North which put such an effort out of reach. President Johnson would try to make the effort, but he had not a fraction of Lincoln's political skill, and the job was too much for him. He

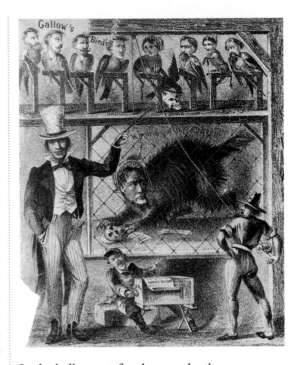

In the indictment for the assassination of the President, the U.S. government went so far as to invoke the name of a former foe, charging the eight defendants with "combining, confederating, and conspiring, together with . . . Jefferson Davis . . . and others unknown, to kill and murder . . . Abraham Lincoln. . . ." This unsubstantiated charge unleashed a wave of rhetoric and propaganda, such as the cartoon (above) linking "Hyena Jeff Davis" to the accused eight. Davis, who had fled Richmond on April 2 in the hope of re-establishing the Confederate government elsewhere, was in Charlotte, North Carolina, when he learned of Lincoln's death. According to a member of his cabinet, Davis' response was: "I certainly have no special regard for Mr. Lincoln; but there are a great many men of whose end I would much rather have heard than his." Government officials were unable to prove that Davis was involved in the assassination of President Lincoln. Imprisoned for two years at the end of the war, he was never charged with treason or any other crime.

The Lonesome Train

Just after 8:00 A.M., April 21, the special nine-car train carrying Abraham Lincoln's body left Washington for Springfield, Illinois, following a route designed to retrace the journey Lincoln took in 1861 to assume the Presidency. The photo above shows the funeral train on a Lake Michigan pier at Chicago. While the engine and some of the cars would change over the course of the journey, the car bearing Lincoln's body remained the same and was always the second from the end. All along the route, even at places where the train slowed but did not stop, people turned out to see "The Lonesome Train," as some took to calling it. A reporter watched the train pass through one small town and wrote that the "men stood with uncovered heads, and the women look on in silence. A number of little children were grouped together, holding in their hands white flags with mourning fringes."

"The Nation Mourns" declared the banner above New York's City Hall on April 24 (left), the day that Lincoln lay in state within. So that Lincoln's body could be formally viewed in cities across the country, the funeral train also stopped in Baltimore, Harrisburg, Philadelphia, Albany, Buffalo, Cleveland, Columbus, Indianapolis, and Chicago. Reporters later estimated that more than seven million citizens either watched the corteges that traveled from the train to the place of honor in each city or else attended one of the many farewell ceremonies. Said one officer who accompanied the funeral train throughout the journey, "More people looked upon the remains of the late Commander in chief during this period than had ever before viewed the form of the man from whom life had departed."

At every stop endless lines of people waited for hours, often in bad weather, to view Lincoln's body; in Cleveland, a special pavilion was set up in Monument Square (above) to accommodate the mourners. Over the course of the entire journey only one photograph was taken of Lincoln's body lying in state. Jeremiah Gurney, Jr., took the picture (below right), which also shows Rear Admiral Charles Davis on the left and Brevet Brigadier General Edward D. Townsend on the right. After seeing the photograph Secretary of War Edwin Stanton deemed it inappropriate to the somber occasion; he ordered the negative destroyed, along with all known copies. The one print to survive did not surface until 1952.

was never able to use what might have been his greatest asset—the wholehearted support which the two most famous Northern generals, Grant and Sherman, would have given to an attempt to put Lincoln's policy into effect.

No one in the North, after Lincoln's death, had anything approaching the prestige which these two soldiers had, and Johnson could have used them if he had known how. But Sherman's experience following the rejection of his "treaty" left him embittered, deeply disgusted with anything smacking of politics; thereafter he would be nothing but the soldier, letting the people at Washington commit any folly they chose to commit, and President Johnson never understood how to soften him. And Grant before long became estranged, not because he opposed what Johnson wanted to do, but simply because Johnson could not handle him. In the end he would be counted among Johnson's enemies because the radicals were able to take advantage of Johnson's clumsiness and Grant's own political innocence.

So things happened in the familiar and imperfect way that every American knows about. The Union was reconstructed, at last, at the price of bitterness and injustice, with much work left for later generations to do. A measure of the amount of work bequeathed to those later generations is the fact that more than a century after Appomattox the attempt to work out a solution for the race problem—that great untouchable which, many layers down, lay at the abyssal depth of the entire conflict—would initially still be looked upon as a sectional matter and would still be productive of sectional discord. In the anger and suspicion of the reconstruction era the chance that the thing might be approached rationally, so

that it could perhaps be solved rather than simply shoved aside and ignored, flickered out like a candle's flame in a gale of wind.

NOTHING COULD BE DONE rationally at that time because wars do not leave men in a rational mood. Bone-weary of fighting in 1865, the American people greatly desired magnanimity and understanding and a reasonable handling of vexing problems; but those virtues had gone out of fashion, and they could not immediately be re-established. What happened after the war ended grew out of the hot barren years when anger and suspicion went baying down the trail of violence: the years in which bitter appeals to unleashed emotion had made the fury of a few the common affliction of all . . . years of desperate battles, of guerrilla snipings and hangings, with a swinging torch for town and home place and the back of a hard hand to silence dissent. These had created the atmosphere in which men tried to put the Union back together, to turn enmity into friendship, and to open the door of freedom for a race that had lain in bondage. The wonder is not that the job was done so imperfectly, but that it was done at all.

For it was done, finally; if not finished, at least set on the road to completion. It may be many years before the job is really completed; generations before the real meaning and the ultimate consequences of the Civil War are fully comprehended. We understand today a little more than could be understood in 1865, but the whole truth remains dim.

Here was the greatest and most moving chapter in American history, a blending of meanness and greatness, an ending and a beginning. It came out of what men were, but it did not go as men had planned it. The Almighty had His own purposes.

On May 3 Lincoln's body reached Springfield, Illinois, where the whole town, including the Lincoln family home (above), was draped with mourning black. In an account of the entombment at Oak Ridge Cemetery, May 4, a correspondent wrote: "People stood on tiptoe, anxiously peering over each other's shoulders, each one determined, if possible, to satisfy himself. . . . The ceremonies having terminated, the doors of the vault were closed. . . . Thus we buried him; thus we leave him—the great, the good, the martyr President."

Joining the Peace

Even as the nation returned to itself at the end of the war, united once more, each individual soldier had to return to himself—or try to. Winslow Homer's painting *The Veteran in a New Field* (above) was the ideal, in its harmonious title and in the image of a man resuming his rightful place. For many, though, the aftermath of the war was a struggle to find something, or someone, worth returning to. The South offered so few prospects that many Confederate veterans left for other countries or for the North. Ironically, the traditions and institutions of the victorious North seemed as much changed, as "gone with the wind," as those of the vanquished South. Confined by hard-pressing progress or stultified by the lack of it in their respective regions, restless veterans on both sides found that the far West continued the

adventure that the war had started. A Northerner described his malaise: "The change from this wild life, where we do not care a fig for a man who does not rank us, and where we march into a man's yard, then enter his home and tell the man of [the] house that his family has too much room & that he must move up stairs & we will occupy the balance and do sundry & diverse other impudent things; to the more peacable association of home is indeed great."

If some old soldiers couldn't, in their hearts, leave the war behind, others had the harsher evidence of their wounds to remind them, and those who were disabled were granted modest pensions. Eastman Johnson painted *The Pension Agent* (above) in 1867, a scene that was sadly commonplace: a veteran crippled in the service having to plead his case to a government auditor.

CHAPTER 16

A Sound of Distant Drums

T he Civil War left America with a legend and a haunting memory. These had to do less with things that remained than with the things that had been lost. What had been won would not be entirely visible for many years to come, and most people were too war-weary to look at it anyway, but what had been lost could not be forgotten. The men who had marched gaily off in new uniforms and who had not come back; the dreams that had brought fire and a great wind down on a land that meant to be happy and easygoing; the buildings the war had wrecked, the countryside it had scarred, the whole network of habits and hopes and attitudes of mind it had ground to fragments—these were remembered with proud devotion by a nation which had paid an unimaginable price for an experience compounded of suffering and loss and ending in stunned bewilderment.

North and South together shared in this, for if the consciousness of defeat afflicted only one of the two sections, both knew that something greatly cherished was gone forever, whether that something was only a remembered smile on the face of a boy who had died or was the great shadow of a way of life that had been

From the first months of the peace, remembering the Civil War became and remained an important and enduring part of the American experience. Soon after the conflict veterans' organizations formed to keep war memories alive; their annual conventions always included displays of memorabilia, like the medals shown above. In the North and the South a day was set aside every year to honor Civil War soldiers, both living and dead. The precursor of Memorial Day, it was known earlier as Decoration Day, a time to decorate gravestones with flowers. Henry Sandham's painting (right) shows Union veterans parading through Boston on Decoration Day, led in the front row by high-ranking old soldiers, such as Oliver O. Howard (extreme left) and William Tecumseh Sherman (extreme right).

On June 11, 1865, one of the first postwar ceremonies to consecrate a battlefield monument was held on the hallowed ground at Bull Run. Alexander Gardner photographed the dedication of the monument to all Union soldiers who had fought at the First Battle of Bull Run. A reporter present noted that the "dedicatory services were of a simple, but impressive character."

destroyed. People clung to the memory of what was gone. Knowing the cruelty and insane destructiveness of war as well as any people who ever lived, they nevertheless kept looking backward, and they put a strange gloss of romance on what they saw, cherishing the haunted overtones it had left.

As the postwar years passed the remembrances became formalized. In cities and in small towns the Decoration Day parade became a ritual; rank after rank of men who unaccountably kept on growing older and less military-looking would tramp down dusty streets, bands playing, flags flying, ranks growing thinner year by year until finally nobody remained to march at all. In the South the same ceremonial was performed, although the date on the calendar was different; and in both sections orators spoke at vast length, reciting deeds of bravery and devotion which somehow, considered from the increasing distance, had the power to knit the country together again. Their stereotyped speeches were oddly made significant by the deeds which they commemorated.

The South had the bitterer memories, and it wrapped them in a heavier trapping of nostalgia. Decaying plantation buildings, with empty verandas slowly falling apart under porticoes upheld by insecure wooden pillars, became shrines

OPPOSITE: After the war the nation faced its obligation to properly inter the hundreds of thousands of battle dead who lay buried where they fell. While this picture shows crews working near Cold Harbor, Virginia, the scene was the same at Stones River, Antietam, Olustee, Port Hudson, and a hundred other places.

The South remembered its fallen soldiers in song and honored them in stone, but it could very nearly see them in carefully preserved uniforms such as the one below. Once worn by a private in a Louisiana volunteer regiment, the frock coat and dress gloves are accompanied by a photograph of the original owner. Like many of the uniforms used in the Civil War, it is of a much higher quality than standard issue, having been hand-sewn or embroidered, probably by loved ones at home. As a memorial, such a uniform would remind a family both of its soldier and of the emotions with which he was sent from home to war. The South gave up, proportionally, even more of its sons, brothers, and husbands than the North, and was a long, long time in letting them go.

"Many years have passed, and we see today/A few soldiers left who were the boys in gray," wrote a respectful Southern poet in 1931. "They are bent with age, and their step is slow,/And they cannot march as of long ago,/But we can love and honor them while they live. . . ." The love and honor of the South for its former soldiers was expressed in many ways, from the propagation of cemetery monuments (right) to the organization of reunions for increasingly frail veterans (some are shown, above, in Richmond, Virginia, in 1922). On a national level, the two sides met again in a number of notable "Blue and Gray" reunions, usually held on a significant anniversary of a major battle. At Gettysburg in 1938 a thin line of gray-haired survivors of Pickett's Charge crossed that field of death one last time (opposite top). And even as these mainstream commemorations were taking place, groups such as the North Carolina Cherokee Confederate veterans of the famous Thomas Legion (opposite bottom) recalled their own service and sacrifice.

simply because they somehow spoke for the dream that had died, the vitality of the dream gaining in strength as the physical embodiment of it drifted off into ruin. There were cemeteries for both sections—quiet, peaceful fields where soldiers who had never cared about military formality lay in the last sleep, precisely ranked in rows of white headstones which bespoke personal tragedies blunted at last by time. There were statues, too, with great men frozen in cold marble, presiding over drowsy battlefields which would never again know violence or bloodshed.

And, finally, there was the simple memory of personal valor—the enduring realization that when the great challenge comes, the most ordinary people can show that they value something more than they value their own lives. When the last of the veterans had gone, and the sorrows and bitternesses which the war created had at last worn away, this memory remained. The men who fought in the Civil War, speaking for all Americans, had said something the country could never forget.

OPPOSITE: As the United States passed into the twentieth century and confronted the profound uncertainties of the modern age, it was comforting to know that one-time fierce adversaries could set aside their animosities to become friends. Civil War reunions, ostensibly created to allow aged warriors to recall past glories, provided the nation with unforgettable images of reconciliation. Gettysburg's fiftieth anniversary drew some 57,000 Union and Confederate veterans: members of America's newest generation were shown fields where history had been made (top left) while old soldiers gathered to retell their hard-earned war stories (top right). In a ceremony freighted with symbolism, survivors of Pickett's division marched to the stone wall on Cemetery Ridge and shook hands with the very men in blue who had tried so hard to kill them fifty years earlier (bottom).

ABOVE: One of the most famous monuments of the thousands built to preserve the memory and meaning of the Civil War is Boston's *Shaw Memorial*, honoring Colonel Robert Gould Shaw and the 54th Massachusetts (Colored) Regiment. This unit suffered heavy casualties, the young colonel among them, in an unsuccessful attack on Fort Wagner, near Charleston, South Carolina, in 1863. Shaw's death, occurring as he led one of the nation's first black regiments, made him a martyr among many Northern abolitionists. Efforts to create a memorial began in 1865, but it wasn't until 1881 that enough funds had been raised to commission the piece from the distinguished American sculptor Augustus Saint-Gaudens. Shaw's family rejected an initial clay model for an equestrian statue of Colonel Shaw alone: they insisted that some of his men also be portrayed. It took Saint-Gaudens another fourteen years to work out a solution to the problem, creating what one art critic described as a "fusion of traditional equestrian and [bas-]relief sculpture." In addition to Shaw shown in profile mounted on his horse, twenty-three black soldiers are portrayed. The *Shaw Memorial* was unveiled on May 31, 1897, amid a great ceremony. Among the speakers was Booker T. Washington, the president of Tuskegee Institute, who declared that his heart went out "to those who wore gray as well as to those clothed in blue. . . ." More eloquent than any speech, though, was the moment when Sergeant William H. Carney, who had won a Medal of Honor for saving the 54th's national flag at Fort Wagner, came forward bearing the standard once more. "In dramatic effect, I have never seen or experienced anything which equalled this," wrote Washington. "For a number of minutes the audience seemed to entirely lose control of itself."

"And so good-bye to the war," wrote Walt Whitman in the text for a speech that he never gave. Although Whitman also asserted in that speech that the "real war will never get in the books," countless symbols remain to inspire succeeding generations in the quest to touch its undying spirit. The imagery of the Civil War is unending: a traditional equestrian statue of Major General Winfield S. Hancock at Gettysburg (opposite page); a more contemporary sculpture honoring North Carolinians on that same battlefield (left); the silent lines of battle at Antietam National Battlefield (overleaf). And looming over it all are the words and deeds of the nation's sixteenth President, Abraham Lincoln, whose legacy is defined by that fiery trial and the modern nation that emerged from it.

With malice toward none; with charity for all; with firmness in the right, as God gives us to see the right, let us strive on to finish the work we are in; to bind up the nation's wounds; to care for him who shall have borne the battle, and for his widow, and his orphan—to do all which may achieve and cherish a just, and a lasting peace, among ourselves, and with all nations.

—Abraham Lincoln, *Second Inaugural Address*

Acknowledgments and Selected Bibliography

This edition of *The American Heritage New History of the Civil War* would not have been possible without the vision of Richard M. Ketchum, who was the creator and editor of the first edition of the book.

Many individuals contributed their time and expertise to create this new edition, and must be mentioned here: Thank you to Richard Snow, Frederick Allen, and Barbara Strauch of *American Heritage* for their guidance and expertise; Stephen Sears for his ideas for the new edition and for his wonderful picture suggestions; Julie Fenster for her line editing; Marianne Cohen for her copy editing and proofreading; Kathy Huck for helping in the final stages of production; and Cathy Hemming, Erin Boyle, and Roni Axelrod of Viking Penguin for their support of the project.

Selected Bibliography

The following books were the main sources for the anecdotes and quotations that appear in the captions and sidebars, and are recommended for those readers interested in pursuing further their study of the Civil War.

General

Buel, C. C., and Robert U. Johnson, eds., *Battles and Leaders of the Civil War*. New York: Castle Books, 1888 (reprint).

Commager, Henry Steele, ed., *The Blue and the Gray: The Story of the Civil War as Told by Participants*. Indianapolis: Bobbs-Merrill, 1950.

Chapter 1: A House Divided

Davis, William C., *Jefferson Davis: The Man and His Hour*. New York: HarperCollins, 1991.

McPherson, James M., *Battle Cry of Freedom*. New York: Oxford University Press, 1988.

Oates, Stephen B., *With Malice Toward None: The Life of Abraham Lincoln*. New York: Harper & Row, 1977.

Stampp, Kenneth M., *The Peculiar Institution*. New York: Random House, 1956.

Chapter 2: The Opening Guns

Chesnut, Mary Boykin, *A Diary from Dixie*. New York: Houghton Mifflin Company, 1949.

Current, Richard N., *Lincoln and the First Shot*. New York: Washington Square Press, 1963.

Doubleday, Abner, *Reminiscences of Forts Sumter and Moultrie in 1860–1861*. New York: Harper and Brothers Publishers, 1876.

Swanberg, W. A., *First Blood: The Story of Fort Sumter*. New York: Charles Scribner's Sons, 1957.

Chapter 3: Real Warfare Begins

Dowdey, Clifford, *The Seven Days: The Emergence of Robert E. Lee*. Boston: Little, Brown & Company, 1964.

Hess, Earl J., and William L. Shea, *Pea Ridge: Civil War Campaign in the West*. Chapel Hill: University of North Carolina Press, 1992.

Sears, Stephen W., *To the Gates of Richmond: The Peninsula Campaign*. New York: Ticknor & Fields, 1992.

Sword, Wiley, *Shiloh: Bloody April*. New York: William Morrow and Company, 1983.

Chapter 4: The Navies

Cochran, Hamilton, *Blockade Runners of the Confederacy*. Indianapolis: Bobbs-Merrill, 1958.

Davis, William C., *Duel Between the First Ironclads*. Baton Rouge: Louisiana State University Press, 1975.

Jones, Virgil Carrington, *The Civil War at Sea* (3 volumes). Austin, TX: Holt, Rinehart & Winston, 1960.

Milligan, John D., *Gunboats Down the Mississippi*. Annapolis: Naval Institute Press, 1965.

Chapter 5: Confederate High-Water Mark

Hafendorfter, Kenneth A., *Perryville: Battle for Kentucky*. Owensboro, KY: McDowell Publications, 1981.

Hennessy, John J., *Return to Bull Run: The Campaign and Battle of Second Manassas*. New York: Simon & Schuster, 1993.

Krick, Robert K., *Stonewall Jackson at Cedar Mountain*. Chapel Hill: University of North Carolina Press, 1990.

Sears, Stephen W., *Landscape Turned Red: The Battle of Antietam*. New York: Ticknor & Fields, 1983.

Chapter 6: Stalemate at Home and Abroad

Cozzens, Peter, *No Better Place to Die: The Battle of Stones River*. Chicago: University of Illinois Press, 1990.

McWhiney, Grady, *Braxton Bragg and Confederate Defeat*. New York: Columbia University Press, 1969.

Marvel, William, *Burnside*. Chapel Hill: University of North Carolina Press, 1991.

Stackpole, Edward J., *The Fredericksburg Campaign: Drama on the Rappahannock*. Harrisburg, PA: Stackpole Books, 1957.

Chapter 7: The South's Last Opportunity

Bearss, Edwin C., *The Campaign for Vicksburg* (3 volumes). Dayton, OH: Morningside Books, 1986.

Coddington, Edwin B., *The Gettysburg Campaign*. New York: Charles Scribner's Sons, 1968.

Furgurson, Ernest B., *Chancellorsville 1863: The Souls of the Brave*. New York: Alfred A. Knopf, 1992.

Stewart, George R., *Pickett's Charge*. New York: Houghton Mifflin Company, 1959.

Chapter 8: Men at Arms

Billings, John D., *Hardtack and Coffee, or the Unwritten Story of Army Life*. Alexandria, VA: Time-Life Books, 1982.

Casler, John O., *Four Years in the Stonewall Brigade*. Dayton, OH: Morningside Books, 1981.

Wiley, Bell Irvin, *The Life of Billy Yank*. Baton Rouge: Louisiana State University Press, 1981.

Wiley, Bell Irvin, *The Life of Johnny Reb*. Baton Rouge: Louisiana State University Press, 1980.

Chapter 9: The Destruction of Slavery

Connelly, Thomas L., *Autumn of Glory: The Army of Tennessee, 1862–1865*. Baton Rouge: Louisiana State University Press, 1971.

Cornish, Dudley Taylor, *The Sable Arm: Black Troops in the Union Army, 1861–1865*. Lawrence, KS: University Press of Kansas, 1956.

Cozzens, Peter, *This Terrible Sound: The Battle of Chickamauga*. Chicago: University of Illinois Press, 1992.

Sword, Wiley, *Mountains Touched with Fire: Chattanooga Besieged, 1863*. New York: St. Martin's Press, 1995.

Chapter 10: The Northern Vise Tightens

Castel, Albert, *Decision in the West: The Atlanta Campaign of 1864*. Lawrence, KS: University Press of Kansas, 1992.

Marszalek, John F., *Sherman: A Soldier's Passion for Order*. New York: The Free Press, 1993.

Trudeau, Noah Andre, *Bloody Roads South: The Wilderness to Cold Harbor, May–June 1864*. Boston: Little, Brown & Company, 1989.

Trudeau, Noah Andre, *The Last Citadel: Petersburg, Virginia, June 1864–April 1865*. Boston: Little, Brown & Company, 1991.

Chapter 11: Two Nations at War

Bakeless, John, *Spies of the Confederacy*. Philadelphia: J. B. Lippincott Company, 1970.

Marvel, William, *Andersonville: The Last Depot*. Chapel Hill: University of North Carolina Press, 1994.

Starr, Louis M., *Reporting the Civil War*. New York: Collier Books, 1962.

Stern, Philip Van Doren, *Secret Missions of the Civil War*. Chicago: Rand McNally, 1959.

Chapter 12: Total Warfare

Davis, Burke, *Sherman's March*. New York: Random House, 1980.

Kerby, Robert L., *Kirby Smith's Confederacy: The Trans-Mississippi South, 1863–1865*. New York: Columbia University Press, 1972.

Wert, Jeffry D., *From Winchester to Cedar Creek: The Shenandoah Campaign of 1864*. Carlisle, PA: South Mountain Press, 1987.

Wills, Brian Steel, *A Battle from the Start: The Life of Nathan Bedford Forrest*. New York: HarperCollins, 1992.

Chapter 13: The Forlorn Hope

Beringer, Richard E., Herman Hattaway, Archer Jones, and William N. Still, Jr., *Why the South Lost the Civil War*. Athens: University of Georgia Press, 1986.

Kennett, Lee, *Marching Through Georgia*. New York: HarperCollins, 1995.

Royster, Charles, *The Destructive War*. New York: HarperCollins, 1991.

Sword, Wiley, *Embrace an Angry Wind: The Confederacy's Last Hurrah: Spring Hill, Franklin, and Nashville*. New York: HarperCollins, 1992.

Chapter 14: Victory

Barrett, John G., *Sherman's March Through the Carolinas*. Chapel Hill: University of North Carolina Press, 1956.

Davis, Burke, *To Appomattox: Nine April Days, 1865*. New York: Rinehart & Company, 1959.

Gragg, Rod, *Confederate Goliath: The Battle of Fort Fisher*. New York: HarperCollins, 1991.

Trudeau, Noah Andre, *Out of the Storm: The End of the Civil War April–June 1865*. New York: Little, Brown & Company, 1994.

Chapter 15: End and Beginning

Bishop, Jim, *The Day Lincoln Was Shot*. New York: Harper & Brothers, 1955.

Davis, Burke, *The Long Surrender*. New York: Random House, 1985.

Gaddy, David Winfred, James O. Hall, and William A. Tidwell, *Come Retribution: The Confederate Secret Service and the Assassination of Lincoln*. Jackson: University of Mississippi Press, 1988.

Searcher, Victor, *The Farewell to Lincoln*. New York: Abingdon Press, 1965.

Chapter 16: A Sound of Distant Drums

Connelly, Thomas L., *The Marble Man: Robert E. Lee and His Image in American Society*. Baton Rouge: Louisiana State University Press, 1977.

Foner, Eric, *Reconstruction: America's Unfinished Revolution, 1863–1877*. New York: Harper & Row, 1988.

Franklin, John Hope, *Reconstruction: After the Civil War*. Chicago: University of Chicago Press, 1961.

McConnell, Stuart, *Glorious Contentment: The Grand Army of the Republic, 1865–1900*. Chapel Hill: University of North Carolina Press, 1992.

Fiction About the Civil War

Greenberg, Martin H., and Bill Pronzini, eds., *A Treasury of Civil War Stories*. New York: Wings Books, 1985.

Shaara, Michael, *The Killer Angels*. New York: Ballantine Books, 1974.

Slotkin, Richard, *The Crater*. New York: Atheneum, 1981.

Wicker, Tom, *Unto This Hour*. New York: The Viking Press, 1984.

Picture Credits

Abbreviations

AH: American Heritage Picture Collection, New York, NY

BMC: Anne S. K. Brown Military Collection, Brown University Library, Providence, RI

CHS: Chicago Historical Society, Chicago, IL

LC: Library of Congress, Washington, DC

MC: Museum of the Confederacy, Richmond, VA

MFA/KC: Museum of Fine Arts, Boston, MA; M. and M. Karolik Collection

NA: National Archives, Washington, DC

NYHS: Collection of the New-York Historical Society, New York, NY

NYPL: New York Public Library, Astor, Lenox and Tilden Foundations, New York, NY

SRF: Seventh Regiment Fund, Inc., New York, NY

USAMHI: United States Army Military History Institute, Carlisle, PA

VM: Valentine Museum, Richmond, VA

WP: West Point Museum Collections, U.S. Military Academy, West Point, NY

WRHS: Western Reserve Historical Society, Cleveland, OH

Front Matter

ii-iii Sanford R. Gifford, *Fort Federal Hill at Sunset—Baltimore*: SRF. **iv** Winslow Homer, *Pitching Quoits*, 1865: Courtesy, Fogg Art Museum, Harvard University Art Museums, Cambridge, MA, Gift of Mr. and Mrs. Frederic Haines Curtiss. **v** AH. **vi** AH. **ix** AH.

Chapter 1

x LC. **1** Courtesy, David Frent, Political Americana, Oakhurst, NJ. **2** Top: Collection of Everson Museum of Art, Syracuse, NY, Gift of Andrew D. White; bottom: Drawing for *The County Election*, Lent by the People of Missouri, Courtesy, Bingham Trust, St. Louis, MO. **3** Gift of Mrs. Huttleston Rogers, © Board of Trustees, National Gallery of Art, Washington, DC. **4–5** The Museums at Stony Brook, Stony Brook, NY, Gift of Mr. and Mrs. Ward Melville, 1950. **6** Top left: Drawing for *Stump Speaking*, Courtesy, Bingham Trust; bottom right: AH. **7** Photograph © 1991, Detroit Institute of

Arts, Collection of Detroit Institute of Arts, Detroit, MI. **8–9** Courtesy, American Antiquarian Society, Worcester, MA. **10** Top: Harry T. Peters "America on Stone" Lithography Collection, National Museum of American History, Smithsonian Institution, Washington, DC; bottom: LC. **11** Bequest of Elizabeth Hart Jarvis Colt, Wadsworth Atheneum, Hartford, CT. **12** Top: MFA/KC. **12–13** Bottom: Library of Virginia, Richmond, VA. **13** Top: Yale University Art Gallery, Mabel Brady Garvan Collection, New Haven, CT. **14–15** Hunter Museum of American Art, Chattanooga, TN, Gift of Mr. and Mrs. Thomas B. Whiteside. **16** Top: Courtesy, American Antiquarian Society; bottom: WRHS. **17** Daguerreotypes copyright © 1977 by the President and Fellows of Harvard College. All rights reserved. Peabody Museum, Harvard University. Copy photographs by Hillel Burger. **18** Top: LC. **18–19** Bottom: Courtesy, Shepherd Gallery, New York, NY. **19** Top: CHS, neg# P&S – 1957.0027. **20** Historic New Orleans Collection, New Orleans, LA, accession no. 1960.46. **21** Top: LC; bottom left: Lloyd Ostendorf Collection, Dayton, OH; bottom middle: Eleanor S. Brockenbrough Library, MC; bottom right: Print Collection, Miriam and Ira D. Wallach Division of Art, Prints and Photographs, NYPL. **22** LC. **23** Top & bottom left, bottom right: LC; top right: Metropolitan Museum of Art, New York, NY, Gift of I. N. Phelps Stokes, Edward S. Hawkes, Alice Mary Hawkes, Marion Augusta Hawkes, 1937. **24** Top left: LC; middle right: Photographs and Prints Division, Schomburg Center for Research in Black Culture, NYPL; bottom: Worcester Art Museum, Worcester, MA, Goodspeed Collection. **25** Top: Harriet Beecher Stowe Center, Hartford, CT; bottom: NYHS. **26** National Portrait Gallery, Smithsonian Institution/Art Resource, New York, NY. **27** Brooklyn Museum, Brooklyn, NY, neg# 40.59.A. **28–29** Top: Sophia Smith Collection, Smith College, Northampton, MA. **29** Bottom right: LC. **30** Top: Kansas State Historical Society, Topeka, KS; bottom: BMC. **31** Boston Athenaeum, Boston, MA. **32** Top left: LC; top right & bottom: Print Collection, Miriam and Ira D. Wallach Division of Art, Prints and Photographs, NYPL. **33** LC. **34** Right: National Portrait Gallery, Smithsonian Institution/Art

Resource; bottom left: LC. **35** Left: LC; bottom right: Courtesy, Illinois State Historical Library, Springfield, IL. **36** Top: B&O Railroad Museum, Inc., Baltimore, MD; bottom: WRHS. **37** Bibliothèque Nationale de France, Paris, France. **38** Top & bottom right: LC; bottom left: Print Collection, Miriam and Ira D. Wallach Division of Art, Prints and Photographs, NYPL. **39** Top: CHS, neg# IChi-20265; bottom: Lloyd Ostendorf Collection. **40** USAMHI. **41** Top left: Georgia Historical Society, Savannah, GA; bottom right: Rare Books and Manuscripts Division, NYPL. **42** AH. **43** CHS, neg# IChi–09975. **44** Both: MFA/KC. **45** Courtesy, Meserve–Kunhardt Collection, Mount Kisco, NY.

Chapter 2

46–47 SRF. **47** Right: MC, copy photography by Katherine Wetzel. **48** AH. **49** Paul Pugliese. **50** Top: WP; bottom: LC. **51** Top: LC; bottom: Print Collection, Miriam and Ira D. Wallach Division of Art, Prints and Photographs, NYPL. **52–53** Top: AH. **52** Bottom: NA. **54–55** LC. **56** AH. **57** NA. **58** Top left: General Research Division, NYPL; bottom right: Connecticut Historical Society, Hartford, CT. **59** Top right: LC; bottom left: CHS, neg# IChi–06782. **60** AH. **61** Both: Print Collection, Miriam and Ira D. Wallach Division of Art, Prints and Photographs, NYPL. **62** Top: MFA/KC; bottom: AH. **63** LC. **64** Top: Print Collection, Miriam and Ira D. Wallach Division of Art, Prints and Photographs, NYPL; bottom: LC. **65** CHS, neg# P&S – 1920.1038. **66–67** Courtesy, Burton Historical Collection of the Detroit Public Library, Detroit, MI. **68** Lloyd Ostendorf Collection. **69** *The Cormany Diaries: A Northern Family in the Civil War*, James C. Mohr, ed., © 1982 by University of Pittsburgh Press. Reprinted by permission of the University of Pittsburgh Press. **70** Eleanor S. Brockenbrough Library, MC. **71** Top left: MFA/KC; top right: from *The Confederate Soldier*, by LeGrand James Wilson, © 1973 Memphis State University Press, Memphis, TN. **72** Top: VM; bottom: Courtesy, Georgia Department of Archives and History, Atlanta, GA. **73** Both: Eleanor S. Brockenbrough Library, MC. **74** WP. **75** Indianapolis

Museum of Art, James E. Roberts Fund, Indianapolis, IN. **76–77** AH. **78** State Historical Society of Missouri, Columbia, MO. **79** Top: LC; bottom: Collection of Richard P. W. Williams, Washington, DC. **80** Missouri Historical Society, St. Louis, MO. **81** Top: Jonathan Brillhart, Murray, KY; bottom: Print Collection, Miriam and Ira D. Wallach Division of Art, Prints and Photographs, NYPL. **82–83** Top: LC. **82** Bottom: LC. **83** Bottom: NA. **84** LC. **85** WRHS. **86–87** Top: Collection of John Crosby Freeman, from *The Civil War: First Blood*, photograph by Lon Mattoon © 1983 Time-Life Books Inc. **87** Top right: VM; bottom: MFA/KC. **88–89** AH/David Greenspan. **90** Lincoln Museum, Fort Wayne, IN, neg# 4471. **91** Culver Pictures, New York, NY. **92–93** BMC.

Chapter 3

94–95 CHS, neg# P&S – 1932.0031. **95** Right: National Portrait Gallery, Smithsonian Institution/Art Resource. **96** Top: LC; bottom: White House Historical Association, Washington, DC. **97** Top: NA; bottom: Print Collection, Miriam and Ira D. Wallach Division of Art, Prints and Photographs, NYPL. **98** Top: LC; bottom left & right: NA; bottom middle: Historical Society of Pennsylvania, Philadelphia, PA. **99** Left: NA; right: LC. **100** WP. **101** Top left, middle right & bottom right: LC; top middle & right: NA. **102–3** AH. **104** Top: National Museum of American History, Naval Division, Smithsonian Institution; bottom: State Historical Society of Wisconsin, Madison, WI, neg# (x3) 50495. **105** LC. **106–7** CHS, neg# P&S – 1920.1645. **108** Top left & right: LC; bottom: MC, copy photography by Katherine Wetzel. **109** MC, copy photography by Katherine Wetzel. **110** Top: LC; bottom: NA. **111** Print Collection, Miriam and Ira D. Wallach Division of Art, Prints and Photographs, NYPL. **112–13** AH/David Greenspan. **114** Top: LC. **114–15** Bottom: Print Collection, Miriam and Ira D. Wallach Division of Art, Prints and Photographs, NYPL. **116** USAMHI. **117** MFA/KC. **118** CHS, neg# P&S – 1920.0922. **119** AH. **120–21** AH. **122** Both: LC. **123** Top: USAMHI; bottom: LC. **124** Left: NA; right: Courtesy, Brian C. Pohanka, Alexandria, VA. **125** Mariners' Museum, Newport News, VA. **126** LC. **127** Top: Yale University Art Galley, Gift of Samuel Rossiter Betts, B.A., 1875; bottom: LC. **128–29** Top: MFA/KC; bottom, both: LC. **130** Both: LC. **131** Top: Boston Athenaeum; bottom: Graphic Arts Collection, Department of Rare Books and Special Collections, Princeton University Libraries, Princeton, NJ. **132–33** AH. **134–35** All: LC. **136** Top: AH; bottom: Greenville County Museum of Art, Greenville, SC. **137** Stonewall Jackson Foundation, Lexington, VA. **138–39** AH/David Greenspan. **140** LC. **141** VM. **142** Both: LC. **143** AH/David Greenspan. **144** NA. **145–47** All: LC. **148** AH/David Greenspan. **149–50** LC. **151** Cooper-Hewitt, National Design Museum, Smithsonian Institution/Art Resource.

Chapter 4

152 Left: Franklin D. Roosevelt Library, Hyde Park, NY. **152–53** MC, copy photography by Katherine Wetzel. **154** Top: LC; background: AH. **155** LC. **156** Christie's Images, New York, NY. **157** Top: MFA/KC; bottom: State Historical Society of Wisconsin, neg# (x#) 50529. **158–59** Art Collection of the Union League of Philadelphia, Philadelphia, PA. **160** Top: Museum of the City of New York, New

York, NY, neg# 60.122.7; bottom: NYHS. **161** Paul Pugliese. **162** LC. **163** Mariners' Museum. **164** Top: LC; bottom: Naval Historical Center, Washington, DC. **165** WRHS. **166–67** NYHS. **168** AH. **169** MC, copy photography by Katherine Wetzel. **170** Bottom left: LC. **170-1** Both: Courtesy, Hagley Museum and Library, Wilmington, DE. **172–73** AH. **174** All: AH. **175** WRHS. **176** Top: LC; bottom: AH. **177** Top: Print Collection, Miriam and Ira D. Wallach Division of Art, Prints and Photographs, NYPL; bottom: CHS, neg# P&S – 1932.0027. **178–79** Both: Historic New Orleans Collection, accession no. 0546-4-L. **180** Top: AH; bottom: LC. **181** Top: Rosemonde E. and Emile Kuntz Collection, Manuscripts Dept., Tulane University Library, New Orleans, LA; bottom: Maryland Historical Society, Baltimore, MD. **182–83** AH. **183** Right: LC. **184–87** All: MC, copy photography by Katherine Wetzel. **188** Top: Franklin D. Roosevelt Library; bottom: LC. **189** BMC. **190** Top: Naval Historical Center. **190–91** Background: AH. **191** Top: Mariners' Museum. **192–93** WP. **194** Top: NA; background: AH. **195** John G. Johnson Collection, Philadelphia Museum of Art, Philadelphia, PA. **196–97** Top: LC. **197** Bottom: Mariners' Museum.

Chapter 5

198 Left: LC. **198–99** Antietam National Battlefield, Sharpsburg, MD; © 1986, Edward Owen/Photographer, Washington, DC. **200** Top, both: LC; bottom left: Maryland Historical Society. **201** WRHS. **202–3** AH; background: AH. **204–5** All: LC. **206** Top: AH; bottom: LC. **207** AH/David Greenspan. **208–9** Top: LC. **209** Top right: LC; middle right: VM; bottom left: NA. **210–11** LC. **212** AH/David Greenspan. **213** Both: LC. **214** Top: LC; bottom: Historical Society of Frederick County, Frederick, MD. **215** LC. **216** Collection of the Corcoran Gallery of Art, Washington, DC, Gift of Genevieve Plummer. **217–19** All: LC. **220** Top left, bottom left & right: VM; bottom middle: LC. **221** Left: NA; right: LC. **222–23** Top: AH. **223** Bottom: LC. **224–25** AH/David Greenspan. **226–27** Top: Antietam National Battlefield, © 1986 Edward Owen/Photographer. **227** Bottom: private collection; photograph courtesy, Henry Groskinsky, New York, NY. **228–30** All: LC. **231** USAMHI. **232–33** Both: LC. **234** Top: NA; bottom: Anitec/Ansco Collection, Binghamton, NY. **235** Both: LC. **236–37** BMC. **238** Top: LC; bottom: Courtesy, Illinois State Historical Library. **239** Paul Pugliese.

Chapter 6

240–1 WP. **241** Right: AH. **242** Top left & right: NA; bottom left: General Research Division, NYPL. **243** General Research Division, NYPL. **244** Top: NYHS; bottom: National Maritime Museum, Greenwich, London, England. **245** LC. **246** CHS. **247** Top: USAMHI; bottom: General Research Division, NYPL. **248** Top: MFA/KC; bottom: NYPL. **249–50** Both: LC. **251** Top: Lincoln Museum, neg# 3542; bottom: White House Historical Association. **252** AH. **253** NA. **254–55** Both: LC. **256–57** Both: LC. **258** Top: AH; bottom: LC. **259** Eleanor S. Brockenbrough Library, MC. **260–61** AH/David Greenspan. **262** Collection of Mrs. Nelson Rockefeller, New York, NY. **264** Both: LC. **265** WP. **266** LC. **267** Top: LC; bottom: Filson Historical Society, Louisville, KY. **268** Both: LC. **269** Both: National Museum of American History, Armed Forces

Collection, Smithsonian Institution. **270–71** AH/David Greenspan. **272** BMC. **273** Top left: Jonathan Brillhart; top right: VM; bottom: Print Collection, Miriam and Ira D. Wallach Division of Art, Prints and Photographs, NYPL.

Chapter 7

274 Left: AH. **274–75** MFA/KC. **276** LC. **277** Huntington Library, San Marino, CA. **278** NA. **279** Top: NA; bottom: CHS, neg# ICHi–07892. **280** Both: LC. **281–83** All: LC. **284** MC, copy photography by Katherine Wetzel. **285** NA. **286–87** AH/David Greenspan. **288** LC. **289** Virginia Military Institute Archives, Lexington, VA. **290** National Museum of American History, Naval Division; Smithsonian Institution. **291** Top: AH; bottom: Louisiana State University, Baton Rouge, LA. **292** Anitec/Ansco Collection. **293** Top: Eleanor S. Brockenbrough Library, MC; bottom: AH. **294–95** AH/David Greenspan. **296** AH. **297** Top: LC; bottom: AH. **298** Ohio Historical Society, Columbus, OH. **299** Both: LC. **300** Old Court House Museum, Vicksburg, MS. **301** Top: MFA/KC; bottom: AH. **302** American Museum, Bath, England. **303** Lincoln Museum, neg# 3686. **304** AH. **305** Both: AH. **306** Top left: NYHS. **306–7** Minnesota Historical Society, St. Paul, MN. **308** Robert E. Lee IV, Bethesda, MD. **309** Top: Courtesy, American Antiquarian Society; bottom: LC. **310** Both: LC. **311** VM. **312** Top: National Baseball Library and Archive, Cooperstown, NY; bottom: First Regiment Infantry Museum, Pennsylvania National Guard; from *The Civil War: Gettysburg,* copied by Larry Sherer © 1985 Time-Life Books, Inc. **313** Art Collection of the Union League of Philadelphia. **314** Top: VM; bottom: MFA/KC. **315** Both: LC. **316** Maine State Archives, Augusta, ME. **317** All: LC. **318–19** AH/David Greenspan. **320** SRF. **321** Both: LC. **322–25** Eastern National Park and Gettysburg National Military Park, Gettysburg, PA. **326–27** All: LC. **328** Top left: AH; bottom right: LC. **329** NA. **330** Both: NA. **331** LC.

Chapter 8

332 Left: Collection of Don Troiani, Southbury, CT. **332–33** VM. **334** Top left: LC; top right: Ohio Historical Society; bottom: Collection of Don Troiani. **335** Left: Eleanor S. Brockenbrough Library, MC; right: VM. **336** LC. **337** Top left: USAMHI; top, middle & bottom right: National Museum of American History, Armed Forces Collection, Smithsonian Institution. **338** All: LC. **339** Top left: Louisiana Historical Association/Confederate Museum, New Orleans, LA; top right: LC; bottom: Gift of Edgar William and Bernice Chrysler Garbisch, photograph by Ron Jennings, © 1991 Virginia Museum of Fine Arts, Richmond, VA. **340–41** NA. **342** VM. **343** Top: LC; bottom: AH. **344** Top: NA; bottom: VM. **345** LC. **346** Wadsworth Atheneum, bequest of Elizabeth Hart Jarvis Colt. **347** Background: AH; bottom: Cooper-Hewitt/Art Resource. **348–49** Philadelphia Museum of Art: Collection of Edgar William and Bernice Chrysler Garbisch. **350** Top: MFA/KC. **350–51** Bottom: LC. **352** Top: AH; bottom: NA. **353** R. H. Love Galleries, Inc., Chicago, IL. **354** Both: LC. **355** SRF. **356** Moravian Music Foundation, Winston-Salem, NC. **357** Top left: BMC; top, middle & bottom right: Music Collection, NYPL for the Performing Arts. **358** Top: MFA/KC; bottom: LC. **359** Top: LC; bottom: Courtesy, Illinois

State Historical Library. **360** Canajoharie Library and Art Gallery, Canajoharie, NY. **361** Top left: NYHS; top right & bottom: LC. **362** Top: CHS, neg# P&S – 1920.0152; bottom: Library Company of Philadelphia, Philadelphia, PA. **363** Top: NA; bottom: LC. **364** Eleanor S. Brockenbrough Library, MC. **365** MFA/KC. **366** Both: LC. **367** Left: LC; right: NA. **368** All: VM. **369** Top: Ellen Kelleran Gardner Fund, Courtesy, Museum of Fine Arts, Boston, MA; bottom: Cooper-Hewitt/Art Resource. **370–71** SRF. **372–73** Gift of Mrs. William F. Milton, 1923 (23.77.1), © 1995 by Metropolitan Museum of Art.

Chapter 9

374–75 Fine Art Museums of San Francisco, San Francisco, CA, Gift of Mr. and Mrs. John D. Rockefeller 3rd. **375** Right: Wadsworth Atheneum, Amistad Foundation Collection. **376** Top: Philbrook Museum of Art, Tulsa, OK; bottom: NYHS. **377** NA. **378** CHS, neg# ICHi-22051. **379** Top: Archive Photos, New York, NY; bottom: LC. **380** Collection of Herb Peck Jr., Nashville, TN. **381** Union League Club, New York, NY. **382** Collections of Henry Ford Museum & Greenfield Village, Dearborn, MI. **383** NA. **384** Top: Chickamauga and Chattanooga National Military Park, Fort Oglethorpe, GA; bottom: LC. **385** Both: LC. **386** Top: LC; bottom: AH. **387** LC. **388–89** AH/David Greenspan. **390–91** Minnesota Historical Society. **392** Top: Print Collection, Miriam and Ira D. Wallach Division of Art, Prints and Photographs, NYPL; bottom: LC. **393** Top: AH; bottom: Print Collection, Miriam and Ira D. Wallach Division of Art, Prints and Photographs, NYPL. **394–95** Top: Courtesy, National Park Service, Conshohocken, PA. **394** Bottom left: AH. **396–97** AH/David Greenspan. **398** Chickamauga and Chattanooga National Military Park. **399** SRF. **400** Courtesy, Colorado Historical Society, Denver, CO. **401** MFA/KC.

Chapter 10

402–3 Greenville County Museum of Art. **404** Top: BMC; bottom: LC. **405** Top left: AH; top right: NA; bottom: MFA/KC. **406** Top: CHS, neg# ICHi-07849; bottom: NA. **407** NA. **408** Courtesy, Meserve-Kunhardt Collection. **409** VM. **410–11** Both: AH. **412** Paul Pugliese. **413** Top: SRF; bottom: LC. **414** AH. **415** LC. **416** SRF. **417–19** All: LC. **420–21** AH/David Greenspan. **422** NA. **423** Top: Historical Society of Plainfield, Drake House Museum, Plainfield, NJ; bottom: CHS, neg# x.308. **424** Top: NA; bottom: USAMHI. **425** Top: LC; bottom: USAMHI. **426** Top left: VM. **426–27** WP. **428–29** All: LC. **430** Top: NA; bottom: LC. **431** WP **432** LC. **433** Top: LC; background: AH. **434** LC. **435** State Historical Society of Wisconsin, neg# (x31) 10058.

Chapter 11

436–37 White House Historical Association. **437** Right: Stack's Coin Appraiser Co., New York, NY. **438–39** Both: NYHS. **440** NA. **441** Top: WRHS; bottom: BMC. **442** Putnam County Historical Society, Cold Spring, NY. **444** Courtesy, Hagley Museum and Library. **445** NYHS. **446–47** All: LC. **448** All: Print Collection, Miriam and Ira D. Wallach Division of Art, Prints and Photographs, NYPL. **449** Top: AH; bottom: MFA/KC. **450** Top: LC. **450–51** Bottom: AH. **451** Top: NA. **452** NYHS. **453** Top: WRHS; bottom:

USAMHI. **454–55** Both: Gettysburg National Military Park. **456** Top: NA; bottom: Eleanor S. Brockenbrough Library, MC. **457** Left: LC; right: NA. **458–60** All: LC. **461** Collection of Newark Museum, Newark, NJ, Purchase 1944, Wallace M. Scudder Bequest Fund. **462** LC. **463** Top left: Lloyd Ostendorf Collection; bottom left, top & bottom right: LC. **464** Left: Library of Virginia; top right: LC; bottom right: Print Collection, NYPL. **465** Top left: CHS, neg# ICHi-22049; bottom right: Ohio Historical Society. **466** Lincoln Museum, #2338. **467** Top: Museum of the City of New York, J. Clarence Davies Collection; bottom: NYHS. **468** Top: Lincoln Museum, #2566; bottom: BMC. **469** Courtesy, Vermont Historical Society, Montpelier, VT. **470** Top: Maryland Historical Society; bottom: General Lew Wallace Study, Crawfordsville, IN. **471** CHS, neg# P&S – 1918.0005. **472** Both: LC. **473** Collection of the Newark Museum. Gift of Mrs. Hannah Corbin Carter, Horace K. Corbin Jr., Robert S. Corbin, William D. Corbin, and Mrs. Clementine Corbin Day. In memory of their parents and Hannah Stockton Corbin and Horace Kellogg Corbin, 1966. **474** Top: State Historical Society of Iowa, Des Moines, IA. **474–75** MFA/KC. **476** Both: Maryland Historical Society. **477** Both: MFA/KC. **478** Top: LC; bottom: *Harper's Weekly*. **479** Top: *Harper's Weekly*; bottom: MFA/KC. **480** Left: Smithsonian Institution; right: NYHS. **481** Courtesy, Atwater Kent Museum, Philadelphia, PA. **482** Both: Lincoln Museum, #2390 and 2613. **483** LC.

Chapter 12

484 Left: Collection of Don Troiani. **484–85** LC. **486** Top: VM; bottom: LC. **487** Left: NA; right: LC. **488** Top left: LC; top right & bottom: AH. **489** Kirby Collection of Historical Paintings, Lafayette College, Easton, PA. **490–93** City of Atlanta, Atlanta, GA, photo courtesy, Henry Groskinsky. **494–95** Both: LC. **496** Courtesy, Mariners' Museum. **497** Top: NA; bottom: Wadsworth Atheneum, Ella Gallup Sumner and Mary Caitlin Sumner Collection Fund. **498** Century Association, New York, NY. **499** Collection of Don Troiani. **500–1** Cincinnati Art Museum, Cincinnati, OH, The Edwin and Virginia Irwin Memorial. **502** Top left: State Historical Society of Missouri; top & bottom right: Kansas State Historical Society. **503** Kansas State Historical Society. **504** Top: VM; bottom: LC. **505** Both: MC, copy photography by Katherine Wetzel. **506** Both: LC. **507** Top: LC; bottom: Historical Society of Pennsylvania. **508** NA. **509** Top: LC; bottom: AH. **510–11** All: WRHS. **512–13** Both: LC.

Chapter 13

514–15 Gift of Mrs. Frank B. Porter, 1922 (22.207) © 1995 by Metropolitan Museum of Art. **516** Virginia Museum of Transportation, Inc. Resource Library & Archives, Roanoke, VA. **517** Both: NA. **518** Top: CHS, neg# ICHi-10523; bottom: Courtesy, New York State Museum, Albany, NY. **519** Collection of the Corcoran Gallery of Art, Gift of the American Art Association. **520** Both: LC. **521** Photograph © Detroit Institute of Arts, Founders Society Purchase with Funds from Dexter M. Ferry, Jr. **522–23** Both: LC. **524** Eleanor S. Brockenbrough Library, MC. **525** SRF. **526–27** NA. **528–30** All: LC. **531** Archive Photos. **532** Collection of Mrs. Patricia Arden, New York, NY. **533** Courtesy, Illinois State Historical Library. **534** Both: LC. **535** Both: NYHS. **536** Top left, middle & bottom: LC; top right: Eleanor S. Brockenbrough

Library, MC. **537–38** AH/David Greenspan. **539–40** LC. **541** Top: AH; bottom: WRHS. **542–43** Courtesy, Museum of American Art of the Pennsylvania Academy of Fine Arts, Philadelphia, PA. Gift of Mrs. Sarah Harrison (The Joseph Harrison, Jr., Collection).

Chapter 14

544 Left: Eleanor S. Brockenbrough Library, MC. **544–45** White House Historical Association. **546** Top: AH; bottom: MFA/KC. **547** Top: AH; bottom: LC. **548–49** Top: LC. **549** Bottom right: AH. **550** Archive Photos. **551** LC. **552** MFA/KC. **553** Top: LC; bottom: NA. **554–58** All: LC. **559** USAMHI. **560** LC. **561** USAMHI. **562–64** All: LC. **565** CHS neg# P&S – 1955.0398. **566** Paul Pugliese. **567** Both: LC. **568** Top: LC; bottom: Bettmann Archive, New York, NY. **569** Appomattox Court House National Historical Park, Appomattox, VA. **570–71** Both: LC. **572–73** WP. **574** Courtesy, Burton Historical Collection of the Detroit Public Library. **575** WP; photograph, Nan Melville, New York, NY. **576** Bennett House, Durham, NC. **577** Eleanor S. Brockenbrough Library, MC. **578** Top: USAMHI; bottom left & right: LC. **579** LC.

Chapter 15

580–81 Ohio Historical Society. **582** CHS, neg# ICHi-11472. **583** Courtesy, Meserve-Kunhardt Collection. **584–85** Both: LC. **586** Left: NYHS; right: LC. **587** Second row from top, left & right: Courtesy, Meserve-Kunhardt Collection; bottom row, left: NA; all others: LC. **588** LC. **589** Courtesy, Ford's Theatre, Washington, DC; © 1986 Edward Owen/Photographer. **590** National Museum of Health and Medicine, Otis Historical Archives, Washington, DC. **591** Lincoln Collection, Brown University Library, Providence, RI. **592–93** Both: LC. **594–95** Top: Illinois Central Railroad, Chicago, IL. **595** Bottom right: George Eastman House, Rochester, NY. **596–97** All: Courtesy, Illinois State Historical Library. **598** Bequest of Miss Adelaide Milton de Groot (1876-1967), 1967 (67.187.131) © 1995 by Metropolitan Museum of Art. **599** Fine Arts Museums of San Francisco, Mildred Anna Williams Collection, #1943.6.

Chapter 16

600 Left: Collection of Don Troiani. **600–1** National Museum of American Art, Smithsonian Institution, Gift of Henry Sandham. **602–4** All: LC. **605** Collection of Don Troiani. **606** Top: VM; bottom: AH. **607** Top: National Museum of American History, Smithsonian Institution; bottom: Museum of the Cherokee Indian, Cherokee, NC. **608** Top left & right: Brown Brothers, Sterling, PA; bottom: Pennsylvania State Archives, Harrisburg, PA, RG-25, Special Commissions. **609** City of Boston, MA. **610–11** Both: Gettysburg National Military Park. **612–13** Antietam National Battlefield. **615** Archive Photos.

Back Matter

617 AH. **623** Eleanor S. Brockenbrough Library, MC. **624** AH. **626** AH. **629** AH.

Endpapers

Colton Map of the Southern States, 1862: Map Division, The New York Public Library, Astor, Lenox and Tilden Foundations.

Index

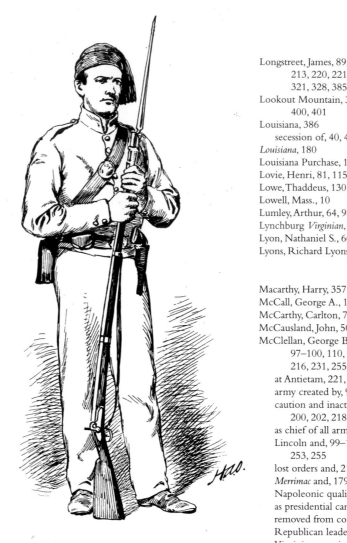